Reflecting on the Names of Allah

Understanding and Connecting to God in our Daily Lives

Jinan Yousef

Al Buruj Press
2020

Published in the UK by Al Buruj Press.

Author: Jinan Yousef
Editor: Louiza Chekhar

Al Buruj Press
Masjid Ramadan
9 Shacklewell Lane
London
E8 2DA
Tel: +447947363946
Website: www.alburujpress.com
Email: info@alburujpress.com

ISBN: 978-967-2420-538

CONTENTS

PUBLISHERS COMMENTS

A true lover strives to know the one they love in the most comprehensive and intimate manner. For a believer in this world, the way to show ultimate love towards his Creator is by dedicating both time and effort to know Him through His signs, beauty and names.

As one continuously ponders on the beautiful names and attributes of Allah, one is paving the way to a more disciplined, purified and content heart.

The more you learn about Allah's names and attributes, the nearer you draw to Him which will ultimately result in greater love for Him. And when that love is alive in your heart, your obedience and worship of Allah will transform to actions enabling you to become a true and obedient servant of His.

We are truly honoured and blessed at Al Buruj Press to present to the world this important and pivotal piece of work. Written with diligence, research and in a manner easy to digest, we ask Allah to bless and accept the efforts of the talented Ustadha Dr. Jinan Yousef. Over the years, Ustadha Dr. Jinan has taught several times for Al Buruj Press, sacrificing her time and energy for which we are most grateful. May Allah reward and elevate her both in this world and the next. Ameen.

We'd like to thank our teacher Shaykh Mohammad Akram Nadwi for kindly reviewing the book and providing a written foreword. Importantly, we'd like to thank all our team members at Al Buruj Press who have played a role over the years organising the classes taught by Ustadha Dr Jinan. Your help will forever be appreciated.

This is an invaluable piece of work necessary to be first digested, for the heart to ponder and then to remain on the bookshelf of every Muslim household; available as a reminder when needed.

> "And to Allah belong the best names, so invoke Him by them." (Holy Qur'an 7:180)

Zayd ul Islam
London, UK
Al Buruj Press Founder
September 2020

ACKNOWLEDGMENTS BY THE AUTHOR

First and foremost, all praise and thanks are to Allah, God, the Most High. Nothing would be possible without His grace, and I am eternally grateful that He guided me to the writing of this book. Whatever good comes from it is due to Him, and any mistakes are mine alone. We ask for His forgiveness for any and all errors.

In completing our thanks to Him, the Prophet ﷺ taught us, *'He who does not thank people has not truly thanked God.'* [Abū Dāwūd] And I would like to express my deep thanks and gratitude to all who helped in the writing and production of this book. Before I do so, I will digress for one moment, as this story truly shows us Allah's wisdom in our lives, even when not apparent in the moment. The events in this story ultimately led to the writing of this book.

I was going through a particularly difficult period in my life and, on a whim, asked Imam Suhaib Webb for advice. Had I not had this problem, I might not have reached out to him. The problem I was facing did not go away – far from it – and had far-reaching consequences in my life. At the time, I prayed to Allah feverishly, and still things seemed to be spiraling downward. At that moment, I knew that I had to have trust. It is easy to trust in Allah when everything is going our way, but what is in our hearts is revealed in hardship. I made the decision to trust in al-Wakīl, al-Ḥakīm, al-Raḥīm, because there had to be wisdom in whatever Allah decreed. More than ten years after this hardship, as I sat reflecting on the privilege and responsibility Allah had given me in writing this book, I realized that I would not be where I am had it not been for that hardship. I would never have asked Imam Suhaib for advice; he would have not seen my writings, which at that point were simply emails to people I knew, and I probably would not have become a writer for SuhaibWebb.com, later VirtualMosque.com. We do not know how the threads in our lives will come together; how a hardship will lead to a chance meeting, which then leads to something greater. As the Prophet Joseph said, *'Indeed, my Lord is subtle towards whomever He wishes. Indeed, He truly is the All-Knowing, the Most Wise.'* [7:100]

And for that reason, I am forever indebted to Imam Suhaib Webb, as he was the catalyst for my public writings and ultimately for the writing of this book. Thank you, Imam Suhaib, for your mentorship, friendship, and guidance, for believing in, encouraging, and providing a platform for a naïve and idealistic twenty-something-year-old so many years ago, and for including me in blessed company. May any good that Allah places in this book, and any other writings, weigh heavily on your scales on the Day of Judgment.

I also would like to thank my fellow WebbAuthors, who have been my sheikhs, scholars and teachers in so many ways, particularly when I first began the series on VirtualMosque.com: Maryam Amir, Ahmed Abdelmageed, Shazia Ahmad, AbdulSattar Ahmad, Jamaal Diwan, John Yahya Ederer, Muhammad Haq, Muslema Purmul, Yusuf Rios, Shafiur Rahman, and Shibli Zaman. Our conversations over the years taught me so much, and I was, and remain always, humbled by your knowledge, character and humility; you all taught me more than you can know. Thank you.

I was honored and blessed to take classes with Sheikh Alaeddine el-Bakri and Sheikh Muhammad Akram Nadwi, to whom I am forever grateful for the many lessons I have learned, which deeply affected my relationship with Allah. Sheikh Alaa, it was an absolute gift to be able to study with you when I was in Berkeley, and I look forward to the day that I can resume, *inshā'Allāh*. Many of the subtle understandings I have learned from both Sheikh Akram and Sheikh Alaa have been incorporated into this book. You are both and will remain in my prayers for all the good you have imparted.

Sheikh Akram in particular, may Allah reward you for taking the time to review this book and write the foreword. Thank you for your teaching, your writing, your commitment to making us think, and all that you do in the pursuit and spread of beneficial knowledge. I have learned as much from your knowledge as I have from your character, your love for Allah, and your humility. May all that you do be a light for you in this world and the next.

Also, my friends who followed and encouraged my writings over the years: though too many to name (that may need its own chapter), I hope that you know who you are, and know what your support meant and still means. May Allah bless you always. I have to mention three individuals specifically who encouraged me to keep writing and to turn this into a book: Maryam Amir, Sanaa Alimia and Ziyaad Lunat – thank you for your constant motivation. It means the world.

Finally, brother Zayd ul Islam and Al Buruj Press, may Allah reward you infinitely for always being diligent and arranging many free or low-cost classes for people, particularly women, and for publishing this book. May you share in its blessing and more.

SOME NOTES

On the names

In a famous narration, the Prophet Muhammad ﷺ said, *'Allah has ninety-nine names and whoever preserves them will enter Paradise.'* [Muslim]

In another version of the narration, these names are listed, and have been used as the basis for the study of the names of God. However, that narration is deemed weak by hadith scholars. A hadith being deemed 'weak' does not necessarily mean that it is wrong, but rather that a number of scholars have contested some of the names contained in it, due to the chain of transmission. Some have devised other ways of knowing His names, such as using only the Qur'an. However, this group has found that the names amount to fewer than ninety-nine. Other have stated that it is fitting to use the Qur'an and sound hadith, which give us more than ninety-nine names. Scholars have said that this is consistent with the Prophet's supplication: *'I ask You by every Name that You have named Yourself, revealed in Your Book, taught any one of Your creation or kept unto Yourself in the knowledge of the unseen that is with You.'* [Aḥmad]

This supplication tells us that there are names that have been revealed to us and names that have not been revealed, so we do not know the actual total number. However, if there is a difference of opinion on the names, then how do we know which names were meant for us to learn as a way of entering Paradise?

In considering this hadith, scholars have said that whoever memorizes *any* ninety-nine *of* His many names will enter Paradise. If one says that they will give you a thousand of their dollars, it does not necessarily mean that they only have a thousand dollars. It means that they have more, but they are going to give you a thousand of them. Similarly, Allah has many names, some which we do not know, but if we learn ninety-nine of them, then we will attain *Paradise,* God willing.

This series uses many of the names found in the classic hadith listing the names of Allah, but also relies on Qur'anic verses and other sound narrations from the Sunnah which contain names not found in the famous hadith.

While a few have interpreted *'preserve'* to mean simply 'memorize', other scholars have said that this cannot be. A good person could memorize these names, as could a bad person; a Muslim and a non-Muslim; one who understands and one who does not. Ibn al-Qayyim stated that *'preserving them'*, as mentioned in the saying of the Prophet ﷺ, means three things:

1. Knowing the names, and the number of names;
2. Understanding what they mean (in their many meanings) and what they indicate; and
3. Calling upon Allah using the names, as He says in the Qur'an: *'To God belong the Best Names, so call on Him using them.'* [7:180] Calling upon Allah can be simply to praise and worship Him, as well as to ask for one's needs.

Thus, it is the person who learns these names, implements their understanding, and connects to God through them who will enter Paradise. This is the purpose of writing this book. Indeed, I hope that it means that we will enter a Paradise of sorts in this world, through knowing God, loving Him, and turning to Him, through the knowledge of His names. As 'Alī ibn Abī Ṭālib taught us: *'The basis of this religion is knowing Him.'* [Nahj al-Balāghah]

On 'Allah' and 'God'

You will notice that, except for the chapter on His name 'Allah', 'God' and 'Allah' are used interchangeably. The word 'God' is used to denote the One Higher, Supreme Being, as opposed to 'god', 'gods' or 'goddess'. Just as Christian and pagan Arabs used, and still use, the Arabic word *Allāh* to talk about the Higher, Supreme Being, 'God' is acceptable for Muslims to use in English. The monotheistic religions worship the same one God – with some differences in *how* we understand Him. Thus, 'God' and 'Allah' are used interchangeably, while understanding that 'Allah' is His unique name.

On the Virtual Mosque series

The series on the names of Allah took four years to complete on VirtualMosque.com, where the articles are still available (and a wonderful reader has compiled them into a PDF, may Allah bless her!), and over three years to turn into this book.

The series on VirtualMosque.com showed my reflections in real time, and contained more personal anecdotes. Over the years, I have studied, learned, and reflected more, so in this book, you will notice that some articles have been completely reworked, while others have significant additions, and others still are largely the same. I have also included names here that were not discussed in the original series, and some of the names in the online series have been omitted here.

On honorifics and salutations

To ensure the flow of the text, the Arabic glyph ﷺ (*ṣallā Allāhu 'alayhi wa sallam* – may Allah's peace and blessings be upon him) is used for the Prophet ﷺ. No other honorifics have been used, but the reader should assume their use for Allah (may He be glorified and exalted), other prophets (peace be upon them), Companions (may Allah be pleased with them) or deceased Muslims (may Allah have mercy on them).

As this book is in English, it will use the Biblical English names for prophets and other people in our shared Abrahamic traditions (e.g. Moses, Jesus).

On references and sources

Translations of the Qur'an mainly relied on Sahih International and MAS Abdelhaleem (Oxford University Press), although others are occasionally used when they bring about the intended meaning more clearly.

As this is not an academic text, when hadith are cited, only the name of the compiler is mentioned, rather than the full reference to the volume and hadith number. Reference will be made to other scholars or books throughout the book without full academic citation, but the bibliography contains all sources used for readers who want further information.

HOW TO READ THIS BOOK

This book is intended to be reflected upon, so my suggestion would be to read it slowly and reflect after each chapter. While the chapters in the book build upon one another, they are also self-contained, so they can be studied selectively, if the reader would like to learn about a particular name or names.

For this reason, some stories may be repeated in different chapters (such as the stories of the Prophet Joseph or Āsiyah, for example), and there will be recurring themes. This ensures that a reader who has chosen to read about a particular name in the middle or at the end of the book will benefit from a full explanation of the story or theme, without having to refer to the chapter where the story is first narrated. This makes it more convenient for the reader to choose where they would like to start, should they so wish. Moreover, it ensures that the reader, whether or not he or she is starting at the beginning and reading in order, can read the book slowly and study it with others. The repetition of stories and themes emphasizes their importance and acts as a reminder for us.

FOREWORD

Any effort to share with others the thoughts and feelings that arise when one tries to know God better and grow in nearness to Him deserves to be appreciated. But it is a particular, personal pleasure for me to introduce these reflections on the names of God by Dr Jinan Yousef. First because she is a former student of mine, but also because I know her to be an observant Muslim, a devout believer, and deeply committed in her pursuit of knowledge and understanding of the religion.

Dr Yousef has spent much time pondering the names of God in the Qur'an, and studying the writings and lectures on the subject of other scholars and teachers. As part of the preparation for writing these *Reflections*, she has lectured on the topic in many gatherings of Muslims in university Islamic societies and community centers. Those who attended these lectures expressed their gratitude to her since she improved their understanding of their Lord, their love for Him and nearness to Him. Their questions and comments on these occasions in turn helped her to improve her arguments and presentation.

Knowing God is the most important responsibility human beings have. It is the means and end for understanding the purpose of our creation and being in this world, and for sustaining beneficial relations with all other creations and for avoiding doing harm to oneself or others. Without the effort to know God, we can never be guided, never live at peace with ourselves and with the world; rather, we will fall again and again into errors that are so persistent we may lose the ability even to unwish them, let alone build the resolve to undo their negative consequences in ourselves and in the world around us.

There are two main ways in which we come to know and reflect on God:

The first is by reflection on one's own creation as one among innumerable other beings, events and processes in the universe, all of which are, individually and as a whole, signs of the will and creative power of God. Such reflection awakens in us wonder and appreciation at the extent and perfection of God's knowledge, power and compassion. It is similar to the wonder and appreciation we feel whenever we see a wonderful building and marvel at the mastery of those who designed and built it. But the knowledge, skill and mastery in the creation of the universe is of an altogether higher order. God cannot be conceived as a designer on the model of any human designer. Our minds cannot encompass the subtlety and intricacy, at the largest or the smallest scale, of the interconnections between living and non-living forms; but we can sense the harmony behind their prolific diversity and beauty, and we can sense their interdependence. From all of that we get some intimations of the Majesty of our Lord. This way of knowing Him is called *'ilm bi-l-ayat*, knowledge through signs or indicators.

The second way is by reflection on God's names, actions and attributes. Just as, when someone introduces another person to us and says: 'So-and-so is a true, honest, kind, generous person', we have a favorable disposition to that person, and an incentive to build further acquaintance with him and get to know him better, so also what God has revealed in the Qur'an of His names and attributes gives us means and incentive to build and improve our knowledge of Him. What He has said about Himself in His Book and on the tongue of His Messenger is said for our benefit, as a courtesy to us, so that we can grow in nearness to Him, and in love for Him. This way of knowing Him is called *'ilm bi-l-sifat*, knowledge through the attributes.

This second way is the subject-matter of this book. The author very succinctly makes this point by saying: ...*one of the most beautiful things about His revealing His names and attributes is that it is the basis of our relationship with Him. We are told that we should love Allah, talk to Him, pray to Him and ask Him, but this may become a burden when we do not understand Him. And so, He reveals His names and attributes for us because He wants us to know Him – when we know Him, we can love Him. Moreover, He reveals from His names and attributes what is necessary for our relationship.*

Why has God revealed His names and attributes to us? Would it not have been enough to command our obedience without introducing Himself to us? Would we not have to obey Him, just because He is our Lord and Master? The answer to this question is No. Because God loves us and is merciful to us, He commands but He does not compel. Relationship with Him requires our consent to it, our desire for it. Moreover, whatever He commands us to do, He always, and He alone, also enables us to do. He does not command what is impossible for us but what is possible, and what is in reality most conformable and agreeable to the nature on which He created us. He commands what is good for us, what raises us in our human dignity, and He enables us to achieve that dignity in appropriate, easy ways that bring us a profound tranquility and steady contentment. Reflecting upon this, the author says: *With these names, God wants you to know Him. It may have been enough for God to say that He is God, and we must obey, without revealing anything else about Himself. But from His Mercy, He has told us His names and attributes in order for us to be able to connect to Him, and have a relationship that is based on hope, awe, and love.*

When God revealed to us His names and attributes, He did so in human language because that is the only language that we would understand well enough to act upon, to translate into regular, established practice. Human language is bound by the limitations of our perceptions and feelings, our reason and imagination. But God and His attributes have no such boundaries. We do not understand Him or we misunderstand Him if we try to conform His attributes to our limitations. The author is fully aware of this, and she puts it nicely: *There are certain things we must be aware of before proceeding. It may be easy to slip into anthropomorphizing God and His attributes because we can only imagine the human 'version' of the name or attribute. But God tells us, "There is nothing like Him: He is the All Hearing, the All Seeing," [Qur'an, 42:11]*

This book is an excellent explanation of the meanings of God's names and attributes. The author has avoided the unnecessary over-definition and fine-tuning of terms that is not useful and is often harmful, but often, alas, typical of speculative theologians. In the pursuit of refined and honed nuances of meaning, such expertise produces only uncertainty, ambiguity, misunderstanding, blurring and troubling the mind and taking it further from God. The aim and achievement of this book is to introduce God in the terms in which He introduces Himself, and thereby make approach to Him easier for willing hearts and minds, and knowing Him a lighter, more pleasant and rewarding manner.

I am confident that this book will help its readers to understand their Lord, to love Him and seek closeness to Him through humility in their devotions and obedience.

Mohammad Akram Nadwi
Oxford, August 2020

INTRODUCTION

Love is an extremely powerful emotion. Love makes lovers choose their beloveds over themselves. Love is a flutter of excitement in the heart, as well as reassuring calm. Love sweetens everything that is difficult. Love gives us meaning.

Some types of love in this world act as anchors for us. They provide us with the emotional safety that we need, and the security to be vulnerable. Love is understanding and kind, but it is also firm, when firmness is ultimately for the benefit of the beloved. However, other forms of love can be destructive. How many of us have witnessed what we thought was love result in heartache, pain, and disappointment?

True love is not fleeting, nor is it temporary, but its permanence takes root in the heart. We might have felt this type of love for certain people in our lives, and we should be grateful for this love.

When it comes to Allah, we know that we *should* love Him. Muslims are taught this from a young age. God says in the Qur'an, *'those who believe are stronger in love for Allah.'* [2:165]

While we often put those we love before what we ourselves want, we might not always choose God in this way. Part of the reason is that true love is based on how much we know someone, our relationship with that person, and his or her presence in, and impact on, our lives. We love our parents and our siblings. We love our friends and spouses. We would quite literally die for our children. If one were to ask the reason for this love, we would have more than a hundred reasons, each reason accompanied by memories and emotions. Our experiences with those whom we love are the basis for our love.

Allah, who created us and knows us more intimately than any human being, knows this about us, and indeed created this tendency in us. Thus, one of the most beautiful aspects of the revelation of His names and attributes is that they form the basis of our relationship with Him. We are told that we should love Allah, talk to Him, pray to Him and ask from Him, but this may feel burdensome when we do not understand God, or have false ideas about Him. And so, He reveals His names and attributes to us so that we can know Him – and when we know Him, we can love Him. Moreover, He reveals those of His names and attributes that are necessary for our relationship. Indeed, knowing Allah's names tells us something about ourselves; when we know that He is the Giver of Peace, for example, it means that we will necessarily go through periods of anxiety, and the antidote is to go to Him for that calm. Knowing that He is the Responder means that there is one who is asking; Him being the Forgiving means that we make mistakes. He also has names that He has not revealed, and they may be names that are not necessary for us to know in this earthly realm. But all of the names that He has revealed are important for our relationship with Him, and our understanding of this world, and our role in it.

With these names, God wants us to know Him. It would have been enough for God to say that He is God, and we must obey Him, without revealing anything else about Himself. But from His mercy, He has told us His names and attributes, so that we can connect to Him, and have a relationship with Him based on hope, awe, and love. Indeed, Ibn al-Qayyim said: '[Love] is the truth by which the heavens and the earth were created, it is the truth which His command and prohibition comprise, and it is the secret to devotion and its unicity; the testimony that there is no one worthy of worship but Allah.' [Madārij al-Sālikīn] He also said that one of the ways to earn God's love is by studying His names and attributes, bearing witness to them, and recognizing them.

There are certain things we must bear in mind before proceeding. It can be easy to slip into anthropomorphizing God and His attributes, because we can only imagine the human 'version' of a name or attribute. But Allah tells us, *'There is nothing like Him: He is the All Hearing, the All Seeing.'* [42:11]

This verse mentions His attributes of hearing and seeing. Human beings hear and see too; however, what is crucial is the preceding statement: *'there is nothing like Him.'* His hearing is not like our hearing and His seeing is not like our seeing. We need other means in order to hear and see: sound, light, the specific body parts and mechanisms that comprise our eyes and ears, etc. But God Almighty does not need these means – His hearing needs neither sound nor ears, and His sight needs no light nor eyes. As the great scholar Imam Mālik said, 'We know the what, not the how.'

We must always keep this in mind when learning the names and attributes of Allah – He is not like us, so we should guard against anthropomorphizing His qualities. This would take us down a dangerous route of applying human norms to Him, and thus imagining Him with similar human weaknesses. His kindness is not like our kindness – it is something we cannot even comprehend. Similarly, His dominion is not like human dominion, because He is above all, and He is the Most Just. This is also why His attributes must be understood holistically – He is both the Most Gentle and the Most Firm, the Giver and the Taker, the Most Merciful and the Most Just. We miss an essential piece of understanding when we focus only on the attributes that we want Him to have, not all of the attributes that He actually has. We have to remember that He is the Creator, and therefore the norms that He has created apply to His creation, not the other way around.

It is virtually impossible to extract all of the secrets of Allah's Beautiful Names, but the intention behind this book is to open a door to connection with God, through knowing Him. In this regard, I know that the book has many shortcomings, and I take full responsibility for them.

Before beginning this book and in order to truly benefit from it, we should have a sincere intention to know Him and become close to Him through knowing Him. We should ask Allah to open our hearts to understanding, and pray for benefit.

AL-HĀDĪ, AL-RASHĪD – THE GUIDE (1-2)

1

AL-HĀDĪ, AL-RASHĪD – THE GUIDE (1-2)

'But sufficient is your Lord as a guide and a helper.'

[25:31]

It would have been fitting to start a book on the names of God with the names most frequently used: Allah, al-Rabb (the Lord), or al-Raḥmān al-Raḥīm (the Entirely Merciful, the Especially Merciful). However, we will begin with His name al-Hādī – the Guide – as well as the related name, al-Rashīd, because the result of knowing God is guidance to Him, God willing. When reading His names and attributes, in addition to knowing God, our intention should be guidance to Him.

The Guide

The Arabic root of the word al-Hādī is *hā-dāl-yā* which, in essence, means to incline towards something. This root gives rise to two main meanings: it is used to describe guidance, as well as gentleness and calm. A gift in Arabic is *hadiyyah*, which is from the same root, because it makes the heart incline towards the giver of the gift; it guides the heart to that person. This is why guidance cannot be forced; at its root is gentleness.

When we think of guidance in religious terms, we tend to think of it as all or nothing – you are either guided or you are not. But guidance is a spectrum, a path which should ultimately lead to Allah and Paradise. Until we get there, God willing, we need further guidance – to continue on the path, to deal with the obstacles, and to not be seduced by the distractions that we may encounter along the way.

Think about it: Why would we go to a guide?

We seek a guide when we are in complete darkness and need someone to guide us out of it.

We seek a guide when we are lost and confused.

We seek a guide when we want a better way.

We seek a guide when we want specific details about the best path.

It is only the arrogant and the heedless who think that they are already sufficiently guided and there is nothing more for them to learn or do; that thought is already a sign that they are in need of further guidance. It takes humility and true intelligence to realize that at every stage, we need to seek guidance from the Ultimate Guide. This is why all Muslims – indeed, the Prophet Muhammad ﷺ himself – recite in every prayer: *'Guide us to the straight path.'* [1:6

Whatever level we are at, we all need some form of guidance.

As for His name al-Rashīd, in *Lisān al-'Arab*, it is stated that: 'Al-Rashīd is the one who directs His servants to what is beneficial for them i.e. He guides them and shows them the way.' The scholar al-Rāzī stated that this word has two related meanings: one is that *rashīd* is related to the word *rāshid* which, when used to describe someone, means that this person has a clear vision that is informed by wisdom and knowledge; the second is related to *murshid*, which means one who guides or directs. Thus al-Rashīd refers to One who directs to the right path with a clear vision as to the intended outcome, informed by wisdom and knowledge. Allah tells us in the Qur'an that our destination is Him and Paradise, and He shows us the way. The difference between direction (*rushd*) and guidance (*hidayah*) is that *hidāyah* is also guidance *along* the path. Moreover, there are levels to *hidāyah*, which is why we constantly ask God for guidance in Sūrat al-Fātiḥah: *'Guide us (ihdinā) to the straight path.'* [1:6]

You can be guided so that you are now cognizant of God, then you can be guided further to better deeds and closeness to Him; ultimate guidance comes in following the Sunnah of the Prophet Muhammad ﷺ in the most excellent manner. *Hidāyah* is also something that penetrates the heart.

Al-Ghazālī states that al-Rashīd is the One who directs you without needing signs. If I have to rely on Google Maps to direct someone, I cannot say that I have this attribute, because I am seeking help to direct someone to the way, but Allah does not need such tools. Thus, God sets us on the path, directing us through His wisdom to our ultimate destination.

In the Qur'an, the words *rushd* or *rashīd* are used in the following contexts: *'They said, "Shu'ayb, does your prayer tell you that we should abandon what our forefathers worshipped and refrain from doing whatever we please with our own property? Indeed you are a tolerant and sensible man (rashīd)."'* [11:87]

God also tells us that He has made clear the right path from the wrong one: *'There shall be no compulsion in [acceptance of] the religion. The right course (al-rushd) has become clear from the wrong.'* [2:256]

Allah is the One who directs us to the destination because He is the One who best knows the way, without needing directions or signs from any other. If you were lost and seeking directions, you would seek it from someone whom you *know* will direct you not simply to one way, but to the best way to the ultimate destination. There are many different apps that we download in order for us to navigate through the best routes; similarly, we should recite the Qur'an and seek to understand the Sunnah to find out which way to God is best.

Types of guidance

Allah's guidance is vast and wide. There is, at a very basic level, general guidance for all of His creation to that which benefits them. God says in the Qur'an: *'He [Moses] said, "Our Lord is He who gave each thing its form and then guided [it]."'* [20:50]

According to scholars, this is the natural 'guidance' of, for example, the bees who collect nectar from flower blossoms and gradually turn it into honey, the child who nurses from his or her mother, and even the capacity to learn that which will benefit us, such as cooking food or developing medicine. These are all possible because of the faculties given to us and other living creatures by God in order to guide us to what is best for us. This is the basic, general guidance.

Then, there is the guidance to God and His straight path. We are told in the Qur'an: *'There has come to you from Allah a light and a clear Book, by which Allah guides those who pursue His pleasure to the ways of peace and brings them out from darknesses into the light, by His permission, and guides them to a straight path.'* [5:15-16]

God is the One who guides us to know Him and His way. The use of our faculties should lead us to this conclusion, and God places signs in the universe, through His Words, and His people.

Many of us may think that it stops here. Once we are guided to believe in God, and perhaps fulfil the basic requirements that the path to Him involves, we may think that we are sufficiently guided. But God tells us that guidance increases: *'Indeed, they were youths who believed in their Lord, and We increased them in guidance.'* [18:13] Allah also says: *'And Allah increases those who were guided, in guidance.'* [19:76]

Guidance does not stop. This increase in guidance means increase in faith, tranquility and steadfastness, increase in good deeds, and increase in understanding. A person who has discovered that there is a path may stop there, reaching out to the Guide only when he or she has strayed or feels lost. But when you have access to the Guide, who can not only show you better and more beautiful ways, but can be with you throughout the journey, why would you not seek His guidance throughout? Indeed, why would you not want this Guide to accompany you throughout your journey?

Finally, there is guidance to Paradise:

> *'And they will say, 'Praise to Allah, who has guided us to this; and we would never have been guided if Allah had not guided us. Certainly the messengers of our Lord had come with the truth.' And they will be called, "This is Paradise, which you have been made to inherit for what you used to do."'* [7:43]

Ultimately, God guides us to Paradise. That is where the Straight Path leads, and we can only reach there with His aid.

The ways of guidance

While we know that God is the Guide in the abstract, *how* does Allah guide us to Him?

Allah guides us to Him and His attributes firstly through the universe. He tells us in the Qur'an: *'He causes to grow for you thereby the crops, olives, palm trees, grapevines, and from all the fruits. Indeed in that is a sign for a people who give thought.'* [16:11]

There are many such verses in the Qur'an, pointing to the signs in the universe. These signs, if properly pondered, should lead us to Allah; who else brought the universe into being, and everything in it? Scientists try to find out the 'how' – the Big Bang theory, for example – but they cannot expand upon a 'why' without recognizing that there is a 'who': God Himself, the Originator. Indeed, the natural guidance that God bestowed us with should enable us to recognize that all things come into being because someone brings them into being – they have a 'creator'. No one assumes that a phone, for example, came into existence because a perfect storm of factors and circumstances led to its invention, without a human hand; it is a basic function of a human's cognitive abilities to recognize that *someone* made the phone.

Indeed, this type of reflection also leads to an understanding of some of His attributes. For example, we can understand that He is the Creator, that He is all-Powerful, that He is the Provider, and that He shows Mercy. The Prophet Muhammad ﷺ, in a society that worshipped multiple idols, retreated to the Cave of Ḥirā to reflect. He reflected on the heavens and the earth, and became more resilient in his conclusions that the idols could not be real; they were not God. That is when he received revelation.

This revelation is the detailed guidance. God tells us: *'Indeed, this Qur'an guides to that which is most suitable and gives good tidings to the believers who do righteous deeds that they will have a great reward.'* [17:9]

While reflecting on the universe may bring us to the realization of the existence of God and some of His attributes, it is His book that further guides us to the details. It informs us of His attributes that we may not reach through reflection, such as His attribute of answering the supplications of His creation. It exhorts us to think, teaches us the meaning of the world around us, and shows us how to worship Him. This is the guidance of His book.

But, as human beings, we may misinterpret some of the guidance that is in the Qur'an. Due to limited knowledge, we may define words differently to what they are intended to mean. And many of us may not connect to words, but rather need to see guidance in action. And that is why God sends us His people: *'Those are the ones whom Allah has guided, so from their guidance take an example.'* [6:90]

The ones whom Allah has guided are, first and foremost, His Prophets, and then those who follow them. Through them, we see guidance and faith in action; when we are truly guided, they are the ones to whom we aspire.

Combining the guidance of the Qur'an and the Sunnah of the Prophet ﷺ, they teach us both to pray and how to pray, to speak well, to fast and how to fast, to help others, to give charity and the best way of giving charity, to establish justice, and so on. And this is also the secret to asking for more guidance in Sūrat al-Fātiḥah; we want to be more like the Prophets, and hence we must constantly be learning and improving.

We must remember that the way of the Prophet ﷺ was the way of moderation. When some Companions came to the Prophet ﷺ to inform him of their acts of worship – praying all night and not sleeping; fasting every single day without a break; never getting married – the Prophet ﷺ corrected them. Putting in effort for the sake of Allah is commendable, but not to the extent that you do not give your body or your family their due rights. Indeed, giving them their rights is part of the worship of God.

In Sūrat al-Kahf, the youth of the cave made the following supplication to God: *'Our Lord, grant us from Yourself mercy and prepare for us from our affair right guidance (rashadan).'* [18:10]

They were being persecuted for their beliefs and had nowhere to turn for refuge but the cave. There, they asked God to show them the best way out of their predicament. In that story, God caused them to sleep for over 300 years, and then showed them that they were on the right path. The tyrant died and the people were then able to follow the youths' example without fear. Thus, remember that sometimes wisdom and direction are not rewarded or appreciated by people, but the fruits will show later, God willing (*inshā'Allāh*).

Finally, Allah guides us through His direct actions with us. We can all point to at least one incident – if not many – in which we have felt God being directly with us. Sometimes it is the response to a verbalized prayer or the actualization of a silent hope. It can be an answer to a question only God knew you had asked, or the coming together of events so perfectly they could only be planned by Him. Or it could be in the biggest test you ever had to endure that forced you to turn to Him.

Regardless of all these means of guidance, we are still required to put in the effort and make that choice to follow guidance. A Guide would not force you to be guided. A Guide will show you the path, and you can choose whether to take that path or not. As Allah tells us: *'The truth is from your Lord, so whoever wills - let him believe; and whoever wills - let him disbelieve.'* [18:29]

But I feel lost...

Sometimes this feeling of being lost can bring us closer to God.

At times, we *need* to feel as though we do not know where we are going, because that is when we start searching. And that is precisely when Allah shows you that He is The Guide (al-Hādī), and how life changes when the Light of God is in it.

Perhaps you started out something with a sense of purpose, but in your journey, you were knocked off the path towards the greater goal. You need al-Hādī. Maybe you are having some sort of mid-life crisis. You need al-Hādī. It could be that you are confused about what path to take in your life that would benefit you in this life and the next. You need al-Hādī. And we cannot for one moment believe that there is no way out and no right path. Allah says in a revelation from God expressed in the words of the Prophet ﷺ (a hadith *qudsī*): *'O My servants, all of you are astray except for those I have guided, so seek guidance of Me and I shall guide you.'* [Muslim]

Guidance can come in numerous ways. It can even come in the so-called 'coincidences' that we experience – which are not coincidences at all – that cause us to reflect or to turn to Allah. How many of us have experienced guidance from where we did not expect it? Indeed, the Prophet's ﷺ Companion 'Umar was on his way to kill the Prophet ﷺ, when he was stopped by someone who said to him that his own sister had accepted Islam. That detour was Allah's guidance. He angrily went to his sister's home, and in a fit of rage, hit her and caused her to bleed. His guilt at that moment

– and guidance can come in a moment – softened his heart to the extent needed for him to hear the message.

So, guidance can take place over time, or in can come in a moment. It can be in sincere advice someone gives you, or in a verse of the Qur'an that you happen to hear or recite, or through an unexpected detour. Our knowledge of Allah's name al-Hādī should cause us to always have our hearts open to His guidance, as well as the conviction that His guidance *will* come, especially for those who seek it.

As Allah gave Himself the attributes of Guidance and Light, how can we ever believe that we will be in darkness for too long?

What about misguidance? Does God misguide too?

Some might say, 'perhaps I am not guided because Allah has misguided me.' They point to such verses in the Qur'an: *'If God so willed, He would have made you all one people, but He leaves to stray whoever He will and guides whoever He will. You will be questioned about your deeds.'* [16:93]

If we do not understand the nature of guidance, and if we do not read the Qur'an holistically, it is easy to misinterpret this verse and other similar verses. As we mentioned above, there are different stages and levels to guidance. At a very basic level, everyone has been sent some of the means of guidance, whether that be through the universe around us, or His books, or His people. Thus, God has guided us by giving us these means. We are told in the Qur'an: *'As for Thamud, We gave them guidance but they preferred blindness.'* [41:17]

The people of Thamūd were given guidance, but they *chose* not to follow it. By nature, a guide does not force us, but shows us the way. Following the Guide is up to us.

As for the person who goes to the Guide and says 'help me to follow the signs and remain on the path', the Guide will be with him or her even more. That person may feel more motivation, closeness to the Guide, and certainty. That is another level or stage of guidance. But it needs a person to make the choice – to *will* – to be guided, and that is the person who will then taste the sweetness of guidance. The person who, out of his or her own volition, *chooses not* to follow God's guidance, will not taste the sweetness of faith – that is the person that is left to stray. Allah tells us about the hypocrites in the Qur'an: '*Why are you divided in two about the hypocrites, when God Himself has rejected them because of what they have done? Do you want to guide those God has left to stray? If God leaves anyone to stray, you [Prophet] will never find the way for him.*' [4:88]

God is careful to tell us that He rejected the hypocrites '*because of what they have done.*' They did not want to be guided and committed acts of treachery; if people do not want to be guided, then *we* cannot put the sweetness of guidance in their hearts. That only comes from Allah. There is the guidance that one chooses to follow, in which one is given the choice, and then because of that, God puts the sweetness of guidance in one's heart, which is itself a form of guidance.

Moreover, while many translations capitalize 'He wills' in the verse above to indicate Allah, in Arabic it can be read in another way: the 'he' in lowercase, referring to the person, not to God. Thus, some scholars understand the 'he' to be not Allah but the person, affirming that if that person *wants* (hence 'he wills' in lowercase) to be guided, then God will help him. God tells us: '*It is not (attributable to) Allah that He should lead a people astray after He has guided them; He even makes clear to them what they should guard against; surely Allah knows all things.*' [9:115]

It is crucial to remember that God's names are al-Hādī – the Ultimate Guide – and al-Rashīd – the One who Directs to the Right Path – so no one who seeks Him will ever be turned away, and everyone is given signs. But we are given the choice in whether we wish to follow the Guide or turn away.

Living with these names

1. Put in the effort to be guided

Take the first step of realizing that He has this attribute, and have the certainty that Allah will not turn a seeker away. Then, ask Him with certainty. Supplicate to Him, pray the prayer for guidance (*ṣalāt al-istikhārah*) and talk to Him. Finally, use the means around you. Re-assess your goals, seek people's advice and take the steps needed to try to find an answer. When we feel an internal instability, these steps may be hard, but God tells us *'And those who strive for Us – We will surely guide them to Our ways.'* [29:69].

Moreover, Sheikh Rātib al-Nabulsī stated that the closer a person is to God, the more likely he is to have this attribute of *rushd*. Allah says in the Qur'an: *'God has endeared faith to you and made it beautiful to your hearts; He has made disbelief, mischief, and disobedience hateful to you. It is people like this who are rightly guided (rāshidūn) through God's favor and blessing: God is all knowing and all wise.'* [49:7-8]

2. Be gentle in guiding people to good

Guide people to the Guide. The Prophet ﷺ said *'by Allah, were Allah to guide a single man through you would be better for you than a herd of red camels.'*[1] [Abū Dāwūd] When Moses and Aaron were sent to Pharaoh, they were told *'speak to him gently so that he may take heed, or show respect.'* [20:44] We should show people the truth in our words and in our actions, and we should do so out of love. This religion is a truly a gift with which God blesses the one who has it, so we should want to spread God's gifts to others because we truly care.

Moreover, Ibn al-Qayyim says: 'God is *rashīd* and He loves *rushd*, and so He makes whom He loves like that [i.e. gives them this quality].' God tells us that He gave the Prophet Abraham,

---

[1] 'Red camels' denotes great wealth.

peace be upon him, this quality: *'Long ago We bestowed right judgment (rushdahu) on Abraham and We knew him well.'* [21:51]

The Prophet Abraham was given wisdom and direction, and thus he was able to direct others in the way that suited them best. He knew how to make his people think when he destroyed all of the idols (21:51-67), and he was able to debate the tyrant in a way that was suited to him (2:258). A person can have this quality in its limited human form by asking God and seeking knowledge in order to gain wisdom (and not simply to 'know a lot').

3. Remember that you cannot force people into guidance

God says in the Qur'an: *'You [Prophet] cannot guide everyone you love to the truth; it is God who guides whoever He will: He knows best those who will follow guidance.'* [28:56]

While we should inform others about our faith, and show them its beauty in our words and deeds, God will put the light of guidance in the hearts of those who choose guidance; we cannot do that. The uncle of the Prophet ﷺ, Abū Ṭālib – who had stood by the Prophet ﷺ through so much – wanted to remain on the ways of his ancestors. He made that choice, and God allowed him that. The Prophet ﷺcould not force him to choose otherwise. Thus, our responsibility is to be people of guidance through our speech and action, all the while knowing that we cannot and should not force people.

AL-RABB – THE LORD (3)

2

AL-RABB – THE LORD (3)

'When his Lord said to him, "Submit", he said "I have submitted to the Lord of the worlds."'

[2:131]

If you were to pick up a copy of the Qur'an, the first thing you would encounter is the opening chapter: Sūrat al-Fātiḥah. This chapter contains seven short verses and they introduce us to the whole of the Qur'an and to God Himself.

The attributes of God mentioned in Sūrat al-Fātiḥah are even more significant because Muslims recite this chapter in every unit of every prayer – indeed, the ritual prayer (*al-ṣalāh*) is not valid without reciting it. Therefore, every Muslim who prays the ritual prayer must have memorized these verses. They may only know two or three other short chapters of the Qur'an by heart, but this chapter is essential. Hence, most will know God by the attributes mentioned in this chapter specifically, even if they do not know anything else. This is also true for someone who does not know anything about Islam, and the first thing they encounter is the opening chapter of the Qur'an.

We are told: *'[All] praise is [due] to Allah...'* [1:2]

If you are unfamiliar with Islam or the Qur'an and are reading it for the first time, you may ask, 'who is Allah that is owed this praise?'

'...Rabb of all the worlds.' [1:2]

Here we are introduced to the first foundation for our relationship with God – He is the Rabb. And what does this word mean? Some of the names of God are 'encompassing names',[2] signifying that the name encompasses many meanings. Al-Rabb is one of these names, as linguistically it means the Master, the Owner, the One who arranges all matters, the Nurturer, the Sustainer, the One who is worshipped, the One who reforms His servants and their affairs, and the One who bestows favors and blessings.

So, God is the owner, who maintains the existence of and cares for the world that He owns and all those in it, ensures its growth, gives gifts to all those who inhabit it, and has full authority over it. This relationship is important to define because there are many theories about God's relationship with us. There are those who believe that God is the Creator, but beyond that, we have no other relationship with Him.[3] There is a modern belief that God – or an overseeing deity – exists and helps us along our path to achieve worldly happiness, but without us being responsible to Him or following His instructions for our lives, especially not those that conflict with our base desires or ego. In the Qur'an, we are told that Allah is the Rabb and, as our Lord, we are responsible to Him and should obey Him. According to Ibn al-Qayyim, the absolute highest level of love is *'ubūdiyyah*, which loosely translates as 'servitude' – as it turns one into a slave (an *'abd)* – to the Beloved. When the Prophet ﷺ was given the choice of being a prophet who was a king or a prophet who was a slave, he chose the latter [Aḥmad]. And the reason he did so is that he understood intimately the honor in being a servant of God, the Rabb, and wanted to humble himself before His Lord. Indeed, choosing this name meant that he could have the honorable title of being *'abdullah* – literally 'the servant' or 'slave' of God.

---

[2] *Al-Asmā' Al-Jāmi'ah* in Arabic

[3] For example, Einstein expressed the belief in a God that created everything in harmony, but that this God does not concern Himself with the doings of mankind. Walter Isaacson, *Einstein: His Life and Universe* (New York: Simon and Schuster, n.d.).

Submitting to and obeying someone other than ourselves appears to go against much of what the modern world teaches us. There is an emphasis on making our own rules, as well as a disdain for authority. But human authority is not the same as divine authority – it is flawed and tainted by self-interest. Despite this, God gives us a choice: we may choose not to obey Him. In the Qur'an, we are told: '*So whoever wills – let him believe, and whoever wills – let him disbelieve.*" [18:29]

At the end of the day, we will all return to Him and are subject to His will. God says in the Qur'an: '*Then He directed Himself to the heaven while it was smoke and said to it and to the earth, "Come, willingly or by compulsion." They said, "We have come willingly".*' [41:11]

The heavens and the earth understood this relationship. Obedience becomes natural once we know *who* the Rabb is; it only becomes burdensome and something to be resisted when we do not understand the nature of our Rabb. Because this word contains elements of care and nurturing, the commands of our Rabb contain the ultimate benefit for us, and help us on our journey towards Him.

Turning to your Rabb

The context of when this name is cited in the Qur'an tells us more about this relationship. The first mention of this name is found in the initial verses revealed to the Prophet Muhammad ﷺ: '*Recite in the name of your Rabb who created.*" [96:1]

Allah's name al-Rabb was the attribute first revealed to the Prophet ﷺ to know his Lord. At that point, the Prophet Muhammad ﷺ had been searching. He was forty years old and had been through much, having been orphaned at a young age. His father had died while his mother was still pregnant with him; his mother then passed away in front of him when he was just six years of age; his grandfather, who had taken care of him after his mother passed, died when he was eight years old. He then moved to his uncle's house with ten other children, and lived with very little means. He worked as a shepherd, witnessed war and peace, and eventually worked in trade. He then married his wife Khadijah when he was twenty-five years old, and had six children: four girls, and two boys who had died in infancy. His was not an easy life, and he witnessed the societal injustices that occurred around him.

So, when Allah revealed His words to him, He told the Prophet ﷺ that He was his Rabb – 'your Rabb' (*rabbuka*) – and this was reassuring to the Prophet ﷺ. There was a Rabb who, despite the Prophet's ﷺ difficulties, was always there. There was a Rabb who, despite injustices that occur, was in control of everything. There was a Rabb who, despite his feeling at times alone and abandoned, had been nurturing him throughout. And, because there was a Rabb of the whole universe and beyond, there was a better way to live in the rules that He has prescribed.

A more contemporary example can be seen in Malcolm X – Al-Hajj Malik al-Shabazz, may God rest his soul – as he described certain events in his life in his autobiography:

> 'And out from where they had been concealed walked two other detectives. They'd had me covered. One false move, I'd have been dead...
>
> If I hadn't been arrested right when I was, I could have been dead another way. Sophia's husband's friend had told her husband about me. And her husband had arrived that morning, and had gone to the apartment with a gun, looking for me. He was at the apartment just about when they took me to the precinct...
>
> I have thought a thousand times, I guess, about how I so narrowly escaped death twice that day. That's why I believe that everything is written.'[4]

---

[4] Alex Haley, *The Autobiography of Malcolm X* (Ballantine Books, 1992), 241–42.

God was taking care of him. When we fully internalize and understand that God is the Rabb, we know exactly to whom to turn in difficult moments. All of the prophets called upon God as 'my Lord' (*rabbī*) when faced with adversity and need. For example:

> '*[Moses] said, "My Lord, indeed I do not possess except myself and my brother, so part us from the defiantly disobedient people."*' [5:25]

> '*And [mention] Zechariah, when he called to his Lord, "My Lord, do not leave me alone [with no heir], while you are the best of inheritors."*' [21:89]

> '*[Noah] said, "My Lord, support me because they have denied me."*' [23:26]

All the above examples give us glimpses into how Allah manifests His Lordship (*rubūbiyyah*) – He is the One who nurtures the orphan, the One to whom we turn because of His power and control over the whole universe, and the One who sustains this world.

What does this mean for you?

Al-Rabb is your Rabb too, who has nurtured you, taught you in ease and hardship, and is the One to whom you can turn in any situation. There is nothing outside of His power and nothing happens without His permission. While others may act as though they are lords, they too are subject to the only true Lord. So, turn to Him and trust Him, and reflect back on your life to see how your Rabb was always there with you and for you.

In the example of Moses, He made a supplication to God. Allah answered his supplication, and then reminded him of how He was there for him even before Moses knew how to ask:

> '*And We had already conferred favor upon you another time, When We inspired to your mother what We inspired, [Saying], "Cast him into the chest and cast it into the river, and the river*

will throw it onto the bank; there will take him an enemy to Me and an enemy to him." And I bestowed upon you love from Me that you would be brought up under My Eye. [And We favored you] when your sister went and said, "Shall I direct you to someone who will be responsible for him?" So We restored you to your mother that she might be content and not grieve. And you killed someone, but We saved you from retaliation and tried you with a [severe] trial. And you remained [some] years among the people of Madyan. Then you came [here] at the decreed time, O Moses. And I produced you for Myself. Go, you and your brother, with My signs and do not slacken in My remembrance. Go, both of you, to Pharaoh. Indeed, he has transgressed. And speak to him with gentle speech that perhaps he may be reminded or fear [Allah].' [20:37-44]

All those times when the world seemed unfair and did not make sense were a preparation for what was to come. Everything in your life, too, that seems to be out of your control, is in the Hands of the Lord. Indeed, God is the Lord of everyone, but He has a special relationship with those who seek Him and try to earn His pleasure in His care for them.

Lord of the worlds, the nations, and those who think

Throughout this book, one thing that must be remembered is that even if words are shared by the Creator and creation, and may help us in understanding the attributes of God, they are not the same in meaning. The word *rabb* – like in English, 'lord' or 'master' – can be used for a human being; the difference is, when used for a person, there must be an addition. For example, the phrase *rabb al-bayt* is often used in Arabic, and means the lord or master of the house or home. But Allah is the only One who is al-Rabb – the complete Rabb.

In the context of Sūrat al-Fātiḥah, we are additionally told that he is *Rabb al-'Ālamīn* – translated as 'the Lord of all the worlds' – which is also a title that is reserved for Him.

The word *al-ʿālamīn* (worlds) also encompasses many meanings. At a very general and basic level, it encompasses all of creation, including humans, jinn,[5] angels, animals and other entities, each of which may be referred to as a 'world.' One says 'the world of angels,' 'the animal world,' 'the human world' or the 'world of the jinn.' This extends to everything big and small; even bacteria and cells are their own worlds. Most of the time we do not even realize the greatness of Allah's creation, making us ignorant of Allah's power over all His creation.

Sheikh al-Shaʿrāwī moreover stated that the word *al-*ʿā*lamīn* refers to the 'thinking worlds' – the emphasis on 'thinking' means that we must use our minds in order to reach Him. Moreover, since God is the Lord of the 'thinking' worlds, then naturally He is also the Lord of the 'un-thinking' – meaning the inanimate.

Finally, the word *al-*ʿā*lamīn* also means that He is the Lord of all the 'peoples' – meaning that He is the Lord of all of the different nations, tribes, and peoples. No matter our language, our skin color, or our culture, He is the Rabb of all of us. He is what unites us; in fact, He created us in this way. Submission to Him does not require us to all be the same, but rather to submit to Him in all of our diversity.

Most religious traditions have this basic understanding of God – the Master, Lord, and Nurturer. Since this word encompasses different meanings, what is the distinguishing feature of this Rabb? What would immediately come to mind when thinking of the word 'lord' or 'master' is authority. But Sūrat al-Fātiḥah immediately clarifies what kind of Rabb He is, as the following verse states: '*The Entirely Merciful, the Especially Merciful.*' [1:2] Elsewhere in the Qur'an, we are told: '*[And] "Peace," a word from a Merciful Lord.*' [36:58]

When you think of the name al-Rabb, you are not meant to think of the relationship as purely one of authority, even though

[5] Jinn are God's creation that we cannot see. Similar to humans, they have free will.

that is a part of the meaning; rather, this is equally a relationship with a loving and merciful Rabb. The next chapter will explore these names of Allah.

Living with this name

1. Worship your Rabb

God says in the Qur'an: *'Indeed, Allah is my Lord and your Lord, so worship Him. That is the straight path.'* [3:51]

'And worship your Lord until there comes to you the certainty (death).' [15:99]

Knowing that Allah is our Rabb is to worship Him wholeheartedly. And that worship has a sweetness, especially when we know *whom* we are worshipping. Thus, part of worshipping Allah by this name is to learn what He has commanded of us so that we can best obey Him.

2. Look back at your life and see how He has been taking care of you all along

Just like the Prophet Muhammad ﷺ, the Prophet Moses, Malcolm X, and many more, look back at your life and see how Allah has been taking care of you. Talk to Him and thank Him for being there with you. Remember that in every hardship there is a lesson from *'a Merciful Lord'*. [36:58]

3. Call upon him like the prophets

All the prophets were close to God and called upon Him with '*Rabbī*' – '*my* Lord'. Many supplications from the Prophet ﷺ also call upon Him with *rabbī*'. He is also your Lord, so call upon Him with all of your heart: *Rabbī!*

AL-RAḤMĀN, AL-RAḤĪM, AL-RA'ŪF – MERCY (4-6)

3

AL-RAḤMĀN, AL-RAḤĪM, AL-RA'ŪF – MERCY (4-6)

'In the Name of God, the Most Merciful (al-Raḥmān), the Most Compassionate (al-Raḥīm).'

[1:1]

Imagine that you had just a few moments to tell someone about yourself; what characteristics would you choose? What defines you? In all your human complexity, you would choose to highlight those things that are important for your relationship with that person. If you are being interviewed for a job, you may focus on the fact that you are hardworking and resourceful, or that you have expertise in the position you are applying for. When you are talking to someone for marriage, you may highlight your kindness and patience. Wherever relevant, you would focus on those qualities that are essential to your relationship.

In defining His relationship with us, God consistently emphasizes two essential attributes, and out of all of the attributes He could have chosen to remind us of *who He is*, God begins with this: mercy (*raḥmah).* These are the names that God has chosen to start the recitation of His words, the Qur'an, at the beginning of every chapter – this is His introduction to us. For those who do not know their Lord except that He is their Lord, it is this attribute that they are supposed to first encounter.

This is not insignificant. First impressions are important and they set the tone for what is to come. God could have impressed upon His majesty, His strength, and His power: they are all part of His attributes. But time and again, just in case we despair, or our hearts harden, or our minds become confused, He brings us back: remember His love and mercy.

Raḥmān and *raḥīm* both come from the same Arabic root, *rā-ḥā-mīm*, which means a combination of tenderness, affection, sympathy and compassion. In showing us what this looks like in action, the Prophet ﷺ pointed to a scene that was occurring right before the Companions' eyes:

A woman was frantically looking for her child in the aftermath of a battle. Imagine the feeling of a mother who, for one moment, thinks she had lost her child, *and* in a battlefield. Imagine her feeling when she finally found him, scooped him up as she wept, and then nursed him. After witnessing this scene, the Prophet ﷺ asked his Companions, *'Do you think that this woman would throw her child in the fire?'* And they said, *'No, by God she would not, if she is able not to.'* He then said, *'Allah the Exalted is more merciful with His slave than this woman with her child.'* [Bukhārī]

This type of mercy – from a mother towards her child – is one that most people can understand. Moreover, the Prophet ﷺ was not general in his example; he could have simply said that God's mercy is more than the mercy of a mother towards her child. But that would be abstract, and some people may not even enjoy that type of relationship with their mothers. They may relate the flaws in that relationship to Allah. The Prophet ﷺ rather demonstrated this mercy through a mother faced with the situation of *losing* her child and *finding* him again. The intensity of *that* mercy, the force of *that* love, the gentleness in *that* affection: Allah is more merciful and loving to His creation than *all that*, and these are the feelings meant to be invoked when we call on Him by these names.

Al-Raḥmān, al-Raḥīm: An essential attribute, a manifestation

God is al-Raḥmān and al-Raḥīm and, as mentioned above, both of these attributes come from the same root. Their different forms show us the types of mercy and how God manifests His mercy.

When Allah tells us He is al-Raḥmān, He is pointing to an essential attribute. The form of the word (the *ān* suffix) indicates an all-encompassing nature, immediacy and expansiveness; for example, one who is filled with anger is *ghaḍbān*; *ḥayrān* is one who is filled with confusion.[6] If someone is described as *ghaḍbān*, you would stay out of his way because of the intensity of his anger, as well the fact that it can be directed at anyone. The one who is *ghāḍib*, however, is less intense, and this word can be used to say that the person is angry for a specific reason or with a person.

So, Allah – who chooses His own names and is not named by others – tells us that His state is one of an all-compassing, immediate, overflowing mercy. This mercy is not limited and touches everything and everyone at this moment: humans and non-humans; men and women; old and young; those who believe and those who do not. Al-Ghazālī states that His mercy 'is all-inclusive in that it includes the worthy and the unworthy, this life and that which is to come and encompasses the essentials, needs and advantages which go beyond them.'[7] The beauty of this name is that, like the name Allah, it is reserved for God alone. His other names and attributes – such as being wise or great – may be used to describe humans although, as we know, His attributes are nothing like ours, even if they share the same name. Regarding al-Raḥmān, God says: '*Say, "Call upon Allah or call upon the Most Merciful [al*

---

[6] Al-Ashqar, *Sharḥ Ibn Al-Qayyim Li Asmā' Allāh Al-Ḥusnā*, 36. Umar Sulayman Al-Ashqar, *Sharḥ Ibn Al-Qayyim Li Asmā' Allāh Al-Ḥusnā* (Amman: Dar al-Nafā'is, 2008), 36.

[7] Abū Ḥāmid Al-Ghazālī, *The Ninety-Nine Beautiful Names of God: Al-Maqṣad Al-Asnā Fi Sharḥ Asmā' Allāh Al-Ḥusnā*, trans. David Burrell and Nazih Daher, The Ghazali Series (Cambridge: The Islamic Texts Society, 1992), 52.

Raḥmān]. Whichever [name] you call – to Him belong the best names."' [17:110]

To show how central mercy is, His name al-Raḥmān is interchangeable here with Allah. Indeed, we are told that when God decreed creation, He also decreed: *'My mercy prevails over My wrath.'* [Bukhārī]

However, language by its very nature is limited. The form of the word *raḥmān*, like *ghaḍbān* and *ḥayrān*, may linguistically indicate that this state is temporary. And thus, the two names tend to come together: al-Raḥmān and al-Raḥīm. The latter indicates permanency and the possibility of deferring its expression. In combining these two attributes, God has covered all the bases – His mercy is all encompassing and immediate, as well as permanent and far-reaching into the future. Al-Raḥīm also refers to the specific manifestation of His mercy. Allah says in the Qur'an: *'And ever is He, to the believers, Merciful (raḥīman).'* [33:43]

While God's general mercy extends to everyone, there is a specific mercy for those who believe in Him. It is only those who believe in Him who experience the mercy of the month of Ramadan or the five daily prayers. It is those with an ounce of faith to whom God will extend His mercy on the Day of Judgment.

Moreover, Allah combines His name al-Raḥīm with His name al-Ghafūr (the Most Forgiving): *'And when those come to you who believe in Our verses, say, "Peace be upon you. Your Lord has decreed upon Himself mercy: that any of you who does wrong out of ignorance and then repents after that and corrects himself – indeed, He is Forgiving and Merciful."'* [6:54]

Sheikh Māhir Muqaddim states that the combination of these two names is an indication of the perfection of God's mercy. The effect of His all-encompassing mercy is forgiveness, over and over again. Moreover, the attribute of forgiveness is mentioned before mercy in this combination because forgiveness is a type of purification from our mistakes, while mercy includes a type of care.

So, we are purified of sin though His forgiveness, and taken care of by Him, through His mercy.

Allah also combines this name with His name al-Ra'ūf. He says: *'And indeed, Allah is to you Kind (ra'ūf) and Merciful.'* [57:9]

The next section will explain the meaning of this name.

Al-Ra'ūf

Al-Ra'ūf is 'the One who has pity (on others), and pity is the intensification of mercy. Therefore, it has the same meaning as *Raḥīm* though in an intensified form.'[8] God says in the Qur'an: *'And never would Allah have caused you to lose your faith. Indeed Allah is, to the people, Kind (ra'ūf) and Merciful.'* [2:143]

So, if al-Ra'ūf is simply a more intensified form of mercy, what is the difference between *raḥmah* and *ra'fah* (kindness, from the same root as al-Ra'ūf)? There are several subtle differences. The first is in relation to when this mercy manifests. For example, if a hardship befalls you, the One who is Merciful – al-Raḥīm – has mercy on you during and after that calamity. He extends His kindness to you during the hardship, and indeed the hardship itself may be from His mercy. But *ra'fah* is mercy *before* the calamity hits, and involves Him taking care of you and warning you so that the calamity can be averted altogether. Sheikh Rātib al-Nabulsī gives an example of parents who are protective of their children. Parents will dress their child in warm clothes during winter so that they do not suffer from the cold. That is *ra'fah*. When a child becomes sick, the parent whose heart aches, and who does everything to get medicine to ease the child's pain, is merciful – *raḥīm*. Imam al-Qushayrī states that *ra'fah* is the highest form of mercy, where God protects His servants by warning them of the deeds that necessitate punishment.

Moreover, the word *ra'fah* can only refer to acts that are manifestly compassionate and kind. One can be merciful – i.e. have *raḥmah* – even though his or her actions appear to be harsh. For

[8] *Ibid.*, 139.

example, a parent may have to force a child to take medicine that is essential to their health. To the child, that may not seem merciful, even though it is. *Ra'fah*, on the other hand, are only those actions that are clearly and outwardly kind and compassionate.

God does not want us to have an ounce of doubt about His mercy towards us. His mercy is not only all-encompassing, with a special kind reserved for the believers on the Day of Judgment, but He is telling us that His warnings to us are out of an intense mercy. He does not want us to go through the hurt and pain we would have gone through had He not warned us. His love and mercy are in both the bitter medicine and the manifest gifts He gives.

What does this mean for us?

In order to understand this amazing mercy in the grand scheme of things, the Prophet ﷺ informs us that, *'Allah has divided mercy into 100 parts, and He retained with Him ninety-nine parts, and sent down to Earth one part. Through this one part, creatures deal with one another with compassion, so much so that an animal lifts its hoof over its young lest it should hurt it.'* [Bukhārī].

When your mother shows affection towards you, or when your spouse covers you with a blanket lest you feel cold, remember that this is only a fraction of the one part of mercy that Allah sent down to Earth. So imagine the mercy He has saved for His people on the Day of Judgment!

This intense focus on mercy should define our relationship with Allah. When we begin reciting the Qur'an, we start by remembering that the One who sent the Qur'an has an essential attribute of mercy – 'in the name of God, the Most Merciful, the Most Compassionate' (*bismillāh al-raḥmān al-raḥīm*). Thus, every single letter, every word, every meaning of the Qur'an has mercy in it. The Most Merciful also sent His Prophet ﷺ *'as a mercy to the worlds.'* [21:107] Through the Prophet ﷺ, we learn what mercy looks like in its human manifestation.

When we look around us, we need to see mercy in the way that everything is created, even in hardship. In all cases of difficulty, the Prophet ﷺ said: '*No fatigue, nor disease, nor sorrow, nor sadness, nor hurt, nor distress befalls a Muslim, even if it were the prick he receives from a thorn, but that Allah expiates some of his sins for that.*' [Bukhārī] None of our pain goes unnoticed.

The culmination of Allah's mercy is in the Paradise that He created, which the Prophet ﷺ described as a place '*no eye has seen and no ear has heard and neither has the thought occurred in any person's heart.*' [Bukhārī] It is this place that we strive to enter, where we will understand that this is what our struggle was for. It is reported that when one of the most miserable people in the world – meaning the person who has only seen struggle and pain in his life – is 'dipped' once into Paradise, God will ask him, '*did you ever face any distress or a thing you hate?*' And that person will respond, '*no, by Your glory! Never did I face anything unpleasant!*' [Aḥmad] Whatever hardship was suffered will feel as though it was nothing, and this is something for us to remember when we go through difficult times: in His mercy, God has prepared for us the ultimate mercy, which will eliminate any form of pain that we ever felt. This is the reward of those who are admitted to Paradise.

Therefore, when we see everything – good and bad – as coming from an All-Merciful source, we can see beyond what is immediately in front of us. When there is hardship, we can search for the mercy in it – what are the lessons we can learn? When there is good, we can praise Him and thank Him.

Moreover, God's *ra'fah* is in His instructing us on the best way to be in this world. When we are faced with things we cannot explain, or suffering that seems too great, it is our responsibility to act. And Allah tells us *how* to act as His vicegerents on this earth. Every suffering will have its end, as '*Allah will bring about, after hardship, ease.*' [65:7] We will only be asked about what we did in the face of it.

While there is much more to say, part of His Mercy can be seen in His other attributes. We see His Mercy in the fact that He is the Lord of the Worlds and is still merciful towards us; in His justice; in His patience; in His wisdom, and more.

Living with this name

1. Have mercy on others

Just as we love that Allah bestows His mercy and kindness upon us, so should we treat others the way that we love to be treated. Muslims by their very nature should exhibit mercy, because we are servants of the Most Merciful. The Prophet Muhammad ﷺ said: *'Those who show mercy to their fellow beings will be shown mercy by the Merciful Lord. So, show mercy to those on the earth, and He who is in the heavens will show mercy to you."* [Tirmidhī]

2. Learn the things that bring about Allah's mercy

While Allah bestows His mercy upon everyone, we mentioned that He has reserved a special type of mercy for His beloved servants. The Prophet ﷺ teaches us what brings about God's special mercy. For example, he ﷺ tells us, *'may Allah have mercy on a man who is kind when he buys, when he sells, and when he makes a demand.'* [Bukhārī] Business can sometimes be cut-throat, where being harsh can be seen as 'getting things done', and all are looking out for themselves. The Prophet ﷺ tells us that kindness should be part of conducting business, and is cause for receiving God's mercy.

Furthermore, he told us, *'may Allah have mercy on the man who gets up at night to pray and wakes up his wife to pray, and if she refuses, he sprinkles water in her face. And may Allah have mercy on the woman who gets up at night to pray, and wakes her husband up to pray, and if he refuses, she sprinkles water in his face.'* [Abū Dāwūd] God has mercy on the couple who encourage each other to do good, and wake each other up gently to pray the voluntary night prayer.

3. Increase mercy in your heart

Living in our own bubble and being consumed with our own issues can numb us to the suffering around us, when we view our problems as being the greatest. This is not to minimize whatever suffering we are going through, but at times we may get caught up in our lives and forget other people. Our hearts may harden, and we may not be able to empathize with the issues and struggles of others. Helping and being with others who are struggling should increase the mercy in our hearts. We can do this through volunteering, for example, for different causes, such as at a soup kitchen, or an organization that provides housing for the homeless, or time with the elderly. Give some of your time, energy and money to stand with people.

4. Follow the one who was sent as a mercy to the worlds

One of the manifestations of God's mercy towards humanity is in his Prophet Muhammad ﷺ. Allah says in the Qur'an: *'And We have not sent you, [O Muhammad], except as a mercy to the worlds.'* [21:7]

If the Prophet ﷺ himself is described as being a mercy to everyone, then the best way for us to become a manifestation of God's mercy is to follow his example. God also tells us: *'So by mercy from Allah, [O Muhammad], you were lenient with them. And if you had been rude [in speech] and harsh in heart, they would have disbanded from about you.'* [3:159]

Part of God's mercy is that He made the Prophet ﷺ lenient and kind. The opposite of that is being rude and harsh, as the verse describes. It is both contradictory and sad that those described as being 'religious' can be the harshest, and this is the furthest one can be from the example of the Prophet ﷺ. Some use the argument that they are simply 'enjoining the good and forbidding evil', but even that principle has its rules. In essence, we should want what it best for others in this life and the next, and our actions should follow that.

For example, during the Battle of Uḥud, which was the most difficult battle for the Muslims, the Companions asked the bleeding Prophet ﷺ to supplicate against their enemy. But he refused and said, *'O Allah! Guide my people for they do not know!'* [Bayhaqī] These are lessons from which we need to learn.

5. Reflect upon the manifestations of Allah's mercy in your life, in times when He has given, and in times when He has withheld

We are all recipients of God's many mercies. Reflecting upon the apparent mercies can help us to see how Allah manifests this name in our lives, and should increase our love and gratitude. We should also remember that part of the definition of mercy that we cited is that, while the action itself may not seem merciful in the immediate, it actually is in the long-term. In our own personal lives, there are many times when something that is perceived as 'bad' turns out to be something good and a mercy for us. Not marrying the one you thought was the love of your life might have been a mercy that saved you from something that would have been far worse. The accident that affected your ability to move may have been a mercy that protected you from engaging in certain types of sin. Losing a loved one and exhibiting patience with that could result in the ultimate mercy of being reunited with him or her in Paradise. So, take the time to reflect on Allah's mercy in your life – the times He protected you, the times He gave to you, and even the times He withheld from you.

AL-MĀLIK, AL-MALIK, MĀLIK AL-MULK – TRUE AND COMPLETE SOVEREIGNTY (7-9)

4

AL-MĀLIK, AL-MALIK, MĀLIK AL-MULK – TRUE AND COMPLETE SOVEREIGNTY (7-9)

'Say, "'O Allah, Owner of Sovereignty, You give sovereignty to whom You will and You take sovereignty away from whom You will. You honor whom You will and You humble whom You will. In Your Hand is [all] good. Indeed, You are over all things competent.'"

[3:26]

God's names must be understood holistically. A human being may be both firm and kind at the same time, their firmness being tempered by their kindness and vice versa. I studied Italian and Spanish in high school, both with very good and fun teachers. The difference was that the Italian teacher was stricter and held us to account on our homework, whereas the Spanish teacher accepted our (many) excuses. Unfortunately, most times we took advantage of the Spanish teacher's laid-back attitude and manifest kindness; students in the Italian class did better in the exams and to this day I can remember much of the Italian grammar.

The way we react to someone who is always kind gives us a glimpse into human nature, and how we interact with God's love and mercy. When we focus solely on God's mercy, it may make us complacent and cause us to ignore what we view as minor faults instead of working on improving them. This is why, in the introductory chapter of the Qur'an, while His mercy is mentioned at the start of the chapter as well as informing us that Allah is our

Lord, we are then reminded: He is the *'Sovereign over the Day of Recompense.'* [1:4]

The meanings

God is al-Mālik (the Possessor), al-Malik (the King), and Mālik al-Mulk (the Possessor of Sovereignty), which may appear to be the same in meaning, but they contain important nuances. Using human examples can initially help us to understand the differences. One may be a homeowner (*mālik al-bayt*) or the king of a country (*malik al-dawla*). Linguistically, *mālik* refers to owning specific things: one could say that they are the owner of the car or of the necklace, but no one would say that they are the 'king' of those things. One would, however, say that they are the king of a country, which is general and does not specifically refer to every single thing in the country. This is the first difference between the two terms.

The second difference is that *mālik* refers to possession, but may exclude the ability to *act* with what one possesses. For example, a person may own property but cannot do whatever he or she wants with it, due to restrictions in the law or when renting it out. *Malik*, on the other hand, means kingship, but a king may not own every single thing – his subjects still own their property, for example, and if he expropriates it, he has to compensate them – even though the king may act as he pleases in general. Thus, these two names complement each other, as God is both King and Possessor. And because the nature of language can sometimes limit our understanding of God's attributes, the third Name, Mālik al-Mulk, completes the full picture: He owns the notion of sovereignty itself.

So Allah is al-Mālik (the Possessor), al-Malik (the King), and Mālik al-Mulk (the Possessor of Sovereignty) to connote His full sovereignty over everything, in this world and the next.

God – the Ultimate Possessor and King

Whoever thinks that they are the sole owner of the things over which they appear to have power, and that they may dispose of things in the way that they like without paying heed to Allah's rules: God is the owner of them. Whatever possessions we might have are ultimately God's, and so we will be asked what we did with God's possessions. In Sūrat al-Baqarah, we are told:

> *'Have you not considered the one who argued with Abraham about his Lord [merely] because Allah had given him kingship? When Abraham said, "My Lord is the one who gives life and causes death," he said, "I give life and cause death." Abraham said, "Indeed, Allah brings up the sun from the east, so bring it up from the west." So the disbeliever was overwhelmed [by astonishment], and Allah does not guide the wrongdoing people.'* [2:258]

The tyrant Nimrod assumed that because he was a king, and could order the lives of people to be spared or ended, that he had true kingship. Even though his logic was faulty, the Prophet Abraham used Nimrod's own reasoning and gave him a bigger challenge: does his kingship extend to the sun?

Everyone who plays the role of a king, or who has ownership over anything, must remember that there is the One above who has ultimate sovereignty over everything. It should cause fear in the hearts of the unjust, and relief in the hearts of the oppressed; the 'ownership' of the tyrants is necessarily temporary, and they will then have to deal with their Maker.

This is not just directed to the tyrants of this world. We will all eventually die, cutting off our links to those things which we think we own, whereas Allah's ownership is enduring. This teaches us not to be so attached to our possessions, knowing that we will all ultimately return to Him. Furthermore, whatever we give away – which, in essence, was given to us by God – is returned to us in one form or another because He is the Owner, and can return things and multiply them. Indeed, any time one gives away his or her possessions for the sake of God, '*He may multiply it for him many times over.*' [2:245]

Moreover, knowing that Allah is Mālik al-Mulk teaches us to whom to turn. In a telling hadith *qudsī*, God tells us:

> '*O my servants. If the first of you and the last of you, humans and jinn, were as God-fearing as the most God-fearing person there is, this would not increase in my dominion in the least.*
>
> *O my servants. If the first of you and the last of you, humans and jinn, were as sinful as the most sinful person there is, this would not decrease in my dominion in the least.*
>
> *O my servants. If the first of you and the last of you, humans and jinn, were to stand as one and ask of Me and I were to give each person what he asked for, it would not diminish what I have, any more than the ocean would be diminished if a needle were dipped into it.*' [Muslim]

This hadith starts off with Allah telling us that He is not in need of our worship. By worshipping Him you are not increasing Him in anything, nor are you decreasing Him in anything by refusing to worship Him. Only you benefit from worship and only you lose from disobedience.

The hadith then ends with something beautiful. Any human we go to for help or to fulfil our needs is necessarily limited, and may or may not be able to give us what we need. Allah tells us that His possession is not limited and does not diminish with giving – so always ask Him. Ask Him with the certainty that it is easy for Him to give to you, easier than it is for a billionaire to give you spare change, and with the humility of knowing that you truly do not own anything.

'My choice'?

When we understand who Allah is, and that He is the ultimate owner, we should re-think popular mantras and slogans. Some slogans contain both truth and falsehood, and are used for both what we consider good and bad. An example is 'my body, my choice', which represents the ideals of bodily autonomy and self-ownership. It is used in conversations around a woman's right to abortion and to sexual consent, and against gender-based violence. However, it is also used more generally as a blanket statement to reject anything that seems to be interference – even if it comes in the form of spiritual advice around notions of modesty – in how we use our bodies. As Muslims, we need to think deeply about the meanings of these popular rallying cries – whether we are of those who outright reject or outright accept them. Our bodies are 'ours' insomuch as they have been given to us by Allah, but they are not completely ours to dispose of as we wish – and this applies to both men and women.

Allah has given us our bodies as a trust. This means that we do have a level of autonomy over our bodies and must treat our bodies with respect as they are gifts from the Most High. This also means that we should not be using our bodies in ways that displease Him. Ostensibly, we have a choice, but we are also accountable; not to people, but rather to God Himself.

Living with this name

1. Take care of God's possessions

When we realize that everything is owned by God and He may do as He pleases, this includes ourselves and what we think we own. Take care of your money and use it in a way that is pleasing to Him by giving money to charity and important causes. Take care of your body by not using it for what He has prohibited or what He hates. Take care of the earth by cultivating it for good and not damaging it.

2. Nothing and everything is out of your reach, depending on how you seek it

When we seek possessions through middle-men, they will always be out of reach, because nothing is truly owned by people. When our mindset is one of belief that people are true owners, we may demean ourselves or act in unjust ways in order to reach that which we seek. Instead we should seek things through the Ultimate King by asking Him and working in the ways that He approves.

3. Be free

Al-Ghazālī defines kingship as being free and able to dispense with everything. Thus, kingship in this world entails detaching ourselves from the passions of this world, which gives us true kingship in the next.

Many of us are beholden to our possessions and we allow things and people to take ownership over our hearts. Realizing that Allah is the true owner enables us to work to be free of being owned by the material things of this world, by recognizing their temporary nature and the brief nature of our ownership, as well as the limited nature of their benefit.

4. Remember that there is a Day of Judgment

This should cause us to know the true value of things. If someone has been given dominion or possessions, this is not necessarily reflective of their value with God, only their actions and internal state are. It behooves us to remember that we will not take any of our possessions to the next realm, only our deeds.

5. Be patient with loss

The Prophet ﷺ advised his daughter, whose child was dying, '*Verily, whatever Allah takes is for Him and whatever He gives is for Him, and everything with Him has a fixed term, so she should be patient and hope for reward from Allah.'* [Bukhārī]

The loss of a child is one of the most difficult things one can go through in this world. It is natural for us to feel this pain deeply. But we can shift our mindset when we remember that the child was God's to begin with, and simply returned to his or her Merciful Maker, just as everything – including our own souls – will. While this may not remove the pain of separation, it does mean that we can look forward to being reunited with whatever we lost with God. Despite us not truly owning anything, Allah recognizes our pain when faced with loss. In His all-encompassing mercy, He prepares for those who are patient and forbearing what will replace that loss, if not in this world, then in the next.

One of the Companions, 'Urwah ibn al-Zubayr, had to have his leg amputated. While he was being visited by a friend, he said, 'if you came to give me condolence for the loss of my leg, I already submitted to Allah with patience to reward me for its loss.' But the guest was there for another reason: to inform him that his son was killed in an accident. Imagine losing your limb and your child at the same time. But 'Urwah said, 'O Allah! You took one child, and left me many... You took one organ from my body, and left me many organs... O Allah! You tested me with my body, and You were kind to leave me with good health. You tested me with the loss of my son, but You were kind in leaving me the rest of my children.' 'Urwah understood that everything is ultimately God's, and chose to focus on that with which Allah blessed him, rather than what he lost.

This does not mean that we cannot be sad, or that it is wrong or spiritually inferior to feel pain due to loss. This is part of being human. But our understanding of God and the nature of this world should mean that this pain can push us towards God rather than away from Him, and that we can be left with hope, not despair.

AL-RAZZĀQ – THE PROVIDER (10)

5

AL-RAZZĀQ – THE PROVIDER (10)

'God is the Provider, the Lord of Power, the Ever Mighty.'
[51:58]

One universal worry of people, no matter the culture, is that of provision. We worry whether we will be able to pay our bills at the end of the month, we worry whether we will be able to afford to pay for our child's higher education, and we may even worry about how we will get our next meal. Being consumed with worry may cause us to forget that God has named Himself al-Razzāq – the Provider – and this has several implications for us.

What is *rizq*?

When we refer to *rizq* or provision, from which the name al-Razzāq is derived, many people assume it is just money and material wealth; however, the definition of *rizq* is all that benefits, as well as something that is bestowed. Therefore, there are two types of *rizq*: the first is the material kind, of which the effects can be seen physically. So, it can be money or any material thing in this world. The second type is internal or moral provision. This can include the provision of the heart, emotional sustenance, and even spiritual *rizq*. While the latter provision is considered the nobler of the two, because its fruits are everlasting, material provision is not necessarily bad. Indeed, the essence of *rizq* is something that brings benefit and is endowed by God. How much it benefits us in the Hereafter depends on how we use our material *rizq* in this world.

The constant Provider of beneficial provision

God, who has named Himself the Provider, creates our *rizq*, and takes it upon Himself to deliver what He has apportioned to His servants. Allah tells us: *'There is not a creature that moves on earth whose provision is not His concern. He knows where it lives and its [final] resting place: it is all [there] in a clear record.'* [11:6]

And because He is al-Razzāq – which is linguistically an aggrandizement of the basic Arabic word for provider, *rāziq* – He provides this sustenance to everyone and continually: Muslim and non-Muslim, woman and man, humans and animals and plants. It encompasses everything on Earth. The rain that nourishes the plants and the animals is provision. The sunshine that provides us with the necessary vitamin D for healthy bones, and increases serotonin production in the brain for a better mood, is provision.

And in case we had doubt, Allah takes an oath by the heavens and earth. He says: *'In the sky is your sustenance and all that you are promised. By the Lord of the heavens and earth! All this is as real as your speaking.'* [51:22-23]

Our acquisition of this provision can happen in two ways: the first, He has made dependent on our striving – the means are considered a form of provision as well – and the second is that which He has written for us independent of our striving. For example, if you apply for tens of jobs and get the job that you want, it is God who provides the means (the ability to make applications) that lead to that job – the provision from the job is made dependent your taking the means that God Himself made available. On the other hand, you may apply for many jobs, and perhaps get an offer from a place to which you did not apply; that is a provision written for you regardless of your striving, and can also be considered a reward for your striving.

The Prophet ﷺ said that a soul will not die until it gets all of the provision that has been apportioned for it [Ibn Mājah]. However, just like the example given above with applying for jobs, receiving our *rizq* requires us to strive – even for the provision written for us regardless, because we do not know what has been written as dependent on our efforts and what has not. All we know is that it has been written – that should comfort our hearts.

Striving for your provision

There is provision that God has made dependent on our effort, as well as the *type* of effort we put in. When we do not put in the necessary effort, it as though we are rejecting God's provision, because the means to sustenance are a form of provision in and of themselves. Rejecting the means is no different to rejecting and dismissing an envelope full of money that arrives in the mail for us that was sent by God. An envelope full of money, and the *means* to obtain an envelope of money, are both provisions. So, we must change the way we conceptualize provision as being only the material result. Once we recognize that means are also provision, this should cause us to be grateful that we have means to utilize, as they are from Allah. While our provision is indeed written, we still need to work for it as though it depended entirely on how hard we try; but in our hearts, we should know that nothing will come to us except what God has written for us.

If we broaden our conception of *rizq*, and truly believe that al-Razzāq is the One who provides it, we will never justify seeking prohibited *(ḥarām)* means of living, because God would never make His provision – whether they are the means or the result of those means – illicit. We need to work in whatever way that we can, in a manner that befits us as Muslims, knowing that it is God who will provide for us – even if everyone around us is engaging in corruption. Remember that striving is not simply an external act, but an internal act as well: it encompasses our intentions and the prayers we make.

We might imagine that, for some, believing that God has written for us our provision means complacency on our part. Yet the example of Hājar – the wife of the Prophet Abraham –

demonstrates to us the striving of someone who completely trusted in God and in His provision. When the Prophet Abraham left Hājar and her infant son in the desert, Hājar was understandably confused. However, she asked Abraham if God had commanded him to do this. When he responded in the affirmative, she knew that whatever God decreed would be good, even if it seemed bad in the moment. This is the first lesson: she had trust in God's wisdom.

Nonetheless, she strived. When her food supplies ran out, and it was harder to breastfeed her son, she ran up and down the mounts of Ṣafā and Marwah seven times, searching for something – anything. Her trust in God – that He was the Provider, the Most Wise and the Most Merciful – did not cause her to simply sit down and wait. God rewarded that striving with the well of Zamzam from which we still benefit today. When we go on *ʿumrah* or hajj (minor or major pilgrimage), we perform what is called *saʿī*, which means striving, emulating the footsteps of Hājar, so that we never forget the lesson of working hard with the means around us.

This perfectly illustrates the concept of *rizq*, as it came from where she did not imagine it would. She fulfilled her part – and Allah gave her what He apportioned for her. This is especially a lesson for those of us who think that there is nothing for us to do – but there is always something to do. Even working to *seek* the means is something for which we will be rewarded, because it shows that we are serious about our striving. And God may give it to us through the channels that we sought or through something completely different. It is simply to show us that our *rizq* is in His Hands, and that He appreciates the wholesome efforts we put in acquiring pure *rizq*.

This example shows that knowing that *rizq* is guaranteed is not an excuse to be lazy or complacent. Indeed, we see examples of this all through the Qur'an, in the Sunnah of the Prophet Muhammad ﷺ, and in the ways of the Companions. Indeed, no one had more trust in God than the Prophet ﷺ, and he did not simply wait for things to come to him or for the angel Gabriel to tell him what to do in any given circumstance. He taught us that *'if you were to rely upon Allah with reliance due to him, he would provide for you just as he provides for the birds. They go out in the morning with empty stomachs and return full.'* [Tirmidhī] The main point here is that the birds *go out* to seek their provision, and we must do the same with complete trust in our hearts.

This understanding of *rizq* is evident in how those who learned from our beloved Prophet ﷺ behaved. For example, the Companion 'Umar said, 'Let not one of you refrain from working for his provision, supplicating to Allah to provide while he knows that the sky does not rain gold and silver.' [*Iḥyā 'Ulūm al-Dīn*] 'Abd al-Raḥmān ibn 'Awf, when he migrated to Madinah without any of his wealth – and he used to be wealthy in Makkah – immediately asked where the market was so that he could work. And these Companions were both amongst the most pious and those promised Paradise.

On poverty and wealth

When we read about God's provision, we might still feel some doubt in our hearts. There are people in the world who starve to death, or are forced into undignified situations because of a lack of means. We may ourselves have been in situations without food or shelter. 'Where is the *rizq*?', we might ask.

Firstly, the Prophet reminds us, *'Do not think of your provision as slow coming, for a servant will never die until he reaches the end of his provision.'* [Ibn Mājah] Even if we go through periods of struggle and seemingly restricted sustenance, we should know that all the provision that has been written for us will come.

Secondly, we must remember not to look at God's names and attributes separately. Allah is the Most Wise, and He tells us that we will be tested in this world with both ease and hardship, wealth and poverty, life and death. Some are tested with few material resources, while others are tested with an abundance of them. And how is the latter a test? If we hoard God's provision, this affects our provision in the Hereafter. It may even affect our spiritual provision, as we should always remember that *rizq* is not limited to the material. Moreover, for some people, a lack of material sustenance may be a blessing. Allah tells us: *'And if Allah had extended [excessively] provision for His servants, they would have committed tyranny throughout the earth. But He sends [it] down in an amount which He wills. Indeed He is, of His servants, Acquainted and Seeing.'* [42:27]

Thirdly, we need to understand that there are consequences for our actions. God reminds us that if we do not rule with justice then there will be corruption on earth that affects everyone. Overusing resources, abusing human beings and hoarding wealth are things that are despised in our religion and God warns us severely against them. We cannot blame God when collectively we have created a system which goes precisely against the way in which He has ordered us to live. So, the test of those with limited means is the hardship in this life – though al-Razzāq may manifest Himself and His provision in ways that we cannot imagine – and the test of those with abundant means is to help and to work to create a system that is more just.

Spiritual sustenance and its effect on material sustenance

Just like we strive for material sustenance, so too should we strive for spiritual sustenance. This is through making the effort to attend circles of knowledge, be devoted during our prayer, reflect upon the Qur'an, and so on. The same effort – if not more – that some of us put into gaining material provision must be put into gaining spiritual sustenance.

This is extremely important, as our spiritual state is not only an indication of our place in the Hereafter, it can affect even our material provision. Part of our striving for sustenance should be to avoid sins. Mālik ibn Dīnār said, 'if you see hardness in your heart, weakness in your body, and deprivation in your provision, then know that you have spoken about what is not your concern.' Of course, we are human, and we will never be able to completely avoid sin. This simply means that we should strive to do the best that we can, refrain from the sins that are considered the most major, while striving to avoid the lesser ones.

But some may question the correlation between our deeds and provision, as many seemingly sinful people appear to receive material *rizq* – and a lot of it. Yet this is a superficial way of looking at things, because provision is of many types. These people may receive their material *rizq*, but God may deny them their spiritual *rizq*. And this is far worse.

One final point is that we may live in times where many forms of earning a living have religiously impermissible or doubtful elements in them (such as interest, for example), even if they are not wholly unethical or outright prohibited in and of themselves. If we fear partaking in forbidden means of *rizq*, we need to seek out specialist scholars who can help us with navigating these issues.

Increasing our *rizq*

While provision has been appointed, it may also be increased by our actions, with the permission of God. Sheikh Rātib al-Nabulsī, Sheikh Māhir Muqaddim, and Sheikh Ṣafwān Ḥanūf list a number of ways in which we can increase our provision, which are summarized below:

God-consciousness (*taqwā*): '*And whoever has taqwa of Allah – He will make for him a way out. And will provide for him from where he does not expect.*' [65:2-3]

Reliance on God (*tawakkul*): '*And whoever relies upon Allah – then He is sufficient for him. Indeed, Allah will accomplish His purpose. Allah has already set for everything a [decreed] extent.*' [65:3]

Prayer: *'And enjoin prayer upon your family [and people] and be steadfast therein. We ask you not for provision; We provide for you, and the [best] outcome is for [those of] righteousness.'* [20:132]

Faith and good deeds: *'And those who have believed and done righteous deeds - for them is forgiveness and noble provision.'* [22:50]

Helping others: The Messenger of Allah ﷺ said, *'Seek out the vulnerable among you. Verily, you are only given provision and support due to your support of the weak.'* [Tirmidhī]

Keeping good relations with family: The Prophet ﷺ said, *'Whoever would like his rizq to be increased and his life to be extended, should uphold the ties of kinship.'* [Bukhārī]

Thankfulness: *'And [remember] when your Lord proclaimed, "If you are grateful, I will surely increase you [in favor]; but if you deny, indeed, My punishment is severe."'* [14:7]

Asking forgiveness and repentance (*tawbah*): *'And said, 'Ask forgiveness of your Lord. Indeed, He is ever a Perpetual Forgiver. He will send [rain from] the sky upon you in [continuing] showers. And give you increase in wealth and children and provide for you gardens and provide for you rivers.'* [71:10-12]

Charity: *'Who is it that would loan Allah a goodly loan so He may multiply it for him many times over?'* [2:245]

Reciting Qur'an: The Prophet ﷺ said: *'The house in which Qur'an is recited is increased in good, and the house in which Qur'an is not recited is decreased in good.'* [al-Bazzār]

Migrating for the sake of God: *'And whoever emigrates for the cause of Allah will find on the earth many [alternative] locations and abundance.'* [4:100]

Living with this name

1. Internal contentment

Knowing that God is the Provider should give us a sense of *riḍā*, which is contentment with what God has given us – and we can still strive for more. But our striving should be with gratitude for what we already have, and without any resentment or bitterness towards God for what others have been given and what we have not been given. Allah reminds us: *'And do not extend your eyes toward that by which We have given enjoyment to [some] categories of them, [its being but] the splendor of worldly life by which We test them. And the provision of your Lord is better and more enduring.'* [20:131]

The provision of our Lord in this verse refers to Paradise. This should inspire us to be with God and obey Him, while looking forward to the true and lasting provision in Paradise for our patience with whatever hardship we have endured. It should also enable us to be content with what He has written for us – and what many of us have is usually more than enough. The Prophet ﷺ reminded us of why we should be content when he said, *'Whoever wakes up safely in his home and is healthy in his body and has provisions for his day, would have acquired all the worldly possessions he is in need of."* [Tirmidhī]

Moreover, this act of contentment may also be the key that God has written to unlock the doors to our material provision. We should avoid being of the people whom Allah describes: *'There are also some who serve God with unsteady faith: if something good comes their way, they are satisfied, but if they are tested, they revert to their old ways, losing both this world and the next— that is the clearest loss.'* [22:11]

God is the Provider but He also tells us that there will be tests in this life. This is why we should understand God's names and attributes holistically – He is the Provider and He is also the Most Wise, meaning that any seeming restriction in our material provision is there for a reason, possibly the increase in spiritual provision.

2. Ethics in seeking provision

We should not seek provision through forbidden means, as that also prevents our supplications from being responded to by Allah. Since God Himself has made some of His provisions dependent on the effort, the means He has provided would never go against His own rulings. The Prophet ﷺ reminds us that *'a soul will never die until it finishes its term and consumes its provision. Thus, be graceful in seeking provision and let not one of you allow the delay in provision to compel him to seek it by disobedience. Verily, Allah does not grant what is with him but by obedience.'* [Al-Albānī]

Ibn 'Abbās emphasized this when he said, 'There is no believer or sinner but that Allah Almighty has decreed his provision from the lawful. If he is patient until it comes to him, Allah will give it to him. If he becomes anxious and consumes something from the unlawful, Allah will decrease his provision from the lawful.' [Ḥilyat al-Awliyā']

And this can truly refer to anything, not just material possessions. A spouse is provision, for example. If we fear never getting married, and engage in illicit relations in order to secure our matrimonial future, this indicates a lack of trust in God. In many places, it is true that the Muslim community makes it hard to get married. But that same community will be questioned by God for their behavior, as will we. There is collective responsibility and also our own individual responsibility. It should go without saying that, if we find that we have made mistakes or committed sins in seeking any type of provision, we can always return to God and seek His forgiveness.

3. Striving

While some provisions are dependent on striving and some are not, God has kept that knowledge hidden from us in order to ensure that we work hard regardless. We should strive for our provision – both internal and external – knowing that God will give us what He has ordained for us, and that He rewards us for our striving using permissible and ethical means.

4. Give from the sustenance that God has given you

We may employ people to do work for us, and in that case, we should pay them promptly – that is their sustenance, and we should not deny people their provision. The Prophet ﷺ said, '*you should pay the laborer his wages before his sweat dries.*' [Ibn Mājah] Moreover, he also warned that '*the procrastination of the rich is an oppression*'. [Bukhārī] Payment is to be given upon completion of work or as agreed on a weekly or monthly basis. We should be wary of being of the people described in this verse: '*And when it is said to them, "Spend from that which Allah has provided for you," those who disbelieve say to those who believe, "Should we feed one whom, if Allah had willed, He would have fed? You are not but in clear error."*' [36:47]

We need to remember that our provision is ultimately from God, no matter how seemingly hard we worked for it. It can therefore be a test for us when we hoard it and refuse to help others with it, or give them what they are owed.

Moreover, God Almighty says in the Qur'an: '*Tell My servants who have believed to establish prayer and spend from what We have provided them, secretly and publicly, before a Day comes in which there will be no exchange, nor any friendships.*' [14:31]

Provision is also spiritual provision, so if we can provide others with spiritual and emotional nourishment, we should do so. Al-Ghazālī describes such people who have been given the means of sustenance for others as 'storehouses of God most high, so that the one whose hand is made a storehouse of sustenance for bodily sustenances, and his speech a storehouse of sustenance for the heart, has been honored with this attribute.'[9]

5. *Ask God for good sustenance*

We all want our provision to be from permissible and ethical sources, and we should ask God for that. One of the supplications of the Prophet ﷺ was, '*O Allah indeed I ask You for beneficial knowledge, and a good provision, and actions which are accepted.*' [Ibn Mājah]

[9] Al-Ghazali, *The Ninety-Nine Beautiful Names of God: Al-Maqṣad Al-Asnā Fi Sharḥ Asmā' Allāh Al-Ḥusnā*, 79.

AL-WAHHĀB – THE BESTOWER OF GIFTS (11)

6

AL-WAHHĀB – THE BESTOWER OF GIFTS (II)

'Grant us from Yourself mercy. Indeed, You are the Bestower.'

[3:8]

How does receiving a gift make you feel? Think of the last time someone gave you a gift, and not just anyone, but someone you love and respect immensely. Receiving gifts gives us joy, a feeling of love and appreciation for the gift giver, as well as the feeling of being special to the person from whom we received the gift. We might even feel shyness or shame if we have neglected our gift-giver, and suddenly find ourselves as recipients of their special gifts.

One of God's Names is al-Wahhāb. The root of this word is *hibah*, which means 'a gift', defined as a 'present free from recompense and interests.'[10] As with many of His names, the Arabic form of the word is as an aggrandizement or a superlative, so al-Wahhāb is the One who constantly showers His servants with gifts – not just on your birthday or special occasions, as human beings do. Allah tells us in the Qur'an: *'Or do they have the depositories of the mercy of your Lord, the Exalted in Might, the Bestower?'* [38:9]

When God mentions two of His names together, He is indicating something to us. He tells us that He is the Exalted in Might, the Bestower, firstly to assure us that no one can stop any gift that He wills to give us (because He is Exalted in Might). Secondly, it

[10] *Ibid.*, 74.

indicates to us the purity of His gifts: He is the Exalted in Might, needing nothing from us, and gives us His gifts not tainted with any desire for power or benefit, as a human gift may be.

And what is the difference between a gift (*hibah*) and provision (*rizq*)? As we described in the previous chapter, while *rizq* is ordained for us, we have to work and strive for it. While some provision is connected to the means that we pursue, other forms of provision are not, but knowledge of that is within the unseen. So we must work for our sustenance, knowing that it is God who provides. If in the course of our efforts, we earn a million dollars, that is the sustenance that Allah had ordained for us – no more and no less.

Hibah, on the other hand, is simply a gift. It has no relation to our striving or effort. It can come through asking God for specific gifts. For example, the Prophet Solomon said, *'My Lord, forgive me and grant me a kingdom such as will not belong to anyone after me. Indeed, You are the Bestower (al-Wahhāb).'* [38:35].

A gift can also be something that we never thought to ask for nor expected. It can be a talent you were born with – the Arabic word for talent is *mawhibah*, from the same root. It can be as simple as a kind word from a loved one, or even a stranger, when we are feeling down. It can be an unexpected phone call from someone we love to whom we have not spoken in a while. It can be a surprise *'umrah* trip (the minor pilgrimage). It can even be your best friend or the people Allah has brought into your life without effort from you, who provide you with spiritual and emotional support. God's mercy itself is a gift, particularly when, despite our unbecoming actions, He bestows it upon us. Even a child – either male or female – is considered a gift. God says: *'He gifts to whom He wills female [children], and He gifts to whom He wills males.'* [42:49]

This should remind us that, despite the erroneous practices and beliefs in some cultures, there is no preference for males or females; both are gifts from God.

The connection between gifts and love

Why would someone bestow a gift? Gifts are given for a variety of reasons. We give gifts to someone who has been on our mind and about whom we care. We also give gifts to those who are far, especially if we have not been in touch with them in a while, to reflect our love for them despite the distance. We give gifts to those we love. The best gifts are from those who know us intimately, because they know exactly what we need and what would benefit us.

While God is far above any analogy, think of what this might mean when Allah gives you a gift. And remember that His gifts are pure, so while our gifts for others may sometimes contain ulterior motives or what we hope to gain by the gift, Allah has no need for us. Thus, His gifts are out of His love, to remind us that we are under His care even when we do nothing to deserve it. Indeed, reflecting upon our gifts should cause our hearts to fill with love for Allah. It is reported that the Prophet ﷺ said, *'The heart is inclined to love those that do good to it.'* [Ibn Ḥibbān]

Some of us may be thinking, 'but I am so far from Allah. Why would He give me gifts out of love?' Our Lord is greater than we imagine. He gives us gifts so that we know that we have a God who does not forget about His creation – even when they go astray. He gives us gifts as a reminder that we can come back to Him at any time. He is far more generous than any human being, who might get offended at our distance from them and choose to ignore or 'cancel' us from their lives. No, He is Allah, al-Wahhāb. He constantly showers us – those near and far – with His gifts, so that we know that we have a generous and giving Lord to whom to return.

Living with this name

1. Be grateful

We should take a few minutes in our day to reflect upon the many gifts of God, both large and small. We can even have a gratitude journal in which we write down God's many gifts, and thank Him for them. Indeed, by doing this we are training our hearts and our minds to constantly recognize Allah's gifts. And what is the result of that? God says, *'If you are grateful, I will surely increase you [in favor].'"* [14:7] Thanking Him for His gifts results in Him giving us more – both spiritually and materially. And the more we are conscious of Allah's gifts to us, the more we are able to realize how blessed we are, increase our love for Him, and thank Him truly.

2. Use His gifts in His way and in His cause

Recognizing God's gifts should cause us to be careful with what we do with them. No one likes for their gifts to be cheapened nor used in the opposite way to that for which they were intended. When God bestows us with gifts, we should be diligent in not using them for what He dislikes. Otherwise, the gift becomes a test for which we will be held accountable.

3. Be a gift-giver

We should always remember that whatever we love from Allah, we should try in whatever human form to give that to people as an expression of our love for God, and as a sign that leads to Him. The Prophet ﷺ said, *'Give gifts, for this will increase your mutual love.'* [Muslim] A gift does not need to be grand or expensive, but can be in the simple, day-to-day things.

AL-'ADL, AL-MUQSIṬ – JUSTICE AND EQUITY (12-13)

7

AL-'ADL, AL-MUQSIṬ – JUSTICE AND EQUITY (12-13)

'And the word of your Lord has been fulfilled in truth and in justice.'

[6:115]

Throughout the Qur'an, God's justice is emphasized, and justice is demanded from us. We are told: *'Indeed, Allah does not do injustice, [even] as much as an atom's weight.'* [4:40]

God further says in a hadith *qudsī*: *'O My servants! I have forbidden oppression for Myself, and I have made it forbidden amongst you, so do not oppress one another.'* [Muslim]

God makes the connection between His divine justice and our actions. If God, who can do anything He pleases, *forbade* injustice for Himself, then it becomes even more incumbent for us – as worshippers of a Just Lord – to apply justice and prevent injustice.

However, some applications of justice may be skewed. For example, two people might have stolen the same amount of money. However, one person stole in order to buy medicine for her sick child, while the other stole from a poor worker. Though they both did something that is outwardly the same, intuitively we would feel that justice would not be to treat them equally. Yet, the law that is theoretically meant to guarantee justice may end up inducing the judge to rule that what each person did was equally wrong – they violated the letter of the same law – so they should receive the same punishment. And so, Allah reveals to us two of His names in order that we might understand the concepts more clearly, as well as His all-encompassing, true justice.

Al-ʿAdl and al-Muqsiṭ – justice and equity

ʿ*Adl* comes from the root *ʿayn-dāl-lām*, which means to make something upright; it is the opposite of transgression. Al-Ghazālī explains that al-ʿAdl means that just actions emanate from Him, and never oppression. Ibn al-Qayyim further states that justice entails putting things in their rightful place, and the Most Just only punishes those who truly deserve punishment, and does not deny those who deserve to be given good, even though it is He who made them deserving. Those who truly understand God's justice are the prophets and those who follow them.[11]

Al-Muqsiṭ comes from the root *qāf-sīn-ṭād*, which means a part or portion of something; *taqassaṭū* means to split something up fairly.[12] This root gives rise to words such as 'scale' or 'balance'. God says in the Qur'an: *'And give full measure when you measure, and weigh with an even balance (bilqisṭās al-mustaqīm). That is the best [way] and best in result.'* [17:35]

Al-Muqsiṭ means the One who is most equitable – because He gives and takes just portions – while *qāsiṭ*, from the same root, actually means 'unjust', because it is someone who transgresses and takes more or distributes unevenly. Allah commands us to be balanced, and He is al-Muqsiṭ: The One who is most equitable, balanced and just. The legal system allows us to see this. Two people may be killed by two different persons respectively and so the assumption is that they should both be punished similarly. But what if one of the killers was the aggressor, while the other was acting in self-defense? Moreover, what if the person acting in self-defense was a twelve-year-old? All these things matter to our judgment. Taking all of these things into account is part of being equitable

[11] Al-Ashqar, *Sharḥ Ibn Al-Qayyim Li Asmāʾ Allāh al-Ḥusnā*, 86.
[12] Ibn Manẓūr, *Lisān al-ʿArab, available online at:* http://wiki.dorar-aliraq.net/lisan-alarab/قسط

and just. If we look at punishments in the Islamic legal system, one might think that the punishment for stealing, for example, applies simply for the act of stealing, regardless of who stole and what they stole. But anyone versed in Islamic jurisprudence (*fiqh*) knows this is not the case, and this is why the caliph 'Umar suspended the punishment for theft when there was a famine; the circumstances matter.

In some translations of the Qur'an, *'adl* and *qisṭ* are both translated as justice, but here we will use the term 'equity' for *qisṭ* to differentiate between the terms.

What is justice?

There are many theories of justice and the best way to achieve it. In essence, it is being fair and equitable. However, there is something essential in which we should have conviction: God's clear rules and commandments are all justice. While they may be implemented in unjust ways – for example, against the weak and not against the strong – we should be careful not impose our modern understandings on the rules that are clearly established.

Standing firm for justice

The scholar Ibn Taymiyyah is reported to have said that God will protect a just nation even if they are not believers, and He would bring down an unjust nation even if they were believers. Belief is not just lip service; it is expressed in action. So crucial is the principle of justice to our faith that God also says:

> *'O you who have believed, be persistently standing firm in justice, witnesses for Allah, even if it be against yourselves or parents and relatives. Whether one is rich or poor, Allah is more worthy of both. So follow not [personal] inclination, lest you not be just. And if you distort [your testimony] or refuse [to give it], then indeed Allah is ever, with what you do, Acquainted.'* [4:135]

God tells us to uphold justice even if it is against our families or even our own selves. When we understand that Allah has named Himself the Most Just, it should reassure our hearts that even if we do not see justice now, there will be justice eventually. Moreover, it should push us to strive to establish justice, because we are servants of the Most Just.

God's justice – and indeed, justice in His name and religion – is highlighted in different stories in the Qur'an, and we will discuss one story here, one that is not often mentioned. The context in which it was revealed is important to understanding the significance of this story. In Madinah, the demographics were very different to the demographics in Makkah; there were the tribes of the Aws and the Khazraj – who were historically enemies, but many of their members accepted Islam – as well as Jewish tribes, and hypocrites (those who pretended to be Muslim but harbored animosity towards Islam and Muslims).

A man from the Aws was awarded a shield of armor from a battle in which they were victorious. Armor was considered precious at that time, as not many people were able to acquire it. But two days later, his armor was stolen. The man's cousin said that he saw a man from the Khazraj steal it; that man was a new Muslim.

To ascertain the truth, the Prophet ﷺ informed him that they had to check in his house, but the armor was not there. People from the tribe of Khazraj said that it was the Jewish neighbor who stole the armor. Indeed, they found it buried in the backyard. The Prophet ﷺ was mad at the accuser; how could he accuse an innocent person of theft?

In any case, it seemed that the matter was solved. The Muslims prayed the evening prayer (*'ishā'*) together and everyone retired to their homes. But something happened at night: God sent the Angel Gabriel to the Prophet ﷺ to declare that the Jewish man was innocent, and it was indeed the man who was originally accused who stole the armor. This was revealed in Sūrat al-Nisā (the fourth chapter in the Qur'an), in verses 105-113.[13]

The accused man had stolen the armor, but he asked his relatives to protect him, so they all conspired with him to protect him. But God knows all, and al-'Adl revealed these verses before the morning prayer (*fajr*) so that the Prophet ﷺ could declare it after prayers. It was crucial for God to reveal this verse and the Jewish man's innocence because the injustice would have occurred in His name and by His Prophet ﷺ.

The Jewish man did not accept Islam. This is important to point out. Allah is al-'Adl, and He is the Most Just; He commands us to be just for its own sake. Inviting people to Islam (*da'wah*) is important, but justice is established for its own sake, and not for other purposes, as noble as they may be.

This story highlights to us God's justice. The issue was not about tribes, or a favored group; Allah's justice is true justice which only favors the group that establishes His justice.

This should also cause us to fear when we commit injustice and claim it in the name of God; our Lord was quick to make clear that the Jewish man innocent against the Muslim because injustice cannot be associated with His way. The Prophet Muhammad ﷺ immediately declared his innocence to all the people, and in this was a lesson to all those who believe: justice is paramount.

When it comes to injustice, we need to reflect inwardly. We sometimes fail to uphold our covenant to God. He has commanded us to be just, but we do not act in such a way. We allow small transgressions in our daily lives, and only complain when something affects us directly. This can even be at the most basic level; do we believe rumors about people without being absolutely certain about the evidence? Do we give people the chance to explain themselves?

[13] The story can be found in the exegesis of al-Baghawī, Ibn Kathīr, and others

As Muslims, as servants of al-ʿAdl, we can never ever give up on striving for justice on all levels. Allah says in the Qur'an: *'O you who have believed, be persistently standing firm for Allah, witnesses in justice, and do not let the hatred of a people prevent you from being just. Be just; that is nearer to righteousness. And fear Allah; indeed, Allah is Acquainted with what you do.'* [5:8]

It may be that a rumor about someone we dislike is easily believed because of our preconceived notions: that too is an injustice. It extends to whom we hire for jobs and whom we overlook; how we treat our children; how we run our places of worship and organizations and more.

Ultimate justice

We see manifestations of Allah's justice both in this world and the next. That said, not everything will see the justice that we expect in this world, or in the time that we want. This is why, in the opening chapter of the Qur'an (Sūrat al-Fātiḥah), we are taken through a summary of the messages of the Qur'an as well as God's attributes. His Mercy is emphasized twice [1:1; 1:3]; we are told that He is the Lord [1:2]; we are informed that He is the Ultimate Sovereign of the Day of Judgment [1:4].

The Day of Judgment in this verse is actually referred to as the 'Day of Recompense' (*yawm al-dīn*). This is the day that the debts will be paid, and ultimate justice will be served. God also says about this day: *'Today each soul will be rewarded for whatever it has done; today no injustice will be done. God is swift in reckoning.'* [40:17]

This chapter lets us know two very important things: We will either be treated with God's mercy or His justice – but no one will be wronged.

Thus, we might live to see the demise of the Pharaohs of this world or we might not. At the same time, while it might seem that the person committing the injustice has 'won' in the short-term, we need to look beyond the superficial. We do not know what Allah has written for the unjust after he or she dies, nor do we know what spiritual nourishment this person has been denied because of his or her transgressions. And ultimately, there is the Day of Judgment, when '*the record of their deeds will be laid open and you will see the guilty, dismayed at what they contain, saying, "Woe to us! What a record this is! It does not leave any deed, small or large, unaccounted for!" They will find everything they ever did laid in front of them: your Lord will not be unjust to anyone.*' [18:49]

Moreover, as God is the Knower of the Unseen and Witnessed, He is the only One who knows what thoughts are going through our minds when we commit a wrong. He knows whether we had a malicious intention or whether we did something out of heedlessness or ignorance. Allah tells us, '*We will set up scales of justice for the Day of Resurrection so that no one can be wronged in the least.*' [21:47]

This is why we are taught that a person may give something that is seemingly small, but be rewarded greatly for it, and vice versa. We are told of a prostitute who gave a dog water and was given Paradise [Bukhārī and Muslim], but of an ostentatious, wealthy philanthropist who was punished [Muslim]. To an outsider, it might not make sense; the philanthropist was more generous than the prostitute in terms of what he gave, and the prostitute was outwardly more sinful than the philanthropist. But God knows the individual circumstance of each person, and distributes His justice accordingly. The prostitute was sincere, and the philanthropist was not.

Also, it could be that God tests one person with loss, but He tests another with wealth. Perhaps He blesses you by giving to you, and He blesses others by taking away from them. He may delay something for me, and hasten it for you. It may take you years to get something that you want – blood, sweat and tears – and for someone else, it requires no effort at all. But if you knew all that God knows, you would understand that His decree is ultimate justice and mercy that is specific to you and your circumstance.

Indeed, this is why Allah tells us: *'God does not burden any soul with more than it can bear.'* [2:256]

Moreover, in a hadith *qudsī*, it is reported that Allah says:

> *'Verily, from amongst My slaves is he whose faith cannot be rectified except by being inflicted with poverty, and were I to enrich him, it would surely corrupt him. Verily, from amongst My slaves is he whose faith cannot be rectified except by wealth and affluence, and were I to deprive him, it would surely corrupt him.'* [Ṭabarānī][14]

When you are tested with an affliction, and yet you see someone else who may have sinned worse than you seem to get off easy, remember that God is al-Muqsiṭ. He reveals this name to us in order to teach us to look deeper, and to understand that al- Muqsiṭ would never wrong anyone; it is simply that He has knowledge and wisdom that we do not. All that we see in the universe – and in our lives – will make sense in the end, and we will come to know His attribute clearly.

Living with these names

1. Commit yourself to justice

Justice is at many levels, and true submission to the Most Just is to work for justice at all levels. Al-Ghazālī says that only God is capable of true justice, but we can emulate this characteristic partly by insisting on justice *from* ourselves *for* others, and being forbearing with other people. These are some ways of striving for justice:

[14] This hadith has been classed as weak, but some scholars permitted using the hadith because the meanings align with what we understand of Allah's justice and mercy. Ibn Taymiyyah alluded to the meanings found in this hadith in *Majmū' al-Fatawa*, where he states that, 'It could be that, for some people, poverty is more beneficial than wealth, while wealth is more beneficial for others...'

- With yourself: Justice concerning ourselves means to rein in our anger and passions, according to Al-Ghazālī. Rage can cause us to commit injustice because we lose the ability to think clearly, and so we must ensure that our anger is guided by wisdom and our religion. Every time we transgress—by crossing the limits of God—we harm ourselves. Even if we do not see the immediate effects, these things affect us spiritually. So be just with yourself.

- With your family: We know that charity starts at home, and so does justice. We cannot be unjust to our siblings, abusive towards our spouse, or unfair in the treatment of our children, and claim to be servants of the Most Just.

- With your community: The Prophet ﷺ told us, *'The believer who mixes with people and patiently bears their annoyance will have a greater reward than the believer who does not mix with people and patiently bear their annoyance."* [Tirmidhī] It may sometimes be disheartening to deal with a community that only gives lip service to the principles of justice, but *this* is Islam: to strive for justice when it is most difficult, to continually improve, and to be just not only to humans, but also to the environment and to the animals. It applies as much to the rejection of gossip as it does to the establishment of equitable mosques where all members of the congregation are respected.

- With wider society: As we have heard many times, justice is not 'just us'. The Prophet ﷺ stood with the oppressed in his society *before* they became Muslim. He was witness to a treaty when he was young – *Ḥilf al-Fuḍūl* – that guaranteed the rights of the weak, and said that if the Quraysh had offered to sign such a treaty with him after Islam, he would still accept.

- For God: Being committed to justice at all these levels for the sake of Allah means that we cannot transgress. We do not choose our 'group' over others. Allah is the Truth and the Most Just, and thus we need to seek truth and justice in all our interactions, even if it is against ourselves.

2. Always remain hopeful and be certain that He is the Most Just

When you see a situation that is unjust and feel helpless to change it, remember that God is the source of justice. Nothing passes without His knowledge and there will be ultimate justice.

3. Remember that Allah will not test you with more than you can bear

While it our tests might seem to be unfair or unjust, we are reminded in the Qur'an: *'God does not burden any soul with more than it can bear.'* [2:286]

Allah tests us to build us because we have potential. In the grand scheme of things, His decree is most equitable and therefore the most just.

4. Understand people's circumstances

It is reassuring to us that God looks at our individual circumstances. Just as we love that from Allah, we should afford people the same gesture. That person who does not pray regularly may be going through a difficulty affecting their faith, and is not leaving their prayers out of malice. That individual who appeared to have committed a wrongful act was actually unaware of the implications of their actions. The friend who has not called you for a while may be dealing with issues of his or her own. The family member who does not show you affection, may have their own emotional baggage. So, reach out to help them.

AL-SHAKŪR – APPRECIATION AND GIVING (14)

8

AL-SHAKŪR – APPRECIATION AND GIVING (14)

'They will say, "Praise be to God, who has separated us from all sorrow! Our Lord is truly most forgiving, most appreciative."'

[35:34]

When someone gives you a gift, the polite response would be to thank that person to convey appreciation and gratitude. The word used for 'thanks' in Arabic is *shukran*. Linguistically, the Arabic root of this word – *shīn-kāf-rā* – is used to describe something that increases and grows what is given to it. For example, the animal that produces much milk is *dābbah shakūr*, or a land that grows a lot of crops is *arḍ shakūr*. When we think of the concept of appreciation and gratitude, we should naturally think of how much God has given us, and that we should give back to thank Him and appreciate Him.

But God has named Himself al-Shakūr, the Appreciative. This is astounding: The Lord who has given us everything we have *appreciates* the little that we do, and gives us back even more. Al-Ghazālī tells us that al-Shakūr rewards the few good deeds we do with many blessings, and rewards us for what we do in the limited time we are here on earth with eternity and unlimited favors in Paradise. God says in the Qur'an: *'That He may give them in full their rewards and increase for them of His bounty. Indeed, He is Forgiving and Appreciative.'* [35:30]

Sheikh Māhir Muqaddim counts the different dimensions of this name. He says that al-Shakūr:

1. Appreciates the smallest of deeds, He appreciates the deeds all the time, and His appreciation is unlimited. Allah tells us: *'And whoever commits a good deed — We will increase for him good therein. Indeed, Allah is Forgiving and Appreciative.'* [42:23]
2. Forgives our many mistakes, while accepting even the little good that we do
3. Appreciates the gratitude and thanks of His servants by bestowing upon them even more blessings
4. Expresses His appreciation and love for His righteous servants to the angels, who express it in the Heavens, so much so that this servant is honored on Earth
5. Bestows many blessings, while being content with meagre thanks
6. From His perfection, He bestows upon His servant, leading the servant to express thanks, thus providing both the cause and means of thanks
7. Despite His bestowing of many blessings, He accepts the few good deeds we do in response
8. Rewards those who leave something for His sake by compensating them with that which is better than what they left

Manifestations of appreciation

What does Allah's appreciation look like? The Prophet ﷺ tells us:

> *'Whosoever relieves from a believer some grief pertaining to this world, Allah will relieve from him some grief pertaining to the Hereafter. Whosoever alleviates the difficulties of a needy person who cannot pay his debt, Allah will alleviate his difficulties in*

both this world and the Hereafter. Whosoever conceals the faults of a Muslim, Allah will conceal his faults in this world and the Hereafter. Allah will aid a servant (of His) so long as the servant aids his brother.' [Muslim]

God appreciates the goodwill we show to others and the help we provide by giving to us what we gave in a way that is befitting His majesty – He gives it to us in this world and in the Hereafter, when it truly matters. Additionally, the Messenger of Allah ﷺ said, *'While a man was walking on a road, he found a thorny branch in the road and he moved it aside. Allah appreciated his deed and forgave him.'* [Bukhārī]

Allah appreciates the deeds that are done for all creatures, not simply humans. The Prophet ﷺ narrates to us a story of a man who was extremely thirsty, and found a well, which he climbed down to fetch water to quench his thirst. He then saw a dog that was panting out of thirst. Recognizing that the dog felt the exact same thirst that he was feeling a few minutes ago, he climbed back down the well in order to give the dog some water. God appreciated his action (*'fashakara Allahu lahu'*) and forgave his sins [Bukhārī and Muslim]. A similar incident is narrated regarding a prostitute who gave a dog water. Despite her grave misdeeds, Allah still appreciated her kind act. Indeed, God reminds us: *'Is the reward for good [anything] but good?'* [55:60]

The incident of Moses with the two women is also instructive. When he fled Egypt because he feared injustice under Pharoah for his accidental killing of a man, and arrived at Madyan, he saw that there were two women who appeared to be facing some difficulty. Despite his own troubles, he was concerned and asked them what the matter was, and they told him, *'We do not water until the shepherds dispatch [their flocks]; and our father is an old man.'* [28:23] So Moses watered their flock for them, and retreated to the shade, asking Allah for whatever good He could give him. He did not expect nor ask anything of the women he had helped. And how did God appreciate his action? This small act of kindness led him to the family of Shuʿayb, where he was given refuge and stability. He married one of the women that he helped, and was protected and separated from Pharoah for all those years. Sometimes Allah will reward a simple, righteous act that seems to be unrelated to your needs at the time with fulfilling needs that you did not know you had. Moses never asked for companionship, or a home, or a loving family – all he knew he needed was safety, and perhaps food and drink. Indeed, Moses ignored his own immediate need at the time (he had arrived after a long journey, presumably needing nourishment and sustenance) to fulfil the needs of the women; he preferred others – strangers, no less – over himself. Allah is more generous, and more appreciative, and so He fulfilled Moses's immediate and long-term needs and gave him more.

For this reason, the Prophet ﷺ urged us to do good deeds no matter how small; giving even half a date in charity can protect us from the Fire [Bukhārī]. Indeed, from Allah's appreciation, one good deed done by a person is recorded as at least ten good deeds, and can be recorded as up to 700 deeds, or even more [Bukhārī]. Even though Allah sent down His book for us a reminder and so we that we can reflect on its words for our own benefit, He appreciates our recitation. The Prophet ﷺ said, '*Whoever recites a letter from the Book of Allah, he will receive one good deed as ten good deeds like it. I do not say that Alif Lām Mīm is one letter, but rather Alif is a letter, Lām is a letter, and Mīm is a letter.*' [Tirmidhī]

God even appreciates our intention. The Prophet ﷺ describes two men who had different means: one man upon whom God had bestowed wealth and knowledge, and he acted upon that knowledge and gave from his wealth; another man whom Allah had given knowledge but no wealth. The second man said, 'if I had the wealth he had, I would do the same.' The Prophet ﷺ said '*They are rewarded the same*', simply for having a sincere intention to do good [Ibn Mājah]. We are also told by the Prophet ﷺ that whoever intends to do good but is not able to do it, God rewards him or her for the intention. Now this might make one worry. Is the same applicable if a person intends to do bad? No: if a person intended to do something bad but stopped himself, God appreciates that the person did not go through with what he had planned, and also rewards him for that. [Bukhārī] The Prophet ﷺ also said, *'Verily, Allah has pardoned my nation for their bad thoughts within themselves as long as they do not speak of them or act upon them.'* [Muslim]

Because God has the best and most perfect attributes – meaning that words cannot express their depth, so when we say that God is appreciative, the appreciation is unimaginable by the human mind – He teaches us to put in the effort no matter what, because that effort is never lost. In Paradise, the people will be told: *'This is your reward. Your endeavors are appreciated.'* [76:22]

It is not about the result, but rather the effort that we put in; this is what God loves and appreciates. The Prophet ﷺ tells us that *'the example of one who recites the Qur'an with great difficulty is that of one who receives a double reward.'* [Bukhārī]

Difficulty and lack of ability should not stop us from striving – because Allah appreciates the effort we put in. We should go out of our way to help someone, not expecting anything in return, and someone down the road may do the same for us as a reward from Allah. It could be that we help someone today, and God will send someone to help us when we are in trouble, or He could save something even more special for us on the Day of Judgment.

Other names of Allah relating to al-Shakūr

Some of us may still express doubt. Would Allah really appreciate the meagre deeds that we do when we also struggle with sin? Firstly, God reminds us: *'Surely our Lord is indeed Ever-Forgiving, Appreciative,'* [35:34] and *'He is most forgiving, most appreciative.'* [35:30]

God knows us and our self-doubts. He appreciates the fact that we are trying despite not always being able to be consistent, and assures us that He will also forgive us for whatever mistakes we make if we seek His forgiveness, while also rewarding us for the good.

Secondly, it feels nice to be recognized. While good deeds should ideally be done purely for God, there is the human side of us that wants someone to know and appreciate what we have done. Or at other times, we may intend to do something good but everything goes wrong – and no one knew that your intention was to do good. To this effect, God tells us, *'And ever is Allah Appreciative and Knowing.'* [4:147]. Allah knows your deeds and your efforts, and He rewards and appreciates what people may overlook.

Remember that with God, the cycle is never-ending. When we deal with human beings, we could give someone a gift and he or she responds with a thanks or a gift in return, but it ends there. With Allah, He tells us that when we thank, He gives us more. So, it is a cycle of increase and encouragement for us to be grateful and constantly do good.

Living with this name

1. Be grateful to God and give thanks

Knowing that Allah is appreciative of the little that we do should humble us and cause us to be even more grateful to Him. Being grateful to God and giving thanks to Him involves reflecting upon and recognizing His blessings; giving thanks with our words; and giving thanks with our actions. Allah tells us, *'And if you should count the favors of Allah, you could not enumerate them. Indeed, Allah is Forgiving and Merciful.'* [16:18]

Recognizing the infinite blessings should, at the very least inspire us to thank God. And our Lord is so generous and appreciative that for the incomplete thanks that we give (incomplete because it is impossible to count, let alone thank Him for, all His blessings), He gives us more. He says, *'And [remember] when your Lord proclaimed, "If you are grateful, I will surely increase you [in favor]."'* 14:7]

Moreover, the Prophet ﷺ reminds us that *'Whoever is not grateful for small things will not be grateful for large things.'* [Daylamī]. Recognizing the small things enables us to see how our life is in fact filled with good, even if the good is small, and enables us to be even more appreciative when even bigger blessings come our way; the opposite is true as well. And for those who are grateful, the Prophet ﷺ told us, *'The first to be called to Paradise are those who always praised Allah in times of ease and adversity'*; in another narration, he said, *'those who praised Allah in every situation.'* [Ṭabarānī] We should train ourselves to always be aware of and express thanks for the different blessings of God.

Finally, we should give thanks with our actions by using the blessings to obey Him, and not to disobey Him.

2. Do not belittle any good deed, and strive for the great ones

The Prophet ﷺ taught us not to *'belittle any good deed, even meeting your brother with a cheerful face.'* [Muslim] Why? Because even that seemingly miniscule deed is appreciated by al-Shakūr. Even if this act is derided by people, it matters to God. Now imagine if we did even greater and bigger deeds? What would happen if we helped someone come out of debt? Or restored someone's hope in Allah?

3. Remember that your intention and your effort are what matter the most

Only we and Allah know our intentions and our true efforts, and we will be judged according to them. While people may only see and appreciate our achievements, Allah appreciates our sincere efforts and our big intentions for His sake. We must realize that our efforts are not only appreciated by God, but they are beloved to Him because they show that we truly believe in and care about His appreciation, and recognize that success only comes from Him.

4. Sincerity is built through postponement

Allah being al-Shakūr does not necessarily mean that we will immediately see the appreciation for our efforts. Sometimes al-Shakūr postpones the signs of His appreciation to build our sincerity. Will we give up on doing good because we do not see the immediate fruits of our actions? Indeed, the Prophet Joseph remained steadfast even though it appeared that his integrity was being punished rather than appreciated! He was a pious son, yet his brothers tried to kill him. He was chaste, yet he was put in prison. He helped his cellmates by interpreting their dreams, and then he was forgotten in prison for years. But Joseph was patient, and He had conviction in the wisdom of God, and in His appreciation. So he continued doing good, and his deeds were appreciated by Allah, who returned his family to him, ensured that everyone knew of his innocence, and gave him a lofty position as overseer of the food rations. And that was just in this life. We can only imagine what Allah has saved for him in the next life.

5. Appreciate and thank people

The Prophet ﷺ taught us that *'The one who does not thank people has not thanked God.'* [Abū Dāwūd] Just as we love our deeds to be appreciated by God, so too should we appreciate people's good actions and efforts.

AL-QUDDŪS – UNIMAGINING GOD: THE HOLY, THE PURE (15)

9

AL-QUDDŪS – UNIMAGINING GOD: THE HOLY, THE PURE (15)

'Everything in the heavens and earth glorifies God, the Controller, the Holy One [Al-Quddūs], the Almighty, the Wise.'

[62:1]

There are varying conceptions (and misconceptions) about God. Different religions understand the Divine Entity in different ways. As Muslims, the Qur'an clarifies for us who Allah is, His attributes and how they manifest in our lives, and emphasizes that He is nothing like His creation.

The last point is extremely important because, without realizing, we tend to anthropomorphize God anyway. Since we are used to dealing with human beings who have flaws, we filter our understanding of the Creator through our experiences with His creation, incorrectly attributing those characteristics to Allah. For example, when we sin, we treat Him like a human being who cannot forgive completely, simply because we have never met a person who has been able to fully forgive. When we see what appears to be evil in the world, we use human logic to conclude that God must not be merciful, or that He does not have full knowledge or power, or to deny His existence completely. And this is because we assume that what we think we know – and only what we think we know of the outward – is the only explanation that exists. When we misunderstand God, we are pushed away from Him and the path that leads to Him. When we see Him as a human being, even if subconsciously, we also attribute to Him the flaws and imperfections of a human being.

Part of this is a normal part of being human. God is the Most Merciful, the Forbearing and the Generous – and these are attributes we can comprehend because they manifest themselves in human forms. We see one dimension of these different attributes: mercy in the acts of kindness around us; forbearance when we are given a second chance; generosity when we are given much more than expected. We understand these attributes at a very basic level because we experience them, and they can give us a glimpse into the attributes of God.

But this becomes problematic when, as mentioned above, we project these understandings, with all their mistakes, unto God. The Qur'an tells us, in no uncertain terms, *'Nothing is like Him.'* [42:11]. Whatever mercy, forbearance or generosity we experience in this world, they are not even a fraction of God's mercy, forbearance and generosity. It is important to keep this in mind. Imam Aḥmad ibn Ḥanbal said that whatever comes to our minds in terms of conceptualizing God, we should know that He is not that. Our minds literally cannot comprehend God's majesty.

Our occasional conflation of divine attributes with human imperfections is what leads us to attribute negative human qualities to God. This is why Allah invites us to know Him via His ninety-nine names, which He calls the *'Most Excellent Names (al-Asmā' al-Ḥusnā).'* [7:170] They are described as the 'most excellent' or 'most beautiful' or the 'best' to point us to the fact that when these names are used to describe Him, they are in their absolute best, most perfect form – a form which we cannot conceptualize because it does not exist in human beings. Thus, while human language gives us a peek into His names and attributes, they cannot truly encompass Him because language is limited, and God is not. For example, there are names that introduce us to His mercy and beauty, and the fact that we have experienced the human dimension of these attributes makes them easier for us to comprehend. Mercy has a linguistic meaning and an outward manifestation – it is not the same as harshness, for instance. Yet the mercy and beauty of God are on a completely different level; this is why the Prophet ﷺ described Paradise as *'what no eye has seen, what no ear has heard, and what no heart has conceived.'* [Tirmidhī] Yet, the Prophet ﷺ still described some of the beauty of Paradise to bring us closer to understanding by comparing it to things we have seen – such as pearls or rivers – but we have to always keep in mind that it is far greater than anything we can ever imagine or conceive of.

There are also names that show us the attributes of majesty, which should fill us with awe. However, some of these attributes, if not properly understood, may cause us confusion about God. For example, He is al-Qahhār – the Dominator. This attribute on its own might inspire in us awe and fear, but because our only experience with 'domination' is the unfair mortal kind, we might not understand *how* God can also be a dominator, or attribute injustice to His domination. And Allah is far above committing any kind of injustice.

Therefore, in addition to describing all of His names as most excellent (*ḥusnā*), there are specific names which, in their essence, teach us that Allah's attributes are nothing like human attributes. They underlie His names, attributes, and actions, and serve as a reminder that, for example, His mercy is not affected by a lack of wisdom, nor is His overpowering a result of irrational rage.

Al-Quddūs – the Pure, the Holy, the Blessed

Here, we come to Allah's Name al-Quddūs. Allah says in the Qur'an: *'He is God: there is no god other than Him, the Controller, the Holy One.'* [59:23]

In bowing in prayer (*rukū'*), the Prophet ﷺ would occasionally say: *'Exalted, Pure, Lord of the Angels and the Spirit (subbūḥun quddūs, rabb al-malā'ikati wal-rūḥ).'* [Muslim]

After the last voluntary prayer of the night (*witr*), the Prophet ﷺ would also say, *'Exalted is the Sovereign, the Pure (subḥān al-malik al-quddūs)'* three times. [Bukhārī]

Quddūs is an aggrandizement of the Arabic root word *qāf-dāl-sīn*, and can mean 'pure', 'holy' or 'blessed'. It tells us that God is pure from any defect and purified from anything blameworthy. This means that *all* of His attributes are also pure and holy. Just like the example we gave above about His name al-Qahhār, His attributes of majesty are completely pure, so they are free of any imperfection that might accompany a human manifestation of the same word. Indeed, God makes this clear in the Qur'an. Twice, Allah's name al-Quddūs comes after His name al-Malik, which means the Sovereign or King. When people think of a king, it might conjure up particular characteristics of kingship, such as power and authority; it might even summon images of injustice, or of specific kings of this world. Our conception of a king is limited by our imagination and experience. Hence, God tells us that He is al-Malik al-Quddūs, which should remind us not to conflate the human with the divine. He is the King and He is Pure, so there is no oppression or unfairness under Him. At its core, this name teaches us that that God's essence and actions are pure and untainted. Imam al-Ghazālī tells us that al-Quddūs transcends what we consider to be perfection itself.

If our conception of perfect qualities is still imperfect when it comes to Allah – because He far transcends them – what about when we attribute to Him qualities that are negative? As Ibn al-Qayyim reminds us, al-Quddūs is too pure and holy to ever act with oppression.[15] This is important to keep in mind and contemplate over so that we do not attribute blameworthy human attributes to Allah.

Another meaning of *quddūs* is that Allah purifies the hearts and souls of His worshippers and His special servants. Furthermore,

[15] Al-Ashqar, *Sharḥ Ibn Al-Qayyim Li Asmā' Allāh al-Ḥusnā*, 52.

those who have a special relationship with God and are close to Him try constantly to purify themselves from anything that might take them away from Allah. Of course, our purification is from that which God considers blameworthy, and not what Allah Himself is purified from. For instance, a person who is not able to sleep is an insomniac and needs help in order to be able to rest – the fact that he cannot sleep is not a virtue but, rather, a problem. With God, His not sleeping shows His self-sufficiency. And according to Imam al-Qurṭubī, the name al-Quddūs also describes the One who is glorified and revered by the angels. The angels say, *'we declare Your praise and sanctify You (nuqaddisu lak).'* [2:30]

The context of this verse sheds further light. God tells the angels that He will place a vicegerent – a *khalīfa* – on Earth in the form of humans. The angels are surprised because they *know* God's holiness means that He is far above having His actions or creation tainted by impurity. So why would He create human beings, who by their very nature make mistakes? Not only mistakes, but, in the angels' words, *'who cause corruption therein and shed blood?'* [2:30]

Our creation is not an exception to God's purity, but rather, a part of it. Indeed, this should encourage us to live up to the role that God has created for us: that of servant-caretakers of Earth, and true servants to Him.

This is a beautiful point to consider. God, the Holy – and all the meanings this name contains – created *you*. There is *wisdom* in you being here on this earth. So how will you choose to honor God's creation of you?

Finally, Ibn al-Qayyim points to the name 'Holy House' (*Bayt al-Maqdis*), which refers to the whole area encompassing al-Aqsa Mosque and the Dome of the Rock in modern day Palestine. This is the 'Holy House' because people go there to be purified of sins, and whoever visits it for the sole reason of praying there will return from it completely cleansed of his sins.

Remember these beautiful attributes, and remember that Allah is pure in His essence and actions, and thus only perfect mercy, justice, and wisdom can come from Him.

Living with this name

1. Glorify God

Knowing the above about Allah should inspire us to glorify Him. We should have a deep conviction in the purity of His essence, attributes and actions. We should know that our being here is not a mistake, but from God's perfection. We should also reject popular culture that makes jokes about God, and that does not respect the sacred. Allah is al-Quddūs, and there is a certain reverence that is owed to knowing God by this attribute.

2. Sanctify that which God has sanctified

Al-Quddūs has taught us which things are holy, and that He has sanctified certain things. We are commanded to value life, to protect people's honor and to respect our own places of worship, as well as the places of worship of others. We need to learn the things that God has sanctified and give them their proper respect.

3. Purify yourself

We should purify our beliefs from associating anything with God, our time from wrong-doing and idleness, our hearts from heedlessness and other diseases, and our souls from distractions. The practice of *murāqabah* – watching over one's self or cultivating self-awareness – can help us to purify our practice and create vigilance over our inner states.

AL-SALĀM – PEACE (16)

10

AL-SALĀM – PEACE (16)

'He is God: there is no god other than Him, the Controller, the Holy One, Source of Peace.'

[59:23]

Ibn Ḥazm wanted to find something that all people were united upon, despite their differing creeds, preoccupations, and dispositions. He said, 'I have found only one: to be free from anxiety.' We all seek peace and tranquility in some way. We work so that we do not have to worry about how we will get our next meal. We take breaks to rest and give ourselves some calm. We go out for long walks or drives just to get to a place of quiet and stillness.

Something in us constantly desires this serenity. We were created in this way. And the reason we desire peace so much is because the soul craves the divine. The soul's desire for peace in essence is leading us to God because only He can truly bestow peace. We are told in the Qur'an: *'peace (salām) be upon whoever follows the right guidance.'* [20:47]

Yet we sometimes act in contradictory ways. We look for an illusion of complete peace in the material, in other people, or in a certain way of life. But the reason we sometimes see people who do not seem to have much, yet are filled with the light of contentment, and others who appear to have it all but are never satisfied, is precisely because peace comes from al-Salām, and not from this world. If peace is sought through Him, then peace is achieved by

Him. As He tells us: *'Unquestionably, by the remembrance of Allah hearts are assured."* [13:28]

This does not mean that we cannot find any measure of peace in this life. This world is a creation of al-Salām, and so He has created means of peace within it. Indeed, a close friend or spouse, stability, the natural world – they all provide varying degrees of peace and contentment. Knowing al-Salām simply means that we recognize that the source of this peace is God Himself. However, anything that appears to bring us peace, but takes us away from Allah, causes to violate His commandments, or blinds us from recognizing Him as the source, is deception. Indeed, Ibn Al-Qayyim said very beautifully that in the heart 'is a strong desire that will not cease until He is the only one who is sought. In it is a void that cannot be filled except by His love, turning to Him, always remembering Him, and being sincere to Him. Were a person to be given the entire world and everything in it, that would never fill the void.' [Madārij al-Sālikīn]

This does not mean that we cannot take rest in the things of this world, as they are from Allah al-Salām. One of the Companions named Ḥanẓalah was worried about not being in a constant state of remembrance of God. He said to the Prophet ﷺ: 'O Messenger of Allah, when we are in your presence and are reminded of Hellfire and Paradise, we feel as if we are seeing them with our very eyes, but when we leave you and attend to our wives, our children, and our business, most of these things slip from our minds.' The Prophet said:

> *'By Him in whose Hand is my soul, if your state of mind remains the same as it is in my presence and you are always occupied with the remembrance of Allah, the angels will shake your hands in your beds and roads. O Ḥanẓalah, rather time should be devoted to this and time should be devoted to that."* [Muslim]

Al-Salām: the Flawless Source of Peace

We all understand *salām* to be peace, but this word has a number of dimensions. It is not just that God *is* Peace; He is the *source* and *giver* of peace. The root *sīn-lām-mīm* also means to be free from defect. *Salāmah* means safety. So how are these meanings interrelated, and how do they manifest in Allah's beautiful name?

God, His attributes, and His actions are free from fault or blemish; He is flawless. In essence, peace comes with the absence of fault. Peace in society comes with the absence not just of war but also of injustice, and peace in our relationships comes with not just the absence of violence but also of mistrust. Because God is truly flawless, He is real peace and therefore also the bestower of peace.

The ways to peace

We are reminded of God's name al-Salām when we say this supplication after every prayer: '*O Allah, you are the Source of Peace, and from You is peace, blessed are You O Possessor of Glory and Honor.*' [Muslim]

The end of prayer – after we have been in an intimate conversation with God – should be this realization and affirmation that truly God is Peace and from Him is peace. Some of us might sincerely feel this way, but many of us might not. Prayer becomes automated. We might not understand what we are saying. Some of us might even associate negativity with prayer because of the way we were taught the obligation of prayer as children.

But we need to remember that when the Flawless, the Source and Giver of Peace, prescribes something, it is inherently good. And working to find peace within prayer, because of the conviction that God is the Source of Peace, can only bring us closer to Him. Devotion in prayer is not zero-sum. It is a process and a journey that only elevates our soul.

Moreover, Allah tells us: '*A light has now come to you from God, and a Scripture making things clear, with which God guides to the ways of peace (subul as-salām) those who follow what pleases Him, bringing them from darkness out into light, by His will, and guiding them to a straight path.'* [5:15-16]

All of God's rulings and commandments are designed to give us peace, even if they also contain struggle within them. We are commanded to pray five times a day, to eat healthily, to be purposeful in our actions, to cultivate meaningful relationships, and to improve the state of our hearts. These things require effort but, ultimately, they come from the Source of Peace who shows us the way to peace.

The struggle inherent in most matters is a reminder of the nature of this world. But this does not mean that we will remain in this state forever. Al-Salām gives us something to look forward to. He says, *'But God invites [everyone] to the Home of Peace, and guides whoever He will to a straight path.'* [10:25]

Indeed, Paradise is the Home of Peace because it is the place of true perfection, where there is no sadness, nor enmity, nor struggle. That is the home of true bliss.

Spreading peace

When God created Adam, the first human, He said to him: *'Go and greet with peace the assembled angels and listen to how they greet you, for this will be the greeting among your progeny.'* So, Adam said to the angels, *'Peace be upon you.'* The angels responded, *'May peace be upon you and the mercy of Allah.'* [Bukhārī]

Our greeting to one another is '*as-salāmu 'alaykum*', which means 'peace be upon you'. This was the first greeting taught to the first human being, emphasizing the importance of spreading peace. Essentially, when we say *as-salāmu 'alaykum*, we are declaring that we will not harm others, guaranteeing them peace and security. When we submit to the Source of Peace, we should become vessels of peace for others. The Prophet ﷺ made this connection directly when he taught us: *'Verily, Peace (al-Salām) is among the names of Allah He has placed on the earth, so spread it between yourselves.'* [Ṭabarānī]

Indeed, when the Prophet Muhammad ﷺ migrated to Madina, this was his first commandment to the people: *'O people, spread peace, feed the hungry, and pray at night when people are sleeping and you will enter Paradise in peace.'* [Ibn Mājah]

In a new society with different demographics and potential conflicts, the Prophet ﷺ reminded the people that spreading peace and refraining from harming others was of utmost importance. He also laid the foundation for two different aspects of peace: societal and personal. He advised people to feed the hungry, establishing our connection to and relationship with the people around us, and to pray at night, establishing our connection to and relationship with God. This foundation paves the way to peace in Paradise. The Prophet ﷺ also taught us the basis of faith: *'You will not enter Paradise until you believe and you will not believe until you love each other. Shall I show you something that, if you did, you would love each other? Spread peace between yourselves.'* [Muslim]

In order to be at peace with others, we need to find peace within our hearts.

Al-Salām and our hearts

Allah tells us in the Qur'an that the Day of Judgement is *'the Day when neither wealth nor children can help, when the only one who will be saved is the one who comes before God with a heart devoted to Him (qalbin salīm).'* [26:88-89].

A heart that is *salīm* – which comes from the same root as the word *salām* – not only guides us to peace in the Hereafter, as it is the only thing that will benefit us, but it also brings internal peace in this world. The foundation of being at peace can be found in the state of our hearts. When we allow our hearts to make things of this world equal to God, to envy, to hate, and to think ourselves better than others, we are naturally far from being in a state of peace, because our hearts are far from the Flawless Source of Peace. No heart can be devoted to God when it is full of these diseases.

Having any degree of one or more of the diseases of the heart does not mean that there is no hope, or that it is a permanent feature over which we have no control. We are human and it is natural to become influenced by the vices of the world. The real problem occurs when we are oblivious to the fact that we have these diseases and, thus, do not work on the state of our hearts. It would be impossible to be a person at peace – with God, with ourselves, with others – while our hearts are tarnished by envy, miserliness, ostentation, vanity, heedlessness, extreme love of this world, rancor, obliviousness to blessings, and other diseases. Therefore, part of being a servant of al-Salām is to look inwardly at all the obstacles to peace in our own hearts. Few of us will be able to say that we are completely free of every single disease. We might have a mild version of a disease and might be even asymptomatic for most of our lives, until our reaction to an unexpected incident gives away what is in our hearts.

For example, we may usually be happy for other people's achievements, but suddenly find ourselves resentful and envious when someone whom we do not like receives something that we wanted for ourselves. Here, envy means that we wish for the gift to be taken away from that person, while resentment means that we might even feel resentful towards God for bestowing that person with the gift, and not us. These are very subtle manifestations, but the more we work on the state of our hearts through being vigilant, having hope, and doing good, the more we can polish our hearts of these blemishes.

The weight of sins

Sins also weigh heavily on our hearts. The Prophet ﷺ told us,

> *'Verily, when the servant commits a sin, a black mark appears upon his heart. If he abandons the sin, seeks forgiveness, and*

repents, then his heart will be polished. If he returns to the sin, the blackness will be increased until it overcomes his heart. It is the covering that Allah has mentioned: No, rather a covering is over their hearts from what they have earned.' [Tirmidhī]

At times, we might not know why our hearts are in a state of trepidation, or we might not seem to find success or blessing in anything that we do. Again, it behooves us to look inwardly. We should examine the sins that we are committing and return to Allah. This thought should be liberating, because it means that we *can* do something to help ourselves. Indeed, Allah loves those who constantly strive and who turn to Him. We are reminded that, *'All of the children of Adam make mistakes, and the best of those who make mistakes are those who repent.'* [Tirmidhī]

The goal is self-improvement, even if it is one small step at a time.

Living with this name

1. Remember God

Hearts are inclined to find peace in His remembrance. This includes prayer, specific forms of remembrance (*dhikr*), supplication (*du'a'*), and doing things with the intention to please God. Allah should be remembered with mindfulness, rather than a distracted heart.

2. Find peace in your heart through al-Salām

Have a regular practice of examining and reflecting upon the state of your heart. We will find that many of the obstacles to peace can be found in the blameworthy traits which we allow to seep into and spread within our hearts. Moreover, what is in our hearts eventually finds its way to our tongues and our limbs.

3. Spread peace

Start with greeting people with peace and let your actions be an embodiment of peace and keeping others safe from harm.

4. Ask for forgiveness

The Prophet ﷺ tells us that, *'The one who (regularly) says seeks forgiveness, God will relieve him of every burden, and make from every discomfort an outlet, and He will provide for him from (sources) he never could imagine.'* [Abū Dāwūd]

5. Seek reward from God, not from people

When we seek peace outside its true source, eventually we will be disappointed. When we put our hopes solely in results and not in Allah, maintaining good works and activism for good causes can be hard. This is why we should seek peace in God Himself, while utilizing the means of this world that He has given us.

6. Strive for excellence

In this world, we should still strive for perfection or excellence in our deeds because we believe in a Flawless Lord. The Prophet ﷺ said, *'When one of you does something, Allah loves that you do it with excellence.'* [Ṭabarānī]

AL-MU'MIN – SECURITY (17)

11

AL-MU'MIN – SECURITY (17)

'He is God: there is no god other than Him, the Controller, the Holy One, Source of Peace, Granter of Security."

[59:23]

Every one of the names of God opens up a new dimension of our relationship with Him. The more we know and experience of His Names, the more stable we feel our relationship with God. And God is al-Mu'min – the Granter of Security.

Mu'min comes from the Arabic root *alif-mīm-nūn*, which can mean safety, security and protection. Security and protection are not simply in terms of the physical, but include spiritual and emotional security and protection as well. We may have people we feel safe with, and this is an internal feeling that comes from trust. The meaning of the word *mu'min* goes back to affirmation and belief. Keeping this in mind, Allah's name al-Mu'min has a number of dimensions in relation to our relationship with Him:

1. Allah gives people freedom from fear. Allah says in Sūrat Quraysh: *'Let them worship the Lord of this House, Who has fed them, [saving them] from hunger and made them safe (āmanahum), [saving them] from fear.'* [106:4]

   Allah uses the word āmanahum, from the same root, to describe how He had made the Quraysh safe from any fear.

2. He fulfills His promises and thus is believed and trusted. We cannot truly feel safe with someone who cannot be trusted. Allah says in the Qur'an in the story of Prophet Joseph: *'They said, "O our father, indeed we went racing each other and left Joseph with our possessions, and a wolf ate him. But you would not believe (bi-mu'minin) us, even if we were truthful."'* [12:17]

3. He grants belief, and thus ultimate safety, to His servants who seek Him. Allah tells us in the Qur'an: *'It is those who have faith, and do not mix their faith with idolatry, who will be secure (lahum al-amn), and it is they who are rightly guided.'* [6:82]

Protection from fear

We are vulnerable as human beings and, because of that, we feel anxiety and fear. But Allah says: *'God has made a promise to those among you who believe and do good deeds: He will make them successors to the land, as He did those who came before them; He will empower the religion He has chosen for them; He will grant them security to replace their fear.'* [24:55]

True security can only be found with Allah and through faith (*īmān*) in Him. God gives us many examples in the Qur'an of His giving safety from fear, in particular to those who believed in Him, in the time of the Prophet Moses. Pharaoh was quite literally inducing terror in the Children of Israel. In addition to their oppression and ghettoization, he began to murder any newborn boy. It is worth mentioning that his slaughter of babies was due to his own fear of being overthrown, as he had had a dream that someone would come from amongst the Children of Israel and replace him. When your fear is due to your own transgressions against others, there will never be internal nor external security. Similar to Shakespeare's Macbeth, in which the protagonist murders the king out of his ambition for the throne and then has to continue killing others to protect himself, he becomes mad with paranoia and is eventually killed himself. Security can only be found in God and His way.

But for those who have faith in al-Mu'min, God provides for them security from fear, even when they are in the most trying circumstances. When the mother of Moses gave birth and realized that he was a boy, she was gripped by fear, because she knew that Pharaoh's henchmen would soon be knocking on her door to slaughter her child. But Allah says, '*And We inspired to the mother of Moses, "Suckle him; but when you fear for him, cast him into the river and do not fear and do not grieve. Indeed, We will return him to you and will make him [one] of the messengers."*' [28:7]

God gave her respite. Despite her feeling emptiness afterwards, God tells us that He '*strengthened it [her heart] to make her one of those who believe [al-mu'minīn].*' [28:10]

Belief in al-Mu'min makes one a true believer, because we believe and have faith in the One who grants security and faith. Similarly, when Moses and Aaron were told by God to confront Pharaoh, they said, '"*Lord, we fear he will do us great harm or exceed all bounds.*"' But God is al-Mu'min – so '*He said, "Do not be afraid, I am with you both, hearing and seeing everything."*' [20:45-46]

Likewise, when the magicians cast their sticks and ropes, and they appeared to be moving, '*Moses was inwardly alarmed.*' [20:68] And what did Allah say? '"*Do not be afraid, you have the upper hand.*"' [20:69]

Any time we are paralyzed by fear, we should remember that God grants security. And the greater our faith in Him, the more secure we will feel, despite external danger. Perhaps the greatest example from the story of Moses is Āsiyah, the wife of Pharaoh. While her husband's despotism was manifested in its most extreme form outside the palace, eventually Āsiyah would be the object of his tyranny. When he found out about her faith in God, he decided to make an example of her. He tortured her – his own wife! – in the most gruesome ways. Externally, she was destroyed, but in her heart, she did not falter. She was secure, unwavering. God tells us: *'God has also given examples of believers: Pharaoh's wife, who said, "Lord, build me a house near You in the Garden. Save me from Pharaoh and his actions; save me from the evildoers."'* [66:11]

The security of faith that Āsiyah possessed was what enabled her to see beyond this life. She wanted not simply any house in Paradise; the important thing was that it would be near Him. And that was how she could face a tyrant's horrific abuse: faith (*īmān*) in al-Mu'min, who secured her heart.

The examples of the mother of Moses, Moses and Aaron themselves, and Āsiyah show us that through faith in Allah, we are given true security. The Qur'an gives us this reassurance, not just in the stories of those who were firm in faith before us, but in the promises of God Himself.

The One who fulfils His promise and is thus believed

Allah, al-Mu'min, fulfils His promises, and thus He is the One who is believed, and we are granted security in this way. Think of the unstable nature of a relationship with someone who never fulfils their word and thus cannot be trusted. There is no security. But with al-Mu'min, part of the essence of this name and His revealing this name to us, is that we feel secure when He tells us something. We are told in the Qur'an: *'Truly, God does not break His promise.'* [3:9]

Al-Mu'min gives us the Qur'an, informing us of His attributes, the nature of this world, and what we need to do in order to gain nearness to Him. He does not keep us guessing as to His nature or how to be in this life, nor does He ever disappoint a good opinion of Him. Because He has told us this, we believe that He accepts us when we return to Him, that He bestows His mercy upon His creation, and that no one will suffer injustice under Him. Indeed, there is no security with injustice, and God is far from subjecting anyone to an atom's weight of unfairness.

After describing certain characteristics of those on the straight path, Allah says, '*We accept from such people the best of what they do and We overlook their bad deeds. They will be among the people of Paradise -- the true promise that has been given to them.*" [46:16]

Indeed, this promise of God is the promise of eternal security.

The Giver of Eternal Security through faith

God is the Giver of Faith through His sending of messengers, the Qur'an, and the signs in both the natural world as well as those in our own lives. Al-Mu'min gives faith, but He does not force it. When Moses showed up with the miracles, that was from God, so that people could be guided. The magicians, upon seeing Moses' staff turn into a snake that ate their sticks, immediately believed. Pharaoh, upon seeing the same sign (and many others), rejected God. The magicians were given security in the Hereafter through this faith, while Pharaoh was given eternal damnation due to his rejection, transgression and conceit.

Allah says: '*For those who say, "Our lord is God," and then follow the straight path there is no fear, nor shall they grieve: they are the people of Paradise, there to remain as a reward for what they were doing.*' [46:13-14]

Al-Ghazālī explains that by far the biggest fear is – or should be – eternal damnation, and nothing can protect us from that but the profession of faith in the unity of God. That is where true security and safety lie. And Allah being al-Mu'min means that He gives to His creation the means to attain faith – *īmān* – and thus eternal security.

The 'sharing' of a name

While a believer is described as a *mu'min* and Allah's name is al-Mu'min, these characteristics are not alike. God being *al-Mu'min* carries with it all the meanings discussed above. Our responsibilities as believers (*mu'minīn*), on the other hand, mean that we must strive to be true believers in Allah through the various means that He has prescribed. God tells us in the Qur'an:

> *'The desert Arabs say, "We have faith (āmannā)." [Prophet], tell them, "You do not have faith. What you should say instead is, "We have submitted (aslamnā)," for faith has not yet entered your hearts." If you obey God and His Messenger, He will not diminish any of your deeds: He is most forgiving and most merciful. The true believers are the ones who have faith in God and His Messenger and leave all doubt behind, the ones who have struggled with their possessions and their persons in God's way: they are the ones who are true."* [19:14-15]

Thus, achieving true faith is not simply in being labelled a Muslim, but a conscious effort to find security through God. We can learn much from the stories of those who came before us, whose faith in God gradually became stronger. And He strengthens with faith those who strive for Him.

Living with this name

1. Trust in the promise of God

Allah is al-Mu'min, and thus is the One who fulfils His promise and is the One who is believed. We should therefore find comfort in the fact that God makes ease after hardship [65:7], we can widen our vision when we understand that we may dislike something that might actually be good for us [2:216], and we should self-reflect when God tells us that the corruption we see around us may very well be what our own hands have wrought [30:41]. Belief (*īmān*) in the promise of God means that we are secure in our hearts and secure with Him.

2. Give other people security

The Prophet ﷺ emphatically declared: *'By God he does not believe, by God he does not believe, by God he does not believe!'* The Companions asked, 'Who, O Messenger of Allah?' The Prophet ﷺ replied: *'He whose neighbor is not safe from his misdeeds.'* [Bukhārī] Imam Al-Ghazālī stated that the most worthy person of being called 'faithful' is the one who keeps others safe from himself or herself.

3. Speak the truth and let your actions affirm the truth of your speech

Mu'min is also to believe or affirm the truth. Allah's actions and speech in the Qur'an confirm one another and there is no contradiction. Sheikh Rātib al-Nabulsī advises that our actions must correspond with and affirm our speech. So, when we say we believe, we should ask ourselves, where is the proof of that in our actions?

4. Guide others to safety

The most deserving person to be called a *mu'min* is one who guides others to what will give them ultimate safety and security; one guides others to al-Mu'min Himself. While we know that it is only Allah who guides, guidance here means that we advise with wisdom and inform others.

AL-MUHAYMIN – COMPLETE CONTROL (18)

12

AL-MUHAYMIN – COMPLETE CONTROL (18)

'He is Allah, other than whom there is no deity, the Sovereign, the Pure, the Perfection, the Bestower of Faith, the Overseer.'

[59:23]

If you make a big mistake – whether at school, work, or at home – and someone tries to reassure you, this reassurance can only go so far. If you heard that fifty percent of the class failed in exams, and your friend comforts you by saying that you are probably of those who passed, it may only help slightly – your friend is not the one grading your paper, nor does he or she have insider knowledge. If cuts are being made at work and you are worried about your job, your colleague may attempt to make you feel better by listing why you will most likely keep your job. It may make you feel a little more confident, but your colleague is not the boss. He or she does not control the company.

But when the reassurance comes from the teacher grading the paper or the CEO of the company, that is when you can be sure that you will be ok. They are the ones who are in control.

God has revealed those of His Names that are relevant for us to know and live by. Knowing our potential fear of situations where we do not know who is in control, God tells us that He is al-Muhaymin, which has three basic, intertwined meanings: complete control, command, and protection. If a soldier, for example, has *haymanah* over a city, it means he has taken control of it and watches over it. Allah also describes the Qur'an as *muhaymin*, meaning that it will guard over all the other scriptures that came before it.[16]

The conditions of complete *haymanah*

While human beings may have some form of *haymanah*, such as the example of the soldier over a city, it is by nature limited. To have complete *haymanah*, three things are required:

1. Knowledge

Complete control and protection cannot occur without complete knowledge. We would not trust someone who does not have full knowledge of a situation, even if they *appear* to be in control. Think of a patient in a hospital whose doctor is replaced. While the new doctor may be just as capable, if he or she does not have full knowledge of the patient's history, the doctor's control over the situation would be deficient. God is al-'Alīm – the All-Knowing – and 'Ālim al-Ghayb wa al-Shahādah – the Knower of the Unseen and the Witnessed – having full knowledge of everything on Earth, as well as what is in your heart.

2. Ability

For someone to exercise full control over something, he or she has to have the ability. Again, while human beings may be able to exercise some control over some situations, if the ability is lacking, so is the control and protection. God is al-Qadīr – the Most Able.

3. Continuity

Finally, people may exercise control over a short period of time. A tyrant, a president, a CEO – all of their control will be limited. Whereas God is al-Bāqī, the Everlasting, and His control and protection transcend time.

---

[16] Al-Oadah, *In the Company of God*, 45.

Thus, God is the ultimate *muhaymin*, because His control and protection are complete and all-encompassing. People may have limited forms of control but, like a CEO who gives some control to the managers, that control is subject to the CEO's will; he or she can remove the power given to them. Moreover, when a human being has *haymanah*, it is for his or her benefit. But with Allah, His all-encompassing control and protection ultimately benefit us.

Worry and the protective wing

Connecting to this name is the ultimate antidote to excessive worrying and stress. We must have conviction that God is in control, watching over everything, and bestowing His protection. Nothing escapes His knowledge nor His power. We all worry a little about a number of things, but reflecting upon this name should afford us a measure of peace and confidence. One of the ways the word *haymanah* is used in Arabic is to describe a bird that covers her chicks with her wings, thereby providing them comfort and protection. We should think of al-Muhaymin covering us with His protection whenever we feel that things are outside of our control and we have no shelter.

Living with this name

1. Supervise, take control over and protect your inner state

We mentioned the different dimensions of *haymanah* – control, possession, and protection – and this is what we should do with our hearts and internal states. We need to take possession over our own hearts, control their negative passions, and protect them by inculcating in them the good traits that God praises in His servants.

2. Find calm with the knowledge of His control and protection

Human beings desire control, and when we lose it, it causes much anxiety and stress. Reminding ourselves that God is al-Muhaymin should enable us to let go of that desire, because we cannot truly control anything – only by His will. Thus, we should focus on those things that Allah has placed under our control in this world, and let go of the things that are outside that realm.

3. Do not oppress people

When we are given control or authority over people, that should be exercised as a trust. Any oppression that occurs under our control will render us accountable for it. Just like God gave us control over certain people, He may give others control over us.

AL-'AZĪZ – STRENGTH FROM DIGNITY (19)

13

AL-'AZĪZ – STRENGTH FROM DIGNITY (19)

'Your Lord alone is the Almighty (al-'Azīz), the Merciful.'

[26:9]

There are different types of strengths and sources of strength. Someone may appear strong physically, while others are strong mentally, and others still have both types of strength. Some derive their strength from an inherent dignity while others project strength that is based on oppression. We know that God is the Almighty, and His Name al-'Azīz teaches us the different dimensions of God's might.

The meanings

Al-'Azīz comes from the root *'ayn-zā-zā*, and al-'Azīz has several meanings. It means the invincible that no one can overpower, the dignified, the strong, and the One who is needed. The Qur'an alludes to all of these meanings. In the story of the Prophet David, when a man came to him to rule on a dispute with his brother, the man said: *'This is my brother. He had ninety-nine ewes and I just the one, and he said, "Let me take charge of her," and overpowered me with his words.'* [38:23]

The word for 'overpowered' here is *'azzanī*, from the same root. The Qur'an is also described as *'azīz*, and God teaches us that: *'it is an unassailable Scripture.'* [41:41]

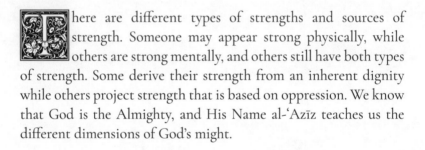

In the story of the Prophet Solomon and the Queen of Sheba, the Queen said: '"*Indeed kings - when they enter a city, they ruin it and render the honored of its people humbled. And thus do they do.*"' [27:34]

The 'honored' people are the *a'izzah*, from the same root. God also says in the Qur'an about two prophets who were rejected by the people: '*so We strengthened ('azaznā) them with a third.*' [36:14]

These are the different ways that the concept of '*izzah* (strength and dignity, from the same root as al-'Azīz) are used in the Qur'an. So what does that mean for Allah?

Exalted in Might

When we bring together all of the linguistic meanings, we understand that al-'Azīz is the One who is exalted in might, who can overcome and is not overcome, who is unassailable, invincible, who humiliates those who transgress, and who is honored. Allah shows us the manifestations of His name in the Qur'an. During the Battle of Badr, the Muslims were outnumbered: 313 to 1000. Allah tells them that He sent them angels as reinforcements, and we know that the Muslims were victorious during the battle. But Allah reminds us: '*God made this a message of hope to reassure your hearts: help comes only from God, He is mighty and wise.*" [8:10] It was al-'Azīz who defeated, and not the angels. The angels were simply a reassurance for the hearts of the believers, but it is God who is mighty, and it is God who defeated those who wanted to harm them. In the same chapter of the Qur'an, Allah tells us that, '*The hypocrites and those who have sickness in their hearts said, "These people [the believers] must be deluded by their religion," but if anyone puts his trust in God, God is mighty and wise.*' [8:49]

The hypocrites did not believe in God's might. They thought that the Muslims were deluded for going out to fight when they were so outnumbered. But God reminds us that, if we put our trust in Him – by taking all the necessary precautions, obeying Him, and trusting Him in our hearts – God is able to give us strength and victory. He is both mighty and wise, and so when God al-'Azīz commands us, there is wisdom in His commandment.

Al-'Azīz warns people of wronging others, and reminds us of His strength. Regarding people taking advantage of the property of orphans under their care, Allah says:

> *'They ask you about [the property of] orphans: say, "It is good to set things right for them. If you combine their affairs with yours, remember they are your brothers and sisters: God knows those who spoil things and those who improve them. Had He so willed, He could have made you vulnerable too: He is almighty and wise."'* [2:220]

Allah reminds people that the orphans are essentially defenseless, so those who have been given the responsibility of caring for them and their property should not take advantage of that. God has the power to make the caretakers vulnerable too, because His is the Almighty. Allah has even harsher words for those who plot against the Prophets and the righteous. He says in the Qur'an: *'They made their plots, but, even if their plots had been able to move mountains, God had the answer. So, do not think [Prophet] that God will break His promise to His messengers: He is mighty, and capable of retribution."* [14:46-47] This means that no matter what those who wish harm upon the messengers do, God is mightier than them and is able to execute a just retribution for their plots and actions. So al-'Azīz is the One who is invincible, able to overpower those who think they can overpower His people.

Finally, a related name from the same root is al-Mu'izz, meaning He gives *'izzah* (strength and dignity). *'Izzah* is the opposite of humiliation. Because Allah is al-'Azīz and al-Mu'izz, He gives honor, dignity and strength to whomever He wills, particularly His righteous servants. Allah says: *'The believers, both men and women, support each other; they order what is right and forbid what is wrong; they keep up the prayer and pay the prescribed alms; they obey God and*

His Messenger. God will give His mercy to such people: God is almighty and wise." [9:71]

Al-Qurṭubī states that Allah is al-'Azīz in that He is mighty over those who harm the servants He describes in this verse, and is wise in how and whom He overpowers. Ibn Kathīr says that Allah mentions His name al-'Azīz at the end of this verse to indicate that for those who seek strength in Him through the ways that He outlines in the verse, God will surely strengthen them. Allah also says, *'They say, "Once we return to Madinah the powerful (al-a'azz) will drive out the weak," but power (al-'izzah) belongs to God, to His Messenger, and to the believers, though the hypocrites do not know this.'* [63:8]

Those who only believe in the material may doubt this, but this verse affirms that power, strength, and dignity are from God.

Strength and dignity are from Him

God is al-'Azīz, and so He gives *'izzah* to His righteous servants. As mentioned earlier, in the Qur'an, we are told of two Prophets who were sent to a people in Sūrat Yāsīn: *'When We sent to them two but they denied them, so We strengthened them with a third, and they said, "Indeed, we are messengers to you."'* [36:14].

In this story, the prophets were trying to call people to God. But the people rejected them and continued with their transgressions. So God gave them strength by sending with them a third prophet. This is an important point. When we do something sincerely for Allah, and we behave with dignity and strength, then God Himself will give us strength and reinforcement from where we could not imagine. He gives us true *'izzah*, because only He can.

Might is not oppression

Many of the verses we saw above that end by telling us that Allah is the One Exalted in Might (al-'Azīz) also mention an additional name. The name al-'Azīz is frequently paired with either Allah's names the Wise (al-Ḥakīm) – forty-two times – and the Merciful (al-Raḥīm) – thirteen times – because some people might interpret *'izzah* to simply mean defiance and exercising strength, whether justified or not. But God's strength is always tempered by wisdom and mercy. His is not an overpowering of oppression or haste.

This name is also paired with His names the All-forgiving (al-Ghafūr) twice and the Perpetual Forgiver (al-Ghaffār) three times. While God is indeed the Almighty, this does not negate His forgiveness. Indeed, God forgives all those who turn to Him. One of the people who believed during the time of Moses said to his people, '*You invite me to disbelieve in Allah and associate with Him that of which I have no knowledge, and I invite you to the Exalted in Might, the Perpetual Forgiver.*' [40:42]

Knowing that God is the Almighty should induce a feeling of awe within us, but this should not paralyze us. It should not make us feel that God is quick to punish, or that He exercises power just for the sake of it. If we ever commit wrongs and are set straight by God exercising His strength over us – maybe we took advantage of the weak financially, and He causes us to lose our wealth; perhaps we mistreated those deemed weaker than us, and suddenly find ourselves at the mercy of someone who does not show mercy – this does not mean that that is God's final judgment over us. On the contrary, the fact that we see these lessons as a sign of His might is a mercy, and we can be hopeful in His forgiveness if we rectify our ways, make amends, and return to Him; He is both mighty and forgiving.

Moreover, the pairing of these names has implications for us. When we try to be servants of al-'Azīz, we must remember that it is God who gives strength, and that can be internal or external. When we have *'izzah*, it should not turn into arrogance or harshness, rather it should be accompanied by wisdom and mercy. Moreover, being forgiving does not negate strength. Indeed, only those who are strong and secure internally can truly forgive slights against them.

Strength through God

When we obey God, that is a source of strength and dignity. God tells us: *'And let not their speech grieve you. Indeed, honor ('izzah) belongs to Allah entirely. He is the Hearing, the Knowing."* [10:65]

People seek strength and dignity from many worldly things that, in essence, may only temporarily strengthen us – yet that strength may not be not based on dignity. Following God's path ensures that al-'Azīz is with us, and that brings internal strength, external aid, and dignity.

For example, the Prophet ﷺ taught us one of the dimensions of the concept of *'izzah.* He said: *'Seek the things you need with self-respect and dignity (bi 'izzati anfus), for all matters run according to Divine Ordainment."* [Ibn 'Asākir][17]

This means that we should not act in undignified ways or ways that are displeasing to Him when we seek, for example, our sustenance. The true servants of al-'Azīz are those who derive their dignity from Him, and thus respect themselves and have an inner strength.

Living with this name

1. Fear only Allah

Allah cannot be overpowered. We sometimes fear people because of what we perceive to be their strength over us. But Allah is al-'Azīz, and we should always remember this when we are faced with those who exercise strength in unjust ways. Āsiyah, the wife of Pharaoh, was physically and socially weaker than her husband. But she feared only God, because she knew that He is al-'Azīz. And through that, she was able to stand up to Pharaoh, and God eventually humiliated and destroyed him.

[17] Collected by Ibn 'Asakir and related by 'Abdullah bin Bisr. The chain has been censured by al-Suyuti

2. Be strong for and through Him

The Messenger of Allah ﷺ said, *'The strong believer is more beloved to Allah than the weak believer, but there is goodness in both of them. Be eager for what benefits you, seek help from Allah, and do not be frustrated. If something befalls you, then do not say: If only I had done something else. Rather say: Allah has decreed what he wills. Verily, the phrase "if only" opens the way for the work of Satan."* [Muslim]

We should work on our strength, remembering that strength includes physical strength, but is not limited to that. It is mental, emotional, and spiritual strength. The hadith above mentions the strong believer, and then proceeds to talk about seeking help from Allah, and how to deal with something befalling us. This shows that strength is also the ability to face the hardships of this world, and they cannot be faced by physical strength alone.

3. Strengthen people

The Prophet ﷺ said, *'Whoever is humiliated before a believer and he does not help him when he is able to do so, Allah will humiliate him before the creation on the day of judgment.'* [Aḥmad] Indeed, this point is related to the one above. If we do not work on our own strength, how can we help others?

4. Go to God with humility

He is al-'Azīz and true *'izzah* belongs to Him, and this should humble us, particularly when we have been given strength over others. The Prophet ﷺ tells us, *'no one humbles himself for the sake of Allah except that Allah raises his status.'* [Muslim] The ultimate honor lies in our prostrating to God, both in our prayers and in our hearts.

5. Being strong does not mean being harsh

Having strength or *'izzah* does not mean being harsh, uncompromising, or unforgiving towards others. Allah pairs His own name al-'Azīz with His names the Most Merciful, the Most

Wise, the Most Forgiving, and the Perpetual Forgiver. So, we need to change our understanding of strength, if strength to us means simply being able to defeat others. The Prophet ﷺ taught that *'no one forgives except that Allah increases his honor ('izzah).'* [Muslim]

6. Be dignified

Part of the meaning of *'izzah* is honor and dignity. As humans, we sometimes derive our strength and dignity from worldly sources such as wealth, status or even ethnicity or nationality. If we perceive that they will give us *'izzah*, then they are what we will pursue; without them, we may feel a sense of inferiority and project this onto other people, harming ourselves and others. Yet God is the One who truly strengthens and gives honor, and true dignity comes in servitude and obedience to Him. When our pursuits are in His name and for Him, we break free of the power that worldly matters have over us. One of my favorite statement comes from the Companion, 'Umar ibn al-Khaṭṭab, who said, *'We were indeed a very lowly people. Allah raised us to honor and greatness through Islam. If we forget who we are and wish other than Islam, which elevated us, the One who raised us surely will debase us.'*

AL-JABBĀR – THE COMPELLER, MENDING THE BROKEN (20)

14

AL-JABBĀR – THE COMPELLER, MENDING THE BROKEN (20)

'The Compeller, the Truly Great; God is far above anything they consider to be His partner.'

[59:23]

Some of the names of God contain many different meanings, sometimes seemingly opposing meanings, which is why it is useful to understand the linguistic root of each name.

God's Name al-Jabbār indicates both majesty as well as beauty. The Arabic root of the word is *jīm-bā-rā*, which gives rise to meanings such as to compel, to be strong, as well as to mend what is broken.

Jabbār over the tyrants

As God is the Compeller, this Name demonstrates God's Majesty and Strength over His servants. Only He can compel everything according to His divine will, yet nothing and no one can compel Him.

In the Qur'an, the word *jabbār* is used to describe human beings as tyrannical. This is because tyrants try to compel people to submit to their will. God says in the Qur'an, *'In this way God leaves the doubting rebels to stray— those who dispute God's messages, with no authority given to them, are doing something that is loathed by God and by those who believe. In this way God seals up the heart of every arrogant tyrant [jabbār].'* [40:35]

Yet, God is al-Jabbār as well as the Most Merciful and the Most Just. His attributes are holistic and the perfect form of each attribute – His compulsion is never oppressive. Therefore, when we call upon God al-Jabbār, we are seeking strength from Him knowing only He can compel and change events. This is a name for all tyrants to know, because God can compel them under His will, and they will have to answer for their oppression.

But this name is not only for tyrants. We should also be vigilant over our own selves and guard against 'breaking' people, particularly those weaker than us. Allah might manifest His force over us due to our wrongful actions against others.

Mending the broken

The Arabic word for a splint that is used to help a broken bone to heal is a *jibeera*, which is from the same root as *jabbār*. The splint compels the bone to heal in the right way and restores it to its whole, unbroken state.

Moreover, a supplication (*du'ā'*) that is frequently made is '*Allah yijbur bi khaṭirik*', which is difficult to translate, but roughly has the meaning 'may Allah console your heart' or 'May Allah mend your heart.' People say this to ask God to give the person for whom they are praying whatever his or her heart desires. Some of the scholars would supplicate '*ya jābir kull kasīr*' when they were faced with overwhelming difficulty, meaning 'O You who mends everything that is broken.' Allah has named Himself al-Jabbār, and this means that He will mend what is broken – we need to be sure of that.

And as human beings, we do feel broken at times. It can be for any number of reasons, such as hurtful words from others, emotional exhaustion, or the death of someone close. Sometimes it is difficult to pinpoint exactly the source of the brokenness. Whatever the reason, we should turn to the One who can mend everything that is broken, and the One who can console the hearts.

How many times did God comfort the heart of the Prophet ﷺ? When the people of Quraysh mocked the Prophet ﷺ for not receiving revelation for a certain period, Allah comforted Him with these words:

> *"Your Lord has not forsaken you [Prophet], nor does He hate you, and the future will be better for you than the past; your Lord is sure to give you so much that you will be well satisfied. Did He not find you an orphan and shelter you? Did He not find you lost and guide you? Did He not find you in need and make you self-sufficient? So, do not be harsh with the orphan and do not chide the one who asks for help; talk about the blessings of your Lord.'* [93:3-11]

The Prophet ﷺ still faced difficulty, but his heart was put at rest by God Himself. When the Prophet ﷺ was rejected by the people of Ṭā'if after going there to seek their protection, and was chased away with stones and derision, he turned to Allah – not to pray against the people who harmed him, but to ask for His mercy. He was broken. He had lost his beloved wife and his uncle. And Allah comforted him through a young boy by the name of 'Addās, who saw the Prophet ﷺ and brought him some grapes. After talking with him and realizing that he was a prophet, the young boy kissed his bleeding feet. That is al-Jabbār. He then mended the heart of the Prophet ﷺ in a different way: through the miraculous journey of al-Isrā wa al-Mi'rāj, when the Prophet ﷺ traveled from Makkah to Jerusalem, and from Jerusalem to the Heavens in one night.

The journey itself did not accomplish a great victory, nor did it help to convince the Quraysh that he was a Prophet. On the contrary, the people of Quraysh mocked him even more for claiming that he had travelled to Jerusalem and back in one night! But God honored him after all the hardship he had gone through. It was a comfort and a spiritual support. Imagine how the Prophet ﷺ must have felt after the journey, after being subjected to so much heartbreak and pain before.

And this should be a lesson for us; when we are broken, we should turn to the One who can mend our broken hearts. Our lives might not change drastically. But He may console us through the kind word of someone that brightens our day, or someone who helps us with our problem. It may even be something greater. But He will mend what is broken.

Living with this name

1. Do not break people

The worst thing we can do is be *jabbārīn*, compelling people until they break. God can compel tyrants and He can cause our evil deeds to return to us in worse forms. If we are of those people who have hurt others in extreme ways, this does not mean that we cannot return to God. Perhaps the punishment of having the bad things we did return to us can bring us to know God, who can mend everything. Something bad happening to us in this world that brings us back to God is a blessing and ultimate mercy, because there is still time to seek forgiveness and mend our ways.

2. Help those who are broken

Sufyān al-Thawrī said that he had not seen an act of worship better for getting close God than consoling the heart of one who is broken. We should strive to be the means by which people are comforted, consoled, and helped – spiritually, emotionally, and physically.

3. Go to God when you are broken

The worst thing one can do is turn away from God when one feels defeated. This is the time to go to Him and sincerely plead with Him to help. God would not have given Himself this name had He not wanted the broken to come to Him to be healed.

4. Say this prayer between the two prostrations

One of the approved supplications between the two prostrations is: 'O Allah, forgive me, have mercy on me, guide me, console me (*ijburnī*), grant me well-being, and provide for me.' [Tirmidhī; Ibn Mājah][18]

[18] Transliteration: *Allāhumma ighfir lī, warḥamnī, wahdinī, wajburnī, wa 'āfinī, warzuqnī*

There are differences of opinion on whether one should say one of the confirmed supplications or make his own supplications, and whether this is for the obligatory of voluntary prayers.

AL-KABĪR, AL-MUTAKABBIR – GOD IS GREATER (21-22)

15

AL-KABĪR, AL-MUTAKABBIR – GOD IS GREATER (21-22)

'So it will be, because it is God alone who is the Truth, and whatever else they invoke is sheer falsehood: it is God who is the Most High, the Most Great (al-Kabīr).'

[22:62]

In this world, it may often feel that there are many issues that are bigger than us which we cannot affect, or which are too big to overcome by ourselves. The problems of the world and our personal troubles often feel burdensome and overwhelming. It can be all-consuming. Yet part of the reason Allah reveals His names to us is for reassurance, and we declare the attributes in this chapter in particular every day, multiple times a day. Because our Creator knows us better than we know ourselves, He knows that there may be a tendency to feel the weight of the world on our shoulders, and He thus enjoins us to internalize the meanings of these names daily. These names are: al-Kabīr (the Most Great) and al-Mutakabbir (The Proud), from the same root *kāf-bā-rā*. He is the Most Great, and He alone possesses rights and attributes above those of everyone else.

Al-Kabīr

An Arabic speaker may use the word *kabīr* to describe something that is great or big physically. In Sūrat al-Anbiyā, God describes for us the Prophet Abraham destroying the idols. He says,

> *'He broke them all into pieces, but left the biggest one [kabīran lahum] for them to return to. They said, "Who has done this to our gods? How wicked he must be!" Some said, "We heard a youth called Abraham talking about them." They said, "Bring him before the eyes of the people, so that they may witness [his trial]." They asked, "Was it you, Abraham, who did this to our gods?" He said, "No, it was done by the biggest [kabīruhum] of them –– this one. Ask them, if they can talk."'* [21:58-63]

The Prophet Abraham left the biggest idol, which is understood to have been the biggest physically but also perceived to be the greatest by those who worshipped it. Thus, the word *kabīr* can also be used for things that intrinsically have (or are perceived to have) greatness.

When it comes to Allah, as Sheikh Rātib al-Nābulsī states, God's greatness is that He is not confined by size nor by our mental conceptions of Him. He is truly Great – al-Kabīr. God says in the Qur'an: *'That is because Allah is the Truth, and that which they call upon other than Him is falsehood, and because Allah is the Most High, the Grand (al-Kabīr).'* [22:62]

Whatever we imagine as great or big, we need to remember that Allah is al-Kabīr and therefore He is *akbar* – i.e. greater – than anything we can ever conceptualize or think of or face. The words used to call us to prayer are *Allāhu akbar* — 'God is greater.' When we reflect upon these words, the result should be the realization that God is indeed greater than whatever is occupying us at the time and we should get ready for the prayer. In the call to prayer itself, it is as though Allah is explaining to us *why* we should prioritize the prayer. We are told: Allah is greater (*Allāhu akbar*) than everything in this world, so come to prayer (*ḥayya 'alā al-ṣalāt*) and come to success (*ḥayya 'alā al-falāḥ*). Indeed, the Prophet ﷺ taught us that one of the most beloved deeds to God is to pray on time [Bukhārī]. Our dedication to pray on time is an internalization of the meaning of God's greatness; we are prioritizing Him and the deeds that bring us near to Him, because He is greater.

Indeed, the prayer itself is a constant reminder of that. We start the prayer by proclaiming: *Allāhu akbar* – God is bigger; He is greater. He is greater than the world we are about to leave behind. We might be consumed by making money – He is greater than our money. We might be beaten down by our problems – He is greater than our problems and is indeed the solution to them. We may be infatuated with a human being's seeming grandeur – Allah is greater.

The reminder in our prayer about His attribute of greatness should help us to turn to al-Kabīr when the things of this world seem overwhelming and too great for us to handle. After almost every change of position, we declare that Allah is Greater, just in case our mind wanders to the affairs and issues of this world. Allah is greater.

In our day-to-day affairs, we should remind ourselves to always choose the most ethical and God-conscious way, because truly al-Kabīr is greater than any worldly benefit we might perceive to come out of illicit or improper means. The Prophet ﷺ said, '*Verily, you will never leave anything for the sake of Allah Almighty but that Allah will replace it with something better.*' [Aḥmad]

Similarly, whenever it seems that an oppressive person or system is too great to be brought down or dismantled, we should remind ourselves that Allah is greater. We should be in awe of and obedient to the One who is truly great, and not those who present a façade of greatness.

Moreover, knowing that Allah is *kabīr* should humble us and prevent us from oppressing. Indeed, this name is paired with His name al-'Aliyy (the Most High) in a context in the Qur'an that should be striking for anyone who reflects. In verse 34 of the fourth chapter, which talks about men's maintenance of women, and is sometimes misused by people to justify violence or harm against a wife,[19] the verse ends with '*Allah is Ever Most High, Most Great*

[19] Discussion of the meaning of this oft-misunderstood verse would be beyond

('Aliyyan Kabīran)'. Ibn Kathīr, al-Ṭabarī, and others, state in their exegesis of this verse that the mentioning of these two attributes at the end of the verse is a threat or warning to men who consider transgressing against women, for Allah al-'Aliyy al-Kabīr is the *walī* (the Guardian Protector) of women, and will take vengeance against men who oppress and transgress against them. Al-Ālūsī states that Allah mentioning His name al-'Aliyy is in order to say that because He is higher, and still chooses to overlook our faults, so too should spouses overlook faults the faults of one another [instead of committing aggression]; while it is paired with al-Kabīr as a reminder that He is even greater and is capable of punishment against those who oppress.

Al-Mutakabbir

From the same root we get Allah's name al-Mutakabbir, which is usually translated as the Proud, the One who possesses all grandeur, or the Truly Great. It is mentioned in the Qur'an in Sūrat al-Ḥashr: *'The Compeller, the Truly Great; God is far above anything they consider to be His partner.'* [59:23] Allah also says, *'And to Him belongs [all] grandeur [kibriyā] within the heavens and the earth, and He is the Exalted in Might, the Wise.'* [45:37]

This name, with is majestic connotations, is exclusive to God alone. He is al-Mutakabbir because He has elevated Himself above the traits of creation. And this is a name of praise for God because He has exclusive rights or attributes above other people. However, it would be a blameworthy trait for human beings, because it would connote arrogance. Arrogant people are those who see that they have attributes above others, and therefore see themselves as elevated above others, holding them in disdain.

---

the scope of this book, but the following source is useful in this regard: Nazir Khan, Tesneem Alkiek and Safiah Chowdhury, Women in Islamic Law: Five Prevailing Myths, Yaqeen Institute, 24 July 2019. See also lectures by Sheikh Muhammad Akram Nadwi and Hafidha Maryam Amir.

Living with these names

1. Be humble

God says, *'There is no doubt that God knows what they conceal and what they reveal. He does not love the arrogant.'* [16:23]

God alone is al-Mutakabbir – He has elevated Himself above the traits of His creation. As human beings, if we find that we consider ourselves greater than others for whatever reason – be it wealth, status, beauty, race, ethnicity, color or nationality – it is as though we are competing with God for His grandeur. The Prophet ﷺ told us, *'Do not ask about three people: a man who competes for the robe of Allah Almighty, for His robe is grandeur and His garment is might, a man who doubts in the matter of Allah, and one who despairs of the mercy of Allah.'* [Aḥmad]

Indeed, the Prophet ﷺ warned that *'Whoever exalts himself or carries himself with arrogance, he will meet Allah while He is angry with him.'* [Aḥmad]

So, what is arrogance, and how can we guard against it? The Prophet ﷺ reminded us, *'No one who has the weight of a seed of arrogance in his heart will enter Paradise.'* Someone replied, 'But a man loves to have beautiful clothes and shoes.' The Prophet ﷺ clarified, *'Verily, Allah is beautiful and He loves beauty. Arrogance means rejecting the truth and looking down on people.'* [Muslim]

Some types of arrogance are obvious. The Prophet ﷺ said, *'The worst of my nation are the garrulous, the braggarts, and the pompous. The best of my nation are those with the best character.'* [Bukhārī, al-Adab al-Mufrad]

When we see someone who brags, mocks and mistreats others, and is very obviously ostentatious, we can recognize this blatant form of arrogance. But arrogance can be extremely subtle. We need to interrogate the tension we feel in our hearts when someone seemingly 'less' than us – for whatever reason – corrects us or is elevated above us. When al-Fuḍayl bin 'Iyāḍ was asked about humility, he said, 'It is to humble yourself for the truth, to act in accordance with it, and to accept it even if you hear it from a child.'

The Companions were very aware of this and guarded themselves even against hidden forms of pride and arrogance. For example, 'Umar ibn Al-Khaṭṭāb was seen carrying a heavy water container on his back when he was the caliph. He was told that he should not have to do that, being the caliph, and that it was unbefitting of his position. But 'Umar replied that a delegation had visited Madinah and, due to the respect and deference that they gave to him, he felt some pride enter his heart; so, he wanted to destroy it through this action.

2. Be strong

This story perhaps best highlights the meaning of this name: When I was in high school revising for my exams, I received a text message from my aunt. The text message read, 'When you have a problem, don't ever say "O God, I have a big problem." Rather, say, "Hey, problem! I have a big God!" and everything will be ok.' What immediately came to my mind was *Allāhu akbar* (Allah is greater). We should feel a sense of calm when we hear or say *Allāhu akbar*, and we should internalize this phrase when we face difficulties, because nothing is too great for God. Nothing is too difficult. He is greater than our circumstances. We should work hard, because Allah is greater than the obstacles. We should be strong, because when al-Kabīr is with us, we can do and overcome so much more than we thought or expected.

3. Prioritize

Knowing that Allah is al-Kabīr, and that He is Greater, should teach us to prioritize. We often elevate or choose worldly things over what God has prescribed because, in our hearts, those things are greater. When we choose sin over obedience, it is because we see the pleasure or perceived benefit as a result of that sin, in that moment at least, as greater. But Allah is al-Kabīr, and He is and remains greater than anything we could choose in this world. When we choose and prioritize God above the things of this world, we should know that God will elevate us in the Hereafter because of that choice.

4. Prayers are a reminder of God's greatness

The most oft-repeated phrase in prayer is *Allāhu akbar.* We begin the prayer with it and we repeat it throughout. This is a reminder of God's greatness and indeed of the greatness of the moment we are in: standing before Him, in deep conversation with Him. If we are truly devoted in prayer, our worries should melt, and our hearts should be strengthened. Internalizing these meanings may take time, but Allah guides to Him those who seek Him.

AL-KHĀLIQ, AL-BĀRI', AL-MUṢAWWIR – CREATING, INNOVATING, FASHIONING (23-25)

16

AL-KHĀLIQ, AL-BĀRI', AL-MUṢAWWIR – CREATING, INNOVATING, FASHIONING (23-25)

'He is Allah, the Creator, the Inventor, the Fashioner; to Him belongs the best names. Whatever is in the heavens and earth is exalting Him. And He is the Exalted in Might, the Wise.'

[59:24]

Those who spend time in nature – whether in the desert at night in full view of the starlit sky, or on a nature reserve, or simply in a park surrounded by trees and flowers – have at some point felt the awe that comes with witnessing the beauty of the natural world. Allah tells us in the Qur'an,

> *'In the creation of the heavens and earth; in the alternation of night and day; in the ships that sail the seas with goods for people; in the water which God sends down from the sky to give life to the earth when it has been barren, scattering all kinds of creatures over it; in the changing of the winds and clouds that run their appointed courses between the sky and earth: there are signs in all these for those who use their minds.'* [2:164]

The purpose of a sign is to lead us somewhere or to a conclusion. In everything in the universe is a sign that should lead us to God: the Creator (al-Khāliq), the Producer (al-Bāri') and the Fashioner (al-Muṣawwir). These names might seem synonymous or similar, but there are nuances that reveal to us the intricacies of the nature of His creation.

Al-Khāliq is translated as the Creator, and it is a general name. This name alone is mentioned in this form in the Qur'an eight times, but reference is made to His creating more than 200 times. In reference to human beings alone, Allah mentions how He created us over eighty times. While many explanations have been given about this name, when we say that He is al-Khāliq, we are referring to His determining (*taqdīr*) that something is brought from non-existence to existence. That is the essence of this name. Allah says that He *'has created (khalaqa) each thing and determined it with [precise] determination (qaddarahu taqdīrāh).'* [25:2] And His determination of what to bring into existence is a result of His ultimate wisdom. Indeed, He says, *'We have created all things in due measure.'* [54:49]. Others have said that it also means invention and innovation, and the One who determines what is brought into existence without help or aid.

Al-Bāri' – the Producer – is more specific, and refers to the manifesting or bringing of what has been determined into existence, without fault. Al-Muṣawwir – the Fashioner – is He who specifies the particular, unique form of what He has created and produced. Allah says, *'it is He who shapes you all (yuṣawwirukum) in the womb as He pleases. There is no God but Him, the Mighty, the Wise.'* [3:6]. What is especially lovely in this verse is that, after telling us that Allah Himself shapes us in the wombs as He pleases – how beautiful it is that God has chosen how we look, and our shapes! – it reminds us that He is al-'Azīz, indicating His might and power in creating, and al-Ḥakīm (the Most Wise). It is this second attribute that should warm our hearts when we reflect on its relationship to the first part of the verse. The way we look, and our forms, have been determined by the Most Wise. There is wisdom in our different looks, expressions, shapes and forms – even the aspects we have had since birth, with which we might struggle.

Through these names, Allah calls us to reflect on the different aspects and stages of creation. God says:

> *'We created man from an essence of clay, then We placed him as a drop of fluid in a safe place, then We made that drop into a clinging form, and We made that form into a lump of flesh, and We made that lump into bones, and We clothed those bones with flesh, and later We made him into other forms — glory be to God, the best of creators!'* [23:12-14]

The images of the development of a fetus are stunning if we take the time to simply think about it. There are many videos one can find where this development is simulated. Simply thinking about what we used to be – nothing, then out of millions of sperm, one fertilizes an egg, and that develops into a human being with a soul and thoughts and feelings and hopes and dreams – is enough to feel the awe of being one of God's creation. Imagine every single part that had to come together in such a precise way to create you, as you are today. Indeed, the above verse ends with *'glory be to God, the best of creators!'* because that is the natural reaction to contemplating our own selves.

Human beings cannot be true 'creators' in the ways we described above. The infamous sheep Dolly is recognized as and called a 'clone'. The sheep was not created from nothing; rather, it was copied from what already existed, using materials that were already there. Dolly is considered to have three 'mothers': the first provided the egg, the second the DNA, and the third carried the cloned embryo to term. Without God's original creation, Dolly the clone could not exist. God says, *'People, here is an illustration, so listen carefully: those you call on beside God could not, even if they combined all their forces, create a fly.*" [22:73]

The key word in the verse is 'create' – human beings cannot bring something into existence that did not already exist, nor can they do it without help. Actually, the process of cloning and making things from what Allah has already given us simply shows us the grandeur of God's creation, that He has put within a single cell all the information needed to produce something similar from it. Likewise, when a couple who cannot conceive, or have difficulty conceiving naturally, undergo IVF treatment, this procedure assists them by fertilizing the mother's egg in vitro. The embryo is then transferred back to the woman's uterus, where it is hoped that it will result in pregnancy. These all build upon God's original creation and use it in ways that seem novel to us, but they cannot rival nor even come close to God's creation of a human being from nothing – *'when He decrees a matter, He only says to it, 'Be,' and it is.'* [3:47]. Moreover, Allah tells us:

> *'He created the heavens without any visible support, and He placed firm mountains on the earth — in case it should shake under you — and He spread all kinds of animals around it. We sent down water from the sky, with which We made every kind of good plant grow on earth: all this is God's creation. Now, show Me what your other gods have created. No, the disbelievers are clearly astray.'* [31:10-11]

In these timeless verses, Allah was saying to the people then, and is still saying to us now: 'compare what you have 'created' to what I have created.' This is a direct response to people who use science and its (no doubt impressive) developments and achievements to deny God's creation. Modern science – and, indeed, everything – owes its existence to God. Whatever comes from it that seems novel is only novel to us; we manage to be so impressed with ourselves – to the degree that we elevate ourselves above God – for solving a problem or inventing something, rather than being in awe that God has created solutions and means to build upon within His creation.

The Prophet ﷺ said, *'Every disease has a cure. If a cure is applied to the disease, it is relieved by the permission of Allah Almighty.'* [Muslim] If we were to truly reflect on this statement, we would come to the realization that what we do is more akin to discovery and bringing different pieces together – which is praiseworthy and remarkable, no doubt – because Allah has placed within His creation the means for that. This is not to disparage or show contempt towards scientists – we respect them and the good they bring into this world – but simply to demonstrate the fallacy of using science to turn away from God rather than turn to Him.

The importance of reflection

All of Allah's names require us to think about them and reflect upon their manifestations in our lives, in order to connect to Allah through them. And this is especially true for the names in this chapter. Allah tells us in no uncertain terms:

> *'Indeed, in the creation of the heavens and the earth and the alternation of the night and the day are signs for those of understanding. Who remember Allah while standing or sitting or [lying] on their sides and give thought to the creation of the heavens and the earth, [saying], "Our Lord, You did not create this aimlessly; exalted are You [above such a thing]; then protect us from the punishment of the Fire."'* [3:190-191]

Reflection is an act of worship, especially purposeful contemplation that leads us to God. And because there are signs in His creation, they lead us to His majesty and grace. Allah asks us, *'Do they not contemplate within themselves? Allah has not created the heavens and the earth and what is between them except in truth and for a specified term."* [30:8] This contemplation is meant to lead us to Allah, the Truth.

Indeed, the Messenger of Allah ﷺ told the Companion Abu Dharr, *'O Abu Dharr, shall I not show you two qualities that are easy on your back and heavier on the scale of good than others?'* Abu Dharr said, 'Of course, O Messenger of Allah.' The Prophet ﷺ said, *'You must have good character and observe long periods of silence. By the one in whose Hand is the soul of Muhammad, no one can behave with deeds more beloved to Allah than these two.'* [Ṭabarānī] The Companions took this to heart. When the wife of the Companion Abu al-Dardā' was asked what the greatest act of worship was that her husband used to do, she replied, 'reflecting deeply' (*al-tafakkur*).

Long periods of silence are for the purpose of reflection. The great scholar, al-Ḥasan al-Baṣrī said: *'An hour's contemplation is better than a year of voluntary night prayer (qiyām).'* This is not to say that praying the voluntary night prayer is not important – but devoid of reflection, even this most virtuous act becomes empty and mechanical. Indeed, reflection is the path to God. The Prophet ﷺ, before receiving revelation, would isolate himself for periods of time in the cave of Ḥirā. 'Ā'ishah said that he would '*yataḥannath*', which some have translated as 'worship.' However, this worship is not what we know today as the ritual acts of worship, because they had not been revealed yet. So, scholars said that this means that he would reflect upon the creation of the heavens and the earth.

Living with this name

1. Reflect on this world

A practical exercise to undertake in order to understand these names is to take some time to truly reflect on the beauty and creation of this world. One way is by stepping outside and simply seeing and observing – spending time in nature. Another way is to watch documentaries or read books that go into depth into the creation of God. The Prophet ﷺ said, *'Reflect deeply upon the creation.'*[20]

2. Reflect upon His blessings

Reflection is not simply about the grandeur of the creation. The Caliph 'Umar ibn 'Abd al-'Azīz said, 'Speaking in remembrance of Allah Almighty is good, and thinking about the blessings of Allah

[20] The continuation of this hadith is "*...but do not reflect upon the essence of the Creator. Verily, his essence cannot be known other than to believe in it,*" [Musnad al-Rabī'; *Hasan* (fair) according to Al-Albani]. This is because conceptualizing Allah accurately without projecting our human understandings is difficult, if not close to impossible, and is a way for Satan to sow doubt.

is the best act of worship.' Nothing brings more comfort to the heart than realizing the infinite ways in which Allah has blessed us.

3. Do not abuse His creation

Allah tells us, '*And [He] has subjected to you all that is in the heavens and all that is in the earth; it is all as a favor and kindness from Him. Verily, in it are signs for a people who think deeply.*' [45:12-13] When we realize that Allah created everything, this should instill in us a deep respect for the creation of God. When Allah subjects something (e.g. animals) to us, it is not for the purpose of misusing it, but rather to utilize it in ways that recognize and respect His blessings upon us. We should not be wasteful, nor should we abuse the environment or animals, because we recognize that they have been created by Allah.

4. Worship Him

When Allah describes those who '*give thought to the creation of the heavens and the earth,*' this leads them to say, '"*Our Lord, You did not create this aimlessly; exalted are You [above such a thing]; then protect us from the punishment of the Fire.*"' [3:191] Allah's creation are signs, and the signs lead to Him. The modern wellness industry encourages us to be in nature and reflect, but the aim is connection to the self, or to an abstract 'universe' or 'mother nature' – in essence, using creation to go back to creation or a false deity, rather than the Creator – al-Khāliq. Indeed, we were foretold this: '*and there are many signs in the heavens and the earth that they pass by and give no heed to ––most of them will only believe in God while also joining others with Him.*' [11:105-106]

However, people who truly and deeply reflect are led back to Allah. They comprehend that because God has created this universe, there is a purpose ('*You did not create this aimlessly*'); this understanding leads them to glorify God ('*exalted are You*'); they then realize that they will be returned to Him, and so they desire

His mercy (*'then protect us from the punishment of the Fire'*). We should infuse our worship with this understanding.

5. Understanding God's wisdom

Since Allah is the Creator, the Inventor and the Fashioner, then He also knows how His creations works and what is best for them. If we buy a gadget from a producer and then face problems with it, we know that the best way to fix it is with the advice of that producer. We can try to take a cheaper or more convenient route – which may work if this somehow leads to whatever the producer would have done – but we create more problems when we go to someone who imposes the wrong solutions, without reference to the one who made the gadget.

Similarly, Allah tells us, *'We created man –– We know what his soul whispers to him: We are closer to him than his jugular vein.'* [50:16] All of God's commandments and rules are for our ultimate benefit in this life and the next. There might be nuances, of course, and differences of opinions on certain matters, and that is from His wisdom and mercy. Thus, we should trust that the Creator has decreed for us the most optimal way to be in this world.

6. You are special

There is a popular quote that states, 'The same God that created mountains and oceans and galaxies thought that the world needed one of you too.' [unknown author] God says that in our very selves, there are signs for those who reflect. The greatest sign is that the Almighty God, who created things that we see as magnificent and grand, created us too – each person, individually. This should remind us to reflect on our purpose and our relationship with the very One who fashioned us Himself, and to cultivate a relationship with Him. You are not purposeless, and you are special to the One who made you.

AL-LAṬĪF AL-RAFĪQ – SUBTLE AND KIND (26-27)

17

AL-LAṬĪF AL-RAFĪQ – SUBTLE AND KIND (26-27)

'How could He who created not know His own creation, when He is the Most Subtle, the All Aware?'

[67:14]

We all desire to be treated with gentleness and kindness. Gentleness does not need to be some grand gesture, but is in the simple daily acts. Gentleness manifests in the smile of a stranger when we are down, or the phone call of a friend who wants to ask about how we are. It can even be the correcting of a mistake in a kind way, rather than harshly. We all appreciate this type of treatment, and indeed our hearts warm to the one who expresses this gentleness.

And Allah has named Himself al-Laṭīf – He who is Benevolent and Subtle with His servants. In Arabic, the word *laṭīf* comes from *luṭf* (gentleness) or the Arabic three-letter root *lām-ṭā-fā*, and while it carries many meanings, at its core this word is about gentleness, subtlety and kindness. Ibn Al-Qayyim explains that God's *luṭf* is of two types: that God knows the subtleties of everything, and that He treats His servants with gentleness. Further, Allah is al-Rafīq, which means gentle and beneficial. The word *rafīq* is also used to mean a companion as one travels.

So, when we say that God is *laṭīf* with His slaves, as well as *rafīq*, it means that He is always with us, knows all of the thoughts and emotions that go on within us, and His protection and presence with us are subtle. For example, someone might say something that you need to hear in a particular moment, without your expressing this need. Perhaps a piece of medical information you happened upon casually ends up coming to you later when you need it. Maybe the train you missed, in spite of the frustration you felt as a result, got you to your destination even faster, because the train you missed ended up getting delayed. Al-Laṭīf knows the subtle realities of our hearts, and He gently sends us what we need.

We are told in the Qur'an, *'My son, if even the weight of a mustard seed were hidden in a rock or anywhere in the heavens or earth, God would bring it [to light], for He is all subtle and all aware.'* [31:16]

Allah frequently combines His name al-Laṭīf with His name al-Khabīr, the All-Aware. The meanings of these names reinforce one another, as al-Khabīr is the one who is aware of the inner realities of things. Allah is aware of the internal and the external, that which is subtle and that which is obvious, and from His *luṭf*, He treats us with His kindness. When someone comforts our hearts, they are manifesting this gentleness with us; in reality, al-Laṭīf knew what our heart needed, and sent someone to console it.

His subtleness and kindness are not simply with regards to our hearts, but also in God's manifestations in the universe. Allah tells us, *'Have you not considered how God sends water down from the sky and the next morning the earth becomes green? God is truly most subtle, all aware.'* [22:63]

The signs are all around us, if we only reflect. The subtle nature of how the rain nourishes the earth, how the night turns into day and the day turns into night, the subtle twinkling of the stars in the darkness of the night, and so much more.

Moreover, God subtly moves us towards our ultimate goal, though we may not realize it and may indeed believe we are moving farther away from it. While the Prophet Joseph went through much hardship – betrayed by his brothers, sold into slavery, wrongfully accused and jailed – he was eventually declared innocent, made a minister, and reunited with his family. We are told: *'And [Joseph] took them up to [his] throne. They all bowed down before him and he said, "Father, this is the fulfilment of that dream I had long ago. My Lord has made it come true and has been gracious to me— He released me from prison and He brought you here from the desert — after Satan sowed discord between me and my brothers. My Lord is most subtle (laṭīf) in achieving what He wills; He is the All Knowing, the Truly Wise."'* [12:100]

Joseph had no way of knowing in the moment that the hardships he went through would lead to ultimate good. He only knew to trust in Allah throughout and persevere. Every small event that happened had a purpose that led Joseph to where he was at the end of the story – fulfilling the prophecy. But that is how subtle God is, and this should teach us to trust in Him.

Living with this name

1. Be gentle

When we see the way al-Laṭīf and al-Rafīq treats us with benevolence and gentleness, we cannot but try to be a source of gentleness for others, as a way of being grateful to God for His kindness to us. The Prophet ﷺ said, *'Allah is gentle and loves [seeing] gentleness.'* [Muslim]

Moreover, he also said, *'Show gentleness (rifq), for if gentleness is found in anything, it beautifies it and when it is taken out from anything it damages it.'* [Abū Dāwūd]

Gentleness in our demeanor is a gift from Allah. Indeed, He made the Prophet ﷺ so. Allah says, *'So by mercy from Allah [O Muhammad], you were lenient with them. And if you had been rude [in speech] and harsh in heart, they would have disbanded from around you."* [3:159]

This should really cause us to pause – Allah tells us that were His beloved Messenger ﷺ harsh-hearted, people would have disbanded from him! We should ask ourselves, how do we treat people? How do we convey religious knowledge? Do people turn away from us, or do they turn to us?

2. Call people to good through your actions

Al-Ghazālī advises calling people to good and to the truth by 'one's good qualities, pleasing comportment, and exemplary actions, for they are more effective and more benign than eloquent exhortation.'[21]

3. Recognize Allah's subtle kindness

In the story of Joseph, every step, every seemingly 'random' event had a purpose that led to Joseph fulfilling the dream he was given as a child. We should stop and reflect on all the minutiae of our lives and marvel over Allah's subtle guidance and presence with us. We should appreciate the simple kindnesses we experience in life as a manifestation of Allah's *luṭf* and *rifq*.

[21] Al-Ghazālī, *The Ninety-Nine Beautiful Names of God: Al-Maqṣad Al-Asnā Fi Sharḥ Asmā' Allāh Al-Ḥusnā*, 98.

AL-WĀḤID, AL-AḤAD – THE ONE AND ONLY (28-29)

18

AL-WĀḤID, AL-AḤAD – THE ONE AND ONLY (28-29)

'Say, "He is God the One."'

[112:1]

In terms of its theology, Islam has a basic, simple premise: that God is One, Indivisible, Unique. He is not many, nor is He split into parts. He is not Father and Son, nor Father or Son at different times. In one of the shortest chapters of the Qur'an, God instructs the Prophet ﷺ to *'Say, "He is God the One (Aḥad)."'* [112:1]

This was revolutionary for the prevailing context at the time of revelation. The majority of Arabs were polytheists. While they understood that there was a Supreme Being, they worshipped the idols to bring them closer to Him. The Qur'an spoke to Christians too. God says, *'The Messiah, Jesus, the son of Mary, was but a messenger of Allah and His word which He directed to Mary and a soul [created at a command] from Him. So, believe in Allah and His messengers. And do not say, "Three"; desist - it is better for you'* [4:171]

At the core of Islam is the central truth that God is One; He is al-Wāḥid (the One) and al-Aḥad (the Unique). This negates any other supposed divine entity. And since God is One, He needs to be one in our hearts as well.

The One and Only

Both of these names come from the same root and represent His oneness, but they are used in different contexts. Al-Wāḥid means the One, and scholars have specified that this 'one' is not a number, but rather He is One in that He is singular, without any equal. Allah is al-Wāḥid in His essence, meaning that He cannot be divided or split into parts. Al-Aḥad indicates His uniqueness and is used when negating the existence of anything else. These names bring us back to the essence of Islam. They bring us back to what this religion is really about: Allah; One, Unique.

While Allah is described as *aḥad* once in the Qur'an, the chapter in which it appears (Sūrat al-Ikhlāṣ) is described as equivalent to one third of the whole Qur'an.[22] This chapter mentions only two names of Allah – al-Aḥad and al-Ṣamad. Scholars have said that around one third of the Qur'an contains reference to the names of God, and these two names are encompassing of many of the meanings of His names. This chapter was revealed in response to those who asked, 'what is the lineage of your Lord?' or 'you say your God is the creator, but who created Him?'

Aḥad is used in Arabic to negate, so one would say '*lā aḥad*' to mean 'no one'. If you wanted to use this term to affirm, there has to be something added to it; for example, *aḥadukum* means 'one of you'. However, *aḥad* on its own can only refer to Allah, because it signifies His utter uniqueness. This provides the basis for understanding His other names, especially those that seem to have human dimensions. For example, human beings may exhibit mercy or kindness. But God is *aḥad* – completely unique and one. There is no comparison between what mercy or kindness a human

[22] The Prophet ﷺ told his Companions: *'Is it difficult for one of you to recite a third of the Quran in a single night?'* That was difficult for them, so they said, 'Which one of us can do that, O Messenger of Allah?' The Prophet ﷺ said, *'The chapter, "Allah, the One, the Refuge" (112:1-2) is worth one-third of the Quran.'* [Bukhārī]

can manifest and what Allah manifests. God tells us at the end of this chapter: *'No one is comparable to Him.'* [112:4]

This chapter was incredibly special to the Companions. It gave comfort to them, and affirmed God's oneness in their hearts. One of the Companions, who led the others in prayer during travels, always recited Sūrat al-Ikhlāṣ. He was asked why he would recite this chapter so frequently. He replied, *'It is because this chapter describes the Most Merciful, and therefore I love to recite it.'* When he heard the man's reply, the Prophet ﷺ said: *'Tell that man that God loves him.'* [Bukhārī and Muslim].

In another narration, a man said, *'O Messenger of Allah, I love this chapter, 'Say: "He is Allah, the One."''* [112:1] The Messenger of Allah ﷺ said, *'Your love for it will admit you into Paradise.'* [Bukhārī]

The name al-Wāḥid is paired with His name al-Qahhār frequently in the Qur'an. Al-Qahhār is the Dominator. While human beings are seemingly able to dominate others, Allah reminds us that He alone is able to dominate all. Additionally, human beings seldom, if ever, dominate alone. They need armies and their back-ups. Allah does not need back-up. Allah can dominate others alone.

The effect of the unity of God on one's heart

Bilāl was an Abyssinian slave and a Companion of the Prophet ﷺ. The teachings of Islam in a tribal society were ground-breaking. Human beings were equal as servants of God – indeed, human beings are all slaves of God. The best people are those who are most God-conscious – not those who are from a particular tribe or ethnicity, and it is not dependent on whether one is a slave or free. Bilāl, like other Companions, found this liberating. As a Muslim, he stood on equal footing with someone like Abū Bakr, who was of the nobles of Quraysh.

When Bilāl accepted Islam, the people of Quraysh were furious, and they tortured him in response. In the face of their physical torment, Bilāl would repeat one phrase: *'Aḥadun aḥad. Aḥadun aḥad. Allāhu aḥad.'*

God is One, no other.

But Bilāl did not simply say that God is Wāḥid; he said that God is Aḥad. With this, Bilāl was negating any other claimed divinity. This conviction in the oneness of God and all that implied gave Bilāl the strength to face his oppressors. Because, in reality, they had no power; only God has true power. They had no strength; only God has strength. There is nothing equal to Him, so not even their beating him could force Bilāl to leave his beliefs. A similar effect happened to the magicians in the story of Moses. They realized that they needed to direct their hopes and fears to God, because Pharaoh had no share in them. And even when Pharaoh threatened to crucify them for their defiance, their hearts were filled with hope in, and fear of, God – not Pharaoh. So they were able to stand up to Pharaoh's transgressions. Their hearts were in true submission to the One, not in submission to the delusions of the world.

These names should negate any other false idol in our hearts. This, at its core, is what the effect of these names should be. God should be One and Incomparable in our hearts, and thus our love for Him should be incomparable to any other love.

Living with this name

1. Submit

God told the Prophet Muhammad ﷺ to *'Say, "What is revealed to me is that your God is one (wāḥid) God –– will you submit to Him?"'* [21:108]

The effect of knowing that God is One should be that we submit wholly and fully to Him, associating no other partners, not even in our hearts, with Him. It is to submit our desires to what pleases Him. The Messenger of Allah ﷺ said, *'None of you have faith until his desires comply with what I have brought.'* [Ibn Abī 'Āṣim]

Conviction in Allah's oneness will weigh heavily on the scales. The Prophet ﷺ said: *'Allah will save a man of His community, the record of whose sins fills ninety-nine books, each book extending as far as the eye can see. Against all this will be weighed the one good deed that he has, which is his witnessing that there is no god but Allah and that Muhammad is His Messenger, and it will outweigh all the rest.'* The Messenger of God ﷺ then said: *'Nothing is of any weight compared to Allah's name.'* [Aḥmad]

The question we need to ask ourselves is: 'Is Allah One in my life? Do I direct everything to Him – from fears and hopes to needs?' Realizing that He is One is to know that there is no love like His love, that there is no One who gives like Him, and that there is no One else who can fill the void – only Him, the One. Knowing that He is al-Wāḥid al-Aḥad reminds us that this life is about Him. He is our ultimate goal. This life is temporary; its joys and pains will disappear, and this knowledge should negate our worldly attachments and our submission to them. Allah tells us in the Qur'an: *'Our God is One, so devote yourselves to Him. [Prophet], give good news to the humble, whose hearts fill with awe whenever God is mentioned, who endure whatever happens to them with patience, who keep up the prayer, who give to others out of Our provision to them.'* [22:34-35] This is submission to the oneness of God in action.

2. Be sincere

Knowing that Allah is al-Aḥad should remind us that anything we put above Him is a false idol; this means that sincerity to Him is of utmost importance. Our actions and intentions should be directed towards His pleasure and love. The effect of this is that we should not 'see' the praise or criticisms of people any more (unless it is for constructive purposes and subjugating our egos). We might do things for praise, but we may or may not receive it. Even if we do receive it, this praise will slowly wither. If we prevent ourselves from doing the right thing because of what people will say or do, their reaction becomes a false idol that we subtly worship alongside

Allah. Our actions are insincere because we do not desire God through them. However, if His oneness is realized in our hearts, that is when we actualize true freedom. His oneness and uniqueness force us to say to ourselves, 'I cannot put my desires on an equal footing with God. He is al-Aḥad.' The weight of that knowledge should negate our lower desires and those elusive things that we worship – be they money, status or anything else. The Prophet ﷺ said, '*Allah Almighty said: The most beloved act with which my servant worships me is sincerity for my sake.*' [Aḥmad]

And what does this sincerity mean? Sa'īd ibn Jubayr said, 'Sincerity is to not associate partners with Allah in one's religion, and to not display ostentation in good deeds to anyone.' Indeed, having a desire to display our good deeds is a sign that a part of us wants reward and recognition from people, and not solely from God. The Prophet ﷺ actually called this 'the lesser idolatry' and said that it was his greatest fear for his nation. When he was asked by the Companions what the 'lesser idolatry' was, he answered '*It is ostentation. Allah Almighty will say to them on the Day of Resurrection, when people are being recompensed for their deeds: Go to those for whom you made a show in the world and look, do you find any reward with them*?' [Aḥmad]

While it is good to be public about some of the good that we do, as an encouragement to others, we should be vigilant over the state of our hearts, and try to do at least some (if not most) good works in secret, in order to protect them from the part of us that desires to receive something of this world through them. The Companion 'Umar ibn al-Khaṭṭāb said, 'Whoever purifies his intention, Allah will take care of his affairs between people. Whoever embellishes for people what Allah knows is not in his heart, Allah Almighty will disgrace him.'

Of course, some of us might read this and feel fear; we might obsessively question our intentions for every action and become immobilized by this fear, even stopping ourselves from doing good because of the worry that it is not done for God. This is a trick of

Satan – his ultimate goal is to persuade you to leave good deeds and ultimately despair. Ibn Ḥazm counseled, 'Satan sets his traps, under the cover of finding fault with hypocrisy. It can happen that someone refrains from doing a good deed for fear of being thought a hypocrite. If Satan whispers such an idea in your ear, take no notice; that will frustrate him.' [Mudāwāt al-Nūfūs] The quest for sincerity is meant to beautify our good works, and not cause us to forego them. The key is to work on the state of our hearts simultaneously.

3. Be Aware

There may be come cultural practices, whether traditional or contemporary, that we think are harmless, but they contain elements of idolatry (*shirk*). The Messenger of Allah ﷺ said, '*Whoever hangs an amulet around his neck has committed an act of idolatry.*' [Aḥmad] An amulet by definition is worn to give protection, and this was said in a context when some men had come to give the pledge of allegiance to the Prophet ﷺ, and one of them was wearing an amulet. Hence, we should be careful about taking things like 'good luck charms' lightly. This also applies to partaking in rituals where other deities are invoked. We should respect our fellow humans and their beliefs – this should be a given – but we also have to remain resolute in our own beliefs, and ensure that we do not taint them with questionable practices.

4. Renew your faith

Being unaffected by the temptations of this world (or at least having the ability to resist them) requires constant work and reminders. The Prophet ﷺ told his Companions: '*Renew your faith.*' They said, 'O Messenger of Allah, how can we renew our faith?' The Prophet ﷺ said: '*Say often, "there is no god but Allah (lā ilāha ill Allāh)."*' [Aḥmad]

Regularly reminding ourselves that there is no god but God Himself – essentially, that He is al-Wāḥid al-Aḥad – forces us to contemplate what we have elevated to the status of something to be worshipped, even if this is subtle. It compels us to ask ourselves, 'is there really no other god in my heart?'

5. Witr

Another related name is al-Witr (the Unique, Single). The Prophet ﷺ said, *'God is witr and loves what is witr. So perform witr prayer (the optional last prayer of the night). O followers of Qur'an, observe witr (prayer).'* [Tirmidhī]

Witr is difficult to translate, yet it has the meaning of being unique, single (i.e. without a pair), and 'odd' in terms of numbers. Because God Himself is unique and without pair, He loves this special voluntary prayer, which is also called *witr* as it is prayed as a single unit (*rak'ah*).

AL-ṢAMAD – REFUGE (30)

19

AL-ṢAMAD – REFUGE (30)

'Allah, the Eternal Refuge.'

[112:2]

In Sūrat al-Ikhlāṣ, those who asked about the Lord whom the Muslims worshipped were told two important things: He is al-Aḥad (the One, explained in the previous chapter), and al-Ṣamad (the Eternal Refuge). Sūrat al-Ikhlāṣ thus summarizes Allah's attributes, which means that knowing that He is al-Ṣamad is crucial.

Knowing that God is One should lead us to the knowledge that Allah is al-Ṣamad, and all that implies for us in our daily lives. Since He is indeed One, Indivisible, Unique, then this negates any power, self-sufficiency, or dominion outside of Him. If God is One in our hearts, and we do not make anything equal to Him, we are reassured by being told that He is al-Ṣamad. In the dictionary, *ṣamad* is defined as: the eternal; to remain unaffected or unchanged; to intend or turn to; something that is solid, with no holes or emptiness inside; and the ultimate Master who is obeyed. We say *ṣumūd* (from the same Arabic root *ṣād-mīm-dāl*) to mean 'remain firm and steadfast'. Al-Ghazālī states that al-Ṣamad is 'the One to whom one turns in need and the One who is intended in our desires, for ultimate dominion culminates in Him.'[23] Ibn al-Qayyim states that He is also the One to whom the hearts flee both

[23] Al-Ghazālī, *The Ninety-Nine Beautiful Names of God: Al-Maqṣad Al-Asnā Fi Sharḥ Asmā' Allāh Al-Ḥusnā*, 131.

in hope and reverence. He is the One and Only, to whom we turn for all our needs.

Indeed, the Prophet ﷺ said, *'By Him in whose Hand is my soul, he has asked Allah by his greatest name, for which he answers when called upon and he gives when asked,'* when he heard a Companion making the following supplication: *'O Allah, I ask you by my testimony that you are Allah, there is no God but you, the One, the Eternal Refuge, who does not give birth and was not born, and to whom no one is equal.'* [Tirmidhī]

This supplication contains the two names mentioned in Sūrat al-Ikhlāṣ. If you know that God is One and al-Ṣamad, you know that your needs can only be fulfilled through Him.

And we have many needs. We have material needs, spiritual needs, emotional needs, intellectual needs, and physical needs. The name al-Ṣamad encompasses so many meanings, which tell us that all of our needs can by fulfilled through turning to Him and living in the way that He has prescribed. There are some needs that we can verbalize, and others that remain within our hearts. There are tangible things we ask for, and sometimes we just want internal serenity. When the Prophet ﷺ and the Companions migrated to Madinah, they were not used to the conditions there, and many Companions fell ill. They missed Makkah. The Prophet ﷺ turned to al-Ṣamad and asked Him to make Madinah as beloved as Makkah, and Allah gave him that. Indeed, only al-Ṣamad could give them that, because they were all in the same situation. They all felt sadness, and you cannot give what you do not have. Al-Ṣamad, on the other hand, is unshakeable. We can be confident and assured, because the One we are turning to is the Master, unaffected by the changes around us. Human beings by their very nature may not be able to fulfill every need or desire of ours, because they too rely on others. Not al-Ṣamad; He does not waver, no matter the circumstances.

This is why the Prophet ﷺ encouraged us to turn to God for all of our needs, even the most minor ones. He said: *'You should ask Allah for all of your needs, even if the strap of your sandal breaks.'* [Tirmidhī, Ibn Ḥibbān] The Prophet ﷺ also made a comprehensive supplication where he asked for both this life (*dunyā*) and the next (*ākhirah*):

> *'O God, set right for me my religion which is the safeguard of my affairs. And set right for me the affairs of my world wherein is my living. And set right for me my Hereafter to which is my return. And make the life for me (a source) of abundance for every good and make my death a source of comfort for me protecting me against every evil.'* [Muslim]

When Ibn 'Abbās, the cousin of the Prophet ﷺ, was young, the Prophet ﷺ taught him the meaning of living with Allah al-Ṣamad. He said to him,

> *'Young man, I will teach you some words. Be mindful of Allah and he will protect you. Be mindful of Allah and you will find him before you. If you ask, ask from Allah. If you seek help, seek help from Allah. Know that if the nations gathered together to benefit you, they will not benefit you unless Allah has decreed it for you. And if the nations gathered together to harm you, they will not harm you unless Allah has decreed it for you. The pens have been lifted and the pages have dried.'* [Tirmidhī]

One who has certainty in al-Ṣamad lives the reality of the above hadith. When we know that He is al-Ṣamad, we turn to Him for all of our needs, and know that there is truly no power outside of Him.

Striving

Turning to Allah for all our needs does not negate the need to strive and using the physical means around us. Turning to al-Ṣamad means recognizing where all these physical means come from, and that they can only work with the help of God. When Moses felt that he could not go to Pharaoh because he was not as eloquent as his brother Aaron, he went to God first and said, *'And appoint for me a minister from my family—Aaron, my brother. Increase through him my strength and let him share my task.'* [30:29-32]. He turned to al-Ṣamad to provide for him the means that he would need.

Living with this name

1. Go to Allah with every need; rely only on Him

Knowing that He is unshakeable, that He is eternal, and that He is the refuge should give us confidence in Him and help us to turn to Him for all our needs.

2. Be a refuge for people, and remind them of God

Allow people to turn to you and offer them your help. The Prophet ﷺ told us that *'the best of people are those that bring most benefit to the rest of mankind,'* [Ṭabarānī] and that *'if Allah wants good for a person then He uses him."* [Aḥmad] Al-Ghazālī says: 'The one whom God has appointed to be a model for His servants in fulfilling their worldly and religious duties, and who secures the needs of His creatures by his word and action—to that one God bestows a share in His attribute. But the absolutely eternal is the One to whom one turns to in every need, and He is God—may He be praised and exalted.'[24]

3. Learn His names

One way of being certain that God is al-Ṣamad is by learning His other names and attributes. In some ways, this name becomes a gateway to understanding His other names because it contains so many meanings. When we put the effort to become close to God, His attributes become more apparent to us.

[24] Al-Ghazālī, 131.

AL-QĀHIR, AL-QAHHĀR – DOMINATION (31-32)

20

AL-QĀHIR, AL-QAHHĀR – DOMINATION (31-32)

'One Day — when the earth is turned into another earth, the heavens into another heaven, and people all appear before God, the One, the Overpowering (al-Qahhār).'

[14:48]

Allah's names al-Qāhir and al-Qahhār come from the Arabic root *qāf-hā-rā*, which means 'to dominate over' or 'to subdue from above'. The difference between the two is in their intensity: al-Qāhir informs us that God is able to dominate all of creation from above, and al-Qahhār emphasizes to us that He is able to subdue and overpower even the most powerful and most numerous.

These names should inspire in us awe and reverence for God. There should be a healthy fear in us that prevents us from committing injustice because we know that we cannot escape al-Qāhir al-Qahhār. No matter how much power we think we have over others, Allah is *qāhir* over us.

However, for some of us, hearing that God has a name which means to dominate over or subdue might cause a crippling terror, rather than a fear which remedies our faults. Yet knowledge of this name should not be paralyzing. Indeed, Allah tells us in the Qur'an, *'So flee to Allah.*" [51:50]

Fear of anything other than Allah causes us to flee from them. Fear of God should induce us to flee *to* Him, because He accepts all those who turn back to Him. Moreover, fearing being overpowered by human beings is because this domination tends to come with injustice. Subjugation is not considered a positive trait when it is applied to human beings. The word *qahr* (domination) itself causes fear. To say that you have felt *qahr* because of someone's actions indicates that they wronged you in some way, and you were the weaker party. Allah clarifies to us His name when He says in the Qur'an: *'He is the Supreme Master (al-Qāhir) over His creatures, the All-Wise (al-Ḥakīm), the All-Aware (al-Khabīr).'* [6:18]

Allah reminds us through the above verses that He is the Most Wise and the One who is Best-Acquainted with everything. His domination is balanced by His all-encompassing wisdom and knowledge not just of the outward things, but also the hidden elements of which we as human beings are not aware. Indeed, God is the Most Just, and His overpowering is an expression of justice rather than a negation of it.

Qahhār over the Tyrants

Many people, when given dominion or power over others, misuse it. We see this all around us. We witness the actions of oppressive leaders, exploitative bosses, abusive spouses, and violent authorities. Some might ask, since Allah is al-Qahhār, why has He not overpowered the oppressors? Why are they allowed to persist in their tyranny and abuse, causing long-lasting destruction and pain?

We have to remember not to divide and separate Allah's attributes; this is part of the reason why names which sometimes seem contrasting are mentioned together. In the verse above, God is reminding us that there is ultimate wisdom in whom He chooses to subdue at any point in time. But His domination will come, at the right time, because He is Just. Indeed, the Prophet ﷺ said that injustice is one of the categories of sins whose punishment is hastened in this life. [Bukhārī, al-Adab al-Mufrad]

Moreover, because He is Wise and Generous, He gives people opportunities to return before subjecting them to punishment. Pharaoh represents the worst type of tyrant. He divided people, oppressing a group of them, slaughtering babies, and claiming he was god. In respond, Allah sent Moses and Aaron to speak to him, not to fight him. Pharaoh was shown different signs. Finally, after rejecting all the signs and insisting on oppression, he was drowned. He was drowned while attempting to overtake and subdue Moses and the children of Israel, and Allah subdued him. Every tyrant will get his or her day, and often it is in the most humiliating of ways. Sometimes it is at the hands of those very people they were oppressing. The Prophet ﷺ told us that, '*Verily, Allah Almighty will give respite to the wrongdoer until He seizes him and he cannot escape.*' Then the Prophet recited the verse, '*Such is the seizure of your Lord, when he takes hold of the cities while they are doing wrong. Verily, his seizure is agonizing and severe.*' [11:102] [Bukhārī and Muslim]

Moreover, Allah subdues people in subtle ways as well. A person may exhibit dominance externally, but God can subdue their hearts and their souls, such that they never experience internal peace nor pleasure. They may never experience sweetness in relationships nor gratification in their possessions. That is another manifestation of His *qahr*.

So, when we see that there are different types of oppressors in the world, this should not cause us to doubt God's name. These persons will see the wrath of al-Qahhār, in its different manifestations. Indeed, the worse their oppression and the longer it goes on for, the more immense their punishment will be. And the greatest manifestation of Allah's name al-Qahhār will come on the Day of Judgment.

Al-Qahhār on the Day of Judgment

As Muslims and believers in the Day of Judgment, we must always remind ourselves that this world, and everything in it – from its pleasures to its pains – are temporary. This world will test us and try us. We might be tried by the abuse of others, by our witnessing the oppression of others, or even our own mistreatment of other people. Allah reminds us in this regard: '*The Day they come forth nothing concerning them will be concealed from Allah. To whom belongs [all] sovereignty this Day? To Allah, the One, the Prevailing (al-Qahhār).*' [40:16]

It is a reminder that we will all be returned to Him, and anyone who had grand delusions of power and grandeur will see that it was a mirage. Indeed, Allah states that He is the One, the Prevailing. Oppressors needed their henchmen and their armies. They needed the systems they built in order to dominate over others. But Allah has no need for support or reinforcement – He is One, al-Qahhār. No army in the world can stand against God alone.

Anyone who harmed others in this world will be subdued and will receive justice. We will all stand before God, and we will be questioned. If we oppressed others, we will be asked about what we did, and all those we harmed will receive justice. If we were witnesses to injustice against others, we will be asked about what we did about it with whatever means we possessed. And if we were of the oppressed, then on that Day, we will see Allah subdue our oppressors.

Fear oppressing others

This should remind us that this name is not just relevant for those who clearly have much power, like statesmen or leaders. Some of us are given a degree of control or influence over others in different contexts, where we can choose to exercise that authority in righteous and just ways, or misuse that power. Perhaps we are employers, or religious leaders, or simply someone with higher social standing than others. Allah commands in the Qur'an: '*So as for the orphan, do not oppress [him] (fa lā taqhar).*" [93:9] The word *taqhar* comes from the same root of the name al-Qahhār. A person taking care of an orphan might not view him or herself as being given power, if their position in society appears to be mediocre or low. But they do exercise power in that relationship; indeed, there are different power dynamics in various relationships. If ever we are intoxicated by the power we have been given – in whatever form it is –and we are tempted to abuse those over whom we have been given control, our knowledge and fear of al-Qahhār should subdue any perceived pleasure we may get from misusing our powers.

Do not fear oppressors

Those who manifest unjust *qahr* in this world only retain this power temporarily, and this reminds us where to direct our fear. The example of the magicians in the story of Moses is instructive, as they had every reason to fear Pharaoh's punishment. He threatened to cut off their hands and feet, and to crucify them, for recognizing the truth that Moses brought. They said to him, *'decree whatever you are to decree. You can only decree for this worldly life.'* [20:72]. They chose Allah even when faced with the very real and immediate oppression of Pharaoh.

Perhaps even greater than the magicians was Āsiyah, who was also subject to the torment of her husband for daring to believe in Allah and the message of Moses. She was killed in the most gruesome way for her belief. But she, too, knew not to fear Pharaoh. She knew that his power was not real, and it was limited. She knew that He would face al-Qahhār in this life and the next – and he did, and he will.

Of course, Āsiyah and the magicians attained a station so lofty that it can seem out of reach for us. For that reason, sometimes mentioning these stories from the Qur'an does the opposite of inspiring us; it may make some of us despair because we feel so far from these examples. 'We cannot even get the basics right, let alone stand up to a tyrant!' we think.

But the stories in the Qur'an are not narrated for us to despair. Allah gives us the best examples. He shows us that certainty in Him can bring one to that elevated station – but not everyone will be asked to reach that station. Allah does not test us with more than we can bear. We should find hope in the fact that the magicians and Āsiyah were not prophets, nor were they people who spent their lives in religious upbringings or amongst religious families. But they dominated their lower desires and stood up to fear, and they were able to stand up to a tyrant.

So, while Āsiyah and the magicians are given to us as examples of those who truly feared only Allah, who gave up the wealth of this world for nearness to Him, in our own lives, this will look very different. But choosing Allah over our fears is still beloved to Him no matter what level it is at. For us, knowing that Allah is al-Qahhar might be to stand up to a bully. It may be to stand up to the oppression of our own souls. And while it may not be easy, we are rewarded for trying.

Living with these names

1. Dominate your lower desires

The idea of emulating God's beautiful attributes is easy to conceptualize. We all know that we should manifest mercy and forgiveness, for example, as He is the Most Merciful and the Most Forgiving. But in what way should we be 'dominators' or 'subduers' in our own lives? Al-Ghazālī counseled that we should subdue our greatest enemies: Satan and the lower self. We need to conquer our negative passions so that Satan does not use them to lure us. Indeed, love of power is one such passion or disease of the heart, and it is this disease that can cause us to enact the worst injustices against others. So, we must be wary of these diseases of the heart and do our best to overpower them.

2. Use that fear to stop a sin, particularly against others

To know that Allah is al-Qahhār is to extinguish the desire for sin in the heart. Because God is the Dominator, we should fear that al-Qahhār could take our soul while we are committing a sin.

Appearing to be allowed to continue in evil deeds – particularly against others – does not mean that Allah will not manifest this attribute. Allah says: *'So when they forgot that by which they had been reminded, We opened to them the doors of every [good] thing until, when they rejoiced in that which they were given, We seized them suddenly, and they were [then] in despair.'* [6:44]

Moreover, the surest way to earn the wrath of al-Qahhār is to oppress others. Al-Qahhār may manifest Himself in different, subtle ways, and not just in the most apparent fashion. Being unable to find peace and being in constant agitation is one such way. Another is that, just as we are hurting or oppressing those weaker than us, He may place someone above us to dominate us. Therefore, we should be diligent in exercising beauty, fairness and justice in all our relationships, particularly where we have been given authority. The fear we have of al-Qahhār should cause a positive type of paralysis: one which prevents us committing injustices against others. A practical initial exercise is to reflect on at least one thing that we may be doing and commit to stopping it. We can and should also seek forgiveness from those we feel have wronged in the past.

3. Stand for the oppressed

Oppressors wish to instill fear in the hearts of those they oppress. Abusive partners do this, for example. They make the victim feel as though they cannot leave, because the consequences would be direr than staying in the relationship. But knowing that al-Qahhār is above them should remind us that their power is a façade and delusion. And we should try to be of those who remove the oppressive *qahr* that people manifest in this world. Indeed, the Prophet ﷺ taught that we should *'help [our] brother, whether he is an oppressor or is oppressed.'* He was asked, 'O Messenger of Allah, we help the oppressed, but how do we help an oppressor?' The Prophet ﷺ said, *'By seizing his hand (i.e. by stopping him).'* [Bukhārī and Muslim]

4. Balance fear and hope

Many of us shy away from discussing the names of Allah that represent His majesty, and which generate fear in our hearts. On the one hand, it is so much more reassuring to focus on those attributes that enable us to relax and feel good. On the other, for some of us, it may be that all we heard about Allah growing up were these attributes that struck fear in our hearts. We may be healing from the trauma of feeling that Allah is 'out to get us', and the only relationship we could have with Him was one of obedience or punishment. But this explanation of al-Qahhār should put those incorrect beliefs to rest. The fear we are meant to feel is more a state of being alert to our shortcomings. We cannot forget that His names are to be looked at holistically. He is indeed al-Qahhār, but He is also al-Ḥalīm (the Most Forbearing, who is not quick to punish and indeed forgoes punishment for those who return to Him) and al-Laṭīf (the Subtle, the Most Kind). We should always have this in mind when thinking about Allah.

AL-QARĪB AL-MUJĪB – CLOSER TO YOU THAN YOURSELF (33-34)

21

AL-QARĪB AL-MUJĪB – CLOSER TO YOU THAN YOURSELF (33-34)

'My Lord is near, and ready to answer.'

[11:61]

Start this chapter by pausing for a moment and thinking of the closest person to you. Is it your best friend? Your sibling or cousin? Your spouse? One of your parents? Maybe your grandmother?

When you think of someone who is close to you, you probably think of the person you know best and who knows you best, who has been there for you through the good times and the bad, the one whom you know you can call at any time and he or she will be there for you. You know this person will understand. You trust in this person's advice and judgment. You are certain that, were you ever to need anything, this person would do their best to help you. He or she truly cares. And nothing gives you more pleasure than just being with this person.

Who is that person for you?

While the people we feel closest to are truly gifts from the Most Merciful, a gift by which Allah consoles our hearts and provides the companionship we need and crave in this world, we sometimes focus so much on the gift that we forget that the giver of the gift is al-Qarīb al-Mujīb – the Near One, the Answerer of prayers. All the traits that we described in the paragraph above, Allah is all that and more. And He reminds us of that – of His closeness to us, His knowledge of us and the secrets of our hearts, His answering our needs and wants – by revealing these names to us.

Even our best friends might fail us or might not be able to be there for us at certain times. They may be too physically far, too emotionally occupied with the things going on in their own lives, going through their own mental stresses, or something as simple as the time difference between our hometowns might make that connection all the more difficult. They are humans, so we too have to pay attention to their needs, and we may not want to burden them with our troubles. And we so are left with a void because that closeness – or the comforting feeling of closeness – is missing.

But Allah?

He is always there.

He is always near.

He always answers.

For all those times when we have felt distant from those closest to us, for all those times when we were lonely, and for all those times when we could not understand why no one was there, perhaps it was a nudge from al-Qarīb al-Mujīb – connect to Him, ask Him.

The meanings

Al-Qarīb is, very simply, the Near One. He is close to us in His knowledge of us, His knowledge of the secrets of our hearts and the thoughts in our minds, and in His watching over us and being with us. Of course, this closeness is not a physical closeness, as Allah cannot be contained physically, but He is even closer to us than someone who is sitting by our side, whom we can physically touch. God says in the Qur'an, '*We created man – We know what his soul whispers to him: We are closer to him than his jugular vein.*' [50:16]

Knowing that Allah is close to us is comforting enough. But we have needs and wants that we would like to have fulfilled. A person who is close to us, while they might love us enough to *want* to fulfil all our needs and wants, cannot do so – simply because they are themselves limited in what they can do and in their own resources. Not Allah. He is al-Mujīb – the Answerer of prayers. He responds to us when we ask of Him, helps us when we need Him, and even answers the prayer of our heart before we ask.[25]

Al-Qarīb – He is close to you

Before discussing Allah's name al-Mujīb, it is important to really consider al-Qarīb, and to truly internalize how close Allah is to us. Asking Allah when we feel far from Him affects the way in which we ask Him, and what we believe about how He will answer.

We discussed above the ideal close relationship. But even the relationships with people to whom we think we are close can break down sometimes. You might have thought that someone knew you, but realized that he or she did not. Perhaps you were close at some point, but ceased to be so because one of you changed. Sometimes it is difficult to verbalize the words we are feeling in our hearts, because we do not know if it will reach the other person. And sometimes we fear being vulnerable.

What about Allah? He says in the Qur'an: *'[Prophet], if My servants ask you about Me, I am near.'* [2:186]

For all those times when you have wondered whether God is near or far, He does not use an intermediary to answer this question. He does not tell the Prophet ﷺ *'tell them'*, as He does in response to other questions. When it comes to our relationship with Him, He answers us directly: *'I am near.'*

If you have ever wondered, does God really hear me? He answers: *'Indeed, He is Hearing and Near.'* [34:50]

[25] Ahmad Ibn Ajiba, *Allah: An Explanation of the Divine Names and Attributes*. Translated by Abdulaziz Suraqah (USA: Al-Madina Institute, 2014), 105.

And if you have ever questioned whether He would hear the supplications of your heart, He tells us: *'Indeed, my Lord is near and responsive.'* [11:61]

One of the fruits of being close to someone is feeling safe and understood. And if you have ever felt lonely, Allah says in the Qur'an, *'and He is with you wherever you are.'* [57:4]

The One who named Himself al-Qarīb is inviting us to be close to Him, and He does not close the door to the servants who seek Him. Moreover, the way this name is mentioned in the Qur'an – either alone, or with His names the All-Hearing and the Answerer – teaches us something: Allah is close to us, He hears us, and He responds to our supplications. He hears our inner thoughts even when we do not articulate them, and knows the prayers of our hearts. Sometimes even our best friends do not understand what we are going through. Allah is so close to us that He hears our thoughts, our reflections, our unuttered questions and the secret supplications of our hearts. There may even be times when we think of something that we want, but never ask for it, yet somehow, God gives it to us. There may even be times when *we* do not know what we want, and yet somehow we get that thing we need, sent by the Most High.

Because is He is near – al-Qarīb.

It is comforting to know that God is so close to us. It can, however, still feel limited. You may have a friend who knows you and is close to you, but who cannot help you when you need it. Yet God is not only closer to us than anyone else, He is also the Responder: al-Mujīb.

The Near One is the One who Responds

How amazing is it that the nearest one to us is also the one – the only One, truly – who can give us what we need and want. The Prophet ﷺ taught his cousin, Ibn 'Abbās, an important lesson when he was young: '*If you ask, ask from Allah. If you seek help, seek help from Allah.*' [Tirmidhī]

This does not negate the necessity of working with the means we have. Indeed, the means of this world are provided by God, and He requires us to work with them. The Prophet ﷺ prepared for everything he had to face, he sought advice, *and* He asked God. It may be that you ask for something, and Allah facilitates for you the means by which to achieve that for which you asked.

This is not a religion of complacency. Knowing that Allah is al-Mujīb should actually increase what we think we can achieve, both in this world and the next, because we know that He answers – what we are responsible for is the effort. Indeed, this name should inspire us to be spiritually ambitious, because we know that He will aid us.

When we ask Allah, it is an affirmation of our knowledge of and belief in His names and attributes. Having utmost belief that He responds means knowing that He is Near, that He is All-Hearing (al-Samī'), All-Knowing (al-'Alīm), that He is the Most-Affectionate (al-Wadūd) and Merciful (al-Raḥmān), and the Most Powerful (al-Qādir). Asking Him therefore leads us to know His other names. When Allah gives us that for which we asked, we truly know that He is the Gift-Giver (al-Wahhāb) and the Most Generous (al-Kar*īm).*

For this reason, the Messenger of Allah ﷺ said, '*When one of you supplicates, let him be determined in the supplication and he should not say: "O Allah, give me if you will." There is none to coerce Allah.*' [Bukhārī and Muslim] The scholar al-Nawawī said, that 'being determined' means 'to have good expectations of Allah Almighty in answering you.' We also end up learning about His other names and attributes when it appears that we did not receive that for which we asked, and the relationship between His nearness to us and His response is important. You may ask something of someone who does not know you, and they might give you exactly what you ask for, but it turns out that what you want is bad for you. This person may have responded, but their response was to your detriment. Not Allah. He knows us so intimately that when He gives, it is exactly what we need. And this introduces us to His wisdom (al-Ḥakīm).

Ibn 'Aṭā'illāh said, 'If in spite of intense supplication, there is delay in the timing of the Gift, let that not be the cause for your despairing. For He has guaranteed you a response in what He chooses for you, not in what you choose for yourself, and at the time He desires, not the time you desire.'

What prevents us from asking?

There are two main reasons why we do not ask: we do not believe that God can or will answer us, for a variety of reasons, or we believe that we can do it without His help.

The second reason is a form of arrogance. In the verse in which God tells us to call on Him and He will respond [40:60], He mentions those who are *'too proud'* to worship Him – they do not call on Him, and thus they disdain His worship. This is considered one of the diseases of the heart, and a fatal one, as it makes us turn away from God.

But here we will be expounding in more detail upon the first reason. God tells us that He is al-Mujīb, so we should have utter confidence that He will respond to our supplication (*du'ā'*). The Prophet ﷺ said: *'Verily your Lord is Generous and Shy. If His servant raises his hands to Him (in supplication) He becomes shy to return them empty.'* [Aḥmad and others]

God loves that we go to Him. Sometimes God will not give us something unless and until we ask, even though He can give it to us whenever He wills. And so, we come to know our Lord and experience certainty in His attributes. The Prophet ﷺ tells us to ask God with certainty that He will respond. [Tirmidhī]

In order to build our certainty in al-Mujīb, God tells us stories of how He manifests this name in the Qur'an: *'Remember Job, when he cried to his Lord, "Suffering has truly afflicted me, but you are the Most Merciful of the merciful." We answered him, removed his suffering, and restored his family to him, along with more like them, as an act of grace from Us and a reminder for all who serve Us.'* [21:83-84]

The Prophet Job was afflicted with a disease for eighteen years, and never once did he complain of it or resent God. Before contracting the disease, he was blessed with abundant wealth for fifty years and was always grateful to God for what he had been blessed with. He never once blamed Allah when he lost everything, and if we look at his *du'ā'*, he called on Allah by His Majestic Names, and recognized that it was truly only God who could help him. And when Allah responded to him, He did not just remove the affliction, but gave him more. We should always think the best of Allah and recognize that even as He is the One who responds, He is also the Most Generous. And the most hopeful part? Allah says that His answer was *'an act of grace from Us and a reminder for all who serve Us'* – a reminder that when we are afflicted, we need to turn back to Allah. God makes ease after hardship, puts eases within hardship (Prophet Job, for example, had his wife, who stood by him and took care of him throughout the illness, even when others abandoned him) and can cure our afflictions when we turn to Him. We should be patient as Job was patient, and certain as he was certain that he had a Merciful God, even as he was being tried. So whenever harm afflicts you, remember this prayer.

Allah then tells us about Jonah: *'And remember the man with the whale, when he went off angrily, thinking We could not restrict him, but then he cried out in the deep darkness, "There is no God but You, glory be to You, I was wrong." We answered him and saved him from distress: this is how We save the faithful.'* [21:87-88]

The Prophet Jonah was sent to a people who initially disbelieved. He did not wait for the sign from God telling him what to do next but left them in anger – essentially giving up on them – because of their disbelief and rejection. So God made a huge whale swallow him, and he remained there in its belly, saying the supplication above: *'There is no God but You, glory be to You, I was wrong.'*

What is so special about this prayer? That Prophet Jonah recognized his wrongdoing, and that all power lies with God. He kept saying this *du'ā'* until God responded. Sometimes, when we do something wrong, we feel too ashamed to turn to God and ask for His help. But this was not the way of the prophets. Knowing that you can turn to Him despite your wrongdoings signifies your firm belief in His Name. Allah said of Jonah in another chapter: *'If his Lord's grace had not reached him, he would have been left, abandoned and blameworthy, on the barren shore.'* [68:49]

Allah responded to Jonah and delivered him from his distress, and when he returned to his people they all believed, because they had witnessed the signs that they were told about. Allah, in His infinite mercy, reminds us at the end of the story: *'this is how We save the faithful.'* [21:88] When you are distressed and under great difficulty, before asking for something, say this *du'ā'* and recognize your wrongdoings to Allah – He will, God willing, forgive you and respond.

Then God proceeds to tell us about the Prophet Zachariah: *'Remember Zachariah, when he cried to his Lord, "My Lord, do not leave me childless, though You are the best of heirs." We answered him – We gave him John, and cured his wife of barrenness.'* [21:89-90]

Zachariah and his wife were very old and so could not bear children, but as we see here, Zachariah implored only Allah, and called him by His attribute as the Best of Heirs (*Khayr al-Wārithīn*). Thereafter, God made Zachariah's wife fertile again, and they had John, who was also a prophet. After informing us of His gift to them, Allah tells us of the good they used to do; that *'they were always keen to do good deeds. They called upon Us out of longing and awe, and humbled themselves before Us.'* [21:90]

They would constantly do good deeds, always calling on God with fear and hope, and they were not arrogant, but humble. These are some of the qualities from which we should learn and with which we should adorn ourselves; they will, God willing (*inshā'Allāh*) make us closer to God, and of those to whom God responds.

God gives us these three examples: the example of one who had everything and was afflicted with loss; the example of one who had wronged himself; and the example of one who desired something that he did not have. All of them called to God, and He responded, not because they were prophets, but because they turned to Him. In every verse Allah reminds us that this is the way He will treat the believers; this treatment is not exclusive to the prophets.

But sometimes it does not feel like He is close, nor that He answers...

Imam Suhaib Webb once said, 'If you feel far from Allah, ask yourself, who moved?'

Sometimes, *we* put emotional distance between us and Allah. It is not that He is far, nor that He does not answer. There are reasons for this that need to be explored.

The first reason for this feeling is the way in which we conceptualize God. For whatever reason, it may feel that we could never be close to Allah. Closeness to God is only for the saints, and not for people like us. But Allah tells us that He is close to us, and He is inviting us to bring ourselves closer to Him. We need to get out of our heads and just take that first step to Him. The issue is not with Allah, but rather with how we feel about ourselves. We should remember that we ask Allah based on who He is, not based on who we are.

The second reason is that we put distance between ourselves and God knowingly. We disobey Him without remorse. One thing that may block our *du'ā'* from being answered is that we earn money through illegitimate means. When someone earns money from illegitimate sources, it also ceases to be a private matter, but rather it harms others (e.g. selling alcohol). We cannot harm or take advantage of others for a living and then expect that Allah will give us that for which we ask – although He may still give to us in order to remind us of His grace. Moreover, it shows a lack of trust in Him, because our belief is that we can be supported through means that He has deemed reprehensible. This does not mean that we can never be close to Him; our repentance to Him is a sign of our desire to be of His beloved servants, and He accepts all those who seek closeness to Him in the right way.

Thirdly, it may be hard to have certainty in this attribute when we are going through hardship and feel that there has not been an answer to our prayers. In fact, sometimes it may seem that the situation is getting worse. Is He truly close to us, knowing what we are going through, and does He really answer prayers when the situation is prolonged?

The Prophet ﷺ said, *'The supplication of any worshipper will continue to be responded to, as long as he does not ask for a sin or breaking the ties of kinship, and as long as he is not hasty.'* It was asked, 'O Messenger of Allah, and what does it mean to be hasty?' He responded, *'A worshipper says, "I have prayed and prayed, and I don't see that it will be accepted," so he gives up hope of being answered and leaves his supplication.'* [Muslim]

This is an important point. We do not put a time limit on when God can or should respond. While He is al-Mujīb, He is also al-Hakīm (the Wise). Perhaps we hate a thing and God puts good in it, and perhaps we love a thing and it is bad for us. One might ask, so what is the point of asking if I do not get that for which I ask, when I ask for it?

In reality, when we have faith that God will answer, we will get more than that for which we ask, because God gives us what we need and what is best – so much so that we may even forget that thing for which we were asking initially. The Prophet Job just wanted to be cured of his illness, but God gave him more – he got health, riches, and family. Mary's mother wanted a son who would serve God, but God gave her a daughter – this was not the son for which she had asked, and she might have been disappointed. But God showed Mary's mother, and all of us, the station of Mary as an example to all believers – men and women – of piety and closeness to God. In fact, she even reminded the Prophet Zachariah to ask God for what appeared to be impossible, and that is when he asked God for a child.

We have to remember to entrust our affairs to the One who takes care of them with all of His attributes, and who gives us what we truly need. The Prophet ﷺ said: *'There is no Muslim who calls upon Allah, without sin or cutting family ties, but that Allah will give him one of three answers: He will quickly fulfill his supplication, He will store it for him in the Hereafter, or He will divert an evil from him similar to it.'* The Companions said, 'In that case, we will ask for more.' The Prophet ﷺ said, *'Allah has even more.'* [Aḥmad]

The scholar Ibn Ḥajar explained, 'Every single person who makes *du'ā'* will be responded to, but the actual responses are different. Sometimes the exact matter that was prayed for is given, and sometimes, something equivalent to it is given.'

Moreover, in a beautiful hadith, we are told of a believer who appeared not to receive that for which they were asking God in this world. When the Day of Judgment comes, and this person is admitted to Paradise, he finds that the answer to his supplications were deferred to Paradise, where they were even greater than what the he had ever imagined. He then wished that none of his supplications had ever been answered in this life.

Additionally, the scholar Ibn al-Jawzī stated that appearing to receive no response is a test and demands patience. Will we give in to the whispers of Satan that may create doubt in our minds, or do we fight him with our conviction in and love for God?

We need to remember that our prayers are never, ever lost. We should never stop asking – Allah will either shower His mercy upon us in this world or will save something infinitely better for us in Paradise, where we will reside, God willing, for eternity. Supplications are a way of accumulating spiritual wealth in ways we could never imagine.

The connection between being near and responding

In the verse in which Allah tells us that He is close, He follows it with: *'I respond to those who call Me, so let them respond to Me, and believe in Me, so that they may be guided.'* [2:186]

Ibn al-Qayyim stated that while God is close to all of His creation, He is specifically close to those who ask from Him.[26] Thus, one of the ways to increase in closeness to God is to ask Him for our all our needs and wants. This shows how different God is to human beings. One of the ways to ensure *distance* from people is to constantly ask from them. Indeed, even if you were once close to someone, your persistent asking for favors would put a heavy burden on them, and may make them turn away from you or think that you are trying to take advantage of them.

Not so with God. We are told to ask from Him, because asking from Him is a recognition of how close He is to us. Indeed, when the Prophet ﷺ said that the *'closest that a servant is to his Lord is when he is in prostration,'* he followed it up with, *'so increase your supplications therein.'* [Muslim]

So, asking from God is both a sign of and way to gain closeness to Him. We can only feel comfortable asking someone to whom we feel close – the closer we are, the more comfortable we are in asking for even the smallest things – and the amazing thing is that *by* asking Him, we can gain closeness to Him.

---

[26] Al-Ashqar, *Sharḥ Ibn Al-Qayyim Li Asmā' Allāh Al-Ḥusnā*, 177.

Living with these names

1. Understand His names

One of the best ways to come close to God is to know Him, and the best way to know Him is to understand His Names and attributes, which are in and of themselves an invitation to closeness.

We can only be close to those whom we know really well and who know us in return. Often, when we tell people about ourselves, it is because we want them to know us; the more we share about ourselves with someone, and the more we know about them, the closer we become to each other. Allah wants us to know that He is close and He responds, so He tells us this and many other facts about Himself. Re-read some of the names in this book and get re-acquainted with Allah.

2. Prayer

The root of the word *ṣalāh*, the Arabic word for the ritual prayer, means to turn completely towards something with all your being.

Prayer was given as a gift to us so that we can connect with Allah and be *with* Him. If we do not know how to connect through prayer, we can attend a course or follow an online guide.

3. Ask Him in all circumstances

God tells us specifically to ask Him – *'Call on Me and I will answer you'* [40:60] – and He tells us to call on Him when we are in trouble. He does not condition it with 'only the pious of you' or 'only those who are worthy' (otherwise we would all be in trouble!), but He tells us: *'Who is it that answers the distressed when they call upon Him? Who removes their suffering? Who makes you successors in the earth? Is it another god beside God? Little notice do you take.'* [27:62]

God reminds us that no one can truly help us except Him, so we should be asking Him for help when we are distressed, as well as using the means around us. Moreover, it is reported that the

Prophet ﷺ reminded us that, *'For whomever the door of du'ā' opened, for him the doors of mercy are opened.'* [Tirmidhī] This means that whoever calls upon God – and does not stop for any reason – the doors of mercy will be opened for him or her. This will take a form that only God knows.

Moreover, we are told to be persistent in asking God. The Prophet ﷺ told us, *'Do not stop making du'ā', because nobody who makes du'ā' is forsaken.'* [Ḥākim]

So ask Him for closeness; ask Him for your needs; ask Him for His help.

4. 'Respond' to God and be there for people

Imam al-Ghazālī states that we should first be responsive to Allah in following His commandments. We all sin and make mistakes, but the point is to strive to do the best that we can. Moreover, being close to Allah does not mean being disconnected from His creation, but rather the opposite. It is important to respond to the servants of God, by assisting people if we are able, and if not, then by being kind. We should look after people, visit the sick, and stand in solidarity with the oppressed. Thus, we will find nearness to Him.

AL-TAWWĀB – TURNING BACK (35)

22

AL-TAWWĀB – TURNING BACK (35)

'He turned to them in mercy in order for them to return [to Him]. God is the Ever Relenting (al-Tawwāb), the Most Merciful.'

[9:118]

Imagine waking up one day and realizing that you are lost, or reflecting on your life and recognizing that something is not right. Somewhere along the way, something went wrong, and you strayed away from the center – from your true home. This realization should lead you to desire to return. But to be able to return, there must be something *to which* to return, and it is vital that you know what that is.

God tells us that He is al-Tawwāb; He is the One to whom we return. While the common translations of al-Tawwāb are the 'Accepter of Repentance' or the 'Ever-Relenting', in actuality, this name means so much more.

The Arabic root of the word al-Tawwāb is *tā-wāw-bā*, which means to turn from something towards something else. Thus, when it comes to God, this name has two main meanings: first, Allah Himself turns towards us and, second, He accepts whenever we return to Him – in fact, He loves welcoming us back.

God turns to us

The first meaning of al-Tawwāb is that God Himself turns to us. The nature of this turning manifests in different ways: God turns to us in His mercy, for example, to inspire us to turn back to Him.

It could be that, after being far from God, He sends you something good that reminds you of Him, and encourages you to turn back to Him. It could be a blessing that comes out of nowhere that you know you did not deserve, and this reminds you that no matter where you are, God is there for you. Al-Ghazālī states that Allah facilitates the causes of repentance through the manifestation of His signs, or through His book, which both counsels us and warns us.

His turning towards us could even be through a hardship or a test that comes along, which compels us to turn back to God. It is in that moment – a moment of being under immense stress or pain – that we realize our need for God. One of the great Islamic scholars, Mālik ibn Dīnār, was not always as pious as he later became. Actually, he was far from it – he lived a depraved, unethical life. This continued until he lost the most precious thing he had: his daughter, who died as a child. In her short life, his daughter encouraged him to do good, and he found himself wanting to be better because of her. Initially after her death, he became worse because of the grief, drinking away his sorrows. After being intoxicated to the degree of passing out, Mālik ibn Dīnār had a dream about her. This dream reminded him that his daughter was with Allah now, and would be waiting for him at the doors of Paradise – this is what caused him to turn back to God and turn his life around, benefiting both others and himself by becoming a scholar.

Whatever causes us to return to Him – whether it is a verse (*āyah*) in the Qur'an, an article, a friend who reminds us, a difficulty, or even the realization of a sin committed – it comes about only because He has turned to us, and wants us to turn back to Him. These are all ways by which He shows us that we need to return. And when we do turn back, time and time again when we find that we have strayed, we become one of the *tawwābīn*: those who constantly return. Returning is not a mark of shame – it is a special status with God because, as He tells us in His book, *'God loves those who turn to Him (al-tawwābīn).'* [2:222] So by returning to God from mistakes or sins or heedlessness, we become beloved to Him. How kind is God, who focuses on how far we have come, and not how far we were.

One of the Companions of the Prophet ﷺ, Kaʿb ibn Mālik, made a big mistake; he abandoned his people in their time of need. It was during the Battle of Tabūk, which was an especially difficult battle and there were not enough riding animals for everyone, yet Kaʿb himself had two. He procrastinated leaving until he could not catch up with the expedition. When he saw who remained, it was only those who were ill, incapacitated, or the hypocrites. And he was among them.

When the army came back more than a month later, Kaʿb was worried. He contemplated lying to the Prophet ﷺ. But he knew that even if he lied to the Prophet ﷺ, God knew why he had truly stayed behind, so he chose to tell the truth and bear the consequences.

This is where repentance shows its sincerity. Kaʿb and two other men who were truthful about their reasons for staying behind were reprimanded and told to wait for God's decree. In the meantime, no one would speak to them. This, of course, seems harsh, and many of us would feel disheartened. We would wish that we had lied. We would feel that our repentance was not accepted, otherwise why would we be punished like this? To add to an already difficult situation, some of the Arab tribes heard about his temporary excommunication and invited Kaʿb to join them against the Muslims, saying they would support him. Some of us might have decided to join them, giving up on ourselves.

Yet the story of Kaʿb ibn Mālik teaches us not to give up after turning back and repenting sincerely. Kaʿb refused their invitation. He continued praying to God, seeking forgiveness, and asking for His grace – and the reward for that was being remembered in the Qur'an for eternity in this verse:

> *'And to the three men who stayed behind: when the earth, for all its spaciousness, closed in around them, when their very souls*

> *closed in around them, when they realized that the only refuge from God was with Him, He turned to them in mercy in order for them to return [to Him]. God is the Ever Relenting, the Most Merciful.'* [9:118]

God records the three men as among those people whom He has accepted, and in this is a lesson. God does not leave those who turn back to Him. In fact, He turns to them in mercy even before they turn to Him. The apparent lag in feeling this acceptance or facing hardship after repentance is simply a lesson that the All-Merciful is teaching us. And if you are patient, and turn to Him even in that scenario, you will get something you could not have even imagined. As Allah reminds us: *'God will find a way out for those who are mindful of Him, and will provide for them from an unexpected source; God will be enough for those who put their trust in Him.'* [65:2-3]

Our turning to God

In the story of the creation of Adam and Eve, both were put in Paradise and told to enjoy everything within it, except for a particular tree. The Qur'an tells us Satan whispered to them both, and they both ate from the tree, sharing the responsibility. They felt terrible; they were the first human beings to whom God had given everything, yet they forgot and followed their desires. And in this moment, God revealed His attribute of acceptance to them: *'Then Adam received some words from his Lord and He accepted his repentance: He is the Ever Relenting, the Most Merciful.'* [2:37]

And this was a lesson to Adam, Eve and their progeny until the end of time: God wants us to turn back to Him so much that He teaches us how to do this, and never leaves us. Once He has taught us and revealed this attribute, it is up to us to take that step and turn back to Him, no matter what state we are in. As God tells us: *'Do they not know that it is Allah who accepts repentance from His servants and receives charities and that it is Allah who is the Accepting of repentance, the Merciful?'* [9:104]

Acceptance with mercy and wisdom

God shows us the nature of His acceptance in how He pairs this attribute with His other attributes. He frequently reminds us that He is both the *'Ever-relenting, Most Merciful."* [49:12]

By combining these two attributes, God tells us He accepts us out of His Mercy, and this means that no matter how far we are, we can always return. Moreover, the name al-Tawwāb refers to our returning to Him after being far away, and so He removes the harms we have incurred upon ourselves, while al-Rahīm refers to God bestowing His blessings upon us after we return to Him.

God also reminds us that He is the Most Wise (al-Ḥakīm). We are told: *'And if not for the favor of Allah upon you and His mercy…and because Allah is Accepting of repentance and Wise.'* [24:10]

Because God is the Most Wise, the form of His acceptance will be different depending on our state. Just like the story of Ka'b bin Malik, a hardship after turning back to God does not mean that He has rejected us. It is an invitation to look deeply and rectify ourselves even further; were the hardship not there, we would never truly improve and become better. In His wisdom, He teaches us in both hardship and ease, with gentleness and firmness. God also teaches us different ways to turn back to Him. For example, if we have spent our lives harming other people, the first step may be to return to God. But true repentance would be to make amends with the people we have harmed. Similarly, if one forgets an obligatory act during the hajj or *'umrah* pilgrimage rituals, the expiation is to donate a slaughtered sheep to the needy. Thus, the wisdom of God is that when we return to Him, we also benefit other people.

Back to open arms

'God loves those who turn to Him and He loves those who purify themselves.' [2:222]

If we come home and find that our clothes are dirty, torn, or messy, we remove them. We take a shower and wash our clothes. And what happens afterwards? We feel good. We feel clean. We may get dirty again tomorrow, even if we try to avoid it, but we will shower again and wash our clothes again. We do not avoid taking a shower or washing our clothes because we are sick of getting dirty. Rather, we accept that going about our business means that our bodies might smell and our clothes may get soiled, even with all our attempts to keep them clean; still we enjoy and feel invigorated by the feeling of being cleansed again. This is analogous to our relationship with sins and mistakes. The fear that we will slip into sin again – indeed, the same sin even – should not prevent us from going back to God and trying to do better.

Turning back to God might feel like something that causes us shame, because we have to admit that we are at fault. We think of human beings who would turn us away, and think that God may react in the same way. But when we return to Allah, it should not feel heavy. It should actually be a liberating act because we are doing something that He loves. We are actually making Him happy. The Prophet ﷺ tells us: *'Verily, God is more delighted with the repentance of His slave than a person who lost his camel in a desert land and then finds it.'* [Muslim]

Think of this example for a moment: imagine being lost in the desert and losing your only means of transport. Imagine the feeling of despair and confusion. Now imagine the relief and joy when you find your camel again. It is not simply happiness, but a feeling of ecstasy. That is as close as we can get, as human beings, to imagining how God feels when we turn back.

Do not let guilt keep you from going back; rather, go back because you love God, and because He loves those who return to Him and is happy with their repentance.

Living with this name

The conditions of repentance from sin are the following, as stated by some scholars:

1. Turn back in whatever state you are

To whom does the idea of turning back apply? We might think that it is just for people who have made huge mistakes. The truth is, though, we all need to turn to God. We could be a person living life in complete disobedience or a person who is heedless, simply doing deeds robotically and not much more. So how does one return? The answer is to take it step-by-step. Your return to Allah is the first step, a beautiful step. It includes seeking forgiveness from Him for what has passed. The next step is to work on yourself and work on your surroundings. Pick something that you need to work on, or something that you need to stop doing. Work on it for a while until it becomes habit, or is easier to do. Then add a second habit. Do not be discouraged if you feel that your development is slow and you didn't suddenly turn into Super-Muslim. Remember that the Prophet ﷺ said: '*The most beloved of actions to Allah are the most consistent ones even if little in amount.*' [Bukhārī]

2. If you are doing something that is wrong, stop

If you know that your actions are wrong, the first step is to regret those actions, recognizing that they are indeed wrong. This does not mean hating yourself or despairing. Rather, you recognize the act that you did or the state that you are in as something not good, which needs to change. After this recognition, try to stop the sin in that moment. Sometimes we do not stop the sin because we think that we will be unable to continue desisting, and that we will slip back into it. But that should not matter – stop in the moment when you can, even if you fear going back to the wrongdoing the next day. Do not sabotage yourself with negative thinking, which is akin to saying 'let me hurt myself now, because I will probably hurt myself again tomorrow.' When you stop the wrongdoing, intend never to do it again – use affirming language and encourage yourself by reminding yourself of the good you are doing in that moment. Ask Allah to help you. Change your environment to one that aids you in your endeavor. Ask your friends or family to hold you accountable.

But what if you fall into it again? Remember: hate the sin, not yourself. The Prophet ﷺ told us, *'All of the children of Adam make mistakes, and the best of those who make mistakes are those who constantly return.'* [Tirmidhī] The issue is not the mistake itself, but what we do afterwards – and if we are of those who constantly turn back, then we fall into the realm of those who have God's love, *inshā'Allāh.*

3. Make amends with people

If your mistake or wrongdoing involved the rights of another person, you should return the rights you have violated, if you can. If you cannot, supplicate for that person and try to benefit them in other ways.

4. Do good

Someone may ask, what do I do afterwards? Start with what is obligatory, because that is what brings us close to Allah. Even if you are a person who already does the obligatory, work on improving; an example of this is learning how to be more devoted during the ritual prayers. Then add the extra deeds. You can do them simultaneously of course, but do not prioritize the extra over the foundational. Many of us are familiar with Allah's saying: *'Nothing endears My servant to Me more than doing of what I have made obligatory upon him to do. And My servant continues to draw nearer to Me with the supererogatory (nawāfil) so that I shall love him.'* [Bukhārī]

What is crucial is to get aid – from a good friend, your spouse, or your mentor. Even if you do not have that aid now, keep seeking it – Allah is the Guide, and He is the Provider; He will provide.

GHĀFIR AL-DHANB, AL-GHAFŪR, AL-GHAFFĀR– GOD'S COVER OF FORGIVENESS (36-38)

23

GHĀFIR AL-DHANB, AL-GHAFŪR, AL-GHAFFĀR – GOD'S COVER OF FORGIVENESS (36-38)

'Tell My servants that I am the Forgiving, the Merciful.'

[15:49]

Of the things that create a mental barrier between us and God are our sins, mistakes and missteps. Many of us have felt disheartened because we messed up. Perhaps we messed up too many times to count. And maybe we messed up in the worst of ways, and this brings us feelings of shame and unworthiness.

And this results in us feeling that we cannot turn back to God; indeed, that we cannot even have a relationship with Him. How could we, when we make so many mistakes? Yet God tells us that He is the Forgiver of sin, the Oft-forgiving, the Ever-forgiving (Ghāfir al-Dhanb, al-Ghafūr, al-Ghaffār) – and these names are a *response* to all of us who wonder what happens regarding our mistakes when we ask God for forgiveness. What does it mean that Allah forgives and what is the nature of this forgiveness? Are we supposed to live in a constant state of guilt because we are sinners?

Many of us already call on God by these names, and worship Him by these attributes, even if we do not know the actual nuances of the names. Many others ignore this attribute altogether. But in giving Himself three names from the same root, God tells us,

'I have you covered, no matter the nature of your mistakes and transgressions.'

So, what is the difference between them, and what does this mean for us?

Maghfirah (Forgiveness)

The three aforementioned names come from the same Arabic root: *ghayn-fā-rā*, which linguistically means to cover and protect. When Muslims say '*rabbī ighfir lī*' – which is usually translated to 'My Lord, forgive me' – what we are actually asking Allah for is to cover our sin and protect us from it.

Allah tells us in the Qur'an: '*God does not forgive the joining of partners with Him: anything less than that He forgives to whoever He will.*' [4:48]

In other words, God tells us that He forgives *everything*; the only sin He does not forgive is to die while still associating another deity with Him. This *maghfirah* is a covering and protection in this life and the next. God covers our sin in this life and protects us from its effect, and covers the sin up in the Hereafter and protects us from the Hellfire.

Whom does He forgive?

Our nature as human beings is that we will mess up. This is not a condemnation, simply a reality that we live with. In our relationship with God, we sometimes use this idea to distance ourselves from Him, believing that we will never be worthy of a relationship with Him. But it is strange that we apply this to our spiritual relationship and not to our worldly relationships. We also constantly make mistakes in our relationships with others. We do things that subjectively cause other people to become angry with us, and sometimes our transgressions are objectively wrong. But most of us do not give up on relationships because of our own mistakes (the mistakes of others are another issue). We especially do not give up when the person whom we love loves us even more in return, and is accepting of our mistakes, helping us to get past them and work through them. Indeed, our love and appreciation of that person makes us *want* to be better and want to be even closer to them. His or her acceptance of us makes us unafraid to look hard at ourselves and admit our mistakes. Indeed, a relationship like this is one of hope and constant growth, not censure and dejection.

God is far above any analogy, but the above example serves to show the logical fallacy of distancing ourselves from God because we are sinners. Allah knows that – He created us! – and His telling us that is not an insult to us. It is rather recognizing our fallible nature so that we can focus on what we can do within the reality we live in. But it does not stop there. Allah *empowers* us with the knowledge that He forgives; this tells us that we have a loving, accepting Lord, *and* it is a testament to our ability to become better.

Allah gave Himself three different names from the same root to drive this point home. He invites us to call on Him by these names, so that we can be forgiven, transform, and become better. These names are meant to both humble us and empower us. God tells us that He is, *'Forgiver of sin (Ghāfir al-Dhanb) and Accepter of repentance, severe in punishment, infinite in bounty. There is no god but Him; to Him is the ultimate return.'* [40:3]

Furthermore, He says: *'If any of you has foolishly done a bad deed, and afterwards repented and mended his ways, God is most forgiving (Ghafūr) and most merciful.'* [6:54]

In Sūrat Nūḥ, the Prophet Noah called his people after they had committed grave injustices, and said to them, *'Ask forgiveness of your Lord: He is ever forgiving (Ghaffāran).'* [71:10]

The number of times and the contexts in which these names appear give us a glimpse into their nuanced meanings. Ghāfir al-Dhanb occurs once in the Qur'an, and tells us that God forgives sin. Some of us might be dismayed. God forgives sin? How many times? And what type of sins? We have way too many to count!

Then God reminds us that He is al-Ghafūr more than ninety times in the Qur'an. Al-Ghafūr is the One who forgives over and over and over again. While this is more reassuring, some of us might still be skeptical. Maybe it is not the number of sins, but that we have sins we are too ashamed to talk about because they are truly *that* bad. And so He tells us that He is al-Ghaffār. This name relates to intensity: God forgives the gravest of sins. Allah tells us that He has covered all bases. No matter how many sins, or even the type of sin, you have committed, God will cover and protect you from them, *if* you seek His forgiveness.

Allah tells us in a beautiful narration: *'O son of Adam, so long as you call upon Me and ask of Me, I shall forgive you for what you have done, and I shall not mind. O son of Adam, were your sins to reach the clouds of the sky and were you then to ask forgiveness of Me, I would forgive you. O son of Adam, were you to come to Me with sins nearly as great as the earth and were you then to face Me, ascribing no partner to Me, I would bring you forgiveness nearly as great as it.'* [Tirmidhī]

What is beautiful is that God Himself *invites* us. We are told in the Qur'an: *'Their messengers said, "Can there be doubt about Allah, Creator of the heavens and earth? He invites you that He may forgive you of your sins, and He delays your death for a specified term."'* [14:10]

When God forgives, we are protected from our mistakes, and sometimes, our mistakes are erased completely.[27] On the Day of Judgment, when our books of deeds are open, Allah will ask us, *'Do you know this sin? Do you know that sin?'* and the believers' reply will be, 'Yes, O Lord,' until we have been reminded of all of our sins, and we think that we will be condemned. Allah will say, *'I covered up your sins during your life, and I will forgive your sins today.'* [Bukhārī and Muslim] Then we will be given our books of good deeds. That is the beauty of Allah's forgiveness.

At a higher level, God may even *replace* our bad actions with good. Allah says in the Qur'an: *'Except for those who repent,*

[27] See God's Name, *al-'Afuw* (chapter 48)

believe and do righteous work. For them Allah will replace their evil deeds with good. And ever is Allah Forgiving and Merciful.' [25:70] This is the highest level of acceptance: acceptance of our return and forgiveness of our mistakes. God will change our heedlessness, our mistakes, and our sins into good deeds. We may see mountains of good deeds on the Day of Judgment and think to ourselves, 'when did I do that?' Then we will be told that God accepted us and turned all the bad that we did into good.

Be aware

Knowing that Allah forgives should give us hope, fill us with love, and energize us with the knowledge that we will be accepted and can work to be better. But we should balance fear and hope so that we do not purposefully disobey Him and say that we will repent later – after all, this is a form of insolence in the face of God's magnanimity, and will ultimately harm ourselves and others because every prohibited thing has been prohibited for a reason. Sometimes that reason is obvious, while at other times, there are deeper metaphysical factors at play. This is part of the Unseen (*ghayb*) – those things that cannot be accessed using our senses – and the believers are described as those who believe in the *ghayb* [2:2-3].

Another thing to keep in mind is ensuring that we do not publicize those things that God does not love. The dominant culture celebrates the publicizing of depravity in an effort to normalize those things that God hates. It is seen as transparency, rebellion and, more insidiously, 'authenticity'. This logic seeps its way into our own Muslim psyche and is then covered in an 'Islamic' veneer. We regard sinning in private as hypocrisy and so we publicize our mistakes. The real issue is that publicizing the sin is not even to seek help or to talk about our struggles, but for the sake of this ill-defined 'authenticity.' However, the Prophet ﷺ taught us:

> *'All of my nation will be forgiven except the mujāhirūn (those who sin openly and/or publicize their sins). It is a part of sinning*

> *openly when a man does something at night, then the following morning when Allah has concealed his sin, he says to someone, 'I did such and such last night,' when all night his Lord has concealed him and the next morning he uncovers what Allah had concealed.'* [Bukhārī and Muslim]

This hadith refers to talking about our missteps and normalizing them or gossiping about them, rather than talking about them to ask for advice or seek help. If we feel guilty that people might think that we are better than we really are, we should emulate Abū Bakr al-Ṣiddīq, the closest Companion of the Prophet ﷺ, who supplicated: 'O Allah, You know me better than I know myself, and I know myself better than these people who praise me. Make me better than what they think of me, and forgive those sins of mine of which they have no knowledge, and do not hold me responsible for what they say.' Indeed, the Andalusian scholar Ibn Ḥazm has an entire section in his book, *Mudāwat al-Nufūs,* on being concerned with Allah's words, rather than the people – whether what they say about us is good or bad.

Am I supposed to live in a constant state of guilt because I am always doing wrong?

For some of us, when we hear about sin and forgiveness, it does not fill us with hope, but rather with dread. Talking about sin in the modern world is seen as outdated and negative; indeed, it becomes a source of hopelessness. Today's messaging tells us that we are already good; if we directly hurt others then we should apologize, but our personal failings are our own – they have nothing to do with God.

Our religion does not operate on either extreme premise – that there is no sin at all, on the one hand, or that committing sin defines us forever. Rather, we are told that human beings have a choice to do good deeds or bad. When we do bad deeds – deliberately, or out of ignorance or forgetfulness – God tells us how to rectify that fault, to give us hope. And it is inevitable that we will make mistakes, because we are not perfect. This hope enables us to see that we can still be with God and that we can always become better. As the scholar Timothy Winters stated, 'True religion invites us to become better people. False religion tells us that this has already occurred.'[28] The purpose of knowing that God is the Most Forgiving is to empower us to change. It benefits us physically, emotionally, and – of course – spiritually.

It is hard to turn to someone after making a mistake – usually due to embarrassment or fear – but we are invited to do just that with God. It is a testimony to our relationship with Him that we are even able to turn to Him to ask for His covering and His help. Seeking forgiveness also improves our character. We are forced to be humble because we know that we are not perfect and that there is room for improvement. It prevents us being arrogant or looking down on other people because we are focused on rectifying ourselves and recognizing our own flaws. Knowing that God is forgiving should also soften our hearts and make us more forgiving towards other people.

The act of seeking forgiveness from the One who forgives should also change our relationship with bad actions – they do not define us, as long as we try to combat them. Moreover, it should change the way we *think* about our bad deeds. There is now an abundance of psychological research on how setbacks can fuel creativity because we are *forced* to think in new ways. Similarly, when we find it difficult to stop doing a particular sin because we have accustomed ourselves to it and it has become a habit or even part of the wider culture, we have to think of creative alternatives to replace it. Those who socialize around drugs and alcohol, for example, can simply cut themselves off, or they can find a better and more purposeful substitute instead. That act in and of itself has the blessing of God.

[28] Abdal-Hakim Murad, "Contentions 2," Masud.co.uk, accessed January 7, 2017, http://www.masud.co.uk/ISLAM/ahm/contentions2.htm.

Moreover, knowing that God is the Most Forgiving means knowing that He appreciates our effort, and this enables us to focus on those things that are within our control – it is not all or nothing. We will only be asked about whatever we have the ability to change, nothing else. This in itself is empowering because every change – no matter how small – is appreciated.

The benefits of seeking forgiveness

There are also spiritual benefits to seeking forgiveness that are only known in the metaphysical realm:

1. Seeking forgiveness from God brings uncountable blessings. We are told: '*"Ask forgiveness of your Lord. Indeed, He is ever a Perpetual Forgiver. He will send [rain from] the sky upon you in [continuing] showers. And give you increase in wealth and children and provide for you gardens and provide for you rivers."*' [71:10-12]
2. Our hearts are polished and cleansed. The Prophet ﷺ told us: '*When a slave commits a sin, a black spot appears on his heart, but if he gives it up, seeks forgiveness and repents, his heart will be cleansed.*' [Tirmidhī]
3. It opens the doors of relief from hardship. The Prophet ﷺ told us: '*The one who (regularly) seeks forgiveness, Allah will relieve him of every burden, and make from every discomfort an outlet, and He will provide for him from (sources) he never could imagine.*' [Abū Dāwūd]

Living with these names

1. Reflect on your state

While we are taught to constantly seek forgiveness verbally, it truly starts in the heart. Sometimes we say blessed words without considering what they mean. For this reason, it is important to reflect on our states and actions, in order to become more aware of our reality, and what we need to do to get better. This ensures that we are always evolving for the better, because we are always seeking to improve.

Some of us may worry as we struggle with bad thoughts. But the Prophet ﷺ reminds us that, *'Verily, Allah has pardoned my nation for their bad thoughts within themselves as long as they do not speak of them or act upon them.'* [Muslim] We might all battle with bad or unsavory thoughts, but the most important thing is that we do not act upon them. Indeed, we are rewarded for the act of resisting acting upon them. The more we work upon diminishing these thoughts by ensuring that what we allow to enter through our senses is wholesome, as well as being with righteous company, the easier it is to transform ourselves internally, God willing.

2. *Ask for forgiveness in abundance*

One of the best ways to seek forgiveness was taught to us by our beloved Prophet ﷺ. He said:

> *'O Allah! You are my Lord! None has the right to be worshiped but You. You created me and I am Your slave, and I am faithful to my covenant and my promise as much as I can. I seek refuge with You from all the evil I have done. I acknowledge before You all the blessings You have bestowed upon me, and I confess to You all my sins. So I entreat You to forgive my sins, for nobody can forgive sins except You.'*

He also said of this supplication: *'Whoever says it during the day with firm faith in it, and dies on the same day before the evening, he will be from the people of Paradise; and if somebody recites it at night with firm faith in it, and dies before the morning, he will be from the people of Paradise.'* [Bukhārī]

This supplication is so powerful because it is an admission of our faults in the face of all the blessings we have been given, as well as an expression of hope because we truly know that He forgives, and that He is the only One who forgives in such a way. Most human beings would say, 'after all I have done for this person, he or she has the audacity to treat me this way!' and would not forgive after the first or second mistake. Not Allah. He is the Perpetual Forgiver who *loves* to forgive and love us when we choose to return.

We should accustom ourselves to seeking forgiveness as the Prophet ﷺ did, multiple times in a day. Indeed, God describes the righteous who are rewarded with Paradise as *'those who say, "Our Lord, we believe, so forgive us our sins and protect us from suffering in the Fire," those who are steadfast, truthful, truly devout, who give [in God's cause] and pray before dawn for forgiveness.'* [3:16-17]

3. Go to God with good deeds

Part of seeking forgiveness is to try to make up for the bad deeds with good. Indeed, it is the good that we do that can cause us to be forgiven. We are told in the Qur'an to *'establish prayer at the two ends of the day and at the approach of the night. Indeed, good deeds do away with misdeeds. That is a reminder for those who remember.'* [11:114] This was revealed after an incident in which a man felt extremely guilty for kissing a woman to whom he was not married. He did not persist in his action – he most definitely did not seek to justify it or blame her – but took responsibility and sought forgiveness; however, he still felt bad. So, Allah revealed this verse to remind him (and us!) to do good after seeking forgiveness and stopping the sin. Indeed, doing good is a way of getting out of the paralysis of guilt. Some of us might believe that we cannot do any good because we committed a heinous sin, and our good just won't be accepted. But Allah reminds us that good deeds can do away with the bad.

4. Be in gatherings of the remembrance of God

As much as Islam is about our personal relationship with Allah, community is also essential. Our community can aid us in doing good and bringing us closer to Allah. The Prophet ﷺ reminded us that the angels seek out gatherings where people have come together to remember God, and they speak to Allah about those people. Allah then says to the angels: *'You are My witnesses that I have forgiven them.'*

One of the angels will reply: 'So-and-so is not really one of them; he came for some other reason.' And Allah will respond, *'They were all in the gathering, and not one of them will be excluded (from forgiveness).'* [Bukhārī]

A wonderful practice to develop is to come together with friends and family to remember God, His blessings, and learn about Him and His book. Dedicating some time to this brings blessings and forgiveness to the whole gathering.

5. Forgive others if you want God to forgive you

We are taught to treat people the way we would love for God to treat us. When Allah advised Abū Bakr to forgive his nephew, who had slandered his own daughter, He said, *'They should forgive and forebear. Do you not love that Allah should forgive you? And Allah is Forgiving, Merciful.'* [24: 22]

An important point here is that forgiveness should not be confused with naïveté. If people have wronged us, forgiveness is to forgive in our hearts, meaning not to harbor any ill-will or anger towards them. This often needs time. On the outside, forgiveness is that we continue to treat them well.[29] It does not have to mean that we have to entrust them with our secrets as a show of forgiveness, for example, particularly if they appear not to have changed. We can learn lessons from interacting with people and adjust our behavior accordingly without harboring resentment.

[29] This general rule would not apply in cases of, for example, sexual assault or other forms of serious abuse. Individual circumstances will need to be considered, and it is best to discuss these cases with licensed therapists and trained scholars.

AL-'ALĪM, AL-ḤAKĪM, AL-KHABĪR, 'ĀLIM AL-GHAYB WA AL-SHAHĀDAH – THE ALL-KNOWING, THE MOST WISE, THE ALL-AWARE, KNOWER OF THE UNSEEN AND THE WITNESSED (39-42)

24

AL-'ALĪM, AL-ḤAKĪM, AL-KHABĪR, 'ĀLIM AL-GHAYB WA AL-SHAHĀDAH – THE ALL-KNOWING, THE MOST WISE, THE ALL-AWARE, KNOWER OF THE UNSEEN AND THE WITNESSED (39-42)

'My Lord is most subtle in achieving what He will; He is the All Knowing, the Truly Wise.'

[12:100]

Being in this world and observing its events can bring their own struggles. It is difficult to process what appears to us to be loss, injustice, and a lack of fairness. We might not understand sometimes why something for which we worked hard does not work out, or why 'bad things happen to good people.' We may even be confused when it seems like the occurrences of this world defy what we understand of God's names and attributes. Allah is al-Mujīb, but our specific prayer appears to have been left unanswered. Allah is al-'Adl, but there is much injustice. Allah is al-Raḥīm, but there is so much cruelty.

These are some of the reasons why it is so important to look at Allah's names completely and not divide them. His names complement one another and give us a picture that is more whole, helping us in our relationship with Him and in understanding this world. Indeed, understanding His names and attributes is one of the ways to achieve internal strength and tranquility.

Perfect knowledge

There are certain names that underlie His other names and attributes. The first name is al-'Alīm (the All-Knowing): God knows what is and what could be, what was and what could have been.

Another of Allah's Beautiful Names is al-Khabīr. The Arabic root of this word is *khā-bā-rā*, which means 'to know', 'to be aware of the real inner nature of something', or 'to be an expert in something because you know both the inner and the outer.' Both Al-Ghazālī and Ibn al-Qayyim state that when knowledge (*'ilm*) is related to hidden secrets, it is called awareness (*khibrah*). Thus, God is al-Khabīr (the All-Aware), whose knowledge encompasses both the inner and outer nature of things. He knows not only our actions, but also the state of our hearts. He knows the outward actions that He has ordained and their hidden benefits, which only those who are aware will truly appreciate. The Prophet ﷺ was asked whether God knows what we keep hidden inside of us, in terms of thoughts and feelings, and the Prophet ﷺ answered in the affirmative. [Muslim] Indeed, *'it is God who is All-Knowing and All-Aware.'* [31:34]

While God tells us that He is al-'Alīm and al-Khabīr, which already encompass His knowledge of everything, He emphasizes this point to us further with another name. The name 'Ālim al-Ghayb wa al-Shahādah (Knower of the Unseen and the Witnessed) alerts us to the fact that there are things that we cannot reach with our senses – they are in a realm we cannot access – and God knows them. Part of our frustration with see around us is that we assume that the outward is all there is. But just as human beings have both an inward and outward reality, so too do the events, happenings, and experiences of this world. Allah tells us in the Qur'an:

> *'He has the keys to the unseen: no one knows them but Him. He knows all that is in the land and sea. No leaf falls without His knowledge, nor is there a single grain in the darkness of the*

earth, or anything, fresh or withered, that is not written in a clear Record.' [6:59]

God emphasizes His knowledge of the different realms, as He tells us, *'Such is He who knows all that is unseen as well as what is seen, the Almighty, the Merciful.'* [32:6]

For this reason, we need to take a step back when we assume that we know all there is to know and make a judgment based on that. This is especially so when things do not go our way. Allah tells us: *'You may dislike something although it is good for you, or like something although it is bad for you: God knows and you do not.'* [2:216]

This does not mean that we cannot judge things at all. Most of the time we need to act upon what we see; this is why we have faculties, and why we have been told about right and wrong. But we should not assume that we know is all there is to know.

Of course, awareness of everything does not tell us about what one does with that knowledge. Allah's knowledge includes acting upon it in the best way.

The Most Wise

Al-Ḥakīm is the Most Wise. For human beings, knowledge does not necessary result in wisdom. There are intelligent scientists who are impulsive, smart businessmen who make the wrong decisions, and intellectuals who cannot even relate to other people's lives. Many of us may know people who know a lot, but we would not describe them as wise.

Thus, there are two branches related to acting with wisdom: one is knowing, and the other is acting with this knowledge. Allah is both the All-Knowing and the Most-Wise – He possesses all the knowledge and, as al-Nabulsī states, He 'does the proper thing in the proper way in the proper place and the proper time.'

Whenever Allah decrees something in our lives, we must have certainty that it has been decreed with all His knowledge and His wisdom. So, whenever things do not go our way, or as we assumed they would, we need to put our trust in the One who truly knows what is best. How many of us can look back and see that a hardship, a closed door, or a painful memory, actually ended up providing some benefit in the long term? And even if we cannot see the wisdom now, our knowledge of this name should instill in us the conviction that there truly is wisdom and we will come to know it, whether in this life or the next.

All-Knowing and Forbearing

There is a purpose in how Allah chooses to pair His names. God tells us in the Qur'an that *'God is all knowing and benign [ḥalīm] to all.'* [4:12] He is both al-'Alīm and al-Ḥalīm, meaning that despite His knowing everything about us – our intentions, our actions, our secrets – He does not hasten any punishment but indeed keeps His doors of forgiveness open to us. This name comforts those of us who worry about what we do, and fear that God's knowledge of us means that there is no hope – He reminds us that He is Forbearing and is not out to get us.

The manifestations of knowledge and wisdom

God shows us these attributes in the Qur'an, particularly in the stories of the Prophet Joseph, as well as Moses and al-Khaḍr, and 'Āishah in the incident of *Al-Ifk*, in order to teach us about the nature of His knowledge and wisdom.

The Prophet Joseph had a dream as a child, which he told to his father, the Prophet Jacob. After warning him not to tell his brothers his dream, Jacob said, *'"This is about how your Lord will choose you, teach you to interpret dreams, and perfect His blessing on you and the House of Jacob, just as He perfected it earlier on your forefathers Abraham and Isaac: your Lord is all knowing and wise."'* [12:5]

The Prophet Jacob taught his son that God is All-Knowing and Wise at this crucial juncture. When you know this about your

Lord, you can look at the events that happen in your life through that lens. You can focus on what you need to do, and leave what is outside of your control, always maintaining hope in Allah and faith that He knows best.

Indeed, this is what transpired in the life of Joseph. His brothers wanted to get rid of him, and threw him in a well. There, he was apparently rescued by a caravan of people, who subsequently sold him to a wealthy minister in Egypt. After he grew into a young adult, the wife of the minister tried to seduce him, and went on to accuse *him* of making a pass at her. To justify her actions after the story became the city's gossip, she arranged a dinner in her mansion so all of the aristocratic women could see how beautiful Joseph was – here they exclaimed that he could only be an angel. Joseph was put in prison just to separate him from her and her plotting. He interpreted the dreams of his cellmates, but when one was released, he forgot to advocate for Joseph after he left. Eventually, after years in prison, Joseph was asked to interpret the dream of the king. This finally opened the door for him to occupy a high position in the land before and during the famine.

Joseph, we must remember, was a righteous child. He was beloved to his father. He received a dream informing him of his prophecy. And yet, he went through all these hardships. He spent literally years away from his family, as a slave, and then more years in prison, with people speculating over his virtue.

If one did not know that God is the All-Knowing and the Most Wise, it would be easy to question Him. It would be easy to resent the events that are outside of our control, so much so that we might even think that there is no point in working with the means within our control. But when his family was brought to Joseph in Egypt, and he was reunited with them, Joseph said to his father:

> *'Father, this is the fulfilment of that dream I had long ago. My Lord has made it come true and has been gracious to me –– He released me from prison and He brought you here from the desert*

–– after Satan sowed discord between me and my brothers. My Lord is most subtle in achieving what He will; He is the All Knowing, the Truly Wise." [12:100]

Looking back on his life, Joseph could see God's wisdom in everything that had happened to him. His father had taught him Allah's attributes, and his certainty in them allowed Joseph to remain righteous and steadfast throughout. Looking back on his life, God's wisdom became even more apparent.

This story is not simply about recognizing the wisdom in events after all is said and done. We learn from Jacob to trust in God's wisdom when we are in the midst of hardship. When his sons took their brother Benjamin with them to Egypt, and returned without him, explaining that he had been accused of theft and detained, *'their father said, "No! Your souls have prompted you to do wrong! But it is best to be patient: may God bring all of them back to me –– He alone is the All Knowing, the All Wise."'* [12;83]

Jacob was in the middle of his second crisis – losing another son. But he trusted in God's wisdom. Indeed, as the situation became worse, he increased in hope. He knew that God knew all and He is the Most Wise, so however difficult it was, or appeared to be from the outside, he knew that there was wisdom in the trial – even if he could not see it at that moment.

A similar lesson is found in the story of Moses and al-Khaḍr. Al-Khaḍr was given special knowledge from God that was not known to anyone else – He revealed part of the Unseen to him. Moses asked to travel with al-Khaḍr so that he could learn from him, and al-Khaḍr asked a question that is directed to us as well: *'"How could you be patient in matters beyond your knowledge?"'* [18:68] Moses promised that he would be patient, and traveled with al-Khaḍr on three journeys.

In the first journey, some poor fishermen helped Moses and al-Khaḍr cross the river on their boat. Instead of helping them, al-Khaḍr damaged their boat, and Moses was horrified. Al-Khaḍr replied, *"'Did I not tell you that you would never be able to bear with me patiently?'"* [18:72] Al-Khaḍr continued doing things that baffled Moses – causing the death of a child of good parents, mending a wall in a village whose people were inhospitable to them – to the point that Moses was not able to be patient. And so, al-Khaḍr finally explained: *"'I will tell you the meaning of the things you could not bear with patiently: the boat belonged to some needy people who made their living from the sea and I damaged it because I knew that coming after them was a king who was seizing every [serviceable] boat by force.'"* [18:79]

Al-Khaḍr knew that there was a king who was confiscating functioning boats, hence, the damage meant that the king would not take their boat; the fishermen would be able to fix it, and then continue to use it. He knew that the child would grow up to be of the worst transgressors, and his passing before this was a mercy to the parents, as difficult as it was for them. The mending of the wall was not about the hostile villagers at all, but rather about two orphans whose father had left them a treasure underneath the collapsing wall. Moses, of course, had no access to the Unseen; hence, he reacted in the way many of us would. But God teaches us that there is an unseen realm, and He knows what is in it. It may be that something outwardly seems bad, but through it, we are being protected from an even greater harm.

Finally, in Sūrat al-Nūr, we are told of a great slander that was propagated against ʿĀishah, the beloved wife of the Prophet Muhammad ﷺ, and a righteous Companion, Ṣafwān bin al-Muʿaṭṭal al-Sulamī. Ṣafwān had helped ʿĀishah to return when she was accidentally left behind after the end of a military expedition. When they returned to Madinah, some of the hypocrites saw them, and spread a slanderous rumor about them. This continued for over a month, and even involved many of the virtuous Companions. There was discord in the community. Gossip spread. One might wonder why the Prophet ﷺ did not receive revelation to declare her innocence immediately and put a stop to the smears and speculations, rather than allow them to circulate.

But Allah says, '*do not consider it a bad thing for you [people]; it was a good thing.*' [24:11] The community was meant to learn some important lessons. It is worth quoting the entire section of the Chapter here:

> '*When you heard the lie, why did believing men and women not think well of their own people and declare, "This is obviously a lie"? And why did the accusers not bring four witnesses to it? If they cannot produce such witnesses, they are the liars in God's eyes. If it were not for God's bounty and mercy towards you in this world and the next, you would already have been afflicted by terrible suffering for indulging in such talk. When you took it up with your tongues, and spoke with your mouths things you did not know [to be true], you thought it was trivial but to God it was very serious. When you heard the lie, why did you not say, "We should not repeat this -- God forbid! -- It is a monstrous slander"? God warns you never to do anything like this again, if you are true believers.*' [24:12-17]

Through this ordeal, Allah was teaching the Muslims lessons about thinking well of others, defending the honor of people, the status of gossip and slander as great and severe sins, and not to belittle that which God has deemed grave. The section ends with, '*God makes His messages clear to you: God is all knowing, all wise.*' [24:18]

While this lesson was taught to the Companions so that both they and we can heed God's warning about such matters, it is unfortunate that we see these very same problems (and worse) rife in some communities, with baseless accusations becoming rampant and amplified on social media. We should ask ourselves who we are when gossip spreads: are we of those '*think well of their own people and declare, "This is obviously a lie"*? Or are we the '*accusers [who did] not bring four witnesses*'? Or those who speak about '*things you did not know [to be true]*? Or those who said, '*We should not repeat this -- God forbid! -- It is a monstrous slander*'?

And if we are of those who defend others against such lies, yet still feel disheartened that it appears that accusers are getting away with their defamation, we should remember that, '*A painful punishment waits in this world and the next for those who like indecency to spread among the believers: God knows and you do not.*' [24:19]

There is another subtle point in this story that highlights God's wisdom and kindness. Through most of the trial, 'Āishah was oblivious to what was happening. She narrates herself that, 'After we returned to Medina, I became ill for a month. The people were propagating the forged statements of the slanderers while I was unaware of anything of all that.' [Bukhārī] She only suffered the emotional pain of knowing what people said for a short period before it was revealed by Allah, the Most High, the Most Wise, that what was being said was a terrible slander.

Her illness at that time might have been viewed as something that 'just happened'. However, it shielded her from knowing what was being said for most of the ordeal, to protect her from that pain while the events ran their course. Sometimes we go through periods of discomfort or hurt in one part of our life, not realizing that God is actually protecting our hearts from something that would have been far worse in a seemingly unrelated other part. He is indeed the Most Wise, the Most Merciful, the All-Aware of what our hearts are capable of handling.

The Fully-Aware who created the rules

Part of having faith in these names, which cover every different type of knowledge – hidden and manifest, in the physical or the metaphysical realm, of our hearts or of our limbs – is to have certainty in God's commandments. It is to know that what He has ordained for us benefits us, and what He has prohibited is harmful.

Trusting in God's knowledge and wisdom is to know that what God has decreed is undoubtedly good for us, and what He has prohibited is unquestionably bad for us. His commandments and prohibitions cover what is beneficial in this world and the next, for both our external and internal realities. When we struggle with an obligation or a prohibition because our modern mode of living tells us that these rules are outdated, we need to go back to the One who ordained these rules. Allah, in His mercy and wisdom, has also created certain exceptions and flexibility – but our starting point is to know that whatever has been ordained with certainty (rather than any doubtful matters) comes from the Most Knowledgeable, Wise and Merciful Lord. This same conviction should apply when we ask for or work towards something and do not get it; we have to remember that we see the outward, and not the inward reality.

Indeed, we need to have full faith that our supplications and the tears we shed in the night have averted harm from befalling us, and opened doors to greater goods. We need to know that the restrictions placed upon our actions and behavior have actually *protected* us in many instances. God tells us that *'man prays for harm, just as he prays for good: man is ever hasty.'* [17:11] This haste sometimes prevents us from seeing the hidden wisdom in a situation.

Pay attention to the hidden within our hearts

No one can truly know what is in our hearts – for better or worse. We might present a perfect picture to the world, but internally, we harbor ill-intent. Or on the other side, we might appear to be completely unextraordinary, but we are of God's special people. The key is the state of our hearts, which only al-Khabīr knows.

While sitting in the mosque, the Prophet ﷺ informed the Companions that they could see one of the people of Paradise. It is worth emphasizing that the man he pointed out was not one of the well-known or famous Companions. Naturally, the Companions all wanted to know what this man did to earn such a station. One of them decided to find out, spending a few days with the man to observe his actions. But he could only observe his outward, and what he saw was not out of the ordinary. Nothing was particularly remarkable about him. It could be said that the Companion was disappointed. But he then learned something: this man did not allow himself to sleep at night before ensuring that he let go of any grudge he held against people and forgave them for any wrongs. This was a completely internal action, but it earned him a place in Paradise.

An important point to make is that there should be some congruence between our internal and external states. The Companions did not ignore what was obligatory upon them with the excuse that their heart was sound; such a statement is actually a sign of an ill heart. The Companions prayed, sacrificed their worldly possessions and always strived to be better, but the state of their hearts gave life and true meaning to their external actions.

Living with these names

1. Search for the lessons in life

Having certainty in these names means knowing that there is wisdom in the events that occur in this life, even when they are not immediately apparent. This includes learning from our own mistakes – it is from God's wisdom that He enables us to see the error of our ways, take responsibility for it and work to rectify ourselves.

2. Remember that there is an unseen realm

God knows all that is inaccessible to us. He has revealed some matters of the metaphysical realm that is beneficial for us to know, and has left others hidden. We are thereby given the drive to continue doing deeds that do not appear to give us material or immediate benefit; for example, we are told that giving charity prevents calamities from happening and, indeed, that charity never decreases wealth. This is in opposition to what we see materially –

we cannot physically see calamities being prevented and the money in our bank account or our wallet decreases the moment we give – but our certainty in God's promise ensures that we continue to give, even when we do not have much. Indeed, we know that the money will be returned to us and increased, whether in this life or the next. Moreover, sometimes what is beneficial is hidden within what outwardly appears to be harmful, and vice versa, just as we learned in the story of Moses and al-Khaḍr. We must operate on the basis of thinking well of God – that everything has a purpose, and that God treats us with His mercy – as well as taking responsibility for our actions when there is a correlation (or outright cause-and-effect!) between our bad deeds or misjudgments, and the misfortunes that befall us.

3. Be humble

We all know our own faults better than others, but there are some faults that we do not notice in ourselves, although God knows them. It is important to keep ourselves grounded, and know that no matter how good we think we have become, Allah is All-Knowing of our internal state and we can always improve. The supplication of the angels in the Qur'an is beautiful in this regard: '*They said, "Exalted are You; we have no knowledge except what You have taught us. Indeed, it is You who is the Knowing, the Wise."*' [2:32]

It is important to always attribute what is good to God, because truly all good is from Him. And as we know, whoever is grateful, God increases them in favor [14:7].

4. Be wary of those who claim to know the Unseen

God's emphasis on His knowledge of what is inaccessible to us should make us wary of those who claim to know the Unseen. This matter is so severe that the Prophet ﷺ warned us, '*Whoever goes to a fortune-teller and asks him about something, his prayer will not be accepted for forty nights.*' [Muslim] Indeed, we are also told that whoever '*goes to a fortune teller and believes what he says, has disbelieved in that which God has revealed to Muhammad."* [Abū Dāwūd] It is only God who has true and complete knowledge of the Unseen, even if a fortune-teller appears to be accurate. The Prophet ﷺ stated that even if what the fortune-teller predicts does indeed come to pass, *'they mix more than a hundred lies with it.'* [Bukhārī and Muslim]

5. Increase your knowledge of God

Al-Ghazālī advised that if one knows everything but does not know God, he cannot be a wise person.

We are encouraged to increase our knowledge, as Allah instructs us in the Qur'an: *'and say, "My Lord, increase me in knowledge."'* [20:114] Indeed, Ibn al-Qayyim stated that the All-Knowing loves those who are knowledgeable, and gives His knowledge to those whom He loves.[30]

So, it is important to keep learning in general, in order to better ourselves in this life, but it is equally – if not more – important to keep up our religious knowledge and knowledge of God, because that knowledge brings us closer to Him, our goal in the Hereafter, and also helps us to put this life into context.

6. Ask God for wisdom and seek it

Allah says in the Qur'an, *'He gives wisdom to whoever He will. Whoever is given wisdom has truly been given much good, but only those with insight bear this in mind.'* [2:269] Much of the time, people are obsessed with acquiring more knowledge, whether that is in the religious or the worldly sciences. But although point 5 emphasized the importance of learning, knowledge by itself does not benefit us if we do not know how to employ it. We should strive to be wise, rather than simply collecting information for the sake of it. Moreover, we should seek wisdom wherever we can find it because where Allah has placed wisdom, He has placed good. The Prophet ﷺ taught us, *'The statement of wisdom is the lost property of the believer,*

[30] Al-Ashqar, *Sharḥ Ibn Al-Qayyim Li Asmā' Allāh al-Ḥusnā*, 79.

so wherever he finds it then he has a right to it.' [Tirmidhī] We can benefit from matters outside our tradition, especially if we ensure that we leave out what is not beneficial and only take what is good.

7. Know yourself and work on your heart

Just as we work on our external, we need to work on the internal realities of our hearts. The Prophet ﷺ said, *'Verily, Allah does not look at your appearance or wealth, but rather He looks at your hearts and actions.'* [Muslim]

Knowing that God looks at our hearts – indeed, that only God truly sees our hearts – should drive us to cleanse our hearts of any impurities. Indeed, just like the Companion mentioned above, it can be a secret – one that nobody else knows – that elevates us to a high station with God, simply because we work on the state of our hearts.

8. Understand the inner meanings of outer actions

One of the reasons that we do not connect to our acts of worship is that we focus on the form, to the exclusion of the spirit – we focus on the outward and forget the inward. But all acts of worship have an internal element. Prayer is elevated through our devotion and connection to Allah. Fasting can be transformed from a deed restricted to abstaining from food and drink, to a fasting of the heart. Zakat (obligatory almsgiving) is not simply a donation of money, but an act of gratitude and care. We should care for the internal elements just as much as we do the rituals themselves.

AL-ḤAKAM – THE JUDGE (43)

25

AL-ḤAKAM – THE JUDGE (43)

'Is there any better judge than God for those of firm faith?'

[5:50]

God is al-Ḥakam, and the Prophet ﷺ said: *'Indeed, Allah is the Arbitrator (al-Ḥakam) and to Him is the judgment.'* [Abū Dāwūd]

The Arabic root of al-Ḥakam, *ḥā-kāf-mīm*, means 'to prevent' or 'to restrain'. A ruler is named a *ḥākim* because he prevents opponents from transgressing against one another; he decrees and judges in all affairs. A *ḥukm* is a judgment or decree that is just. *Ḥikmah* (wisdom) also means 'the prevention of ignorance.'

God's name al-Ḥakam means that He is the ultimate arbitrator and judge, whose rulings and decrees no one can overturn, as al-Ghazālī points out.

Al-Ḥakam in this world

The Prophet ﷺ said: *'The reality of faith is knowing that what has passed you by was not going to befall you; and that what has befallen you was not going to pass you by.'* [Ṭabarānī]

One of the basic tenets of the Islamic faith is belief in *'divine determination (qadar) both in its good and in its evil aspects.'* [Muslim] This is oftentimes a confusing topic for many, and some do not know how to reconcile this principle with planning and action.

The Prophet ﷺ was asked, 'O Messenger of Allah, the *ruqyah* (recitations of the Qur'an for healing) we use, the medicines which heal us, and our fortifications against the enemy; do they repel anything from the decree of Allah?' The Prophet ﷺ replied, '*They are part of the decree of Allah.*' [Tirmidhī]

We have been commanded to strive. Indeed, Allah says in the Qur'an: '*And that there is not for man except that [good] for which he strives. And that his effort is going to be seen – then he will be recompensed for it with the fullest recompense.*' [53:39-41]

This teaches us something very important. Our obligations relate to our efforts and the state of our hearts. This is what we will be asked about, and thus what we should focus on. We will not be asked about God's decree – that is none of our business. Thus, it is very important not to be consumed trying to figure out what the future divine decree is, and not to rely on the excuse that 'everything is decreed' to avoid responsibilities. Many people ask, 'how do I know what I am supposed to do?' Being in this world means that we have to strive to make the best decisions, using all the means we have been given – knowing what our religious obligations are, asking advice from those with wisdom about the issues we face, identifying the opportunities as well as the potential drawbacks when making a decision concerning our lives, and then deciding. We will be asked about all of these steps, rather than the outcome itself. Whatever ends up happening is from the decree of Allah. If it works out, we praise and thank Him, and if it does not, we still praise Him, show patience, and learn from the lessons.

Indeed, when the Prophet ﷺ decided that is was time to leave Makkah, using the information that he knew at the time, he resolved to ask help from the people of Ṭā'if. If anyone could have accessed the Unseen in order to avoid making mistakes or 'wasting' effort on something that would bear no fruit, it would have been the Prophet Muhammad ﷺ – he could have asked the angel Gabriel to ask Allah to reveal to him what would happen. He could have been told, 'do not waste your time on the people of Ṭā'if; it is Madina that is decreed for you'. But that is not the point of being in this world, and not what it means to have certainty in divine decree. He did everything required of him as a human being, and what ultimately passed was from the decree of Allah. There was a lesson in Ṭā'if for us: seeing our Prophet ﷺ strive and sacrifice for the truth, so that we would be Muslim today.

There are certain issues that are far above human comprehension. The Messenger of Allah ﷺ heard some Companions arguing about the divine decree, and became angry. He said, '*With this I have commanded you? With this I was sent to you? Verily, the people before you were destroyed when they argued over this matter. I am determined for you not to argue over it.*' [Tirmidhī]

What *is* required of us is to strive in the ways that Allah has instructed, because that is the effort that '*is going to be seen.*' [53:40] We sometimes spend a lot of time trying to figure out what God has decreed, not realizing that a big part of believing in the decree of God means accepting what has occurred in the past, those events which we cannot change. As for the future, we need to work for whatever it is we want to achieve.

Indeed, 'Umar ibn al-Khaṭṭāb reprimanded some people who cited the following hadith of the Prophet ﷺ as an excuse be complacent and avoid working for their provision: '*If you were to rely upon Allah with reliance due to him, he would provide for you just as he provides for the birds. They go out in the morning with empty stomachs and return full.*' [Tirmidhī] 'Umar said to them, 'Let not one of you refrain from working for his provision, supplicating to Allah to provide while he knows that the sky does not rain gold and silver.' They key in the saying of the Prophet ﷺ is that the birds '*go out in the morning*' – they do not stay in their nests and wait for whatever was decreed for them to simply come to them.

Understanding that Allah is al-Ḥakam means working with our limbs and understanding in our hearts this basic truth: '*Know that if the whole world were to gather together in order to help you, they would not be able to help you except if Allah had written so. And if the whole world were to gather together in order to harm you, they would not harm you except if Allah had written so. The pens have been lifted, and the pages are dry.'* [Tirmidhī]

Allah teaches us this through the example of the Prophet ﷺ. When some of the people of Makkah plotted to assassinate him, the Prophet ﷺ was not oblivious. He did not sit back and wait for his would-be assassins to execute their plans, or expect that Allah would simply bestow upon him miracles. Our Prophet ﷺ was sent as an example for us; he strategized meticulously. 'Alī, his cousin, took his place in his bed to buy time, while the Prophet ﷺ escaped with Abū Bakr.

Allah says of this in the Qur'an: *'And [remember, O Muhammad], when those who disbelieved plotted against you to restrain you or kill you or evict you [from Makkah]. But they plan, and Allah plans. And Allah is the best of planners.'* [8:30]

The Prophet ﷺ made it safely to Madinah, despite his would-be assassins being fast on his heels. So, with our physical bodies, we work, like the Prophet ﷺ worked. In our hearts, we know that whatever Allah decrees will come to pass. Knowing that it is our responsibility to put in the effort and the outcome is in Allah's Hands enables us not to lament the things that happen to us, particularly those things outside of our control. Allah tells us: *'God achieves His purpose; God has set a due measure for everything.'* [65:3]

However, we can and should always take lessons in general from events, especially from whatever happens as a result of our shortcomings. We have to realize that Allah has placed us in this world and given us means for a reason. When we fail to utilize them in the best way, Allah might teach us through our failure to achieve what we wanted. And that is part of Allah's decree, as a result of our shortcoming. But God is also the Most Wise: learning from our failures teaches us lessons that we can take forward, that will protect us from future pain, and perhaps we would have never attained this understanding had we not learned from Allah's decree. Indeed, most people who achieve something great in this world are those who learn from their experiences and mistakes, and use those failures to fuel their success. If one with no or little faith can know this, then what about us?

Moreover, Allah's decrees are not necessarily 'fixed'. He may choose to change the decree. The Prophet ﷺ told us: *'Nothing can change the Divine decree except supplication.'* [Aḥmad] He also told us, *'Supplications are beneficial with regard to what has been decreed and what has not been decreed. The supplication meets the calamity that has been decreed and wrestles with it, until the Day of Resurrection.'* [Ṭabarānī]

The truth is that we do not know God's decree – those things that cannot be overturned – nor we will not be asked about His decree. When we desire something, we can pray to Allah for it and work towards it as much as we can. We are rewarded for our supplication to Him, our physical effort, and our hope in Him

Indeed, Islam is submission to God. Part of submission is that we work within our means – because we have been commanded to do so, and given certain means – as well as understanding that ultimately God decides what He allows to pass. Some make the mistake of seeing planning as the opposite of relying on Allah, whereas in fact they are complementary when viewed under the umbrella of submission to Him.

Delays and detours are an inevitable part of life, both literally and metaphorically. Many times, planning can help, but there may be times when it does not. Yet God shows you that He will always get you to where you need to be, although it may not be where you want to be at that time. It may not happen how you envisaged it, but there is always a lesson to be learned from the Most Wise. Understanding the nature of al-Ḥakam – that He is the Most Just, Merciful, and Wise – enables us to see beyond the outward. The Messenger of Allah ﷺ said, *'I am amazed by the believer. Verily, Allah does not decree anything for the believer except what is good for him.'* [Aḥmad]

We learn from this to search for the lessons in Allah's decree, and to think well of Him always. Even if what we see before us outwardly appears to be bad, we need to remember that there is a metaphysical realm. Perhaps our patience in the face of a calamity that has been decreed is what will enter us into Paradise. Perhaps all our long prayers for something that did not manifest in this world are granted to us manifold in the next world. Thus, we focus on what we *can* control – because Allah has given us that control – and leave what we cannot.

The commandments of al-Ḥakam

According to Ibn al-Qayyim, God's rulings and decrees are part of is His *ḥukm*. God says: *'[Say], "Shall I seek any judge other than God, when it is He who has sent down for you [people] the Scripture, clearly explained?"'* [5:50]

God has placed upon us certain responsibilities. We are commanded to commit to the pillars of submission: the testimony of faith, prayer, fasting in Ramadan, almsgiving (zakat) and pilgrimage (Hajj). We must strive to perfect our character, work for justice and remove oppression; we are commanded to invite people to the beauty of our religion and to seek knowledge – all in submission to the Most High.

Part of believing in God as al-Ḥakam is to know that these rulings came from the Most Wise and the Most Just, committing to them to the best of our ability even when we do not understand them or when we feel down. It is easy to say 'I am not feeling my prayer,' and succumb to the urge not to pray; it is easy to think, 'I am in love with someone, but we can't get married right now; why should we deny ourselves an intimate relationship when are in love?' – yet we must strive to uphold His rulings.

Of course, this does not mean that we do not seek to understand God's rulings, nor does this apply to matters in which there is a considerable difference of opinion and there is more than one possible ruling to take. Rather, this refers to the established responsibilities God has decreed upon us.

Al-Ḥakam on the Day of Judgment

'Say, "God! Creator of the heavens and earth! Knower of all that is hidden and all that is open, You will judge between Your servants regarding their differences."' [39:46]

We all know that we will return to God. On the Day of Judgment, He will be the ultimate Judge. He will judge between us regarding that upon which we used to differ, and everyone will receive their just reward. Knowing this should inspire hope and vigilance – hope, because we know that God will rule according to wisdom, justice and mercy; and vigilance, because we will be asked about what we used to do, and so we should ensure that we take care of our responsibilities and avoid oppressing others.

Allah reminds us: *'God decides – no one can reverse His decision – and He is swift in reckoning.'* [13:41] He also tells us, *'Then you will all return to Me and I will judge between you regarding your differences.'* [3:55]

Remembering that we will ultimately be judged by al-Ḥakam can help to make the trials of this world easier. He sees our struggles and knows what we go through, internally and externally, and He appreciates our efforts for Him. He will judge with true justice and equity. Moreover, it should remind us not to be blinded by the judgment of other people: they only judge in this world. We should strive for what is beyond. Whatever discomfort we are made to feel as a result of our commitment to God's way should be assuaged by the knowledge that we will be judged by the standards of al-Ḥakam, and not of those who seemingly wield power in this world.

On human judging

Understanding that al-Ḥakam created the most perfect rules and will judge us according to our efforts in adhering to them should cause us to critically reflect on a popular phrase: 'Only God can judge me'.

On the face of it, this is true. Indeed, al-Ḥakam will judge us and only His judgment matters. We should not be concerned with the judgment of people when we follow the commandments of the Almighty. But the context in which this phrase is usually used is when one chooses *not* to follow the commandments of God and is criticized by others for it. Understanding al-Ḥakam should make us pause, whether we are the ones criticizing or the ones being criticized. We can learn something in this regard from the story of Korah (Qārūn) in the Qur'an.

Korah was given much wealth and riches, but he transgressed. His people advised him:

> *'Do not exult. Indeed, Allah does not like the exultant. But seek, through that which Allah has given you, the home of the Hereafter; and [yet], do not forget your share of the world. And do good as Allah has done good to you. And desire not corruption in the land. Indeed, Allah does not like corrupters.'* [28:76-77]

Korah became defensive. His response to them was, '*I was only given it because of knowledge I have.*' [28:78]

Korah's misdeeds mattered more because they were in public – the Qur'an tells us, '*he came out before his people in his adornment.*' [28:79] Whether we like it or not, or think it is fair or not, being in the public eye means that we have a degree of influence over others. We cannot hide behind justifications of not choosing or not claiming to be role models. Al-Ḥakam will judge us for those actions but also for the fact that they influenced people – positively or negatively. The Prophet ﷺ said, '*Whoever introduces a good practice that is followed, he will receive its reward and a reward equivalent to that of those who follow it, without that detracting from their reward in the slightest. And whoever introduces a bad practice that is followed, he will receive its sin and a burden of sin equivalent to that of those who follow it, without that detracting from their burden in the slightest.*' [Muslim] A similar hadith is mentioned with regards those who call to guidance and to misguidance [Muslim].

Indeed, the Qur'an tells us how the people were influenced by Korah, '*Those who desired the worldly life said, "Oh, would that we had like what was given to Qarun. Indeed, he is one of great fortune."*' [28:78] But those with knowledge never stopped advising: '*those who had been given knowledge said, "Woe to you! The reward of Allah is better for he who believes and does righteousness. And none are granted it except the patient."*' [28:80]

We can learn from this story that there are three types of responsibilities, and they are all connected to how we relate to al-Ḥakam in our respective roles: the responsibility of those with knowledge; the responsibility of the 'influenced'; and the responsibility of the 'influencer'.

As for the first, the responsibility of those with knowledge – those who know the rulings (*aḥkām* – from the same root as His name al-Ḥakam) – is to advise those who are committing the wrongful or doubtful actions and educate them, as well as the general public. This is a great responsibility that comes with accusations of being judgmental or out-of-touch. But just like those with knowledge in the story of Korah, the advice should be given with care and concern for those being advised, and not from a place of superiority, arrogance, or even envy. Those with knowledge pointed out what was wrong with Korah's behavior ('*do not exult*' and '*desire not corruption in the land*') and what Korah should be concerned about instead ('*seek the home of the Hereafter*' and '*do good as Allah has done good to you*'), not forgetting to let him know that He should use at least a portion of what was given to him in this world to seek the Hereafter ('*do not forget your share of the world*'). Moreover, we have to remember that this was their advice to *Korah*, who had transgressed against others, and not one who was well-intentioned or ignorant and messed up. Being in public is not easy and, while the good that people do is out in the open, so are their shortcomings. Therefore, our advice to people should be clear and decisive, but it should also be tempered with wisdom and love for the person being advised; while it is out of our hands whether people choose to follow the advice, we do not want to contribute to them *not* following the advice due to harshness. The scholar Ibn Taymiyyah said that there are three principles of enjoining good and forbidding evil, and they are: knowledge, gentleness, and patience. The priority is for sincere advice to be given in private; no one should revel in the public shaming of a believer, particularly when there was a better route that would have achieved the same result. Moreover, it requires an awareness of not just the person committing the wrongs, but who he or she is affecting. The people of knowledge addressed those who were mesmerized by what Korah had: '*Woe to you! The reward of Allah is better for he who believes and does righteousness. And none are granted it except the patient.*' [28:80]

As for those being influenced, we must always be aware of what we take in and allow to reach our hearts. Being absorbed by the worldly life can diminish the station of the rules and guidelines set by al-Ḥakam in our hearts, and we should seek knowledge and be in good company in order to be aware of what God has decreed. We have to remember that we will not be judged by the standards of this world, but rather by the standards set by al-Ḥakam, and we should not be of those who solely '*desired the worldly life*' [28:80]. Only we are responsible for our actions, and we will not be able to blame popular figures when we stand before the Ultimate Judge. They may be responsible for what they do with their influence, but we will be asked about our actions and choosing to follow their example, rather than the example set by al-Ḥakam. It is important to curate what we allow ourselves to see and hear, particularly when we are bombarded with immorality and dubious matters (see chapters 26 and 35 for advice on this point).

Finally, there are those of us committing wrongs in public, and/or who may have a degree of influence over others, or are outright 'influencers'. When we are criticized for our mistakes, especially those in public, our first reaction might be to get defensive. It is exceptionally difficult to accept harsh criticism or mean-spirited comments robed in religious garb. We never claimed to be saints, and we are not responsible for the actions of others. Indeed, the Qur'an itself says, '*no soul shall bear the burden of another.*' [53:38] We might resist the reproach by stating, 'only God can judge me'. This may be true, but knowledge of and love for al-Ḥakam should cause us to truly care about how He will judge us and to reflect on how well we follow His decrees – meaning we should truly be concerned that 'only God will judge us' as opposed to using this phrase to shield ourselves from the judgment of others. We should constantly seek advice and realize that, particularly in relation to being in public and assuming that role, we have influence over people's ideas and consequent behaviors. We might not be held to account for other people's sins, but we are responsible for the degree to which we influenced them to commit that sin, particularly when we introduce something new that they had never heard about or known of before. Thus, we need to ask ourselves whether we encourage the following of God's rules or discourage it by flouting His decrees and even justify doing so – even if it is in subtle or unintended ways. We have to guard against labelling any religious advice as an attack from the so-called 'haram police', simply because it agitates our lower self (the *nafs*). Indeed, it would behoove us to take Ibn Ḥazm's counsel, when he said, 'Anyone who criticizes you cares about your friendship. Anyone who makes light of your faults cares nothing about you,' [Mudāwāt al-Nūfūs]. This is because those who make light of our faults do not care about our Hereafter. Indeed, Ibn Ḥazm also said that the way to be free from anxiety is to be concerned with the words of Creator, and leave the words of creation (when they do not benefit us for the Hereafter). We should try as best we can to surround ourselves with or at least have access to those who will counsel us honestly and in good faith, so that we can rectify our actions.

It should go without saying that this does not mean that anyone short of perfect should be condemned. We all struggle, and so whichever category we fall into, we need to have mercy on ourselves and on others, and remember that as long as there is an effort to do good and to avoid justifying our sins, we are on the right path, God willing. We need to be true believers and support one another in doing good, while being both firm and merciful with regards to other people's shortcomings. Indeed, this is also something that al-Ḥakam will judge us for.

Living with this name

1. Submit to His judgments by learning the lessons of this name

The Prophet ﷺ reminds us: '*If something befalls you, do not say, "If only I had done otherwise," but rather say, "Allah's Will be done," for "if only" opens the door to Satan's mischief.*' [Bukhārī]

Our duty is to work to the best of our ability, utilizing the means around us and ultimately having trust in God. Sometimes this will require us to pursue something and never give up, and sometimes it will require us to take a different route. How do we know which is the 'correct' way?

Sometimes there is no way to know, and there is no point in beating yourself up about what you assume 'could have' or 'would have' been. God will not ask us about the unseen world, which only He knows. We judge things according to our limited ability, do the best we can, and ultimately leave the outcome to God. We learn the lessons from whatever has been decreed, and look forward, as opposed to backwards.

Ibn al-Qayyim reported that one of the righteous stated, 'Dignity is in humility, honor is in righteousness, and freedom is in contentment.'

2. Be just when you judge

Whenever Allah mentions judgment or orders people to judge, He accompanies it with justice or truth. For example: '*God commands you [people] to return things entrusted to you to their rightful owners, and, if you judge between people, to do so with justice: God's instructions to you are excellent, for He hears and sees everything.'* [4:58]

Even when He instructs His prophets, He emphasizes fairness. Allah says to the Prophet Dāwūd, *'We have given you mastery over the land. Judge fairly between people.'* [38:26]

The Prophet ﷺ also taught us that our state matters when we are making a judgment: *'A judge should not judge between two persons while he is in an angry mood.'* [Bukhārī] He reminds us that emotions influence our judgments.

Finally, we should ask: how would we like God to judge us? The mercy and understanding that we hope to receive from God is what we should give to other people when making a judgment.

3. Learn the judgments that are relevant to you

As mentioned, one part of God's judgments is the duties that He has enshrined upon us. As people of faith, we have a responsibility to learn those rulings that pertain to our individual responsibilities. They are those responsibilities that God has decreed to be of benefit to us both in this life and the next, and thus bring us into beautiful submission to Him.

Another important point to remember is that sometimes virtues that are loved by God are emptied of their true meaning and practiced in such a way that they contravene God's laws. For instance, mercy and justice are both virtues essential to this faith, but they are sometimes defined so broadly that they become slogans that violate God's justice. An example might be the death penalty as punishment for homicide. While this is a very nuanced discussion – some countries weaponize this punishment in a racialized way or only against the poor and weak, and for this reason there may be reason to oppose it to a certain degree and in specific contexts – if we just focus on the death penalty in principle, we will find that, unless the family of the victim forego the punishment, Allah declares this is as the right way to deal with a murderer. Opposing the death penalty in principle (not the unjust application of it) in the name of mercy and justice is denial of those very principles for the victim's family.

4. Remember that what is decreed by God will always be for your benefit

Ultimately, the Judge is also the Most Wise and Most Merciful, so all of His decrees for us contain wisdom and mercy. This includes both the duties He has enjoined upon us, and the occurrences and events of the universe and in our daily lives. We must remember that no decree is without wisdom and mercy; reflecting upon this ensures that we understand the deeper meanings behind our rituals as well as the events that happen in our lives and around us.

5. Restrain or be a ruler over your anger

One way to emulate this characteristic in the human realm is to rule over our anger. Uncontrolled rage rules over the one who feels it, but as humans with dignified souls, we must subjugate our anger using our minds and intellects.

AL-‘ALIYY, AL-A‘LĀ, AL-MUTA‘ĀLĪ, AL-‘AẒĪM – THE HIGH, THE MOST HIGH, THE HIGH ABOVE, THE GREATEST (44-47)

26

AL-'ALIYY, AL-A'LĀ, AL-MUTA'ĀLĪ, AL-'AẒĪM – THE HIGH, THE MOST HIGH, THE HIGH ABOVE, THE GREATEST (44-47)

'He is the Most High, the Most Great.'

[2:255]

Allah's names al-'Aliyy and al-'Aẓīm are found in numerous places in the Qur'an. The Arabic root of Allah's names al-'Aliyy, al-A'lā, and al-Muta'*ālī* – *'ayn-lām-wāw* – means 'to be high and exalted', while the root of al-'Aẓīm, *'ayn-ẓā-mīm*, means 'to be imposing and great'. These Names are general enough that, as Ibn Al-Qayyim says, they encompass all kinds of greatness and all sorts of elevation.

Allah is great and high in His essence, His attributes and His actions. He al-'Aliyy (the High), al-A'lā (the Most High), and al-Muta'ālī (the High Above), whose essence, attributes and actions are far above being tarnished by anything that is lowly. These names emphasize to us that whatever we see as elevated, or whatever we choose to elevate – even our own selves! – Allah is far, far above that. He is al-'Aẓīm whose essence, attributes and actions are all the greatest they can be: His mercy is the greatest we can ever experience, His generosity is the most magnificent generosity there can ever be, and His sovereignty is the most complete and powerful sovereignty there is or ever will be.

Nothing is too great for Him

Allah is the Greatest, and He is the Most High. Whenever we see obstacles as insurmountable, problems as unsolvable, or when people tell us that something is too great for us to achieve, we have to remember that our reliance is on the Greatest: Allah al-ʿAẓīm. When you rely on the One who is higher than any obstacle, greater than any problem, grander than what you want to achieve, your heart is strengthened by al-ʿAẓīm, and what seems to be too great pales in comparison to al-ʿAẓīm.

Allah makes great

A part of Allah's greatness is that He can make great anything in our lives. Your seemingly mediocre job can be made great by Him. He can make great our provision both materially and spiritually – materially in the sense that He increases it, and spiritually in that He makes our provision always more than enough for us, no matter how little we earn. Your small house can be great by virtue of all the blessings that it holds as a home.

Allah also makes great the reward of those who are mindful of Him. He says, *'God will wipe out the sinful deeds and make great the rewards of anyone who is mindful of Him.'* [65:5]

This should help us to re-orient our standards and our intentions. Allah is the One who makes great, and He is the One who elevates, not people. Being mindful of Him elevates our station with Him in the Hereafter and magnifies our reward – that is true greatness. However, the standards of this world can obscure reality.

Whose standards for greatness?

Scrolling through any of our multiple social media channels, we are bombarded with images of those whom the social order has elevated and regarded as great in modern society: models, actors, athletes, businessmen, entrepreneurs, and others. We are impressed by their accomplishments – indeed, they have achieved what is viewed to be important in this world. Society defines them as the standard that we should try to emulate, the station for which we should strive in this world.

While some might have attained impressive feats, what we consider great or elevated is variable in its value. Some have achieved worldly greatness because they have truly done lofty things; they may have sacrificed for others, built hospitals and schools, or found a cure for a disease. Others have achieved worldly elevation because they can dance or sing, because they shock people, because they are or have become wealthy, or because they tap into deep human desires; they become 'influencers'. All these people are actually influencing our image of greatness. And much of what is regarded as great is not great at all – far from it. It assumes that this world is all there is, and so we must live to satisfy our desires and be our 'authentic selves' – whatever that means. Life ceases to be about struggling against lower desires and holding ourselves to a higher standard – a standard set by the Most High – but rather about living 'our (subjective) truth', which is, in essence, feel-good speak designed to ensure that we gratify our *nafs* (lower self). Yet some, or much, of it is considered reprehensible. It goes against what Allah – the Most Great, the Most High – loves.

When we are drawn into this mode of thinking, our priorities become mixed up, and we fail to see things as they really are, but rather only as they appear. Things that are seemingly great impress us easily, and we elevate those things.

Society may elevate money and status, but the Prophet ﷺ reminded us that what is underneath is what truly matters: '*Verily, Allah does not look at your appearance or wealth, but rather He looks at your hearts and actions.*' [Muslim]

We seek approval from people, forgetting that it is God's approval that matters most. The Prophet ﷺ said, '*Whoever acts to be heard, Allah will make him heard. Whoever acts to show off, Allah will show him off.*' [Bukhārī and Muslim] The scholar Imam al-

Nawawī explained this hadith: 'The scholars said it means whoever is ostentatious in his deeds and he publicizes it to people so that they honor him, aggrandize him, and believe he is virtuous, Allah will publicize it to people on the Day of Resurrection and disgrace him.' Moreover, the Companions would say, 'Do not do deeds for anyone besides Allah, for Allah will leave you in the charge of the one for whom you did it.'[31] This means that we are truly under the control of those whose approval we desire. It may not seem like it – after all, we believe that we are being our authentic selves and are acting out of our own autonomy – but in reality, we are captivated by the pleasure our *nafs* receives when we behave in a certain way.

We raise matters up to stations that they truly do not deserve. Empires founded on injustice have been called 'great', and people who have committed massacres have also been referred to as 'great'. Fame, too, becomes a standard for greatness; we pursue and elevate it, and we see people as great just because they are famous. Alternatively, we view ourselves as great because the standards of this world tell us that we are: for our beauty, our educational achievement, our ethnicity and skin tone, or our wealth.

Allah's names al-ʿAliyy, al-ʿAẓīm – the Most High, the Most Great – are a reminder to us not to be duped by this world's standards of greatness. These names of Allah shift our attention: do not be distracted by the shiny lights of this world, and do not forget that the real standards for greatness are those set by God.

Korah (Qārūn) was of the people of Moses, and he was given great wealth, but he tyrannized his people. Despite this, God tells us that, '*those whose aim was the life of this world said, "If only we had been given something like what Korah has been given: indeed, he is one of great (ʿaẓīm) fortune."*' [28:79] They saw him as great because of his wealth, despite knowing that he had transgressed. But God '*caused the earth to swallow him and his home: he had no one to help him against*

[31] Ibn al-Sarī. Kitāb al-Zuhd. (Kuwait: Dār al-Khulafā' lil-Kitāb al-Islāmī, 1985), 2:435.

God, nor could he defend himself.' [28:81] Korah might have satisfied the standard for greatness in the time he lived in – He was living during the time of Pharoah, who claimed to be a god, so one can imagine what was considered 'great'! – but in Allah's eyes, he was the complete opposite of what is truly great.

God reminds us: *'We grant the Home in the Hereafter to those who do not seek superiority ('uluwwan) on earth or spread corruption: the happy ending is awarded to those who are mindful of God.'* [28:83]

When you begin to be overtaken by worldly standards of greatness that are in opposition to God's standards, remember who is truly Great and Most High, and derive your standards from Him. He tells us that the best outcome is for those who are mindful of Him, so honor the things that He honors. God tells us: *'those who honor (yu'aẓẓim) God's rites show the piety of their hearts.'* [22:32]

That is how you can become, in a human sense, 'great'.

Elevation with wisdom

God says in the Qur'an: *'He is Exalted and Wise.'* [42:51]

Because God is far above everything, He is also far above any negative attribute. However, language is limited, and some might interpret God's Name al-'Aliyy as one who is haughty. Allah reminds us that He is indeed the Exalted, and He is also the Most Wise. The nature of His elevation and greatness is not to be compared to that of human beings – He possesses ultimate wisdom. Whatever occurs due to His elevation comes from wisdom.

Rukū' (bowing) and *sujūd* (prostration): reminders

Every action in prayer has both an internal and external dimension. When we bow to God, we say: *'How Perfect is my Lord, the Exalted (al-'Aẓīm).'*

We bring together the physical act of bowing to the Most Great, with a verbal reminder of who He is, in the hope that our hearts will also bow in awe of Him. This happens even more so when we prostrate to Him: we are at our physically lowest point, but we are praising He who is far elevated above everything. We say: *'How Perfect is my Lord, the Most High (al-A'lā).'*

The Prophet ﷺ also said, *'My community (ummah) on that day [the Day of Judgment] will surely have bright faces because of prostration.'* [Aḥmad]

As these meanings permeate our hearts, we have to then remember that our hearts should not bow or prostrate except to Him: al-'Aliyy, al-'Aẓīm. This is why prayer is so important. We not only take the time out to connect to God, but we are also reminded of His attributes at least five times a day, and thus reminded of true reality.

Living with these names

1. Check yourself

A recurring lesson for us is to always check our ego. Indeed, Allah pairs His name al-'Aliyy with His name al-Kabīr as a warning to those who oppress those under their charge (see chapter 15 for a discussion of this pairing). Whenever you feel that you are great or higher than other people according to worldly standards, remember that it is God who is the Greatest and the Most High. Moreover, He raises people and abases others. The Prophet ﷺ told us: *'Whoever humbles himself to God, Allah will raise him.'* [Muslim] This does not conflict with feeling a sense of accomplishment when you achieve a goal, or feeling pleased when you do a good deed. The Prophet ﷺ taught us: *'When a good deed becomes a source of pleasure for you and an evil deed becomes a source of disgust, then you are a believer.'* [Tirmidhī] However, these accomplishments should cause us to return to God and thank Him for what He has enabled us to do. The Prophet ﷺ defined arrogance as *'rejecting the truth and looking down on people.'* [Muslim]

Indeed, the latest research shows that humility is one of four critical leadership factors because, among other things, it fosters a better environment for growth. One who is focused on improving his or her faults and does not see that they are better than others can inspire others to be and do the same.

Remember that God loves great and dignified character, so work on yourself for Him.

2. Re-orient your standards

When we view something as great, our natural inclination is to elevate it, desire it and even emulate it. Do not elevate things higher than they deserve, and do not be deceived by worldly standards if they conflict with those set by God. More and more, we are being sold on striving for impossible beauty standards, making money no matter what the means, and flaunting what we have. The Most Great is the One who defines for us the meaning of greatness. A person can be great and elevated through his or her ethics, character and manners. Indeed, it is Allah who elevates and abases. The best way to be great in the Eyes of God is to follow His beloved Messenger ﷺ.

3. Be reminded through your prayers

Prayer is a world within itself. Prayer is a sanctuary because through it, we turn completely to God and remember our purpose. It reminds us of His attributes, and when we truly reflect, it gives us insight into the world around us. Five times a day we praise His greatness and elevation, ensuring that we are reminded that He is truly the Most High, the Most Great.

4. Remind yourself of God's greatness

Reflect upon the creation of the heavens and the earth, and the tiny minutiae, in order to be in awe of Allah's greatness. There are certain remembrances that we have been taught by the Prophet ﷺ

that bring us back to God and re-center our focus. The Prophet ﷺ stated that, *'There are two statements which are light on the tongue, heavy on the scales [on the Day of Judgment], and beloved by the Most Merciful: Exalted is Allah, and praise be to Him; exalted is my Lord, the Most Great (subḥān Allāh wa biḥamdih, subḥāna rabbī al-'aẓīm).'* [Muslim] When we utter these statements while truly reflecting on them, they remind us that we should be in awe of God.

AL-ḤAYIYY AL-SITTĪR – GRACE (48-49)

27

AL-ḤAYIYY AL-SITTĪR – GRACE (48-49)

'Verily, God the Almighty and Majestic is Modest and Concealing; and He loves modesty and concealment.'

[Abū Dāwūd]

God is al-Ḥayiyy and al-Sittīr; both of these names are found in the sayings of the Prophet Muhammad ﷺ.

Al-Ḥayiyy al-Sittīr

Ḥayiyy is difficult to translate into English. In the dictionary it is defined as the opposite of insolence and impertinence. *Ḥayā*, the noun from the same Arabic root, *ḥā-yā-yā*, is usually translated as 'shyness', but shyness can sometimes also denote timidity, and God is the Most Majestic. So we will use the terms 'demure', 'gracious' and 'shy' interchangeably to describe God, bearing in mind that His *ḥayā* comes from a place of honor, generosity, and majesty, not meekness or submissiveness.

It is also related to His name al-Sittīr, who is the One who covers. In the hadith above, the Prophet ﷺ tells us that Allah is both *ḥayiyy* and *sittīr*, and He loves for His servants to be adorned with these attributes too.

Al-Ḥayiyy – He does not turn you away

The Prophet ﷺ mentions Allah's name al-Ḥayiyy in a different context and with another name. As mentioned in chapter 21, he said: *'Verily your Lord is Generous (karīm) and Shy (ḥayiyy). If His servant raises his hands to Him (in supplication) He becomes shy (yastaḥyī) to return them empty.'* [Aḥmad, Abū Dāwūd, Tirmidhī]

Many cultures have a similar tradition, but in some it is more pronounced than others; it is considered miserly or unbecoming to turn someone away, particularly someone who is in need of you and someone you have the ability to aid. If you cannot give the specific help that was requested or needed, a person who has *ḥayā* and *karam* (generosity) would give an alternative, or at least a part of what was requested. This comes from a place of generosity and dignity, not weakness.

Allah's *ḥayā* is far above the *ḥayā* of human beings, and indeed it is completely different. One of the ways it manifests is that God does not turn you away when you ask Him. You are in need, and He is the Self-Sufficient and the Most Generous; thus, He takes care of those who are in need of Him. This is why the Prophet ﷺ tells us in the hadith above that God will not turn away your hands with nothing. The Most Generous, the Gracious – al-Ḥayiyy – will always give something, and because He knows us better than we know ourselves, He gives what is better for us – either materially or spiritually – than that for which we asked. Sometimes, even when Allah plans to give us what we ask for in the future, He may still give us something at the time of asking, in order not to turn us away with nothing in the present moment. This is al-Ḥayiyy.

In another hadith, also mentioned in chapter 21, the Prophet ﷺ tells us, *'Any Muslim who supplicates to God in a supplication which contains no sin breaking of kinship, God will give him one of three things: either his supplication will be immediately answered, or it will be saved for him in the Hereafter, or it will turn away an equivalent amount of evil (from him).'* The Companions said, 'So we will ask for more.' He replied, *'God is more [generous].'* [Aḥmad]

The Companions understood: if Allah never rejects their supplication, and they would *always* be given something, then why would they not ask for more? Especially since Allah loves those who turn to Him and ask Him. It is not a burden on Allah to be asked or for Him to answer; He is the Self-Sufficient. Indeed, the Prophet ﷺ tells us: '*The Lord descends every night to the lowest heaven when one-third of the night remains and says: "Who will call upon Me, that I may answer Him? Who will ask of Me, that I may give him? Who will seek My forgiveness, that I may forgive him?"*' [Bukhārī and Muslim]

Allah descends every single night for those who cherish those quiet moments with Him, and He is there for us.

Al-Sittīr – He conceals and covers you

Part of Allah being *sittīr* is that He conceals the faults and shortcomings of His servants, and He loves those who conceal the faults of others – it is also part of *ḥayā* that one does not like to spread what is lewd and unbecoming in society. This name is an aggrandizement of *sātir,* from the same Arabic root *sīn-tā-rā*, meaning that God conceals people's faults repeatedly as well as qualitatively – He conceals both the big and the small. This is why backbiting and gossiping are both so detestable to God; He describes backbiting as '*to eat the flesh of your dead brother.*' [49:12] It concerns talking about another person in a way that they would hate, even if what is being said is true. It can involve exposing their sins, which is iniquitous since they themselves are avoiding being public with their personal failings.

Indeed, the Companions hated to expose people's personal sins. Abū Bakr al-Ṣiddīq said, 'Were I to take hold of a drinker of wine, I would prefer for Allah to cover his sin. Were I to take hold of a thief, I would prefer for Allah to cover his sin.'

Of course, there are exceptions. If someone asks us for advice concerning someone he or she wishes to marry or to hire for work, and we know certain characteristics of that person that are relevant to those roles, it is incumbent upon us to share this, but only with those to whom this information is directly relevant. Furthermore, it becomes an obligation, in certain circumstances, to tell people in the community about particular dangerous individuals; for example, known sexual predators. This is because these people's sins are no longer private shortcomings, but rather transgressions against others. Protecting the community is paramount, as is seeking justice for the victims.

Have *ḥayā* and conceal your sins

The Messenger of Allah ﷺ said, *'Everyone from my nation will be forgiven except those who sin in public. Among them is a man who commits an evil deed in the night that Allah has hidden for him, then in the morning he says: "O people, I have committed this sin!" His Lord had hidden it during the night but in the morning he reveals what Allah has hidden.'* [Bukhārī and Muslim]

This is a point upon which it is worth reflecting. Many times, Allah hides our worst deeds and characteristics from people. This is a protection for us and allows us the space to rectify ourselves without the harsh judgment of people, who many times do not forget our slip-ups and choose to define us by them. It also prevents the spread and normalization of immorality in society. This is why we should not expose what Allah has kept hidden; indeed, He will forgive us, unless we reveal what He has concealed. And it is not hypocrisy to keep those deeds concealed. Modern culture convinces us that everything must be laid bare to the world, in the name of authenticity, even though it leads to the justification and normalization of the wrong deeds that we do. We should be too shy before Allah to expose what He has kept covered.

Of course, the purpose of this is not to create a two-faced society in which people act differently in public and in private. We should have spaces to address our struggles and problems. We can confide in those who can help us. One of the purposes of Allah's concealment is so that we can work on our shortcomings, not so that we can persist in them. Indeed, insisting on a sin may lead to Allah lifting His cover from us.

If someone, moreover, comes to us and shows us our faults, we should seriously consider what is being said, regardless of how it is being said. 'Umar ibn al-Khaṭṭāb, said, 'May Allah have mercy on the one who shows me my faults.' [Dārimī]

Ḥayā: the hallmark of a believer

The Prophet ﷺ told us: *'Every religion has a distinguishing characteristic, and the distinguishing characteristic of this religion is modesty (ḥayā).'* [Mālik]

Ḥayā comes from the same Arabic root as the word for 'life', *ḥayāh*. It is said that the level of one's *ḥayā* correlates to how much life one has in his or her heart. Unfortunately, because we sometimes define *ḥayā* as a kind of shy meekness, as opposed to a modesty that comes from a place of dignity and humbleness, this trait is not appreciated. Even worse, it is seen to apply *only* to women, when the Prophet ﷺ told us that this is the characteristic of Islam as a whole, and thus should apply to everyone: men and women, young and old. When the Prophet ﷺ passed by a man from the Anṣār (the Helpers; natives of Madinah who welcomed and supported the Muslim emigrants from Makkah) who was admonishing his brother about modesty, he said, *'Let him be, for modesty is part of faith.'* [Bukhārī and Muslim]

Modesty, or *ḥayā*, is decency and propriety. It applies in both our relationship with people and, more importantly, with Allah.

This attribute of modesty comes out naturally for most when we are before people whom we revere. Imagine sitting in front of an elder; we would be ashamed to be lewd, vulgar or brash. Rather we would be respectful and thoughtful. Similarly, we see that when people attend certain types of formal, serious events, while they may usually dress or act immodestly, they transform for these particular events – court appearances, entering into sacred spaces, and so on. It is an expression of a natural disposition for this trait, which the modern world demeans.

There are several narrations from the Prophet ﷺ praising modesty as a general characteristic. He said, '*Vulgarity is not found in anything but that it disgraces it, and modesty is not found in anything but that it beautifies it.*' [Tirmidhī] He also said, '*Modesty does not bring anything but goodness.*' [Bukhārī and Muslim]

We all appreciate this characteristic when we see it in others: important people who do not draw attention to themselves; rich people who do not boast of their wealth; beautiful people who are unaware of their beauty. And this characteristic is beloved to God too. One of the Companions, al-Ashajj 'Abd al-Qays, said, 'The Prophet ﷺ said to me, "*You have two characteristics that God loves.*" So, I said, "And what are they, O Messenger of Allah ﷺ?" The Prophet ﷺ replied, "*They are forbearance and ḥayā.*"' [Muslim] How beautiful it is to be adorned by characteristics that Allah loves!

The Messenger of Allah ﷺ said, '*If modesty were to take the form of a man, he would be a righteous man. If shamelessness were to take the form of a man, he would be a wicked man.*' (Ibn Abī al-Dunyā) Indeed, the Prophet ﷺ stated that the most modest person of this nation is 'Uthmān ibn 'Affān, a male Companion and one of the ten Companions promised paradise. There was once a poor child who came to 'Uthmān in the mosque, and 'Uthmān wanted to help him without embarrassing the boy or his family. So, he gave the child a garment and put money in the pocket, then – in order to make sure that the money reached his parents – told the child to show the garment to his parents and ask them what they thought of it. The child went home to show his parents his new shirt, and they discovered the money that 'Uthmān put in the pocket. 'Uthmān was not seeking attention; he did it quietly. This is *ḥayā* in giving.

Some people naturally have this characteristic. For those who do not, God gives us the tools to build this attribute. The scholar Imam Zaid Shakir said that Islam provides the environment which enables *ḥayā*. We should enable others to be modest and we should work with one another to foster the best characteristics in ourselves. After all, these characteristics will bind us together in this life and the next. The Prophet ﷺ said: *'Shyness (ḥayā) is from faith, and the people of faith will be in Paradise. Being disagreeable in nature is from crudeness, and crudeness is in the hellfire.'* [Tirmidhī]

A distinction must be made though. *Ḥayā* is not a shyness that prevents you from doing good things or the right thing. Shyness comes from a sense of dignity and God consciousness. As the Prophet ﷺ told us: *'The best struggle is a word of truth in the face of an oppressive tyrant.'* [Tirmidhī] Shyness or modesty should not prevent us from speaking up, because staying silent in the face of an injustice is not *ḥayā*. It does not mean that we do not put ourselves forward for a job that we know we can do well, with the help of God. The Prophet Joseph put himself forward for the job of overseeing the food rations, saying *'Put me in charge of the nation's storehouses, I shall manage them prudently and carefully.'* [12:55] It is important to strike a balance between avoiding ostentation and completely retreating. 'Ā'ishah, the wife of the Prophet Muhammad ﷺ, said, 'How great were the women of the Anṣār; their modesty did not prevent them from seeking knowledge about their religion.' [Bukhārī] These women were modest, but modesty did not preclude women from putting themselves forward and learning – that is the correct interpretation of *ḥayā*.

Modesty is even more paramount in our relationship with Allah. The Prophet ﷺ said, *'I advise you to be modest in front of Allah Almighty as you would be modest in front of a righteous man among your people.'* [Ṭabarānī] Allah sees us when others do not, and it is imperative to have modesty and shyness in front of Him before others.

He also said, *'Be modest before Allah, as is His right.'* The Companions said, 'O Messenger of Allah ﷺ, surely we have modesty, all praise is due to Allah!' The Prophet ﷺ said, *'It is not so. Rather, modesty before Allah, as is His right, is to guard the mind and what runs through it, to guard the stomach and what fills it, and to reflect upon death and trials. Whoever desires the Hereafter, let him abandon the embellishment of worldly life. Whoever does so has been modest before Allah, as is his right.'* [Tirmidhī]

Part of being modest is covering ourselves outwardly – this applies to both men and women, in the ways that have been prescribed by Allah. There are different rulings in terms of what should be covered for men and women based on our biological differences, and it is a personal responsibility to know what is required of us to cover. However, the prohibition of skintight clothes, for example, is applicable to both men and women; it is not from modesty to allow the detailed contours of our body to be seen in public. Once we know these rules, behaving with modesty outwardly might be easier than ensuring the internal modesty described in the above hadith. Internal modesty means guarding our thoughts from unwholesome thoughts, and guarding what we earn, and therefore what we fill our stomachs with. These are all ways that we are modest and shy in front of Allah, because we know that He sees us where others do not. It is appreciation for His covering of our mistakes and all the blessings He showers upon us.

Living with these names

1. Do not expose people

When a heart is filled with heedlessness, hatred or envy, it becomes easy to talk about the scandals of others. If we find that it is easy for us to do so, we need to examine the state of our hearts. There are situations when we must mention others' sins out of justice and in order to protect others, but other than those circumstances, it is beloved to God that we conceal the personal faults and weaknesses of His people. The Prophet ﷺ taught us that whoever conceals the faults of others, God will conceal his or her faults in this life and the next. [Muslim]

2. God is al-Ḥayiyy, so be shy in front of Him

The Prophet ﷺ described a man who travelled on a long journey and was disheveled and covered with dust. This person stretched his hands to God saying, 'O my Lord, O my Lord.' One would assume that God would respond to his supplication – he was a traveler and he seemed to be calling to God from his heart. But the Prophet ﷺ said: *'But his food is haram (forbidden), his drink is haram, all his nourishment is haram, so how can his du'ā' be accepted?'* [Muslim] All of his earnings were from impermissible means; he had no shame to behave before Allah in ways of which He disapproves.

Conversely, if you have shyness before al-Ḥayiyy, then imagine a Lord who does not want to turn you away; a Lord who is there for your every need; a Lord who does not need you, yet loves to give to you even though it brings no benefit to Him. That is Allah. So, have shyness that comes from being in awe of the grace of your Lord. Do not reject His commandments. Give Him the best of what you have – that means giving your best in your prayers, in your interactions with people, and in your charity. Because after all, God has given to you – given you the best of the best – so how can you not give from the best of what He gave you?

3. Have ḥayā with people

Let your modesty come from the dignity that is given to you by God. Do not be ostentatious, crude or lewd. Do not seek attention; ultimately, you do not need it. Immodest people usually seek their sense of worth from people around them. They love the praise or shock they get from people with their behavior. But you know where your sense of worth comes from. You do not need to shock people or receive their praise.

4. Try not to turn people away

The Prophet ﷺ said, *'God will aid a servant (of His) so long as the servant aids his brother.'* [Muslim] Just like you love for God to give you something when you ask, fulfil others' needs; if you cannot, at least try to direct them to where their needs can be fulfilled. When a homeless person asks you for money and you do not have cash, go to the supermarket and buy a sandwich with your debit card. If someone asks you for a ride and you really cannot take them, try to find someone who can, or give them alternatives. You will be emulating the beautiful attributes of the Most Beautiful.

5. Ask God for all of your needs, and Him to cover and rectify your faults

Ask God without fearing any disappointment. Know that He will give you something. Know that He will not turn you away empty-handed. The Prophet ﷺ said, *'Ask Allah to cover your faults and protect you from your anxieties.'* [Ṭabarānī]

AL-ḤAYY AL-QAYYŪM – THE LIVING, THE SUSTAINER (50-51)

28

AL-ḤAYY AL-QAYYŪM – THE LIVING, THE SUSTAINER (50-51)

'And [all] faces will be humbled before the Ever-Living, the Sustainer of existence. And he will have failed who carries injustice.'

[20:111]

According to Ibn al-Qayyim, all of the names of God relate to these two names: al-Ḥayy and al-Qayyūm – the Ever-Living, the Sustainer.[32] This is because al-Ḥayy – which comes from the Arabic root that means life, *ḥā-yā-yā* – refers to His essential attributes: the fact that He is All-Seeing, All-Hearing, that He wills, that He is able, and so on. These all relate to life. He is the Ever-Living who does not die. Allah says in the Qur'an, *'And rely upon the Ever-Living (al-Ḥayy) who does not die, and exalt [Allah] with His praise."* [25:58]

Allah was before there was anything else, and He will remain after everything is gone. There is no life before Him or without Him. Sheikh al-Sha'rāwī said that al-Ḥayy brings together all perfect qualities, because there cannot be a good quality before there is life. When we call on Allah al-Ḥayy, we are recognizing Him as the absolute source of life and thus the source of all perfect qualities.

Al-Qayyūm is an intense form of the Arabic root *qāf-wāw-mīm*, which means 'to stand up or to stand aright', and thus He is the

[32] Al-Ashqar, *Sharḥ Ibn Al-Qayyim Li Asmā' Allāh al-Ḥusnā*, 133.

One by whom all things are eternally managed aright. This name refers to His actions and self-subsistence. Moreover, He gave us minds, and then bodies and limbs to give action to the thoughts in our heads. He is the source of everything needed by the worshipper, from the One he or she worships.

Thus, God is the source of all life and He is, in every second, sustaining this world. This should teach us to trust in Him because truly, He is the One who is managing and taking care of this world, and no one else.

The greatest verses

God tells us in the famous verse, which the Prophet ﷺ described as the greatest verse in the Qur'an: '*God: there is no god but Him, the Ever Living (al-Ḥayy), the Sustainer (al-Qayyūm). Neither slumber nor sleep overtakes Him. All that is in the heavens and in the earth belongs to Him. Who is there that can intercede with Him except by His leave? He knows what is before them and what is behind them, but they do not comprehend any of His knowledge except what He wills. His throne extends over the heavens and the earth; it does not weary Him to preserve them both. He is the Most High, the Tremendous.*' [2:255]

In this verse, we are told of God's Names al-Ḥayy and al-Qayyūm. The verse then proceeds to explain to us the nature of these attributes: that God, the Ever-Living, does not slumber or sleep. That God, the Sustainer, holds dominion over everything in the heavens and the earth, and He preserves everything – not even our knowledge would exist without Him and His permission. This verse should cause us to reflect on the creation of the heavens and the earth, and then leads us to the logical conclusion: that God is the Most High, the Tremendous.

Al-Ḥayy al-Qayyūm

According to some opinions, these are the greatest names of Allah. Once a man prayed to God, saying, 'O Allah, I ask you as all praise is Yours. There is no god except You, You are the Bestower, the Originator of the Heavens and Earth, Possessor of Majesty and Honor. O Ever-Living (*yā ḥayy*), O Self-Subsisting (*yā qayyūm*).'

The Prophet ﷺ heard him and said: *'He has supplicated to God using His greatest name; when supplicated with this name, He answers, and when asked with this name, He gives.'* [Abū Dāwūd]

It is apparent that the Prophet Muhammad ﷺ loved these names of Allah and frequently called upon Allah with them. For example, when the Prophet ﷺ felt any distress, he would say: *'O Ever-Living, O Sustainer, in Your Mercy I seek relief (yā ḥayyu yā qayyūm, bi raḥmatika astaghīth).'* [Tirmidhī]

Moreover, the Prophet ﷺ advised his daughter, Fatimah, to say in the morning and in the evening: *'O Ever-Living, O Sustainer (yā ḥayyu yā qayyūm), by Your mercy I seek help; rectify for me all of my affairs and do not leave me to depend on myself, even for the blink of an eye.'* [Ḥākim]

We recognize in the Ever-Living, the Sustainer of all, that everything is within His control even when it seems that matters are in the control of people. We know that we cannot even depend on ourselves, because we have shortcomings and ill-judgment. We ask Him for His help because we can only rely on Him; He can truly guide us to the right way.

This is why we also call on God when we feel defeated. We ask Him not to leave us to ourselves alone, because we know that when we are with Him, our affairs are okay. We might misjudge, or be led by our desires, or lack wisdom, so we ask the One who constantly manages the affairs of the world not to leave us to ourselves: we ask for His care.

Living with these names

1. Hold on to the source of life

Remember that God came before everything, and He is the Ever-Living who is also the source of life. Everything goes back to Him, and so will we.

2. Have trust in Him

Al-Qayyūm encompasses all of His other attributes that pertain to managing the affairs of His creation, such as being the Trustee, the Protector, and the Most Wise. When you feel unable to manage, call on God al-Qayyūm, like the Prophet ﷺ did when he was under distress. In a beautiful supplication, the Messenger of Allah ﷺ would say, '*O Allah, I have surrendered to you and I have faith in you. I trust in you and I have turned to you. I have contested my opponents for your sake. O Allah, I seek refuge in your power from going astray, for there is no God but you. You are the Living who never dies, while the jinn and humans die.*' [Bukhārī and Muslim]

3. Memorize the Verse of the Throne (Āyat al-Kursī)

It is recommended for a Muslim to read this verse after offering each of the five daily obligatory prayers. The Prophet Muhammad ﷺ said: '*Whoever recites the Verse of the Throne immediately after each prescribed prayer, there will be nothing standing between him and his entering Paradise except death.*' [Nasā'ī]

Moreover, the Prophet ﷺ also recommended reciting this verse every night before sleeping, as God will then appoint an angel to protect you and Satan will be unable to approach you throughout the night's sleep. [Bukhārī]

AL-ḤAMĪD AL-MAJĪD – PRAISE AND GLORY (52-53)

29

AL-ḤAMĪD AL-MAJĪD – PRAISE AND GLORY (52-53)

'The grace of God and His blessings be upon you, people of this house! For He is Praiseworthy and Glorious.'

[11:73]

At the conclusion of every prayer, Muslims recite this prayer for the Prophet Muhammad ﷺ: *'O God, send prayers on Muhammad, and on the family of Muhammad, as you sent prayers on Abraham, and on the family of Abraham; You are indeed Worthy of Praise, Full of Glory. O God, send blessings on Muhammad, and on the family of Muhammad, as you sent blessings on Abraham, and on the family of Abraham; You are indeed Worthy of Praise, Full of Glory.'* [Bukhārī and Muslim]

God is al-Ḥamīd, and *ḥamīd* – in its general meaning – is the one who is praised. When it refers to God, it also means He who is *worthy* of all praise and the best praise. Al-Ghazālī states that this name 'comes down to the attributes of majesty, of exaltation, and of perfection, as they are linked to the repetition of those who continually remember Him, for praise involves recalling the attributes of perfection insofar as they are perfect.'[33]

Al-Majīd, according to al-Ghazālī, is 'one who is noble in essence, beautiful in actions, and bountiful in gifts and in favors.'[34]

---

[33] Abū Ḥāmid Al-Ghazālī, *The Ninety-Nine Beautiful Names of God: Al-Maqṣad Al-Asnā Fi Sharḥ Asmā' Allāh Al-Ḥusnā*, trans. David Burrell and Nazih Daher, The Ghazali Series (Cambridge: The Islamic Texts Society, 1992), 127.
[34] Ibid, 130.

The names al-Ḥamīd al-Majīd are frequently mentioned together because, while God is the Lord whose commands do not need to be explained, out of His nobility and bounty – because He is al-Majīd – He still explains many issues to us in the Qur'an, or through His Prophet ﷺ. He tells us that prayer is prescribed for us so that we may remember Him, and the Prophet ﷺ teaches us that hardships may indeed benefit us. So, God is praised for that bounty. Furthermore, al-Ḥamīd can also refer to the quantity of attributes and goodness God possesses, whereas al-Majīd refers to the glorious and great nature of these attributes. Thus, He is al-Ḥamīd al-Majīd, because He truly possesses all those numerous attributes and qualities that are glorious and necessitate praise – qualities of perfection and goodness.

Indeed, He is also Praiseworthy and Glorious in reference to the rules that He has prescribed, as His law contains exemplary and beneficial guidelines for all His creation. He is also Praiseworthy and Glorious in what He has decreed for us, even if sometimes, in the moment, it seems bad to us. We are shown in the story of Moses and al-Khaḍr in Sūrat al-Kahf that, when some situations seemed outwardly to be bad or unfair, Allah had actually decreed good in them (see chapter 24). Realizing this ultimate wisdom should lead us to al-Ḥamīd al-Majīd, who is truly Praiseworthy and Glorious.

Expressing praise and thanks

Ḥamd (praise), from the same Arabic root as al-Ḥamīd, is closely associated with *shukr*, meaningful 'thanks' or 'thankfulness'. But *ḥamd* is much more encompassing than *shukr*. Thankfulness is expressed to someone for a particular deed or favor, whereas *ḥamd* is praise and gratitude not simply for overt favors, but for the inherent qualities the praiseworthy one possesses. Accordingly, it is said that *ḥamd* is the pinnacle of *shukr*. God says in the Qur'an: *'Everything in the heavens and earth belongs to Him; God alone is self-sufficient, worthy of all praise (al-Ḥamīd).'* [22:64]

Thus, God al-Ḥamīd is the One to whom we turn with gratitude and humility, praising Him not just for those favors for which we feel thankful, but also for His very essence and all His decrees. Sheikh Rātib al-Nabulsī has said that al-Ḥamīd is the only One deserving of true praise, which is why we repeat in every prayer: *'All Praise is due to God, the Lord of the Worlds.'* [1:2]

The importance of this name is that, through it, God teaches us to be attached not simply to His blessings, but to His essence. Allah gives to us, and we thank and praise Him for what He gives. But when we think of al-Ḥamīd, our thanks and praise cease to be solely for the blessing. We are reminded of His inherent and glorious attributes of *majd* (glory, from the same Arabic root as al-Majīd), of al-Ḥamīd Himself, and thus we praise Him whether the situation is good or seemingly bad, because it all comes from Him. When we realize in this life that good came out of a calamity we were facing, or, on the Day of Judgment, when we see how we are rewarded not only for our gratitude for the good, but also for our patience in the hardships, we embody the spirit of praise, and say wholeheartedly: *al-ḥamdu lillah* (all praise is due to God).

And thus, His names: the Praiseworthy, the Glorious.

All praise is due to the Lords of the Worlds

The opening chapter of the Qur'an starts with praise, but does not mention actions. It states: *'All praise is due to God, the Lord of the Worlds. The Most Merciful, the Most Compassionate. The Sovereign of the Day of Judgment.'* [1:2-4] These are all attributes of God, showing that praise for Him is due for His praiseworthy attributes, and not solely for His actions. Thus, one of the best ways to praise Him is to recount His Glorious names and attributes, and get to know Him through them. The more we know His other names, the more certainty we have in His name al-Ḥamīd.

How the Prophet ﷺ praised God

The Prophet ﷺ praised God throughout his life, whether he was in hardship or receiving many beautiful gifts from God. In a famous narration, 'Āishah, the wife of the Prophet ﷺ, saw him praying for so long that his feet became swollen. So, she asked him: 'O Messenger of God, why do you undergo so much hardship despite the fact that God has pardoned for you your earlier and later sins?'

He ﷺ responded: *'Should I not be a thankful servant (afalā akūna 'abdan shakūra)?'* [Bukhārī]

And what did the Prophet ﷺ say as he was praying in the night? Ibn 'Abbās, the cousin of the Prophet Muhammad ﷺ, relates that he used to say when he stood for the *tahajjud* (late night) prayer:

> *'O Allah! Yours is the praise (laka al-ḥamd). You are the sustainer of the heavens and the Earth and all that they contain. And Yours is the praise. Yours is the dominion of the heavens and the Earth and all that they contain. And Yours is the praise. You are the light of the heavens and the Earth and all that they contain. And Yours is the praise. You are the king of the heavens and the Earth. And Yours is the praise. You are the Truth. Your promise is true. The meeting with You is true. Your word is true. Paradise is true and the Fire is true. The prophets are true. Muhammad is true. The Hour is true.'* [Bukhārī and Muslim]

The Prophet ﷺ, throughout his hardships, reflected on the nature of this world. And he saw the majesty of God's attributes in all of creation, and in everything that happens. And with awe, humility and gratitude, he made this supplication with all of his heart.

Paired names

We know that Allah pairs many of His names and attributes in the Qur'an. One of the reasons is to show us how these names relate to each other. Al-Ḥamīd and al-Majīd are paired together in the Qur'an, as well as in the sayings of the Prophet ﷺ, and additionally al-Ḥamīd is paired with al-Ghanī (the Self-Sufficient), al-Waliyy (the Protective Friend) and al-Ḥakīm (the Most Wise).

God says: *'O mankind, you are those in need of Allah, while Allah is the Free of need (al-Ghanī), the Praiseworthy (al-Ḥamīd).'* [35:15]

If human beings are considered self-sufficient, it usually causes them to withdraw from other people. Since they do not need anyone, they may not see any reason to help, or to give, or to be nice to others – yet they are certainly not perfect in their essence. True glory however is that Allah does not need anyone, yet He still gives to people, and acts with ultimate wisdom, and is praised.

Allah also says: *'And it is He who sends down the rain after they had despaired and spreads His mercy. And He is the Protective Friend (al-Waliyy), the Praiseworthy (al-Ḥamīd).'* [42:48]

You might assign someone to be your lawyer, entrusting him or her to protect you. But if the lawyer is careless, and loses your case, you would not praise this person's actions, nor his or her essence. But when Allah is your Waliyy, you cannot help but praise Him, who defends and protects His intimate friends.

God further tells us: *'Falsehood cannot approach it from before it or from behind it; [it is] a revelation from a [Lord who is] wise (ḥakīm) and praiseworthy (ḥamīd).'* [41:42]

Here God is pointing out to us that if we reflected on His decree, we would praise Him for His wisdom. Because while God does as He pleases, He is also the Most Wise, and thus there is always the best wisdom behind His actions.

Living with these names

1. Praise and glorify Allah through the good times and the bad

The Prophet ﷺ told us that *'"Al-ḥamdu lillāh" fills the scales.'* [Muslim] One way of retaining blessings is to thank and praise God for them, and through the bad times, we should remember that ultimately whatever occurs is out of Allah's wisdom. He is both al-Ḥakīm (the All-Wise) and al-Ḥamīd (the Praiseworthy), and therefore we should remember to humble ourselves and praise Him.

2. Write down all of God's blessings upon you

In the Qur'an, Allah states: *'And if you should count the favor of Allah, you could not enumerate them. Indeed, mankind is [generally] most unjust and ungrateful.'* [14:34]

Interestingly, Allah uses the word 'favor' (*ni'mah*) in the singular, as though saying that to even try to enumerate the blessings of one single favor is impossible! To reflect deeply upon just one favor, and to ponder over its impact on our lives, can fill us with so much awe for al-Ḥamīd.

3. Speak well to people

Allah says in the Qur'an, *'And they had been guided [in worldly life] to good speech, and they were guided to the path of the Praiseworthy (al-Ḥamīd).'* [22:24]

In a beautiful reflection, Sheikh Rātib al-Nabulsī says that it is as though the path to God, al-Ḥamīd, is through good speech, as Allah also says: *'And speak to people good [words].'* [2:83]

A beautiful hadith of the Prophet ﷺ states that: *'A person's faith is not upright until his heart is upright, and his heart will not be upright until his tongue is upright.'* [Aḥmad]

4. Praise Allah by using His gifts in His service

The highest form of praise is to use the gifts He has bestowed upon us in His service, and therefore for good. But do not be like those who God says about them:

> *'If anyone alters God's blessings after he has received them, God is stern in punishment.'* [2:211]

If we use God's gifts in ways that are unbecoming, then this is the opposite of *ḥamd*. The result is that our favors could be taken away, or perhaps worse, we could become unable to find the joy or sweetness in those favors. If we look at the story of Korah in the Qur'an, he was given many blessings. He was from the people of Moses, and Allah says, '*We gave him of treasures whose keys would burden a band of strong men.*' [28:76] Yet Korah tyrannized his own people, and had the gall to say, '"*I was only given it because of knowledge I have.*"' [28:78]

He did not attribute His gifts to God, *and* he used them for corruption. And what was the result? '*And We caused the earth to swallow him and his home. And there was for him no company to aid him other than Allah, nor was he of those who [could] defend themselves.*' [28:81]

AL-KARĪM, AL-AKRAM – LIMITLESS GENEROSITY (54-55)

30

AL-KARĪM, AL-AKRAM – LIMITLESS GENEROSITY (54-55)

'Mankind, what has lured you away from God, your generous Lord?'

82:6]

Karīm comes from the three-letter Arabic root *kāf-rā-mīm*. It encompasses all kinds of good, honor and virtue. Indeed, the Arabs would use the word *karīm* for something beneficial, with lasting benefit, and it is also used for something that is weighty and dignified. The adjective *karīm* is used to describe someone who gives without being asked, and exceeds expectations. *Akram* – derived from the same root – is a comparative which denotes more intense generosity and honor.[35] Indeed, if you were to describe someone as generous – *karīm* – you would use *akram* to say that someone else is more generous. God in His essence is *karīm* and *akram* – more generous than even the most generous being – because of His perfection, His Oneness and His uniqueness. When preceded by *al-* (the), the comparative becomes a superlative – *al-Akram* therefore means 'the *most* generous.'

He who is al-Karīm and al-Akram is therefore generous in every single meaning of the word: He is magnanimous when He gives, so much so that He exceeds all expectations and goes beyond what we can imagine, He forgives all mistakes and slip-ups, and He honors the generousand righteous among us.

[35] Al-Ashqar, *Sharḥ Ibn Al-Qayyim Li Asmā' Allāh al-Ḥusnā*, 99.

While the word *karīm* is usually translated simply as 'generous', its meaning is much more expansive. The different meanings described above can all be found in the Qur'an. For example, the Qur'an itself is described in this way: *'That this is truly a noble (karīm) Qur'an.'* [56:77]

This means that the Qur'an is full of benefit and virtues. Indeed, the Qur'an is the word of God, and it teaches us what is best for us in this life and the next, narrating stories to us so that we may reflect on them and benefit.

Secondly, this word also means honor and dignity. Allah says: *'And We have certainly honored (karramnā) the children of Adam and carried them on the land and sea and provided for them of the good things and preferred them over much of what We have created, with [definite] preference.'* [17:70]

How beautiful that God Himself has honored us, and bestowed upon us this sense of honor and dignity. He has preferred humans, the children of Adam, over other creation, even though we are fallible and make mistakes. However, our honor comes from us returning to Allah Himself. Indeed, Satan detests us because he recognizes that we have been honored by God, and strives to get us to behave in the most dishonorable way. Satan said: *'"Do You see this one whom You have honored (karramta) above me? If You delay me until the Day of Resurrection, I will surely destroy his descendants, except for a few."'* [17:62]

When we follow Satan, we put ourselves in a less dignified state than that in which we were created.

Finally, *karīm* means giving far above and beyond. Allah tells us, *'Who will make God a good loan? He will double it for him and reward him generously.'* [57:11] He also says, *'Charitable men and women who make a good loan to God will have it doubled and have a generous reward.'* [57:18]

Whatever we give for His sake is always multiplied. Indeed, we are actually never compensated justly – we are compensated generously! Indeed, only Allah can be truly *karīm* because He is the Self-Sufficient (al-Ghanī). We are told in the Qur'an, "'*If anyone is grateful, it is for his own good, if anyone is ungrateful, then my Lord is self-sufficient and most generous.*'" [27:40]

Human beings' generosity has constraints, because what we have is naturally limited, and we have needs ourselves. Indeed, someone might appear to be generous, but this might in fact be because he or she hopes to gain something from others through this apparent generosity. Not Allah; He has no need of us. Therefore, as the verse above tells us, whoever thanks God, it is for his own good, and whoever is ungrateful, God is self-sufficient and is not harmed by ingratitude. Pairing His name al-Ghanī with al-Karīm (with His self-sufficiency preceding His generosity) tells us that Allah has no need of us, and yet He still gives to us in abundance. Indeed, His generosity in this world even reaches those who are ungrateful, because He is that generous. How many of us have been given blessings, though we knew that we were living in disobedience? How many of are given so much and yet fail to recognize the blessings, forgetting that we even have them? And still, al-Karīm gives to us!

What are the manifestations of al-Karīm?

It is easy to think of generosity in an abstract manner. But what are the manifestations of Allah's *karam* (generosity) in our lives?

God always goes above and beyond what is needed, though we know that He does not need to. He forgives, He follows through and He gives. He gives without being asked – how many blessings do we have that we never asked for? – and when He is asked, He exceeds all expectations. These are some manifestations of al-Karīm:

1. The subtle blessings

Many of the things of this world that give us pleasure or are beautiful do not need to be so. Flowers help a plant reproduce; that is their function. However, they deliver beauty for the eyes and perfume for our sense of smell. Similarly, the purpose of food is to provide us with the nutrients we need to survive; it could be completely bland and tasteless. But food is not just a pleasure for our taste buds, it is a reflection of culture, a reason for people to come together, and an extension of Allah's generosity when we feed others. Nothing in this world just *is*, in that nothing merely fulfills a function; everything is decorated with beauty and other benefits. This is also from the generosity of God.

2. Prayers

We were created to worship and we know that worship includes many different acts, but at the very base level, we all must pray. It is obligatory upon the believer who has reached puberty to pray, and it is something for which he or she will be held accountable. It is sufficient for our Lord to command, and for us – His servants – to obey. But Allah is far more generous. He provides limitless spiritual healing in prayer, and He makes it something that is beloved in the heart of the believers. When we pray, we are forgiven for sins, for example, as we are told: '*When a slave stands and prays, all his sins are brought and placed on his head and shoulders. Every time he bows or prostrates, some of them fall from him.*' [Bayhaqī]

Not only are we forgiven for our slip-ups, not only are we are rewarded for something that is compulsory – the prayer itself – but we are also rewarded for awaiting it. The Prophet ﷺ said: '*A person is considered in prayer as long as he is waiting for the prayer.*' [Bukhārī and Muslim]

We are also given the gift of closeness to Him through prostration. The Prophet ﷺ told us: '*The closest that a servant is to his Lord is when he is in prostration.*' [Muslim]

This is the generosity of al-Karīm, who gives far more than we can imagine, for acts of worship that are obligatory upon us, and which ultimately bring us benefit.

3. Giving to people even when they are insincere

It is easy to imagine God being generous towards those who are 'pious' or 'good'. But His generosity also extends to those whom He knows are insincere, and who are then proven to be so. We are told in the Qur'an, *'When trouble befalls man he cries out to Us, whether lying on his side, sitting, or standing, but as soon as We relieve him of his trouble he goes on his way as if he had never cried out to Us to remove his trouble. In this way the deeds of such heedless people are made attractive to them.'* [10:12]

The Most Generous even relieves the troubles of those who are insincere in their promises and ungrateful after relief comes.

4. Reward for good deeds

Fairness in judging our actions would be to reward a good deed, and condemn a bad deed. Yet God's generosity goes far beyond. The Prophet ﷺ taught:

> *'Whoever intends to perform a good deed but does not do it, then God will record it as a complete good deed. If he intends to do it and does so, then God the Exalted will record it as ten good deeds up to seven hundred times as much or even more. If he intends to do a bad deed and does not do it, then God will record for him one complete good deed. If he does it, then God will record for him a single bad deed.'* [Bukhārī]

We are rewarded for our good actions manifold, and for our intention to do good even if we do not actually do it. We only incur sin if we actually do the sin, but we are not punished for a bad intention that we do not follow through on. How great is Allah, the Most Generous!

5. Forgiveness

Again, Allah demonstrates the different dimensions of His generosity through how He pairs His names and attributes together. Allah says: *'He can reward those who believe and do good deeds: they will have forgiveness and generous provision.'* [34:4]

Forgiving someone is already an act of generosity when that person has done wrong. As human beings, we feel that it shows enough generosity of spirit to forgive someone who has wronged us. But in Allah's forgiveness of our sins, His unique generosity is manifest. He not only forgives, He then also gives generous provision. Pause for a second. Imagine if someone had wronged you, and you not only forgave them, but you also gave them – and continued to give them – generous gifts, as well as taking care of them. Would that not be the epitome of generosity? And Allah is far above this. Moreover, His generosity extends to how He forgives us; God not only cancels our sins, but those sins may even be turned into good deeds in our books.[36]

6. Supplications

Another coupling of Allah's name al-Karīm is with His name al-Ḥayiyy. As we mentioned in chapter 27 on this name, the Prophet ﷺ said: *'Verily your Lord is Generous and Shy. If His servant raises his hands to Him (in supplication) He becomes shy to return them empty.'* [Aḥmad and others]

The pairing of these names is so beautiful, if one reflects. You may ask Allah for something, but in His wisdom He knows that what you want is not good for you now, or not good for you at all. Because He is both al-Ḥayiyy and al-Karīm, He would never give you nothing in response. He never responds 'no', but rather, '"no" to what you think you need, but you can have this instead, which

[36] The Qur'an states, *'those who repent, believe, and do good deeds: God will change the evil deeds of such people into good ones. He is most forgiving, most merciful.'* [25:70]

much better for you.' So ask the One whose generosity knows no bounds!

7. Paradise

We mentioned above that Allah never compensates us justly, but rather generously; Paradise is the ultimate manifestation of His generosity. Imagine being admitted to the most blissful place simply because your good deeds outweighed your bad deeds by just one deed. Imagine that one deed by which Allah chose to admit you to Paradise was half a sandwich which you shared with someone who was hungry. Imagine that your bad deeds actually outweighed the good (even though good deeds are multiplied and bad deeds are not!), but He chose to forgive you and enter you into the place where there is no sadness, nor grief – forever. Moreover, for those who suffered in this world, Paradise removes even the memory of whatever they were afflicted with. The Prophet ﷺ told us of a person who suffered great hardship in his life, but one 'dip' into Paradise will make that person forget whatever difficulty he or she had ever gone through [Aḥmad]. Paradise is a place that we cannot even imagine – where everyone will have what he or she wishes, and every day is more fascinating and beautiful than the day before. Take a minute to just contemplate this.

Living with these names

1. Recognize the worth that God has given you

God created us as human beings, with intellect and the capacity to choose. This dignity was given by God, so as people, we must act in ways that are dignified. We dishonor ourselves by rejecting His worship, lying, cheating, being rude, and ignoring injustice. Indeed, *'in God's eyes, the most honored of you are the ones most mindful of Him: God is all knowing, all aware.'* [49:13]

2. Recognize and be grateful for God's generosity in His dealings with you

Everything good that we have is a result of Allah's generosity. Reflect upon how Allah's generosity exceeds all expectations. It is important to contemplate over what we have, and realize that what we have is truly over and above our basic needs. All that is from the generosity of al-Karīm, which deserves praise and thanks.

3. Be generous

Know that God compensates His servants because He has ultimate Generosity. And generosity, following the definition we gave above, is not simply about being generous with money; we can be generous with our time, as well as having a generous disposition. The Prophet ﷺ would never say 'no' when he was asked for something. [Bukhārī and Muslim] The Prophet ﷺ also said: '*The generous one is close to Allah, close to people, far from the fire; a stingy person is far from Allah, far from people, far from Paradise; and the generous ignorant person is more beloved to Allah than a stingy worshipper.*' [Tirmidhī]

AL-NŪR – THE LIGHT (56)

31

AL-NŪR – THE LIGHT (56)

'God is the Light of the heavens and earth.'

[24:35]

The scholar Ibn al-Qayyim stated that God has named Himself the Light (al-Nūr), and His religion is light, and He has made the abode of those close to Him filled with glimmering light. Light is one of those words that we use to describe a multitude of things, from the rays of the sun to a person having or being 'light'. It is abstract and intangible, but instinctively we know what it means: light is good – it illuminates. Al-Ghazālī said about this name that, through His light, God makes everything visible. It is related to al-Ẓāhir – the Manifest – as well as to al-Hādī – the Guide. In the dictionary, *nūr* is defined as illumination, rays, or anything that gives off light. Ibn al-Athīr said about this name that He is the One by whose light the blind see, and the astray are guided by His guidance.

We can say that light is of two types: Allah's light and created light. Created light can further be split into physical light – such as the light that we get from the sun, for example – and abstract light, such as the light of faith or knowledge.[37] Allah's name is al-Nūr, and thus He is the Light, and He gives light.

[37] Salman Al-Oadah, *In the Company of God: Closeness to Allah through the Beauty of His Names and Attributes*, 2nd ed. (Islam Today, 2011), 225.

True light

God is the Source of all light and, because He is the Light, it is only He who truly illuminates. It is by His light that all darkness is dispelled – both physical and spiritual – yet His physical light is too powerful for us to comprehend in this life. The Prophet ﷺ said, *'His veil is of light. If He were to lift it, the glory of His countenance would ignite everything in creation as it is touched by His gaze.'* [Muslim]

Indeed, we are told in the Qur'an, *'vision perceives Him not.'* [6:103] When Moses asked to see God, He replied:

> *'"You will never see Me, but look at that mountain: if it remains standing firm, you will see Me," and when his Lord revealed Himself to the mountain, He made it crumble: Moses fell down unconscious. When he recovered, he said, "Glory be to You! To You I turn in repentance! I am the first to believe!"'* [7:143]

It is stated that the light of God is too powerful to comprehend in this life – it is otherworldly – and simply being exposed to a fraction of His light made the mountain crumble.[38]

We also know that God's Face has light. The Prophet ﷺ said that, *'with God, there is no day or night, but the light of the heavens and the earth are from His Face.'* [Ṭabarānī] Indeed, on the Day of Judgment, when the sun and the stars fizzle out, the earth will be *'illuminated by the light of its Lord.'* [39:69] The Prophet ﷺ made this supplication:

> *'I seek refuge in the light of Your face by which all darkness is dispelled, and both this life and the life to come are put in their right course against incurring your wrath, or being the subject of your anger. To You I submit, until I earn Your pleasure. Everything is powerless without your support.'* [Ṭabarānī]

The Prophet ﷺ made this *du'ā'* when he was broken at Ṭā'if – when its people rejected him and drove him out with stones and

[38] Umar Sulayman Al-Ashqar, *Sharḥ Ibn Al-Qayyim Li Asmā' Allāh Al-Ḥusnā* (Amman: Dar al-Nafā'is, 2008), 164.

insults. So when you feel that you are in darkness, remember that God is the Light, and He can make the darkest corners brighter than the sun. Indeed, the Prophet ﷺ was then guided to Yathrib, which we know today as *al-Madīnah al-Munawwarah* – the Illuminated City.

This name also relates to darkness in our lives, especially when we see no way out. Sheikh Rātib al-Nabulsī stated that when we are facing a problem, we are in darkness. The solution to that problem is from al-Nūr. This is part of God's illumination.

Spiritual light

What does God Himself say about His light? We are told in the Qur'an:

> *'God is the Light of the heavens and earth. His Light is like this: there is a niche, and in it a lamp, the lamp inside a glass, a glass like a glittering star, fuelled from a blessed olive tree from neither east nor west, whose oil almost gives light even when no fire touches it— light upon light— God guides whoever He will to his Light; God draws such comparisons for people; God has full knowledge of everything.'* [24:35]

This verse in the Qur'an explains the effect of God's Light in a visual way. It tells us to picture a niche, which is a dent in the wall where lamps are placed. These dents are made in a curved shape, in order to spread the light of the lamp all around the room. In order to make sure that this light does not flicker or extinguish, there is an extra protective covering: the glass. This light needs an external fuel – the pure oil from the blessed olive tree – to keep it going. The internal and external lights meet and there is an explosion of lights – light upon light.

Abū al-Mansūr said in his exegesis (*tafsīr*) of this verse that guidance in the heart of a believer is an example of the light that God gives. Indeed, we have all been given a spiritual light from God, and the rib cage is shaped like a dent, which can spread God's light, and the heart is the protective glass. This light of God – this spiritual light, or spiritual vision – is already inside us, but the heart, like the protective glass, needs constant cleansing in order to ensure that the light is not blocked. When this internal light meets sources of light from the outside, such as revelation, there is a meeting of lights that increases the illumination of the heart, as well as how far it spreads. When God talks about the *'blessed olive tree'*, the Arabic word for 'blessed' is *mubārakah*, which actually means 'increased'. So, these sources of light constantly give to and increase the benefit of those receiving the light, and thus we talk about the *barakah*, or blessing, of reciting and understanding the Qur'an, of prayer, and of remembering God. These are all sources of light that keep giving to us.

Thus God tells us that He is Light – meaning that He is the source of spiritual light and vision – and He has put His light in all of us. We need to keep our hearts polished so that this light is not diminished. This light needs to be fed by His revelation, His remembrance, and the example of His Prophet ﷺ, which are all sources of light.

With light, and specifically the light of God, everything becomes clear. There is understanding. There is clarity. And with those come certainty. Ibn 'Abbās, the cousin of the Prophet ﷺ, said that, 'Light is Allah, the Guide, Who guides with His Divine Guidance whomsoever He wills by showing him the truth and inspiring him to follow it.'[39] Allah also tells us, *'God is the ally of those who believe: He brings them out of the depths of darknesses and into the light.'* [2:257]

God tells us that He brings us from darknesses into the light. And this does not just happen in an abstract way. He sends us what we need to illuminate our path. God says: *'A light has now come to you from God, and a Scripture making things clear.'* [5:15]

[39] Mentioned by Sheikh Rātib al-Nābulsī; reference appears to be in Tafsīr al-Ṭabarī.

The light in this verse is the Prophet Muhammad ﷺ, which is why reading his biography and understanding the traditions of the Prophet ﷺ is so important – because everything is made clear by him. We have the best example in him, and through him God makes many things clear for us.

Sheikh Rātib al-Nabulsī, in describing this name, said, 'Allah, All Mighty, is Light, so if you get connected with Him, you derive from His Divine Spiritual Light spiritual comfort and peacefulness, your vision of things and matters is rightly guided.'

This can help us understand the saying of the Prophet ﷺ when He tells us how God describes what happens when He loves a servant:

> *'When I love him, I shall be his hearing with which he shall hear, his sight with which he shall see, his hands with which he shall hold, and his feet with which he shall walk. And if he asks (something) of Me, I shall surely give it to him, and if he takes refuge in Me, I shall certainly grant him it.'* [Bukhārī]

When God loves you, your hearing, sight and actions are all guided by the Divine Light.

Living with this name

1. Recognize the light God has given you

The verse of light teaches us that all of us were given a spiritual light by God. No matter what we are going through or how spiritually low we feel, that light is still there.

2. Feed your spiritual light

Though we all have spiritual light, we must feed this light with the other sources that He has given us. We have to polish the protective glass – our hearts – with His remembrance and prayers, and increase the light by understanding His book and the teachings of His Prophet ﷺ, as well as being with His people.

3. Reflect God's light

All believers should adorn themselves with the most beloved and praiseworthy attributes to Allah, because Allah will make a light for them, and guide others through that light that He has given them.

4. Pray for Light

There are two beautiful supplications from the Qur'an and the Sunnah. In the Qur'an, God teaches us this prayer: *'Lord, perfect our lights for us and forgive us: You have power over everything.'* [66:8]

In this *du'ā'*, we ask for God's divine light and spiritual vision. The Prophet ﷺ would also supplicate to God with this prayer:

> *'O Allah! Make for me Light in my heart, Light in my vision, Light in my hearing, Light on my right, Light on my left, Light above me, Light under me, Light in front of me, Light behind me, Light in my hair, Light in my skin, Light in my flesh, Light in my blood, and Light in my bones. O Allah Grant me Light!'* [Tirmidhī]

AL-ḤALĪM AL-ṢABŪR – FORBEARANCE AND PATIENCE (57-58)

32

AL-ḤALĪM AL-ṢABŪR – FORBEARANCE AND PATIENCE (57-58)

'He will not call you to account for oaths you have uttered unintentionally, but He will call you to account for what you mean in your hearts. God is most forgiving and forbearing.'

[2:225]

There is an underappreciated attribute that accompanies us throughout our lives, to which we seldom pay attention. In our journey, we may be heedless and forget Allah. Our acts of worship may have shortcomings. We may mess up in major ways, repeatedly. And yet, we seldom see the consequences.

We might realize this and become consumed by guilt. We might look at those who seem to have it all together, and wonder whether we can ever be like them. We might give up in our journey to God before we even begin, because we feel that we are starting so far behind everyone else.

Yet, if we realized Allah's names al-Halīm (The Most Forbearing) and al-Ṣabūr (The Most Patient), we would be filled with hope in and love for God – He who sees us and does not punish. On the contrary, He who sees us and appreciates every single small step we take in His way. He who witnesses our imperfect efforts and rewards us for them. He who, in response to our baby steps towards Him, comes running to us.

The name al-Halīm is found in numerous places in the Qur'an, and it describes the One who is unperturbed by the misdeeds of people, who delays punishment and forgives. Its Arabic root, *ḥā-lām-mīm*, means 'reason', and thus Allah al-Halīm shows forbearance out of His wisdom, and is not moved by haste or anger. This name is also the epitome of strength because Allah – the Most Powerful – has the power and ability to punish, but chooses not to do so.

Al-Ṣabūr comes from the same root as *ṣabr* (patience), and is found in the hadith that lists the names of Allah. It means that He is not quick to punish the heedless or even the sinful, or those who mock Him and say false things about Him.[40] He is also patient with the well-intentioned efforts of His servants. Moreover, al-Ghazālī explains that when God brings about an event, He does not delay it due to procrastination like a lazy person would, nor does He speed it up out of haste. For example, in the story of Joseph, which was described in chapter 24 and others, Allah's *ṣabr* was demonstrated: no event happened before its due time. One might be impatient when reading the story and question: 'When will the relief come for Joseph? Why are the people who wronged him allowed to live their lives and get away with it?' But Allah was not moved by haste due to the ill-will of others; Joseph's relief came at the right time. Similarly, in the incident of *al-Ifk* (also described in chapter 24) where 'Ā'ishah was slandered and gossip about her spread, we see the manifestation of Allah's *ṣabr*. He was aware of the people spreading lies about 'Ā'ishah – and Allah Himself described what happened as '*very serious*' [24:15] and that '*a painful punishment waits in this world and the next for those who like indecency to spread among the believers*' [24:19] – but allowed the events run their course in order to teach the believers important lessons about protecting the honor and dignity of others.

Though they are similar, Ibn al-Qayyim distinguishes between the two names by stating that forbearance is wider in meaning, and encompasses patience. Sheikh Salman al-Ouda points out that He demonstrates patience with us by giving to us, despite our heedlessness and transgressions. Allah tells us, '*If God were to*

[40] Al-Ashqar, *Sharḥ Ibn Al-Qayyim Li Asmā' Allāh al-Ḥusnā*, 174.

punish people [at once] for the wrong they have done, there would not be a single creature left on the surface of the earth. He gives them respite for a stated time and, whenever their time comes, God has been watching His servants.' [35:45]

So what are the dimensions of these two names? And how do they manifest?

Allah's patience and forbearance with us

If we take a moment to reflect on our actions and our states, we will find that Allah has been manifesting His *ḥilm* (forbearance) with us throughout our lives. We can all think back to our major and minor mess-ups, as well as periods of heedlessness (perhaps we are in one now!). And still, we find gentle reminders all around us. In fact, because His forbearance is purposeful and from His wisdom, we realize that the reminders of Him were actually *from* Him. Perhaps a friend convinced us to go to a talk at a time when we were far from Allah, or perhaps an email in our inbox (that we would usually never open!) after we committed a wrong reminds us of Allah's forgiveness for those who return to Him and do not despair. These are all manifestations of His *ḥilm* – not only does He forgo punishment, but He sends us subtle prompts in order that we may remember.

Indeed, God's *ḥilm* extends to delaying not only the consequences of our actions, but even the recording of our wrong deeds. The Prophet ﷺ told us: *'The scribe (angel) on the left delays registering the sin of a Muslim for six hours. If he repents (within these six hours), and seeks God's forgiveness, they drop if off. If he doesn't, they write is down as a single sin.'* [Ṭabarānī]

But what if we experience what we regard as a clear punishment for a wrong that we committed? Does that mean that Allah was not *ḥalīm* with us? We have to remember that the root of Allah's name al-Ḥalīm has the meanings 'to be unperturbed' and 'reason'. Allah's forbearance is purposeful and so are His lesser punishments.

If Allah's forbearance causes us to drift farther away from Him and insist on our sins, that would not be wise – and Allah is far above that. Allah demonstrates the purpose of His lesser punishment in Sūrat al-Qalam. This chapter recounts the story of three sons of a righteous man who would allow his garden to be used by the poor. When he passed away, the sons *'swore that they would harvest its fruits in the morning and made no allowance.'* They wanted to deny the poor their share of the garden. So, what happened? *'A disaster from your Lord struck the garden as they slept and by morning it was stripped bare, a desolate land.'* [68:19-20]

Some of us might feel that this punishment was deserved, as what the brothers were setting out to do was truly mean-spirited and dishonorable. But remember that lesser punishments in this world have a purpose from the Most Wise. They are not a final judgement, but rather a notice that we are on the wrong path and need to return. The brothers realized the lesson – *'They said, "Alas for us! We have done terrible wrong, but maybe our Lord will give us something better in its place: we truly turn to Him in hope."'* [68:31-32] And God says, *'Such is the punishment [in this life], but greater is the punishment in the Hereafter, if only they knew.'* [68:33]

God saved them from the punishment of the Hereafter through the wake-up call He gave them in this life. They realized the error of their ways. If God had allowed them to do what they wanted, they would then have faced a greater reckoning in the next life. The point of these punishments is to bring us back. Allah says this in no uncertain terms: *'And we will surely let them taste the nearer punishment short of the greater punishment that perhaps they will return.'* [32:21]

So, the purpose of forbearance is realization and return. If we take advantage of God's *ḥilm*, or if that *ḥilm* increases our heedlessness, we need to be reminded in the most suitable way, even if it hurts us in the moment. And all of this is from God's mercy.

Of course, God's forbearance and patience are not simply manifested by delaying punishment. The other dimension of these names is His patience with and appreciation for our baby steps.

Patience with, and love for, your efforts

Ideally, someone who loves you and wants the best for you shows patience when they see you trying. They do not chastise you when they know that your effort is sincere, even if your progress is slow – the important thing is that you are truly trying. In a school in the United States, a pilot project was initiated in which students were asked to run in the morning before class in order to get their heart rates up, as this would help with mental cognition later in the day.[41] From the outside, it would be easy to assume that the students who fell behind were lazy. But the coach invested in heart rate monitors, so that he could actually measure their efforts. He found that many of the students who finished behind the rest actually put in more work; their heart rates were much higher. They were sincerely trying. And for the purpose of the exercise, this was what was required of them: to get their heart rate to a specific level, as this would help them focus later in the day. He became much more appreciative of their efforts, despite the fact that, from the outside, they looked like underachievers.

Allah is far above any analogy, but He is the ultimate heart monitor. Imagine the One who created you, the One who sends you signs, who encourages you to return to Him... He is al-Ṣabūr (the Most Patient) because He actually witnesses your effort. He is not impatient with those of us who are slowly but surely walking on the path. He is patient when we stray, and keeps the path open to us when we come back.

There is beautiful wisdom in the statement of the Prophet ﷺ: *'The best actions are those which are consistent, even if they are small.'* [Bukhārī and Muslim]

[41] John J. Ratey and Eric Hagerman, *Spark!* (United Kingdom: Hachette Publishing, 2010).

This saying of the Prophet ﷺ epitomizes God's attribute of patience. God does not ask us to become 'Super Muslim' in a day and a night. He does not mind that we take small steps to build ourselves, or whatever is within our capacity. The Prophet ﷺ reminds us to *'do those deeds which you can do easily, as God will not get tired (of giving rewards) till you get bored and tired (of performing religious deeds).'* [Bukhārī] Simply, this tells us that God does not get bored with waiting for us to get our acts together if we are sincere in our efforts. We should put in the determination to become better, but it is okay to start slowly if that is the way that will get us to start. He is patient. Even if we feel that it is difficult to maintain good actions, we should still do whatever good we can, especially when we feel inspired to do so. The frustration that we may feel in not being 'enough', or as 'good', or as consistent, as others, that leads us to think bad of God or forego even trying to better, is from Satan. He wants to make us feel impatient, unworthy and hypocritical, so that we give up – that is his ultimate aim. But Allah? He is patient! Not only that, but He loves those small steps so much that if we take one step towards Him, He comes to us – yes, Allah Himself! – at speed.

The Prophet ﷺ tells us that Allah says: *'Whoever draws close to me by the length of a hand, I will draw close to him by the length of an arm. Whoever draws close to me the by length of an arm, I will draw close to him by the length of a fathom. Whoever comes to me walking, I will come to him running.'* [Muslim]

This tells us that whatever effort we put into our relationship with God, Allah not only accepts this, but He meets us where we are. And if we try, but mess up again? Again, the Messenger of Allah ﷺ told us, *'Allah Almighty said: O son of Adam, if you call upon me and place your hope in me, I will forgive you without hesitation. O son of Adam, if you have sins piling up to the clouds and then ask for my forgiveness, I will forgive you without hesitation.'* [Tirmidhī]

A person who has hope in God, and who turns back to Him when he or she messes up, is met with an abundance of love and forgiveness. So why do you think that when you sincerely intend to become better and take the necessary steps, no matter how small, that He will get bored or tired of you? These thoughts are in direct conflict with His attributes, which He has chosen for Himself and chosen to reveal to us, in order to remind us that our every effort matters. If a school coach can show forbearance and encouragement to his students, after observing their efforts through their heart rates, what about Allah – the Most Patient, the Most Merciful, the Most Affectionate – who is truly privy to our hearts?

Of course, we should not limit ourselves to small actions if we can do greater deeds. We should be ambitious in what we desire to do for God. But this name tells us that, small or large, as long as we put in the effort, Allah loves and appreciates it, and will be patient with us no matter where we are along the road. The fact that the road seems long should not deter us; we have the best and most patient Guide. There will always be something to improve, and that is a good thing, because it means that we can constantly grow and evolve. The Companions themselves slipped up, but they never despaired. Moreover, they were not complacent. They knew their own selves. If it was anger on which they needed to work, then they worked on their anger. If it was prayer, then they focused on that. If it was laziness, then they tried to improve that aspect of their character.

Suhayl ibn ʿAmr was seventy years old when he accepted Islam, and he spent many of his years before becoming Muslim actively fighting the Prophet ﷺ. Someone might say, 'what was the point, after he spent more than two decades showing enmity to the Prophet ﷺ?' But Suhayl ibn ʿAmr had hope in God, and he knew that if God could be patient with his transgressions against His Prophet ﷺ, surely He would be even more forbearing when Suhayl took the steps to rectify his actions. This teaches us that the past only matters inasmuch as we can learn from it, and from our mistakes. What really matters is this moment, now. Do not be frustrated because you feel that you have squandered all of your life in play, and that there is no time to make up for it. Do not be so hard on yourself when you cannot get something right. Simply ask yourself: what can you do now to improve your relationship with God, to improve yourself, to achieve your spiritual goals?

Because Allah is forbearing and patient with those who are far worse: tyrants.

Allah's patience and forbearance with tyrants and transgressors

When Pharaoh declared himself to be a lord, Allah was watching. When he coerced the magicians to do their magic, Allah was witness. When he ghettoized the Children of Israel, Allah knew.

And still, when He sent Moses and Aaron to him, He said, '*And speak to him with gentle speech that perhaps he may be reminded or fear.*' [20:44]

Someone like Pharaoh surely did not deserve forbearance; he was truly the embodiment of evil in all its forms. But we need to remember something: the punishments of this world – indeed, the justice of this world – is limited. When criminals massacre, we would not give them a second chance, and indeed we should not. Still, no matter how we punish them, it could never reach the level of what they inflicted upon others. Even if we do to them exactly what they did to others, it still would not be the same, if they had hurt multiple people.

But, for some, the Hellfire is eternal. And for someone to deserve that, he or she needs to be given multiple chances to return. And this is why Allah is forbearing even with the tyrants. They might still be punished, and may still have to make amends, but they will eventually be atoned for their sins, if they return to God. But if they insist and continue to reject Him, and persist in their tyranny, no one can doubt that the eternal punishment is deserved. This is why no one who is damned to hell can claim that, if they were given a second chance, they would do differently. Allah tells us that they say, '"*Our Lord, remove us; we will do righteousness - other than what we were doing!" But did We not grant you life enough for whoever would remember therein to remember, and the warner had come to you? So taste [the punishment], for there is not for the wrongdoers any helper.'* [35:37]

The story of Pharaoh illustrates this. Even the worst of people is given multiple chances. He, and others, are reminded through gentleness and difficulty, blessing and punishment.

Moreover, this story teaches us about Allah al-Ṣabūr, because everything that happens in this world has a purpose. Allah does not hasten events before their time. While we might have loved to see Pharaoh punished as soon as he committed the first transgression, all the events that unfolded had their purpose. Those who were dedicated to Allah were tested, but they persevered and were rewarded with the highest levels of Paradise, like Āsiyah, the wife of Pharaoh, and this may not have happened otherwise. Allah's forbearance with a tyrant may be the reason that the oppressed are admitted to Paradise.

The paired names

Allah's name al-Ḥalīm is mentioned in the Qur'an, and thus Allah introduces us to the different dimensions of His forbearance through how He pairs them with His other names. Al-Ḥalīm is most often paired with His name al-Ghafūr, the Forgiving. Allah says in the Qur'an: *'The seven heavens and the earth and whatever is in them exalt Him. And there is not a thing except that it exalts [Allah] by His praise, but you do not understand their [way of] exalting. Indeed, He is ever Forbearing and Forgiving.'* [17:44]

This reminds us that Allah's forbearance does not necessarily mean that He will eventually punish the sinners – He tells us that He delays punishment, *and* is forgiving as well. How kind is our Lord, who gives us multiple opportunities to return to Him, and still forgives all our mess-ups as we strive for Him!

Indeed, He is not only forbearing and forgiving, He is forbearing and appreciative (*shakūr*). Some of us might be worried that, as we struggle for Him and make mistakes, our efforts and good deeds do not matter. Allah comforts us by telling that *'Allah is Most Appreciative and Forbearing,'* [64:17] He appreciates your efforts and your good deeds.

Finally, Allah reassures us that His forbearance is not a 'mistake'. He says, *'He will surely cause them to enter an entrance with which they will be pleased, and indeed, Allah is Knowing and Forbearing.'* [22:59]

When people give us the benefit of the doubt, and give us a chance when we mess up, we might feel guilt, because we think, 'they do not really know me – if they did, they would not have given me this chance!' This cycle of guilt is Satan's way of making us feel undeserving, and therefore unable to utilize the opportunity given to us. Allah tells us that He is the All-Knowing; He knows us inside-out and to our very depths, and *still* He is forbearing. This should soften our hearts because Allah is telling us that He knows that we can be better – and this from the One who knows us better than we know ourselves!

Allah also says, *'Kind speech and forgiveness are better than charity followed by injury. And Allah is Free of need and Forbearing.'* [2:263]

He reminds us in this verse that He is al-Ghanī – Free of need. Indeed, all of these pairings show us how utterly and completely unique Allah's forbearance is, and emphasize that His forbearance is not like the forbearance of human beings. People might display forbearance because they want or need something in return, but Allah is free of need. He has no need of us, and His forbearance truly benefits only us.

How generous Allah is, who showers His fallible servants with opportunities to return to Him, despite having no need of them! Indeed, we have a merciful and loving Lord.

No complacency

Although God is patient and forbearing, this does not mean that we should just be wishful thinkers. Wishful thinking is one of the diseases of the heart. A wishful thinker is one who delays and defers for no reason, simply out of laziness, or commits sin heedlessly – ostensibly because he or she hopes for Allah's mercy. This is actually punishable. The true fruit of hope is effort.

Indeed, there is a story related about a scholar who was being asked questions in the mosque. One man came and asked him sorrowfully, 'is there forgiveness for one who has engaged in pre-marital intimacy?' The scholar responded in the affirmative, and told the man the necessary steps to take. Later in the day, another man came and asked hesitantly, 'is there forgiveness for one who has engaged in pre-marital intimacy?' The scholar shook his head and said 'no'. A person who had heard the whole exchange told the scholar after the second man left, 'Two men asked you the same question and you gave them completely opposite answers!' The scholar responded, 'I knew that the first person had already committed the act, while the second person had yet to commit the act. We must always remind people after a bad deed that they can return to God, whereas we cannot make a mockery of God's patience and mercy by reassuring those who intend to commit wrongful acts.'

Living with these names

1. Identify what you need to improve, set a goal, and work towards it

Been missing your prayers? Always wanted to memorize Qur'an? Parts of your character that need improvement? Maybe your relationship with your loved ones needs to be fixed?

Oftentimes, our lack of belief in our abilities, or even the perceived effort required to improve, prevents us from taking the first step. However, we have to remember that everything – from our intentions, to making the effort, to coming back after messing up – is appreciated by al-Ḥalīm al-Ṣabūr. Start with the smallest deed you can, even if it is just making the intention. Keep adding to it, and keep striving. Allah will appreciate your effort and forgive your mistakes, God willing.

2. Be patient with yourself and persevere in doing good. Be patient while awaiting results

Remember that whatever truly has worth can sometimes be the most difficult goal to achieve, and this why patience is so crucial. Patience is to persevere with God-consciousness, despite the odds. As the Prophet ﷺ tells us, '*Whoever persists in being patient, God will make him patient. Nobody can be given a blessing better and greater than patience.*' [Bukhārī] On a long road, patience is the key to a noble destination.

Allah tells us, '*And those who are patient, seeking the countenance of their Lord, and establish prayer and spend from what We have provided for them secretly and publicly and prevent evil with good - those will have the good consequence of [this] home - Gardens of perpetual residence; they will enter them with whoever were righteous among their fathers, their spouses and their descendants. And the angels will enter upon them from every gate, [saying], "Peace be upon you for what you patiently endured. And excellent is the final home."*' [13:22-24]

This verse reminds us to persevere in doing good, no matter how difficult it might be. We should pray even when we do not feel the prayer spiritually, and give even when it is difficult for our hearts. Allah appreciates all the little things that we do for His sake. And, one day in future, we can look back at our efforts and be grateful that we persevered, *inshā'Allāh*.

3. Be patient with the things outside of your control

Exhibiting patience also applies to the events that befall us, as well as when events do not go our way, despite our efforts. We may be wronged even when we try to do good, and may wonder, 'why?'

We can look to the situation that the Companions of the Cave, as well as the Prophet Joseph, experienced. In Surat al-Kahf, the companions of the cave are described as '*youths who believed in their Lord*,' [18:13]. They believed in their Lord when a ruthless king punished anyone who dared to do that. The youth were found out; one might wonder why? But they remained steadfast, and retreated to the cave to escape the persecution, only to be put to sleep by Allah for over 300 years in order that they might witness that their sincere effort in remaining steadfast did not go to waste at all: when they awoke, the entire nation was a believing one. They did good despite the obstacles and even when they were prevented from doing so, and Allah allowed the seed that they had planted to grow. It took centuries, but Allah is patient, and so should we be with regards to seeing the fruit of our good actions.

Similarly, the position of the Prophet Joseph might seem extremely frustrating to an outsider. His dignity and goodness were almost always met treachery and ill-will. But Joseph remained steadfast. He kept his promise to God and was always mindful of Him, doing what was the right, despite the most trying of circumstances.

Still, he was tested, while the people who wronged him seemed to have it so much better. His brothers lived a normal life with their father. The wife of the minister was free while Joseph was imprisoned. His cell-mates were released before he was, and he remained in prison for years.

In the end though, Allah brought Joseph's brothers to him, in need, at the exact time that he had power, respect, trust and authority. Had they come to Egypt at any earlier point, they may have found him a servant or a prisoner. Had Joseph been released before the dream of the king, people might have doubted his innocence, and he would not have been given the position he later enjoyed. God's timing was better than anyone could ever imagine.

Likewise, when we find ourselves wondering why we are in difficulty, or somewhere that we do not want to be, we need to persevere. We need to remain steadfast in doing good and not be hasty for an outcome, when Allah knows best when to bring it about. The Prophet ﷺ taught us to *'know that victory comes with patience, relief with affliction, and ease with hardship.'* [Tirmidhī]

Other tests might come our way that seem not to be lightened in this world. However, we need to remember that how we will be rewarded in the next world is far greater. For example, the Prophet ﷺ said with regards to the death of a loved one: *'Allah Almighty says: "I have nothing to give to my faithful servant but Paradise if I cause his dear friend to die and he remains patient."'* [Bukhārī]

'Umar ibn 'Abd al-'Azīz also said, 'Allah does not grant a servant a blessing and then remove the blessing, then compensate him with patience in place of what was removed, but that what he was granted is better than what was taken away.' Then, 'Umar recited the verse, *'Verily, the reward of the patient will be fulfilled without account.'* [39:10]

4. Be patient and forbearing with other people

Ḥilm and *ṣabr* are attributes with which people should adorn themselves, especially when dealing with others. Allah says in the Qur'an about the Prophet Abraham: *'Indeed was Abraham compassionate and ḥalīm.'* [9:114]

God also tells us in the Qur'an, *'You who believe, be steadfast (iṣbirū), more steadfast than others (ṣābirū); be ready; always be mindful of God, so that you may prosper.'* [3:200]

The Prophet ﷺ said that forbearance is the best characteristic. He also said, *'Clemency is from Allah and haste is from Satan.'* [Tirmidhī]

It is noble to overlook the mistakes of others, especially since we love for Allah to overlook our own faults. Similarly, just as we appreciate Allah's patience with us, particularly when we mess up, we should try to find it in our hearts to be patient with others. The Prophet Muhammad ﷺ told us: *'Whoever curbs his anger, while being able to act, Allah will fill his heart with certainty of faith.'* [Bukhārī]

However, it is crucial to emphasize here that patience and forbearance do not mean allowing abuse to continue. These characteristics are also not an excuse to avoid having difficult conversations that are necessary for the actual improvement of a relationship; the avoidance may end up creating resentment in our hearts towards people who may be hurting us. This is not forbearance, because, as we mentioned, the one who is forbearing is calm and unperturbed in his heart.

Forbearance and patience mean being generous with others with regards to their mistakes, while also standing for justice. Allah's *ḥilm* allows us to return, and when we do not, He may send us a lesser punishment to alert us. Similarly, our forbearance must come from a place of wisdom and strength, and not from weakness or avoidance.

AL-QĀBIḌ, AL-BĀSIṬ – THE WITHHOLDER, THE EXPENDER (59-60)

33

AL-QĀBIḌ, AL-BĀSIṬ – THE WITHHOLDER, THE EXPENDER (59-60)

'Indeed, God is the Price-Setter, the One who takes away (al-Qābiḍ) and gives abundantly (al-Bāsiṭ).'

[Ibn Mājah]

Allah is al-Qābiḍ al-Bāsiṭ: these names can be roughly translated as the Withholder and the Expender. *Qabḍ* means 'to seize', 'to hold' or 'to grip something', while *basṭ* means 'to give in abundance' or 'to expand something'.

These two words are opposites, yet they complement each other. Indeed, according to some scholars, al-Qābiḍ al-Bāsiṭ are of God's 'paired names', which means that they must be mentioned together when applied to God. However, the attributes themselves (not the names, preceded by *al-*) can be mentioned separately when they refer to an action. For example, *'These people have no grasp of God's true measure. On the Day of Resurrection, the whole earth will be in His grip (qabḍatuhu). The heavens will be rolled up in His right hand -- Glory be to Him! He is far above the partners they ascribe to Him!'* [39:67]

Allah also says, *'If God were to grant (yabsuṭu) His plentiful provision to [all] His creatures, they would act insolently on Earth.'* [42:27]

These attributes are also mentioned together: *'It is God who withholds and God who gives abundantly.'* [2:245]

As names, however, scholars say that referring to God with only one of these names would be to render an incomplete meaning. When He restricts, He also expands – there is no restriction without eventual expansion, there is no withholding without eventual giving. The manifestations of *qabḍ* and *basṭ* are many. For example, God takes or holds (*yaqbiḍ*) charity from the rich, by imposing obligatory almsgiving upon them (zakat), and expands (*yabsuṭ)* the fortunes of others by ensuring that the alms reach the poor.

Another meaning of *qabḍ* is that Allah seizes or holds physically. The Prophet ﷺ told us that on the Day of Judgment, *'Allah will say: "The angels have interceded, the prophets have interceded, and the believers have interceded. There is no intercession remaining save that which belongs to the Most Merciful." Then He will seize (yaqbiḍ) a handful of the inhabitants of Hell who never did anything good and take them out of the Hellfire.'* [Bukhārī and Muslim]

We will be expounding upon three manifestations of *qabḍ* and *basṭ* as they relate to provision, life and death, and our spiritual hearts.

Rizq (provision)

The concepts of *qabḍ* and *basṭ* are closely related to provision. It is God who ultimately provides for us – He tells us: *'Say, "My Lord gives in abundance to whichever of His servants He will, and sparingly to whichever He will; He will replace whatever you give in alms; He is the best of providers."'* [34:39]

And because God is the Most Wise, the Most Just, and the Most Merciful, both His withholding from us and His giving to us are part of His wisdom, justice and mercy. He tells us in the verse mentioned earlier: *'If God were to grant His plentiful provision to [all] His creatures, they would act insolently on earth, but He sends down in due measure whatever He will, for He is well aware of His servants and watchful over them.'* [42:27]

God knows us and our states. He sends us provision in due measure, not all at once. While this verse hints at the fact that there are certain hidden matters and subtleties of which we are truly unaware, we can also see that empires or nations that historically had abundant wealth ended up transgressing, believing that their provision meant that that they were above others and untouchable. Allah tells us, *'Allah extends provision for whom He wills and restricts [it]. And they rejoice in the worldly life, while the worldly life is not, compared to the Hereafter, except [brief] enjoyment.'* [13:26]

This is a reminder: some people rejoice when they are given much in this world for purely worldly reasons. However, this world is both temporary and brief. Being granted provision might give us some pleasure in this life, but what are we doing to prepare for the real life in the Hereafter? Whether our provision is abundant or restricted, only what we do with it is of significance. It matters whether we use this provision – however great or little it is – to turn towards God or to turn away from Him. Indeed, Allah says, *'Wealth and children are [but] adornment of the worldly life. But the enduring good deeds are better to your Lord for reward and better for [one's] hope.'* [18:46]

Allah teaches us through this verse that, yes, there is pleasure in wealth and family. But our true focus should be on doing enduring good deeds. And whether our wealth or children end up being blessings or tests is entirely dependent on how we behave with them. Allah also says, *'It is God who withholds and God who gives abundantly, and it is to Him that you will return.'* [2:245]

This should cause us to reflect upon our actions: what have we done with what Allah has given us? Conversely, if we are going through a period of constriction, does that push us to pursue that which is forbidden?

Finally, provision is not simply with regards to material wealth. It can be in knowledge and status, so if we have been given any of those things, we must ask ourselves, how much of it do we give to others?

Life and death

Another manifestation of *qabḍ* and *basṭ* is how God seizes our souls and causes us to die, or releases the souls. He tells us: *'Exalted is He who holds all control in His hands; who has power over all things; who created death and life to test you [people] and reveal which of you does best – He is the Mighty, the Forgiving.'* [67:1-2]

When we sleep, it is described as a 'small death', in which our souls are returned to God. He restores many of them, and withholds others. Knowing that our souls are within the grip of Allah, al-Qābiḍ al-Bāsiṭ, should remind us that our existence is no accident; indeed, our being in this world is purposeful. If we feel overwhelmed by trials and tribulations, we should do as the Prophet ﷺ instructed: *'None of you should wish for death because of a calamity befalling him; but if he has to wish for death, he should say: "O Allah! Keep me alive as long as life is better for me, and let me die if death is better for me."'* [Bukhārī]

An extra day given to us is an opportunity to do good, because Allah has decreed not to seize our souls. It is because Allah knows what is best for us, and He is giving us daily opportunities to do good for Him.

The constriction and expansion of the heart

Many of us go through periods of constriction; our chests feel tight, our hearts heavy, and we find no pleasure in acts of worship. We juxtapose this with the good times, when our hearts feel light, our chests expansive, and we look forward to doing those deeds that bring us close to God. Both of these are from al-Qābiḍ al-Bāsiṭ, He who contracts and He who expands.

Many, if not all, of us wish to be in the latter state always. We may feel terrible about ourselves – failures, in fact – when we are in periods of constriction. Are we unable to taste the sweetness of worship because Allah has rejected us? Are we doomed to a life of difficulty?

But there is purpose in both states. Sometimes this constriction is what brings us back to God. Perhaps the constriction is to teach us to worship Allah in times of difficulty and hardship. It is easy to do good when we feel good, but do we abandon worship when life overwhelms us? It may be to teach us patience in order to raise our rank in the Hereafter. The person who is in a state of constriction can look forward to expansion and lightness afterwards. The Prophet Joseph had to be thrown in a well before coming into the care of the minister. He had to be put in prison before he was given power and reunited with his family. But he understood that it was all from God, and he was able to make the best of his situation. He knew that the relief was coming and he knew that there was a purpose in the constriction.

Moreover, sometimes Allah gives us abundantly in order that we build spiritual fortitude in the good times. This helps us to withstand difficulty when it inevitably comes. For example, Mary, the mother of Jesus, was beloved to God. We are told, '*The angels said to Mary: "Mary, God has chosen you and made you pure: He has truly chosen you above all women. Mary, be devout to your Lord, prostrate yourself in worship, bow down with those who pray."*' [3:42-43] God Himself chose Mary and made her pure – what an incredibly special position to be in. Indeed, she was blessed:

> '*Her Lord graciously accepted her and made her grow in goodness, and entrusted her to the charge of Zachariah. Whenever Zachariah went in to see her in her sanctuary, he found her supplied with provisions. He said, '"Mary, how is it you have these provisions?" and she said, "They are from God: God provides limitlessly for whoever He will."*'' [3:37]

She was accepted by Allah, cared for by a Prophet (Zachariah), and always had provision. This was a period of expansion and growth for her – and indeed, she grew in goodness. We learn from this to utilize periods of expansion to gain closeness to the Most Merciful, rather than use that expansion as a distraction for worldly purposes. Mary was then tested. She was told that she would carry a child, without ever having been touched by a man. This would not only be difficult for her, but scandalous, as she was from a righteous family, and she was known to be pious. During her labor, she was at the point of wishing that she was dead [19:23]; this is how trying it was for her. She was then told to '*shake the trunk of the palm tree*' [19:25] in order to get the dates for her nourishment; imagine being in this position, after being one who previously was receiving provision with no effort. But she was able to withstand and remain firm, and she is forever recorded as an example to the believers. Moreover, relief came after her effort; Allah said to her, '*so eat, drink, be glad.*' [19:26] Such is life of this world, with periods of *qabḍ* and *bāsṭ*; those who know Allah by His names al-Q̱ābiḍ al-Bāsiṭ recognize this reality, and worship Him in the different situations they find themselves in and are rewarded for it, by His grace.

Furthermore, when we are far from God, this feeling of discomfort and narrowness in the heart may be what causes us to go back to God. It is when we desperately want something, which we know we have little power to obtain, and feel the pain of that need, that we turn to God with devotion to ask Him for it. It is when we are in trouble, and have nowhere else to turn, that we realize our need for God. And it is when people desert us that we understand that God was truly there for us all along. Thus, being in a situation of *qabḍ* and recognizing our need for Him can be the very thing that leads us to al-Bāsiṭ and His relief.

Moreover, sometimes the feeling of *qabḍ* is due to our own priorities and misdeeds. We may desire approval, control and security from sources other than God, and when they fail us, a natural feeling of constriction occurs. We may allow the feeling of *qabḍ* to push us further away from God, instead of turning to Him. But God is al-Q̱ābiḍ, and just like a headache tells us that we have not slept well, or a stomach ache tells us that the food we have eaten is bad, this *qabḍ* tells us to reflect on its causes. There is a root cause, and the only way to eliminate the discomfort is to deal with its source. And just like God is al-Qābiḍ, He is al-Bāsiṭ, who can remove even the traces of any constriction we may have felt. The Prophet ﷺ tells us that, '*Verily, Allah Almighty stretches out (yabsuṭ) His hand by night to accept the repentance of those who sin by day, and He stretches out (yabsuṭ) His hand by day to accept the repentance of those who sin by night, until the sun rises from the west.*' [Muslim]

Allah is always there for us. The key is to know that after every hardship is ease, as promised in the Qur'an [65:7], and with hardship are eases [94:5-6]. And the state of the believers is such that, when we are in a state of ease and feeling at rest in our hearts, we are grateful. Sheikh Omar Abdelkafy stated that the heart is like a home. When we are able, it is important to build around the house, so that if a thief decides to rob us, he or she has to get past so much more just to reach the front door. This means that, in times of ease, we should build our faith, good deeds and habits, and knowledge; indeed, the Prophet ﷺ said, '*Do good deeds in the time that you have and take advantage of the moments of gentle breeze from the mercy of Allah. Verily, Allah has moments of gentle breeze from His mercy that He sends upon whomever He wills among His servants.*' [Ṭabarānī] We should take advantage of the times of expansion – of these gentle breezes – so that when we face constriction and Satan tries to attack us in our vulnerable state, if he is successful, he is only successful in getting us to abandon, for example, a voluntary act, rather than what is obligatory upon us. During times of expansion, we should build to such a degree that our later troubles may only cause us to slip from a state of sincere devotion to an acceptable level of practice, rather than from simply skirting by to outright sins.

Living with these names

1. Do not get stuck in constriction

Recognize that being in this world means going through periods of constriction, but we must not allow ourselves to get stuck there. Knowing that Allah is al-Qabiḍ al-Bāsiṭ means having certainty that there will also be periods of expansion. The Prophet ﷺ reminded us that *'victory comes with patience, relief with affliction, and ease with hardship.'* [Tirmidhī] He also reminded us that, *'Whoever would be pleased for Allah to answer him during times of hardship and difficulty, let him supplicate often during times of ease.'* [Tirmidhī] Difficulty and ease are both states in which to become acquainted with Allah, and becoming acquainted with Him during times of ease can help us withstand periods of difficulty.

2. *Be a source of expansion for others and embrace those in need*

As believers, we need to be people who offer relief to others. The Prophet ﷺ said, *'Whoever relieves the hardship of a believer in this world, Allah will relieve his hardship on the Day of Resurrection. Whoever helps ease one in difficulty, Allah will make it easy for him in this world and in the Hereafter.'* [Muslim]

Indeed, we should give from whatever we have been given, because Allah is the One who gives abundantly. He asks us, *'Who will give God a good loan, which He will increase for him many times over? It is God who withholds and God who gives abundantly, and it is to Him that you will return.'* [2:245]

Some people refrain from giving, for fear that it will cause them to lose out, but this verse tells us when we give, Allah will increase it many times over, because only He can give and withhold.

Moreover, the Prophet ﷺ said, *'Whoever embraces (qabaḍa) an orphan of two Muslim parents by feeding him and giving him drink until he is independent of him, Paradise will certainly be necessary for him.'* [Tirmidhī]

Granting people 'relief' does not just mean material relief. We should remind people of Allah as well. Al-Ghazālī states that we should expand the hearts of people by reminding them of the blessings of God and His consolation, and, if need be, remind them also of His majesty, so that this form of constriction (out of feeling awe) can also bring us back to God when we are far.

2. *Withhold speech and action that God does not love*

A positive human manifestation of *qabḍ* is to withhold ourselves from sin. We should withhold our whole beings from committing deeds that Allah does not like, withhold our sight from looking at things that are forbidden, and withhold our tongues from crass and hurtful speech. The Prophet ﷺ said that *'a Muslim is the one from whose tongue and hand the people are safe.'* [Nasā'ī]

Ensure that you do not cause pain or constriction in the hearts of people through callous or merciless speech. We need to withhold our minds from thoughts that are negative and suspicious, which do not benefit people. If you happen to be with people who are committing wrong, withhold yourself from slipping and doing the same.

3. *Balance hope and fear*

These names demonstrate to us the balance we should be cultivating in our hearts. Some people grow up only knowing Allah's attributes of majesty, and this makes them despair. Others only know the attributes of beauty, and this makes them complacent. Yet, there is a middle ground. We should all fear God withholding good from us in this world and the Hereafter due to our actions, and have hope in God generously giving us the good of this world and the Hereafter. The effect of these feelings should be action; fear should prevent us from doing evil, while hope should propel us to do good.

AL-JĀMIʿ –
THE UNITER (61)

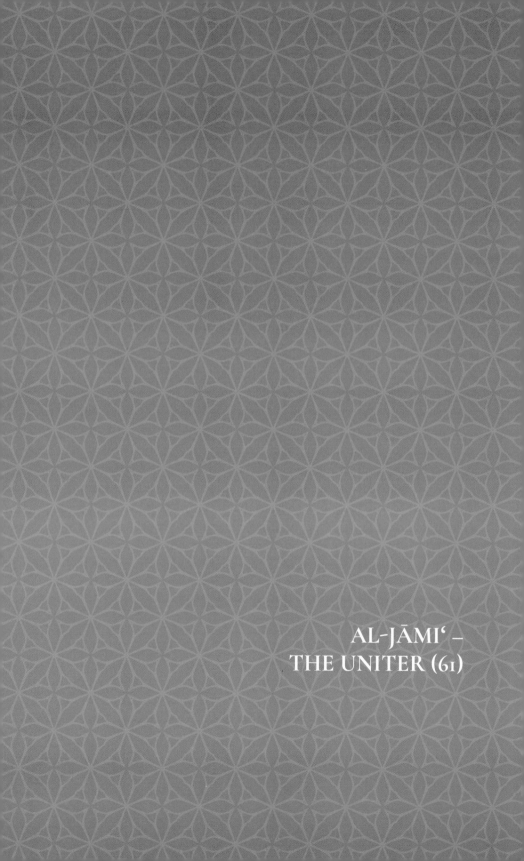

34

AL-JĀMI‘ – THE UNITER (61)

‘Our Lord, You will gather all people on the Day of which there is no doubt: God never breaks His promise.’

[3:9]

Al-Jāmi‘ is found in the hadith that lists Allah’s names, and while it is not used as a name in the Qur’an, Allah gives us many examples of how He unites and brings together. Linguistically, the Arabic root of this name, *jīm-mīm-‘ayn*, means to ‘bring something together’, as opposed to dividing or taking something apart: for example, *yajma‘uhu* (‘he brings it together’), *jam‘an* (‘a congregation’), *jamma‘ahu* (‘he collected them together’) and so on. When we talk about scholarly consensus in Islam, the word for that is *ijmā‘*. The phrase *al-jāmi‘ min al-kalām* refers to speech that contains few words but many meanings, and from this we get the description of the Qur’an as *Jawāmi‘ al-Kalīm* – the most concise and comprehensive speech.

Like all of Allah’s names, there are different dimensions to and manifestations of this name. Allah brings things together what may be similar, or may indeed be opposites, He brings together humankind and jinn on the Day of Judgment (also called *Yawm al-Jam‘* – the Day of Gathering), and He brings together the hearts of people.

The combining and assembly of creation

In the way that Allah has created the world, we find signs. Allah repeatedly praises people who reflect in the Qur'an. He says, for example, *'It is He who spread out the earth, placed firm mountains and rivers on it, and made two of every kind of fruit; He draws the veil of night over the day. There truly are signs in this for people who reflect.'* [13:3]

He also says, *'There truly are signs in the creation of the heavens and earth, and in the alternation of night and day, for those with understanding, who remember God standing, sitting, and lying down, who reflect on the creation of the heavens and earth: "Our Lord! You have not created all this without purpose -- You are far above that! -- so protect us from the torment of the Fire."'* [3:190-191]

These reflections lead to His name al-Jāmiʿ. God says in the Qur'an: *'In livestock, too, you have a lesson – We give you a drink from the contents of their bellies, between waste matter and blood, pure milk, sweet to the drinker.'* [16:66]

In the same chapter, He says again, *'Then feed on all kinds of fruit and follow the ways made easy for you by your Lord. From their bellies comes a drink of different colors in which there is healing for people. There truly is a sign in this for those who think.'* [16:69]

If we take a moment to pause, we find this incredible juxtaposition in God's creation: the way that different bodies contain blood, water, and other substances, and how perfectly they work together, producing for us what is pure; the way that Allah has also brought opposites together, such as hot and cold in one being (we can be feeling cold on the outside but our insides are warm); and how His creations that are similar yet dissimilar are brought together on this Earth, such as different kinds of trees, animals and landscapes. Opposites somehow find perfect harmony, and things that are similar complement one another. We traverse the Earth and observe magnificent deserts, soothing streams, and tropical rainforests, all brought together on the same Earth, created by the Originator, and all with their own purposes. We find male and female, perfectly created for each other. We see different nations and tribes, colors and languages, all brought together by their common humanity and spiritual disposition.

These are some manifestations of Allah al-Jāmiʿ.

The Day of Judgment

God mentions His attribute of *jamʿ* many times in the Qur'an, most frequently in reference to the Day of Judgment. Indeed, He even calls it the Day of Assembly or the Day of Gathering: *'When He gathers you for the Day of Gathering (Yawm al-Jamʿ).'* [64:9]

Allah also says, *'[They will be told], "This is the Day of Decision: We have gathered you (jamaʿnākum) and earlier generations."'* [77:38]

Human beings can gather or assemble in a limited sense, but already we can see the divine nature of this name: Allah brings together everyone – human beings and the jinn, the people of the heavens and the people of the Earth – and judges between them on the Day of Gathering. While we will all be judged alone, we will be taken to Paradise or Hell in groups, brought together based on our deeds. Allah tells us that, *'Those who rejected the Truth will be led to Hell in groups... Those who were mindful of their Lord will be led in groups to the Garden.'* [39:71; 73]

Contemplating Allah's name al-Jāmiʿ, and knowing that we will be gathered again, should inspire us to engage in serious reflection. We are going to be resurrected after we are dead, assembled again after our bones have disintegrated, and the world and all our loved ones have forgotten us. We need to ask ourselves: with whom do we want to be gathered? The Pharaohs of the past, present and future, or the righteous and those beloved to God? Knowing that we will be gathered with those whom we are most like should cause us to reflect on our states and ask ourselves: who am I most like right now? And am I happy to be resurrected with them?

Bringing hearts together

'Hold fast to God's rope all together; do not split into factions. Remember God's favor to you: you were enemies and then He brought your hearts together and you became brothers by His grace; you were about to fall into a pit of Fire and He saved you from it— in this way God makes His revelations clear to you so that you may be rightly guided.' [3:103]

In the verse above, God tells the believers to support one another, and hence Allah tells those who believe to hold firmly to the rope of God *'all together (jamī'an)'*. This way, our hearts are strengthened. Sometimes trying to improve ourselves is a lonely and difficult process. Just like a predator can more easily attack the lone sheep, Satan can make things seem a lot more difficult than they are if we are simply trying to rely on ourselves. But when Muslims support one another, and hold onto the rope of Allah together, our hearts are more easily able to be firm. Even if we have our differences, we can still hold one another up.

Another way God brings us together on a spiritual, internal level is by bringing our hearts together. A different word is used in this context: *allafa. Allafa* connotes gentleness and love. When the Prophet ﷺ migrated to Madinah, the two main tribes at the time, the Aws and the Khazraj, were enemies. Their history was one of bloodshed and vendettas, yet Allah brought their hearts together. Those two tribes went from absolutely hating each other to becoming brothers. God tells us in another verse: *'And [God] brought their hearts together. Even if you had given away everything in the Earth you could not have done this, but God brought them together: God is mighty and wise.'* [8:63]

God reminds the Prophet ﷺ and us that, even if we spent everything on Earth, we would not have been able to bring their hearts together. Yet God united them upon guidance. There were, at times, moments of tension, but those instances teach us patience and perseverance – and the end result is unity.

When we feel that our hearts are divided, we should know that Allah is al-Jāmiʿ. Just like He brought the hearts of the Companions together, God can bring our hearts together too, if we sincerely work on that. So, for example, if we feel tensions with family members, we should ask Allah to soften our hearts and unite us. At the very least, we should work consciously to minimize any external divisions.

Living with this name

1. Reflect on how God brings everything together in this world, and reflect on how He will bring us all together in the next

On one hand, reflecting on how God brings His creation together should inspire a sense of awe in us. Reflecting is a process of taking in the knowledge slowly, opening our senses, and really contemplating the world around us. On the other hand, the greatest gathering is on the Day of Judgment. It is real, and we need to be prepared. When God brings all human beings together in one place, where do we want to be? We are told in the Qur'an: *'Our Lord, You will gather (innaka jāmiʿ) all people on the Day of which there is no doubt: God never breaks His promise.'* [3:9]

God tells us that on this day, there are seven categories of people who are given shade under His throne, when there is no other shade but His: *'a just ruler; a youth who grew up in the worship of God, the Mighty and Majestic; a person whose heart is attached to the mosques; two people who love each other for God's sake, meeting for that and parting upon that; a man who is called by a woman of beauty and position [for illegal intercourse], but be says: "I fear Allah", a person who gives in charity and hides it, such that his left hand does not know what his right hand gives in charity; and a person who remembered Allah in private and so his eyes shed tears.'* [Bukhārī]

This is a reminder – have certainty that you will be brought together with everyone else, and therefore think of which group you want to join. With whom do you want to be brought together? Those whom God shades or those outside His shade?

2. Be a person who brings together what is in your heart and on your limbs

One way of being resurrected and brought together with the righteous is by uniting our hearts and limbs. Al-Ghazālī states that one way for people to emulate this name is to integrate our external behavior and the inner reality of our hearts. Be a person who prays at night and also has mercy with people. Be a person who polishes your heart from spiritual diseases and is also active within the community. Be a person who avoids suspicion and negative assumptions in your heart and also speaks well and brings benefit with your words.

3. Be a person who brings Muslims together, not one who divides them

The Prophet ﷺ told us. *'God's Hand is with the jamāʿah (congregation)'* [Tirmidhī], meaning that God's care and protection is with people who stick together or are united. Sometimes it is tempting to want to be alone or away from others, yet God's blessing comes with the bringing together of people. There is more reward in praying in congregation [Muslim]. Mending relations between two people who are in conflict is better than praying voluntary prayers and giving extra charity [Tirmidhī]. God loves the congregation and, as we have seen, He hates division and discord [Ṭabarānī]. To clarify, unity does not mean that there are no differences. For the most part, the Companions of the Prophet ﷺ were united in their hearts, even though they sometimes differed in strategy, opinion and manner.

So, the lessons for us are two-fold: first, bring people together. Whether it is for prayers, support, or even a family gathering, be a person who brings people together for good. Secondly, do not be a person who engages in petty arguments and discord. You may disagree with someone, but there is no need to get nasty. You can still maintain love and respect, even if a person tests your patience. As God says: *'and do not quarrel with one another, or you may lose heart and your spirit may desert you. Be steadfast: God is with the steadfast.'* [8:46]

This is especially important in the age of social media. Discord is quickly sown within the community on so-called 'Muslim Twitter'. Self-proclaimed 'defenders of the faith' attack others in ways truly unbecoming of believers, instead of taking their differences offline and working through them. Doubt is planted in the hearts of lay-people by discussing obscure matters. Some people are 'cancelled' because of a position they might have taken, rightly or wrongly.

Who are we in the vast world of social media? Do we nurture unity and faith, or do we sow discord and doubt?

If we find that our hearts are affected by the negativity, we should make a conscious effort to limit our online time and, at the very least, ensure that what and who we follow are beneficial for this life and the Hereafter.

4. Do not lose hope

When we say that God is al-Jāmiʿ, this implies that the creation was divided or scattered, and so Allah brings together what was separate and divided to begin with, uniting it all. When you lose something, remember that it is God who can bring it back and unite you with it. As Allah says, *'The Most Excellent Names belong to God: use them to call on Him.'* [7:180]

So ask Allah to unite you with whatever you have lost and, in His wisdom, He may unite you with it in this world, give you that which is greater, or reunite you with something even better on the Day of Gathering.

5. Make this Supplication to bring together the hearts of people

The Prophet ﷺ said,

> '*O Allah, bring our hearts together, reconcile between us, guide us to ways of peace, and deliver us from darkness into light. Keep us away from immorality, outwardly and inwardly, and bless us in our hearing, our seeing, our hearts, our spouses, and our children. Accept our repentance, for you alone are the Relenting, the Merciful. Make us grateful for your blessings, praising and accepting them, and give them to us in full.*' [Abū Dāwūd]

AL-SAMĪʿ AL-BAṢĪR – THE ALL-HEARING, ALL-SEEING (62-63)

❁35❁

AL-SAMĪʿ AL-BAṢĪR – THE ALL-HEARING, ALL-SEEING (62-63)

'They said, "Lord, we fear he will do us great harm or exceed all bounds." He said, "Do not be afraid, I am with you both, hearing and seeing everything."'

[20:45-46]

Allah is named al-Samīʿ al-Baṣīr: the All-Hearing, the All-Seeing. These beautiful names are a reassurance for all of us who have felt or feel alone, misunderstood or afraid. Indeed, Allah knows us so well, and knows everything that we go through, that He chooses to reveal names of His which speak to us and our situations. And through understanding these names, we will learn that we are never alone and never have to be misinterpreted. These names also nurture our own internal vigilance; when we know that Allah hears and sees everything, we learn to guard and beautify our speech and actions. These names also teach us the nature of His divine names and attributes. Allah tells us, *'There is nothing like Him: He is the All-Hearing, the All-Seeing.'* [42:11]

Allah teaches us that there is nothing like Him, and then chooses two names that seem similar to human functions: hearing and seeing. This is deliberate; even those characteristics which we might think we share in common with Allah, are in reality nothing like His attributes. Our hearing and seeing cannot be compared to His hearing and seeing, as this chapter will explore further.

We will discuss these names separately as well as together, as they appear tens of times in combination in the Qur'an, as well as in combination with other names.

The All-Hearing

The Arabic root of al-Samīʿ, *sīn-mīm-ʿayn*, means 'to hear, to listen, to pay attention to, and to accept'. One might assume that Allah's hearing has similarities to our hearing, but in reality, they are nothing alike.

In terms of *what* He hears, Allah hears everything, including everything that is beyond our hearing. There are parts of creation which we do not know make sounds; science has not even concluded whether or not they make a sound. But He hears them. He hears frequencies that no created being can hear; He hears our whispers, as well as what is in our hearts.

In terms of *how* He hears, we as humans need ears, sound waves and an entire system to ensure that we can hear. There are certain frequencies that we cannot access. His hearing needs none of this; He hears all that is accessible and inaccessible to our ears. He hears our unspoken words and all that is hidden in our hearts.

But His hearing is also so much vaster than that. There are two main meanings to His name, al-Samīʿ: the first means that He listens, and the second pertains to His accepting and responding to what He hears. We will examine both.

He hears you

1. Comprehensiveness: He hears and is aware of everything

The first dimension of this name is the comprehensiveness of His hearing. God revealed the following verse when a woman named Khawlah bint Thaʿlabah went to the Prophet ﷺ to complain about her husband: *'God has heard the words of the woman who disputed with you [Prophet] about her husband and complained to God: God has heard what you both had to say. He is all hearing, all seeing.'* [58:1]

When this verse was revealed, 'Ā'ishah, the wife of the Prophet ﷺ, was shocked:

> *'Praise be to God Whose hearing encompasses all voices! Khawlah came to God's Messenger ﷺ complaining about her husband; I was in the next room but I could not hear what she said. Then God revealed [these verses]!'* [Bukhārī]

Though 'Ā'ishah was only separated by a curtain (that was the next 'room'), she could not and did not hear what was being said. Yet Allah heard everything. Indeed, Allah is privy to the words of our hearts and not just what is uttered on our lips. Ibn Al-Qayyim explains that He hears every single person, and one voice does not distract Him from another, nor does He get confused between them, and He hears and understands all languages and all needs. This is reassurance for those who limit Allah's hearing; Allah pairs His name al-Samī' with His Name al-'Alīm thirty times in the Qur'an, so that we know that He not only hears, but He listens and understands.

Furthermore, we are told: *'And if there comes to you from Satan an evil suggestion, then seek refuge in Allah. Indeed, He is the Hearing, the Knowing.'* [41:36] We do not hear Satan's suggestions, nor do we know the form that they take, but Allah does. And so whenever we find ourselves tempted towards what is impermissible, we should seek refuge with God.

Al-Ghazālī similarly affirmed that al-Samī' hears even that which is subtler than whispers or secrets. For Him, the secret is the same as the public, and what is in the heart is the same as what is on the tongue. Allah even hears the thoughts that go through your mind, which you have not even articulated.

The Companions were with the Prophet ﷺ during a journey when people began to exalt Allah loudly. The Prophet said, *'O people, be gentle with yourselves. You are not calling upon one who is deaf or absent; rather, you are calling upon the Hearing, the Seeing.'* [Bukhārī and Muslim] We do not have to shout or be loud in order for Allah to hear us.

Indeed, Allah's hearing and seeing is juxtaposed with the idols that were worshiped by people before Islam. The Prophet Abraham asked his father, '"*O my father, why do you worship that which does not hear and does not see and will not benefit you at all?*"' [19:42] Abraham was incredulous; why would anyone worship something that cannot even hear him or her? How could this idol bring benefit in any way?

2. He hears as a warning; He hears the evil of what people say and is aware of it. He hears what the plotters plot.

The companion 'Abdullāh ibn Mas'ūd narrated that some men were gathered by the Ka'bah, and were discussing whether or not Allah heard them. One of them said, 'Do you think that Allah hears what we say?' Another replied, 'He hears us if we are loud but does not hear us if we are quiet.' Yet another responded, 'If Allah hears us when we are loud, then He also hears us when we are quiet.' [Bukhārī and Muslim] Then, Allah Almighty revealed the verse, *'You were not covering yourselves, lest your hearing, your sight, and your skins testify against you. Rather, you assumed that Allah does not know much of what you are doing.'* [41:22]

This type of hearing should instill vigilance in people: do not think that God cannot or does not hear what is said or whispered. Allah hears the plotters, the slanderers, the gossipmongers, and the foul-mouthed. Allah said with regards to those plotting against the Muslims: *'Do they think We cannot hear their secret talk and their private counsel? Yes, we can: Our messengers are at their sides, recording everything.'* [43:80]

Indeed, He hears what people say about Him and what they ascribe to Him. He says, *'God has certainly heard the words of those who sneer, "So God is poor, while we are rich." We shall record everything they say.'* [3:180]

Allah warns the people that He is not oblivious and indeed hears all. Everything that was said is recorded and will testify on the Day of Judgment. Allah says,

> *'Their ears, eyes, and skins will, when they reach it, testify against them for their misdeeds. They will say to their skins, "Why did you testify against us?" and their skins will reply, "God, who gave speech to everything, has given us speech –– it was He who created you the first time and to Him you have been returned ––yet you did not try to hide yourselves from your ears, eyes, and skin to prevent them from testifying against you. You thought that God did not know about much of what you were doing."'* [41:20-22]

This should cause us to reflect on what we say, and ask ourselves whether we would be happy for our words to be repeated on the Day of Judgment. It should also reassure us that if we were wronged verbally by others, Allah heard it, and knows of our pain.

3. He listens to and will help those who turn to Him; His hearing is reassurance

That Allah listens to us is also very reassuring. When Moses and Aaron were told to speak to Pharaoh, they were understandably afraid. They said: '*"Our Lord, indeed we are afraid that he will hasten [punishment] against us or that he will transgress."*' [20:45] And Allah responded to them to reassure them: *'Fear not. Indeed, I am with you both; I hear and I see.'* [20: 46]

So, when you are feeling lonely or in difficulty, call out to the One who hears everything and sees everything. Talk to the One who revealed this attribute to you, so that you would know that He is there for you. He is the close One who listens to your words when they are spoken, as well as when they are trapped in your heart and you cannot express them. Rest assured that your going through this difficulty has not gone unnoticed.

We all have the need and desire to be heard and to be listened to. We feel closeness and an affinity to those who truly hear and listen to us. We know that they care. Conversely, when even the people who are supposed to be close to us, like siblings or parents, do not take the time to hear us, we feel distant from them.

And it can feel isolating to have no one to listen to us. But Allah, who names Himself and establishes the nature of our relationship with Him, is inviting us to talk to Him. He tells us that He is al-Samīʿ – this name of His lets you know that, whether you choose to turn to Him or not, He hears what is on your tongue and what is in your heart. When you talk to God, it is a one-to-one conversation, even if you are in a crowded room full of people. Do not ever belittle yourself and think that God would not listen to you or hear you. God even hears the thoughts that go through your mind that you have never articulated.

You may be in your room alone right now, or reading this book in a café. Wherever you are, take ten seconds right now to talk to Allah in your heart. Tell Him what is going through your mind. It is certain that no one around you can hear you, but Allah will. He is al-Samīʿ. Indeed, we find that the mother of Mary talked to Allah. We are told, *'[Mention, O Muhammad], when the wife of 'Imran said, "My Lord, indeed I have pledged to You what is in my womb, consecrated [for Your service], so accept this from me. Indeed, You are the Hearing, the Knowing." But when she delivered Mary, she said, "My Lord, I have delivered a female." And Allah was most knowing of what she delivered, and the male is not like the female. "And I have named her Mary, and I seek refuge for her in You and [for] her descendants from Satan, the expelled [from the mercy of Allah]."'* [3:35-36]

This whole scene describes a person who is close to Allah, who talks to Him and expresses her desires, her hopes, her worries and her fears to Him. We should emulate this beautiful practice.

He responds

Within the meaning of His name al-Samīʿ is also acceptance and response. The Prophet Zachariah knew that Allah heard his quiet and seemingly impossible prayer: *'he called to his Lord a private supplication.'* [19:3] When we stand from *rukūʿ* (bowing) in prayer, we say, *'Allah hears those who praise Him.'* This does not mean that God does not hear those who do not praise Him. But 'hearing' in this context implies both awareness and action: He listens and responds. This is why we supplicate to Him after praising Him.

Indeed, to emphasize this point, His name al-Samīʿ is often paired with His names al-Mujīb (the Responder) and al-Qarīb (the Near One). In the hadith cited earlier, the Prophet ﷺ reminded the Companions that they did not need to be loud when they called upon Allah because He is al-Samīʿ al-Qarīb. Allah also tells us in the Qur'an,

> *'Say, "If I should err, I would only err against myself. But if I am guided, it is by what my Lord reveals to me. Indeed, He is Hearing and near."'* [34:50]

Moreover, the Prophet Abraham said, *'"Praise to Allah, who has granted to me in old age Ishmael and Isaac. Indeed, my Lord is the Hearer of supplication."'* [14:39]

Allah's response is part of His hearing and listening to you. Indeed, when the Prophet Jonah was in the belly of the whale, *'he cried out in the deep darkness, "There is no God but You, glory be to You, I was wrong."'* [21:87]. Allah heard him. But not only did He hear, but He also responded to what was never uttered on his lips: He saved him. We are told, *'We answered him and saved him from distress: this is how We save the faithful.'* [21:88]

This is because He is also al-Karīm (the Most Generous). When He hears the thoughts and hopes that remain trapped in our hearts, unable to find expression on our tongues, He still responds, without us even asking. How many of us have had unexpected gifts given to us – the exact gifts we were hoping for without asking for them – knowing that no one ever heard our hopes except God?

Another pairing of al-Samīʿ is with His name al-ʿAlīm – the All-Knowing. When the Prophet Joseph was being plotted against by the wife of the minister and the women of the city to commit indecent acts, he said, '*My Lord, prison is more to my liking than that to which they invite me. And if You do not avert from me their plan, I might incline toward them and [thus] be of the ignorant.*' [12:33]

And this was the response from Allah, '*So his Lord responded to him and averted from him their plan. Indeed, He is the Hearing, the Knowing.*' [12:34]

Allah heard Joseph's plea, and He tells us in the following verse that He averted their plan. God listens – He is al-Samīʿ – and responds. He is also al-ʿAlīm, because He knew of Joseph's desire to stay away from them, as well as the true intentions of the women. But there is another meaning here that highlights to us the wisdom of pairing His names al-Samīʿ and al-ʿAlīm. Allah does not say, '*We sent him to prison*' – even though that is what happened – but rather He points out that He averted the plan of the women because *that* was the point of sending Him to prison. But one might wonder, 'was there no better way to keep the women away from him? Did he have to go to prison?' One might be forgiven for thinking this way in the moment; though he had done nothing wrong (in fact he behaved in the most dignified manner as befitting a prophet and one close to God), he was still imprisoned, and this cast doubt upon his character in society (as a side point, there *is* smoke without fire!). But had he not been sent to prison, he would not have interpreted the dream of the cellmates, which eventually led to his release, a declaration of his innocence and his virtue, and being given authority. Thus, we need to know that Allah is al-Samīʿ and so He hears and responds, but He *also* knows what is best. It may appear to be through a difficulty, but God al-ʿAlım knows that that is best for the future.

For a more comprehensive understanding of how Allah responds, see chapter 21 on His name al-Mujīb.

The All-Seeing

There are two meanings within Allah's name al-Baṣīr: one pertains to His vision and the other to His seeing inner realities.

God is All-Seeing, such that He sees a crawling black ant under a hard rock in the darkest part of the night. He sees in such a way that that nothing is inaccessible to Him, even what is under the earth or above the seven heavens. He sees what is tinier than an atom. He also sees the good that people do and the evil. He is not veiled from the injustices facing people and the torture to which they are subjected. He sees us when we struggle to wake up for *fajr* (dawn prayer) or *tahajjud* (the voluntary night prayer), yet still persevere in doing so. He sees the discomfort on our faces, that no one else can read, when we face difficult situations.

As for inner realities, He sees our pain and all that is in our heart. He even sees the discrepancy between what is hidden from and what is visible to people. He is intimately aware of and sees what is in the metaphysical realm, which we cannot access with any of our senses, let alone our sight.

Al-Baṣīr sees all and nothing is hidden from Him. He is with us wherever we are. Again, this should inspire both vigilance over our actions as well as reassurance: Allah sees.[42]

Al-Samīʿ al-Baṣīr

These names are mentioned frequently together because they are comprehensive: Allah hears and sees. As mentioned above, when Moses and Aaron were told to speak to Pharaoh, Allah emphasizes the attributes that would be most reassuring to them: *'I am with you both, hearing and seeing everything.'* [20:46]

[42] For more on how Allah sees and observes, see the chapter 36 on His name al-Raqīb (the Observant).

Imagine going to face the worst tyrant and knowing that Allah will witness and hear everything. Imagine the strength that comes from that knowledge. It does not mean that the task will be easy, nor that it will not require effort. It means having conviction that Allah is with you. Indeed, it is this conviction that led Moses to say, when he and the Children of Israel were being hunted down by Pharaoh and his army, and the people with him thought they would be overtaken: '*"No! Indeed, with me is my Lord; He will guide me."*' [26:62] This is the ultimate effect of knowing that Allah is with us, hearing and seeing.

Secondly, knowing that God is All-Hearing and All-Seeing should make *us* aware. There are certain things we would not say or do in front of someone whom we love and respect. Knowing that God hears and sees everything should make us vigilant over our speech and actions.

Living with these names

1. Talk to Allah

You know that He can hear you, and that He understands your language. Not only this, but He also hears what you do not know how to express in your heart, and the thoughts that run through your mind. So, speak to Him and tell God what you feel; your troubles and worries, yours hopes and dreams. This does not necessarily mean that you have to ask for something, even though that is also beloved to Him and an essential act of worship. You can just talk to Him, knowing that He hears and listens to you.

2. Guard your speech and actions

Remember that God can see and hear and everything, so guard yourself against evil speech and evil actions. Allah tells us: '*Or do they think that We hear not their secrets and their private conversations? Yes, [We do], and Our messengers are with them recording.*' [43:80]

Forgetting that Allah hears, and failing to cultivate good speech, leads to the misuse of the tongue, and the Prophet ﷺ said: *'The majority of man's sins emanate from his tongue.'* [Ṭabarānī]

Allah has warned us in the Qur'an: *'O you who believe! Avoid much suspicion, indeed some suspicions are sins. And spy not neither backbite one another. Would one of you like to eat the flesh of his dead brother? You would hate it (so hate backbiting). And fear God, verily, God is the one who accepts repentance, Most Merciful.'* [49: 12]

We should guard our tongues from speech that is displeasing to Him.

3. Accustom yourself to hearing and seeing what is beneficial

Listening to what is prohibited, and accustoming ourselves to seeing or watching what is disliked by God, affects our hearts on a subconscious level. Watching sexually explicit scenes in a movie without turning away increases illicit desires and normalizes these types of relationships. Constantly listening to improper speech slowly leads us to speak in the same way, if we are not conscious of it. Listening to slander, for example, is wrong, as many scholars have said that it is just as bad as speaking slander, because it as though the listener is approving the act. In the Qur'an, Allah speaks about the famous incident of slander (*al-ifk*), when Companions were gossiping falsely about 'Ā'ishah: *'And why did you not, when you heard it, say: "We should not repeat this – God forbid! – it is a monstrous slander"?'* [24:16]

We may normalize what God has deemed abnormal and condemned. One of the ways to be grateful for the gift of hearing and seeing is by using these gifts in beneficial ways. We should listen to speech that brings us close to God, that irrigates our mind and increases us in beneficial knowledge, and that makes us see the best in people. Indeed, the Prophet ﷺ was told some negative things that had been said about him, and his response was: *'Let no one among you convey to me what is said about me (in terms of what will give rise to bad feelings in my heart). For indeed I love to come out to you with a pure and clean heart (without having negative feelings about any of you as a result of knowing what you said about me).'* [Aḥmad, Abū Dāwūd, Tirmidhī]

4. Hear and Obey

Allah says about the believers, *'they say, "We hear and obey. Grant us Your forgiveness, our Lord. To You we all return!"'* [2:285] True believers listen to the commandments of Allah and try to obey them as much as they can, although we may slip up.

Allah warns us against being like the hypocrites, when He says, *'Believers, obey God and His Messenger: do not turn away when you are listening to him; do not be like those who say, "We heard," though in fact they were not listening ––the worst creatures in God's eyes are those who are [wilfully] deaf and dumb, who do not reason.'* [8:20-22]

Indeed, the worst of traits is to hear and then choose to disobey. Allah tells us about some of the Children of Israel in the following verse: *'Remember when We took your pledge, making the mountain tower above you, and said, "Hold on firmly to what We have given you, and listen to [what We say]." They said, "We hear and we disobey," and through their disbelief they were made to drink [the love of] the calf deep into their hearts.'* [2:93]

Of course, we will all mess up; these verses do not deny that. But, as long as we are trying to obey, we can be of those who say 'we listen and we obey'. And even if we have found ourselves in a period of willful disobedience, and now wish to return, we are still of those who listen and obey, because we are obeying Allah's commandment: *'ask forgiveness from your Lord, and return to Him.'* [11:52] We maintain hope in Allah, seek forgiveness, and return to Him.

5. Be a good listener

We love for Allah to hear and listen to us. Just as we love to be listened to and to feel understood, we should afford that to those closest to us.

AL-RAQĪB AL-SHAHĪD – THE ALL-OBSERVANT, THE WITNESS (64-65)

36

AL-RAQĪB AL-SHAHĪD – THE ALL-OBSERVANT, THE WITNESS (64-65)

'God is always watching over you.'

[4:1]

Each of the names of Allah nurtures us in a different way, teaching us to be aware of their manifestations in our lives, and opening up to us different paths to connecting with our Creator. When we feel lost, we know that He is al-Hādī (the Guide). When we have needs, we ask al-Mujīb (the Responder). If we are worried about our provision, we hold onto the certainty that He is al-Razzāq (The Provider). God is with us always, in good times and bad, as well as the mundane and ordinary. He is with us through the big events and the tests in our lives, as well as the small and miniscule.

One of the best ways to worship Allah is through the station of *iḥsān* (excellence). In the famous hadith of Gabriel, he asks the Prophet ﷺ about important concepts: Islam (submission), *īmān* (faith) and, finally, *iḥsān*. The Prophet ﷺ described *iḥsān*: *'It is to worship Allah as though you see Him, and though you do not see Him, you know that He sees you.'* [Bukhārī]

Understanding God's names allows us to see their manifestations in every facet of our lives. This is part of what it means to worship Allah as though we see Him; we understand that He is with us every step of the way, because we see the world through the lens of His names. Allah's names al-Raqīb and al-Shahīd teach us how to attain *iḥsān* in the everyday; when we are sitting at home scrolling through social media, when we cook, when we drive or take public transport to work, and when we greet the barista for our morning coffee.

Al-Raqīb is the One who watches over and is observant of everything. A *marqab* – from the same Arabic root *rā-qāf-bā* – is a high place where a watcher stands observe what is beneath. Al-Shahīd is the Witness, as a *shahīd* or *shāhid* is one who witnesses or testifies. So al-Raqīb watches over His creation out of His care, looking after them, while al-Shahīd witnesses all that occurs, and will act as the ultimate Witness on the Day of Judgment. His *shahādah* (witnessing) is a result of His observing, His knowledge of the outer and the inner, and His intimate acquaintance with all that occurs.

Watching over

These names teach us that God is watching over us, all the time, out of His care for us. He says in the Qur'an, *'you are under Our watchful eye.'* [52:48]

This should reassure us and it should also have a profound effect on the way we live. God also says, *'Does he not know that Allah sees?'* [96:14]

While most of us know this theoretically, it is altogether different to live with the impact of that knowledge on our lives. And it should never be an impact that immobilizes; one of the beauties of understanding Allah's names holistically is knowing that while He watches over and witnesses everything, He is also al-Laṭīf – the Subtle and Kind. His watching over us is not uncomfortable; rather, it is subtle, as befits His grace.

Being watchful over ourselves

There is a well-known story of a milk seller in the time when the Companion 'Umar was caliph. One day, he was walking at night, as he usually did to check on the state of the people. He heard a mother ordering her daughter to dilute the milk that they were going to sell with water. The daughter replied, 'Do you not know that 'Umar, the commander of the believers, has forbidden that?' Her mother said, 'Well, 'Umar does not see us now.' The younger woman replied, 'Even if 'Umar does not see us, the Lord of 'Umar sees us.'

The young milk-seller was a regular person. But her faith that Allah is All-Observant, the Witness, prevented her from being blinded by the temptation of greater profits, even in the face of her mother's persistence. She was mindful that God is All-Observant, and thus she was observant over herself. She knew that her decision in that moment would testify either for her or against her on the Day of Judgment, with none other than Allah as the Witness, and so she ensured that what Allah witnessed would save her.

This is one of the effects of knowing al-Raqīb al-Shahīd. We know that Allah watches over us, and thus we should always try to do the right thing, not necessarily just in situations in which our values and integrity are tested. When we find ourselves spending too much time on social media without real purpose, knowing that He is al-Raqīb al-Shahīd simply means reducing the time spent on apps, and making it more intentional. Living with al-Raqīb al-Shahīd means giving up a seat on the train for someone else, or keeping calm when someone cuts us off on the road. It is picking up other people's trash off the street. It is letting go when someone makes an annoying comment. Cultivating this awareness in our day-to-day means that we are more likely to act in accordance with our values when we are tested.

Moreover, knowing that Allah is al-Shahīd should inspire further vigilance, because we understand that everything that Allah witnessed in this world will be laid bare on the Day of Judgment. We are told in the Qur'an about the people of the trench, who were persecuted and killed for their beliefs, and that the persecutors' '*only grievance against them was their faith in God, the Mighty, the Praiseworthy, to whom all control over the heavens and earth belongs: God is witness over all thing.'* [85:8-9] Allah will be the ultimate Witness on the Day of Judgment, and those who committed injustice will face what they did, while Allah's care for His righteous servants will result in Paradise for them.

Living with these names

1. You are never alone

One of the things that should warm our hearts, when we know that God is al-Raqīb al-Shahīd, is the knowledge that we are never, ever alone. When we are up late at night working on an essay, or awake in the early hours of the morning getting ready for work, Allah is with us.

2. Watch yourself

Both al-Ghazālī and Ibn Al-Qayyim stated that the best way to worship God through His name al-Raqīb is to be watchful over our hearts and our actions. This practice is called *murāqabah* and entails guarding one's thoughts, intentions, and inward movements [Madārij Al-Sālikīn]. Just like the milk-seller, being watchful over ourselves inwardly results in righteous action outwardly, God willing.

3. Desire to impress Allah

This name should also make us want to impress God. When we know that our parents, or someone we love, is watching us, we try to do better – so we should do the same when we know al-Raqīb al-Shahīd. He not only sees our bad deeds, but also our good deeds. Let us give more charity because we know that He is watching; let us be good to people despite the fact that we may not be feeling kind or generous in the moment, all for God, because we know that He sees all.

4. Be watchful over that which you are responsible for

The Prophet ﷺ told us: *'Every one of you is a shepherd and is responsible for his flock. The leader of people is a guardian and is responsible for his subjects. A man is the guardian of his family and he is responsible for them. A woman is the guardian of her husband's home and his children and she is responsible for them. The servant of a man is a guardian of the property of his master and he is responsible for it. No doubt, every one of you is a shepherd and is responsible for his flock.'* [Bukhārī and Muslim]

Part of knowing that He is al-Raqīb al-Shahīd is that we become watchful – meaning that we are responsible and caring – over the people or property for which we are responsible.

AL-ḤAQQ – THE TRUTH (66)

37

AL-ḤAQQ – THE TRUTH (66)

'That is God, your Lord, the Truth.'

[10:32]

God is al-Ḥaqq, the Absolute Truth and the Real. 'Truth' is something in which there is no doubt nor mistrust. Moreover, for something to be 'true', it needs to be consistent and everlasting; this definition can only truly apply to God. He is the Truth in His essence, His Divinity and His Lordship, and in His names and attributes. He is the opposite of falsehood. Part of the meaning of this name encompasses justice, because at the very essence of justice is truth. Allah tells us in the Qur'an: *'That is God, your Lord, the Truth. Apart from the Truth, what is there except error? So how is it that you are dissuaded?'* [10:32]

Indeed, the Prophet ﷺ would make this heartfelt supplication when praying at night: *'O Allah, our Lord, praise be to you, You are the Sustainer of the heavens and earth. Praise be to You, You are the Lord of the heavens and earth and all in them. Praise be to You, the Light of the heavens and the earth and all in them. You are the truth and Your word is the truth. Your promise is the truth and Your meeting is the truth. Paradise is the truth, Hellfire is the truth, and the Hour is the truth. O Allah, I surrender to You, I have faith in You, and I rely upon You. I have argued for Your sake and judged for Your sake. Forgive me for what I have done and will do, what I keep secret and what I do in public. None know me better than You, there is no God but You.'* [Saḥīḥ al-Bukhārī]

The meaning of God's name al-Ḥaqq can be found in this prayer. Allah is Truth in and of Himself; His Words (the Qur'an) are truth; His Promise is truth and our meeting with Him is truth; Paradise and Hell are both truth, and the Day of Judgment is truth. Allah is truly the only constant, because He is the Ultimate Truth. This is why we rely on Him and His words. Anyone or anything else might fail us, but not Allah, the Truth.

If we are the creation of the Ultimate Truth, and we worship God who is the Truth, then we have to live this life by the principles of truth. If we truly love God and understand His attributes, then we need to be sincere lovers of truth over all else – even over our own selves and interests.

Understand and be certain of God's truth

We believe that God is the Truth, and we believe that His Words are true. Therefore, what He has promised us is also true. The Qur'an teaches us the truth of our purpose, of accountability for our actions, of return to our Lord, of benefitting others, of cooperating with others for good, of standing up for the oppressed, and of God's presence with us and protection of us when we stand for truth, no matter what oppressor is standing before us.

If we truly believe in the truth of the Qur'an, then we need to understand the purpose of our lives. We must work for something greater. We must take comfort in God's promise when things are difficult for us and, ultimately, be certain of the truth of the Hereafter.

We must also prepare. Knowing that Paradise, Hellfire and the Final Hour are all true should create an urgency in us to learn what will make God pleased with us on the Day of Judgment, enter us into Paradise, and help us avoid being of the people of the Hellfire.

Live 'your' truth?

One of the features of the modern age is relativity; even the relativity of truth itself. Everyone is encouraged to live 'their' truth, implying that everyone's truth is different and subjective. Once we erode the meaning of truth, everyone can feel comfortable following his or her desires, because there is no such thing as objectivity. Indeed, trying to figure out what 'living one's truth' actually means results in no one single answer, and this is the very point. For some, it involves defining for oneself what their truth is and then living 'loud and proud'. It partly involves being prisoner to our emotions, recognizing them as ultimate arbiters of truth. In reality, this is far from what truth is. Allah tells us:

> *'The word of your Lord is complete in its truth and justice. No one can change His words: He is the All-Hearing, the All-Knowing. If you obeyed most of those on earth, they would lead you away from the path of God. They follow nothing but speculation; they are merely guessing. Your Lord knows best who strays from His path and who is rightly guided.'* [6:115-117]

Obscuring truth and making it dependent on unstable and inconsistent foundations makes us believe that we are in control, but in reality, it means that others can define our values for us through subliminal messaging. Indeed, absorbing this idea of the relativity of truth itself shows how successful this messaging is. Allah has foretold this: *'Some He has guided and some are doomed to stray: they have taken evil ones rather than God as their masters, thinking that they are rightly guided.'* [7:30]

Signs of this are that we elevate that which is disliked by Allah, and we define our values in opposition to how al-Ḥaqq has defined them. This type of thinking eventually leads us to ascribing things to Allah that are blatantly false. God warns us:

> *'No! We hurl the truth against falsehood, and truth obliterates it –– see how falsehood vanishes away! Woe to you [people] for the way you describe God!'* [21:18]

Knowing that He is the Truth means turning to Him as our compass in this life. His is the true standard, the objective and constant truth, and everything that comes from Him leads to the truth. Indeed, truth always prevails.

Be a genuine truth-seeker

Al-Ghazālī said that realizing this name makes a person 'so absorbed in the Truth that he has no room for anything else.'[43] Salmān al-Fārisī, one of the Companions of the Prophet ﷺ, was a sincere seeker of truth. The Companions were sitting with the Prophet ﷺ when Sūrat al-Jumu'ah was revealed. When he recited the verse, *'And others who have yet to join them,'* [62:3] a Companion said, 'O Messenger of Allah ﷺ, who are these?' Salmān was among them, and the Prophet ﷺ placed his hand upon him, then he said, *'Were faith to be found as far away as the star of Pleiades, men among these would reach it.'* [Muslim]

Salmān came from a wealthy Persian (*Fārisī*) family, which had a high status as guardians of the fire that they used to worship. However, none of that mattered when it came to the truth. Salmān suffered in his search, was put under house arrest by his father for daring to leave their traditions, and, after accompanying a seemingly pious monk, found that he was corrupt and exploited the poor. These two incidents would be enough to make a seeker abandon his or her journey, and even claim that there is no truth. He was tested externally by his father trapping him, then by losing his wealth in his search; he was also tested internally (i.e. in his faith) when he found out what the monk was really doing. Indeed, some of us make our faith in al-Ḥaqq dependent on the actions of other people. When a seemingly pious person falls from grace, we lose faith. But that person who strayed is not the Truth. That person gave in to falsehood and temptations, and this affirms Allah's truth, because He warns us of such people, and of being such a person.

---

[43] Al-Ghazālī, 125.

Salmān did not make his search for truth dependent upon the actions of fallible human beings. He remained steadfast, and learned from an actual pious monk the signs of the Prophet of Truth ﷺ who would come. He persevered, despite being tested further when he was kidnapped and sold into slavery, and ended up in Madinah. When the Prophet ﷺ arrived in Madinah, Salmān wanted to examine him, looking for the signs the pious monk described to him – and they were all there. He affirmed the truth, and the Prophet ﷺ helped him to obtain his freedom.

Living with this name

1. Be a seeker of truth and stand for truth, whether it is for you or against you

Truly internalizing the meanings of this name should make us seekers and advocates of truth, whether that truth is for us or against us, or whether revealing the truth means that someone else will benefit over us. This might mean that we have to apologize for things we said in the past that we later learned were incorrect, and we should have the humility to be able to look inwardly and assess whether or not we make the acceptance of truth contingent on who said it. Indeed, the Prophet ﷺ defined arrogance as '*rejecting truth and looking down on people.*' [Bukhārī] What should be important to us – more important than our ego or image – is that we are followers of the truth as servants of al-Ḥaqq.

2. Verify information

The Messenger of God ﷺ said, '*It is an evil mount for a man to rely upon what others merely assert.*' [Abū Dāwūd]

In these times of 'alternative facts' and 'fake news', it is very important for us to verify the information that we receive. We should not be part of the problem, spreading sensationalist news when we do not know whether or not it is true. Moreover, we should be active in spreading truth, particularly when falsehood is rampant. One of the most detestable attributes it that of the gossiper, which is defined as a person who spreads news – the 'he said, she said' – without utility and without verification.

3. Take comfort in God, the Truth

It is difficult to rely on anything about which that we are not completely certain, particularly if it is inconsistent or temporary. But God's very essence is truth, and this means that we can rely on Him completely. His essence, actions and words are all true, and will remain true; therefore, we can take comfort in them and rely on them as they will never waiver.

4. Be truthful in all dimensions of truth

We cannot claim to be servants of the Truth if our tongues are busy with lies and falsehood. Allah says in the Qur'an: *'Do not mix truth with falsehood, or hide the truth when you know it.'* [2:42]

One of the signs of the truth of the Prophet ﷺ was that he was known in the community as al-Ṣādiq al-Amīn: the truthful and the trustworthy. When he wanted to publicly announce the message of Islam, he called out to the people, saying, *'If I were to tell you that there is an army behind this mountain ready to attack, would you believe me?'* and their answer was, 'We have never heard you tell a lie before.' This is our example.

He also taught us, *'You must be truthful. Verily, it leads to righteousness and they are both in Paradise. Beware of dishonesty, for it leads to wickedness and they are both in the Hellfire.'* [Ṭabarānī]

Indeed, this whole religion is predicated upon the truth because it is from the Truth and it leads to the Truth. It is stated 'that the religion of Allah Almighty is built upon three pillars: truth, honesty, and justice. Truth is in the body, justice is in the heart, and honesty is in the mind.'[44]

[44] Al-Ghazālī, Iḥyā' 'Ulūm al-Dīn 4/387

Falsehood is not merely speaking blatant lies. The Prophet ﷺ said, *'It is enough falsehood for someone to speak of everything he hears.'* [Muslim] We should ask ourselves, do we repost things that we are unsure about on social media? Do we enter into fruitless conversations about 'he said, she said, this happened, that didn't'? We should truly be wary of contributing to a loss of trust. A man once came to the Prophet ﷺ and asked him, 'When is the Hour?' He replied *'Wait for the Hour when trust is destroyed.'* [Bukhārī] One of the signs of the end of time is that these principles of truth and trust are lost.

5. Be a caller to the Truth

In being callers to truth in general and the Truth more specifically, we must ensure that we fulfill this role with beauty, grace, and humility. It should be done out of love for al-Ḥaqq, and for people to know the *ḥaqq*, and not out of a hidden love of being exalted over others or seeing someone's downfall. We should not be of those who use truth as a stick to beat others with, as a reason to be harsh, or to stroke our egos. How many people have started off calling to truth with humility, and in the end their arrogance becomes the cause of their own spiritual demise? How many have turned people away from truth because of their manners? Truth requires love for the truth to be known. The one calling to truth should constantly be working on his or her soul in order to be a worthy vessel for it, a vessel that people want to drink from.

A specific pitfall of the seeker of knowledge is that, for some, once they have studied a little, they assume that they know all there is to know, and what they have learned is necessarily the *only* truth or correct way. Matters that may contain considerable flexibility or legitimate differences of opinion are viewed as fixed, simply because this person does not know any better, yet anyone who presents an opposing view or is gentle with others regarding these issues is seen to be weak with regards to the *ḥaqq*. Avoiding this pitfall requires the subjugation of the ego, the willingness to listen and learn more, as well as have knowledgeable mentors to guide us and keep us upon truth. One should no doubt be resolute upon those things that are foundational, but one should also be aware of how much (or how little) they know. The Prophet Muhammad ﷺ never compromised on the foundations of faith, but he was willing to be flexible with other issues. One of the matters he never compromised was the *way* in which he called people to truth; as Allah says in the Qur'an, '*[Prophet], call [people] to the way of your Lord with wisdom and good teaching. Argue with them in the most courteous way.*' [16:125]

6. Learn this supplication

The companion 'Umar would make the following supplication: 'O Allah, show me the truth as truth and guide me to follow it. Show me the false as false and guide me to avoid it.'

AL-JAMĪL – THE BEAUTIFUL (67)

38

AL-JAMĪL – THE BEAUTIFUL (67)

'God is beautiful and loves beauty.'

[Muslim]

In an enlightening narration which we first came across in chapter 14, the Prophet ﷺ told us that no one with an ounce of arrogance in his heart will enter Paradise. In seeking to understand what arrogance means, the Companions asked, 'O Prophet of God, what if a person likes to dress well?' The Prophet ﷺ responded, *'God is beautiful and loves beauty. Arrogance is rejecting truth and looking down on people.'* [Muslim]

What is beauty?

We all have an affinity towards beauty in its different forms, and it is important to define what beauty is, since it can be abstract and indeed varies for different people. The Merriam-Webster dictionary defines beauty as 'the quality or aggregate of qualities in a person or thing that gives pleasure to the senses or pleasurably exalts the mind or spirit.' It also adds, 'a particularly graceful, ornamental, or excellent quality.'

In Arabic, two words in general are used for beauty, *jamāl* and *ḥusn*.[45] Beauty can be perceived through sight when we see what we regard as physically beautiful, but it can also be felt in the heart

[45] See this excellent discussion on beauty, its meanings, and the sacred law: Musa Furber, *Beauty and the Sacred Law*, Tabah Essays 4 (Abu Dhabi: Tabah Foundation, 2017).

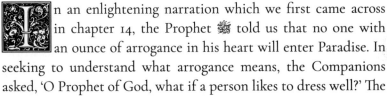

through beautiful attributes, manners, and actions; indeed, we use the word 'beautiful' for a person who possesses both inward and outward forms of beauty.

God is the Beautiful

Allah is al-Jamīl – He is the Beautiful – and all His names are al-Asmā' al-Ḥusnā – the Most Beautiful or Most Excellent. Allah tells us in the Qur'an, *'The Most Excellent Names belong to God (lillāhi al-asmā' al-ḥusnā): use them to call on Him.'* [7:180]

Knowing that Allah is al-Jamīl means knowing that He is Beautiful in His essence, His names, His attributes, and His actions (which includes His creation). None of us can really access Allah's essence as it is far beyond us, so how can we even begin to contemplate His beauty? Yet Allah gives us hints in this world. His actions and creation lead us to His attributes and His names, which then lead in a limited way to His essence. Indeed, Allah al-Jamīl calls the sun, the moon, the stars, the skies, and the mountains 'signs'. And what is a sign except a signal that leads us to something greater than itself – to a logical conclusion, and to the source of that sign? Ibn Al-Qayyim said, 'And it is enough to realize Allah's Beauty when we know that every internal and external beauty in this life and the next are created by Him, so what of the beauty of their Creator?'

If we take just one moment to reflect on the beauty of this world, some landscapes and sceneries can truly inspire awe. The gentle sound of waves, the cascading of a waterfall, the blooming of flowers, and so much more. And this is just worldly beauty. The Prophet ﷺ described Paradise as a place that no eye has seen, no ear has heard of, and which has never come across anyone's mind. Then ponder upon the fact that Allah al-Jamīl is creator of both the beauty of the world that we see, and the unimaginable beauty of the world that we do not – so what of His beauty?

We also see beauty in actions. Allah is beautiful in His Mercy, and His Mercy is manifested in the mercy which He has bestowed upon people, both in the provisions that He gives them, but also in the mercy that His creation show to one another. Look at a mother's ability to forget the pains of childbirth as soon as she holds her newborn in her arms. A father's patient answer to the same question his child has asked for the sixtieth time. A stranger who helps an elderly person cross the street.

Part of the meaning of the hadith which tells us that Allah is Beautiful, and that He loves beauty, is that 'abundant goodness flows from Him, and He loves whoever possesses it (i.e. those individuals to whom His beauty has flowed).'[46] This is all part of God's beauty.

We see beauty in the *qadar* (decree) of Allah. From His beauty, Allah returned the Prophet Moses to his mother as an infant, after he was washed up in front of the palace of Pharaoh, and He returned Joseph to his father after many years of separation. Even in difficulty, if we show *'beautiful patience (ṣabrun jamīl)'* [70:5] – a patience which accepts the decree of God while persevering in doing good – Allah will shower blessings upon us in the Unseen world, and we are ultimately given Paradise in the next world, God willing.

Our faith in God's beauty should strengthen our connection with our Lord. It should increase our love for Him and our longing to return to Him—to be able to see just a glimpse of Him. The Prophet ﷺ made the following supplication: *'I ask of You the joy of looking on Your noble countenance and of my longing to be with You.'* [Nasā'ī] We are inclined towards beauty because God Himself is the Most Beautiful and the source of every internal and external beauty in this world; hence, we supplicate for the joy of looking at God, the Beautiful.

[46] Rāghib al-Aṣfahānī, al-Mufradāt fī gharīb al-Qur'ān (Damascus: Dār al-Qalam, 1412/1991), 202, in Ibid, p. 6

The Beautiful created you

Al-Jamīl created internal and external beauty. It is enough honor for us that Allah created us and fashioned us Himself. Allah says, '*We created man in the finest state.*' [95:4]

The modern 'beauty' industry is predicated upon making people, especially women, feel ugly. They compete with airbrushed models, and only certain, limited types of beauty are held up as the archetype. This skews and constrains what we see as beautiful. Allah created us in different colors and shapes, and all of that is from His perfection and beauty, but industries profit from narrowly defining beauty and making it almost unattainable, except by cosmetic enhancements.

As servants of al-Jamīl, we must fight this commodification of beauty, and see all people as beautiful because they are created by the Beautiful. Beauty is not skin deep, but it penetrates our hearts and souls.

In the different ways that Allah has created us, and in the external differences between us, some are given more outward beauty. The Prophet Joseph was described by our Prophet ﷺ as being '*given half of beauty.*' [Muslim] External beauty can be both a blessing and a test. Indeed, Joseph was solicited by the wife of the governor because of his beauty. When she was blamed by the women of the city, she prepared a banquet for them, giving them sharp knives to cut their fruit, and ordered Joseph to come out so that they could see him. We are told: '*when the women saw him, they were stunned by his beauty, and cut their hands, exclaiming, "Great God! He cannot be mortal! He must be a precious angel!"*' [12:31]

But it was his inner beauty that truly shined. He prayed to be put in prison in order to get away from the women, and was God-conscious throughout. Inward beauty enhances outward beauty and, conversely, outward beauty can be diminished by inner ugliness. An arrogant, rude, and mean person loses any external attractiveness they might have had, except to those who love bad character. When Allah tells us that He loves beauty, this includes the beauty of character and goodness.

He loves beauty

The One who is the Most Beautiful, the source of all beauty, defines what true beauty is, and Ibn Al-Qayyim said that it pertains to two things: firstly, beautifying ourselves outwardly, and secondly, beautifying ourselves inwardly.

Outward beauty is not unimportant – but we have to understand the definition of beauty, which may not always be synonymous with modern-day standards. At the very basic level is to be as clean as we are able to be. We are told that *'cleanliness is half of faith.'* [Muslim] Moreover, people are discouraged from attending the mosque if they have eaten garlic or onion, because the odor bothers the angels and people [Muslim].

At an aesthetic level, we are encouraged to be well-dressed and presentable – again, to the best of our ability, within the guidelines of our faith, and exhibiting the beautiful trait of modesty. This beauty in dressing does not mean that we follow the current fashion trends or strive to wear what is expensive for the sake of it, but simply refers to the basics of striving to have clean clothes that cover our bodies and are dignified, and not appearing ragged or dirty if Allah has given us the means to avoid it. If one has means to dress well, one should do so, as the Prophet ﷺ said, *'God loves to see the effects of His grace upon His servant.'* [Tirmidhī] As the hadith cited earlier explains, dressing well is not considered to be showing off, unless it is done for that purpose, or to show that the well-dressed person is better than others.

However, we should remember that God knows and understands people's circumstances; for some of us, dressing well is very difficult because of a lack of financial means, or the nature of our jobs. God does not pressure a soul above its capacity, so we should understand these principles in relation to our own situation.

Moreover, if what we consider beautiful is touched by what does not please God, it ceases to be beautiful. Our desires and what we consider beautiful are affected and shaped by the messages that bombard us every day in advertisements, social media and movies. God tells us about the hypocrites, '*When you see them, their outward appearance pleases you; when they speak, you listen to what they say.*' [63:4] They looked a certain way, which was pleasing to other people, and they were charismatic when they spoke – but they were hypocrites. Their outward form did not make up for what was missing in their hearts. And this is the crucial point. While we should always aim to look dignified, because we are representing the faith of al-Jamīl, it cannot be at the expense of inward beauty.

The Prophet ﷺ said, '*God does not look at your appearance or your possessions; but He looks at your heart and your deeds.*' [Muslim] So beautifying ourselves outwardly, while commendable, and which can take different forms in different cultures, should be tempered by what is beautiful to God. No matter how elegant a garment is, if it does not cover our *'awrah* (the parts of the body that must be covered), it is not beautiful to God. Once a Companion was wearing a gold ring, presumably because he did not know that gold was prohibited for men. When he heard the Prophet ﷺ say that it is forbidden, he immediately removed it and threw it away. It may have been a beautiful ring, it may have been an expensive ring, but in his eyes it was nothing, because it was not beautiful to the Creator of beauty.

The real beauty, which is evident to anyone, is inner beauty. If the inside is beautiful, it beautifies what is outside. How many of us have met people whose inner light shines through? The Prophet ﷺ describes a '*seemingly disheveled, dusty, negligible person, but if he would swear to God, He would respond to him.*' [Tirmidhī] These are the people of true beauty to God, because of the beauty in their hearts. They are people who love to spend time with Allah, and when they are with others, they are at their service.

And if God loves your inner beauty, what happens? God tells us in a hadith *qudsī*:

> *'When I love him I am his hearing with which he hears, his seeing with which he sees, his hand with which he strikes and his foot with which he walks. Were he to ask [something] of Me, I would surely give it to him, and were he to ask Me for refuge, I would surely grant him it.'* [Bukhārī]

Living with this name

1. Focus on being beautiful to Allah

There is an over-emphasis on external beauty, and on changing our outward appearance to fit modern perceptions of beauty, in our society. The beauty industry is a multi-billion-dollar industry, and there is tremendous pressure on people, particularly women, to look a certain way to be beautiful, which almost always includes revealing one's body. Even with more so-called 'inclusive' body types and faces being portrayed, the emphasis is still on flaunting the outward, rather than on modesty. We must remember that God has given each person their own outward beauty, which does not need to be paraded in order to be validated, and true beauty is internal beauty that is loved by God.

The Companion Jarīr ibn 'Abdullāh, who was considered extremely handsome, reported that the Prophet ﷺ said to him: *'You are an individual whom Allah has given a beautiful appearance, so beautify your character.'*[47] External beauty can be a gift, but it has no impact on our station with God. We should beautify our character, and this beauty in our character should lead others to the beauty of this faith.

[47] Abū Bakr al-Kharā'iṭī, al-Muntaqā min kitab makārim al-akhlāq (Damascus: Dār al-Fikr, 1406/1985), 5, 7., cited in Ibid, p. 10

2. Reflect on the beauty of this world

God, the Beautiful and the Generous, has made the world beautiful. We can connect to this attribute of God through reflecting on the beauty of this world, and then reminding ourselves that it does not even come close to the beauty of Allah, and the beauty of the Paradise that He has created for us.

3. Beautify your world

Unfortunately, there is also ugliness in this world due to the actions of people. To believe in God the Beautiful is to try to remove the ugliness of the world, and replace it with beauty in the form of kindness, generosity and goodwill.

AL-WADŪD – THE LOVING, THE AFFECTIONATE (68)

39

AL-WADŪD – THE LOVING, THE AFFECTIONATE (68)

'Ask forgiveness from your Lord, and turn to Him in repentance: my Lord is merciful and most loving.'

[11:90]

One of the needs of the heart is to feel loved. At the very root of loving someone is that you want the best for your loved one. Some of us have our own definition of what love should look like; indeed, some may engage in destructive behavior just to taste an illusion of love. In Arabic, *ḥubb* describes the internal feeling of love. But, when you are beloved to someone, you want that love to be expressed; *wudd* is about showing externally the love that is in the heart.

Wudd means love, and the expression and manifestation of that love. And God has Named Himself al-Wadūd – the Affectionate – from the same Arabic root, *wāw-dāl-dāl*. This word was specifically chosen to tell us that God is not only loving, but that He shows His love to His servants.

When God loves a servant

Before explaining whom God loves, let us look at what happens when Allah loves someone. The Prophet ﷺ told us: *'When Allah loves someone he calls to [the Angel] Jibreel saying, "O Jibreel, I love such and such a person, so love him." Then Jibreel will call to the angels of the heavens, "Allah loves such and such a person so love him." And the angels will love [that person]. And then Allah will place acceptance on earth for that believer.'* [Bukhārī and Muslim]

It would be enough for God to say that He loves a person, for what more could someone want? But because God is al-Wadūd (the Affectionate) and al-Karīm (the Most Generous), He declares this love to the angels. This declaration does not remain only in the heavens, but descends to the Earth, because God puts acceptance of this person in the hearts of people. What else does God tell us about His love?

The Prophet ﷺ said, *'Allah, the Exalted, has said: "I will declare war against him who treats with hostility a pious worshipper of Mine. And the most beloved thing with which My slave comes nearer to Me, is what I have enjoined upon him; and My slave keeps on coming closer to Me through performing nawāfil (voluntary prayers or doing extra deeds besides what is obligatory) until I love him, (so much so that) I become his hearing with which he hears, and his sight with which he sees, and his hand with which he strikes, and his leg with which he walks; and if he asks Me something, I will surely give him, and if he seeks My Protection (refuge), I will surely protect him."'* [Bukhārī]

God expresses His love for His close servants through giving them knowledge of Him; He expresses His love for the sinners through His forgiveness and pardon; and He expresses His love for all of creation through His provisions and blessings, both internal and external. He even grants praiseworthy characteristics to those whom He loves.

The Prophet ﷺ said, *'Verily, Allah Almighty rewards for gentleness what He does not give for rudeness. If Allah loves a servant, then He grants him the quality of gentleness. No household is deprived of kindness but that they have been truly deprived.'* [Ṭabarānī]

God pairs His name al-Wadūd with His name al-Raḥīm (the Especially Merciful), saying, *'my Lord is merciful and most Loving'* [11:90], as well as with al-Ghafūr (The Most Forgiving), stating, *'and He is the Most Forgiving, the Most Loving.'* [85:14] In general, a person can forgive and show mercy towards people he or she does not love. But God pairs His name the Loving, the Affectionate with His names the Most Forgiving and the Most Merciful, to show that He *loves* to forgive and show mercy, and He *loves* those to whom He shows mercy and whom He forgives.

Indeed, God never leaves His righteous servants and those whom He loves. In Makkah, after the revelation of a few surahs of the Qur'an, revelation stopped. The tribe of Quraysh made fun of the Prophet ﷺ, saying 'The Lord of Muhammad has left him.' So, God revealed the verses, *'By the morning brightness, and by the night when it grows still, your Lord has not forsaken you [Prophet], nor does He hate you.'* [93:1-3] God comforted the Prophet ﷺ with these words. And we too should take comfort – when you are on the right path, God will not leave you. He is with you, and the fact that you are going through hardship does not mean that He hates you or has abandoned you. He will comfort you.

Indeed, al-Wadūd creates love and affection, and He praises this characteristic of *wudd* when it is found between people and in relationships. He tells us in the Qur'an, *'Another of His signs is that He created spouses from among yourselves for you to live with in tranquility: He ordained love (mawaddah) and kindness between you. There truly are signs in this for those who reflect.'* [30:21]

Marriage is not meant to be loveless or devoid of warmth, and we should strive to be affectionate in our relationships with our spouses. Love is, of course, not the dysfunctional, purely lustful, exaggerated version that we see in movies. Indeed, this is why Allah uses the word *mawadda* (from the same root as *wudd* and al-Wadūd) and not, for example *'ishq*, which is another word in Arabic for love, but implies more passion. *'Ishq* is not bad, and it has its place, but it rarely lasts; a lifelong marriage cannot be built solely on the feelings of exhilaration that come with *'ishq*. Rather, marriage is built on tranquility, affection (*wudd* or *mawaddah*) and kindness. This is one of the purposes of marriage.

Allah also reminds us not to write people off, and that He may even put affection between us and between those we consider enemies. He says, *'God may still bring about affection (mawaddah) between you and your present enemies – God is all powerful, God is most forgiving and merciful.'* [60:7]

Indeed, the Prophet ﷺ reminded us to temper the intense feelings we may have for or against others. He said, *'Love whom you love mildly, perhaps he will become hateful to you someday. Hate whom you hate mildly, perhaps he will become your beloved someday.'* [Tirmidhī]

Allah's love for you

Does Allah love you? Some of us may doubt that He does love us. We are filled with flaws, we may think. We sin too much, so how could He love us? Isn't His love reserved for the truly pious, those who rarely make mistakes?

Remember that Allah Himself created you. He honored you by creating you as a human, who has the capacity to know Him. He knows you more intimately than anyone else, even yourself. And He sends His blessings and His signs upon you daily. Take thirty seconds to write down all the blessings you have now, and see how many you can write down. These are from al-Wadūd.

Although He created us, we often worship other idols, like money or status. God blesses us with bounties, yet we attribute those blessings solely to people and forget their source; still He sends us gifts, in order to bring us closer to Him. We make mistakes and are heedless, yet the Prophet ﷺ tells us that *'Allah Almighty will stretch out His hand during the night, turning towards the one who did wrong during the day, and stretch out His hand during the day, turning towards the one who did wrong during the night, until the day the sun rises from the place it set.'* [Muslim]

Why would Allah want you to return to Him if He did not love you, if He did not want to accept you and write your name among the people of Paradise? In a prophetic narration, we are told, '*God is happier about the repentance of one of His slaves than one of you would be about finding your camel which had strayed away from you in the middle of the desert.*' [Bukhārī and Muslim] Think about this narration: *we* are the ones who stray away from God, deliberately or out of heedlessness, and yet He is happy – happy! – when we return, even though we are the ones who need this return.

He keeps the door open to us despite what we might have done. The Prophet ﷺ tells us that Allah says, '"*O son of Adam, so long as you call upon Me and ask of Me, I shall forgive you for what you have done, and I shall not mind. O son of Adam, were your sins to reach the clouds of the sky and were you then to ask forgiveness of Me, I would forgive you. O son of Adam, were you to come to Me with sins nearly as great as the earth and were you then to face Me, ascribing no partner to Me, I would bring you forgiveness nearly as great as it.*"' [Tirmidhī]

And if we leave something for the sake of God – and we know that anything prohibited is bad for us anyway – God replaces it with something greater. The Prophet ﷺ said, '*Verily, you will never leave anything for the sake of Allah Almighty but that Allah will replace it with something better.*' [Aḥmad] How beautiful and kind: in order to reward us and encourage us to leave that which He has prohibited – that in which we should not be engaging anyway – He replaces it with something better!

God makes it so easy to go to Him and be close to Him. The Prophet ﷺ told us:

> '*Whosoever intends to do a good deed but does not do it, Allah records it with Himself as a complete good deed; but if he intends it and does it, Allah records it with Himself as ten good deeds, up to seven hundred times, or more than that. But if he intends to do an evil deed and does not do it, Allah records it with Himself as a complete good deed; but if he intends it and does it, Allah records it down as one single evil deed.*' [Bukhārī and Muslim]

His generosity is so great that not only does He give to us, but if we thank Him for the blessings, He gives us more! God also uses the example of possibly the greatest love – that of a mother to her child – and then says that He has even more love and mercy towards us (see the hadith in chapter 3).

As servants, it is natural for us to love Him, since He is our merciful Creator. But it is amazing that God gives us so much, in order that we can seek to come closer to Him. Sometimes we despair and are unforgiving towards ourselves. But the Prophet ﷺ reminded us that, *'Our Lord descends each night to the earth's sky when there remains the final third of the night, and He says: "Who is saying a prayer to Me that I may answer it? Who is asking something of Me that I may give it him? Who is asking forgiveness of Me that I may forgive him?"'* [Bukhārī]

This is an open invitation to every single person. Some of us may feel so far from Him – where do we even begin? Yet God says in a hadith *qudsī*, *'"If my servant comes closer to Me a hand span, I come closer to him or her an arms-length; and if he or she comes to Me walking, I come to him or her at speed."'* [Bukhārī]

All it takes is one step. That step can be one prayer, and then another. That step can be leaving something He does not love. No matter how small, He appreciates it, and meets you where you are.

How can we not fall in love with al-Wadūd, who showers us with affection daily?

Whom does Allah love?

While Allah has a general love for all His creation, and one that is more specific for the believers, there is an even deeper love for those who strive for Him. Allah mentions in the Qur'an certain types of people whom He loves:

- *Al-muḥsinīn*: The doers of good
- *Al-muttaqīn*: Those who are mindful of Him

- *Al-muqsiṭīn*: The equitable and just
- *Al-mutaṭahhirīn*: Those who purify themselves
- *Al-tawwābīn*: Those who return to Him
- *Al-mutawakkilīn*: Those who put their trust in Him
- *Al-ṣābirīn*: The steadfast and patient

One of these categories is those who return to Him (*al-tawwābīn*). And who can return except the one who was far away? This means He has a special love for those who mess up – and may keep messing up – yet never lose hope in Him and His mercy. They return to Him and try to do better. They are not 'perfect' – there is no such thing as a perfect human, other than the Prophet ﷺ! – but they are all of us, who know our shortcomings but still work on ourselves for Him.

Indeed, to further encourage us, we are told of all the deeds that God loves. For example, the Prophet ﷺ said, *'If the servant glorifies Allah, Allah Almighty says: "Record for my servant an abundance of my mercy." If the servant praises Allah, Allah Almighty says: "Record for my servant an abundance of my mercy." If the servant declares there is no God but Allah, Allah Almighty says: "Record for my servant an abundance of my love."'* [Ṭabarānī]

The Prophet ﷺ also told us, *'The most beloved people to Allah are those who are most beneficial to people. The most beloved deed to Allah is to make a Muslim happy, or to remove one of his troubles, or to forgive his debt, or to feed his hunger.'* [Ṭabarānī]

In our effort to be close and beloved to God, we can strive to do the deeds that He loves.

The One who is loved

Ibn al-Qayyim states that there is another way to understand God's Name al-Wadūd: that He is the Beloved, and thus all of our love and expressions of love should be directed to God Almighty.

Understood in this way, our hearts are directed towards the One who should be the ultimate object of our own love.[48]

Living with this name

1. Love Him

Knowing that Allah al-Wadūd bestows so much affection and love upon us should fill our hearts with an immense love for Him. And as this name teaches us, love is not just about what is in the heart. We should express this love by being obedient to Him. And if we try but find it challenging to do good deeds to the degree that we see the righteous doing, this should not diminish the love in our hearts for Him. Rather, we should love Allah more. The Companion Abu Dharr said, 'I love Allah and His Messenger ﷺ.' The Prophet ﷺ replied, *'Verily, you will be with those you love.'* [Abū Dāwūd]

We should try our best to love God in our hearts and in our actions, and return to Him when we fall, because there is no way that one who truly loves Allah and His Messenger ﷺ can be far from Allah for too long. The heart always yearns to be with the beloved.

2. Do good

> *'Indeed, those who have believed and done righteous deeds – the Most Merciful will appoint for them affection.'* [19:96]

One of the ways in which we can be bestowed with the affection of al-Wadūd is to believe and do good deeds – good deeds are those deeds encouraged by and beloved to Him, and avoidance of those deeds disliked by Him. When we do good deeds, we move into the realm of His love, and He will show us that He loves us. As He is also al-Shakūr (the Appreciative) and al-Karīm (the Most

---

[48] Al-Ashqar, *Sharḥ Ibn Al-Qayyim Li Asmā' Allāh Al-Ḥusnā*, 73. In English, see: Justin Parrott, *Heavenly Affection: Living the Love of Al-Wadūd*, Yaqeen Institute, 9 July 2020.

Generous), the love He will give is so much more than we can ever imagine or conceive of in our minds. The Prophet ﷺ told us that, 'Allah Almighty said: '*My love is a right upon those who love each other for My sake. My love is a right upon those who visit each other for My sake. My love is a right upon those who sit together for My sake. My love is a right upon those who maintain relations for My sake.*' [Aḥmad] These are some of the ways to gain God's love.

3. Follow the Prophet ﷺ, the beloved of God

Allah told the Prophet ﷺ in the Qur'an: '*Say, "If you love God, follow me, and God will love you and forgive you your sins; God is most forgiving, most merciful."*' [3:31]

We should study the biography of the Prophet Muhammad ﷺ, and learn from his character and his way, in order to be like the beloved of God ﷺ.

4. Love one another, and love for others what you love for yourself

The Prophet ﷺ said, '*Verily, among the servants of Allah are people who are neither prophets nor martyrs, yet the prophets and martyrs will admire them on the Day of Resurrection due to their position before Allah Almighty.*' The Companions said, 'O Messenger of Allah, tell us who they are.' The Prophet ﷺ replied, '*They are people who love each other with the spirit of Allah, despite having no shared family relations or wealth. By Allah, there will be light on their faces and they will be upon light. They will not fear when people are afraid and they will not be sad when people are grieved.*' [Abū Dāwūd] As believers, we should carry a special love for one another that is based in our belief in and love for Allah.

The Prophet ﷺ also said, "*None of you will have faith until he loves for his brother what he loves for himself.*" [Bukhārī and Muslim] Al-Ghazālī succinctly shows what it means to adorn oneself with the characteristic of being *wadūd*. He says:

> 'One is loving-kind among God's servants who desires for God's creatures what he desires for himself; and whoever prefers them to himself is even higher than that as the messenger of God – may God's blessing and peace be upon him – said, when his tooth was broken and his face was struck and bloodied: 'Lord, guide my people, for they do not know.' Not even their actions prevented him from intending their good. Or as he commanded 'Ali: 'If you want to take precedence over those who are close to God, then be reconciled with those who broke with you, give to the ones who excluded you, and forgive the ones who wronged you.'[49]

Indeed, we should love people enough to want what is best for them. This includes loving for other believers all types of good, and specifically loving for those who do not believe in the faith of Islam to be guided.

5. *Express love*

Just as we love for Allah to express His love for us, so too should we express love towards those whom we love. The Prophet ﷺ encouraged this, when a Companion who was with him said about another person who passed by, 'O Messenger of Allah, I love this man.' The Prophet ﷺ asked, *'Have you told him?'* He replied that he had not. The Prophet ﷺ said, *'Tell him.'* So, the Companion went to the other man and said, 'I love you for the sake of Allah.' The man replied, 'May Allah, for whose sake you love me, also love you.' [Abū Dāwūd]

This teaches us another important lesson. It is more common in general for women to verbally express love to one another, while some men may only verbally express love to the women in their families, but this hadith shows us that we should all be expressive in our love. It is not a negation of masculinity, but rather a beautiful

---

[49] Al-Ghazālī, *The Ninety-Nine Beautiful Names of God: Al-Maqṣad Al-Asnā Fi Sharḥ Asmā' Allāh Al-Ḥusnā*, 119.

trait for both men and women to have. The Prophet ﷺ, who is the epitome of righteous masculinity, was asked, 'Which person is most beloved to you?' Pause here and reflect on the fact that the Companions did not shy away from talking about and expressing love. This question was not strange nor out of the norm. The Companion was not mocked nor censured for asking this question. The Prophet ﷺ responded, *'Āʾishah.'* This gives us pause again: the Prophet ﷺ did not hesitate to express his love for his spouse in front of others. The Companion who questioned him then said, 'I mean, among men?' The Prophet ﷺ then said, *'Her father (Abū Bakr).'* [Bukhārī and Muslim]

Another way to express love is through giving gifts. The Prophet ﷺ encouraged us to *'Give each other gifts and you will love each other.'* (Bukhārī, al-Adab al-Mufrad)

These two examples show us that there are multiple ways to show and foster love. The book, 'The 5 Love Languages',[50] by Gary Chapman explains concisely and clearly that people have different love languages, and one can learn from his writings and research how to better relationships by expressing love in the most meaningful way to the other person.

6. Adorn yourself with the characteristics that God loves

Allah loves gentleness, as we saw above. The Prophet ﷺ also told one of the Companions that, *'You have two characteristics that Allah loves: forbearance and patience.'* [Muslim] He also reminded us, *'The most beloved people to Allah are those with the best character.'* [Ibn Ḥibbān] We should learn the characteristics that God loves and beautify ourselves with them, in order to be of those beloved to Him.

[50] There are different versions of the book for the various types of relationships.

7. Make this supplication

The Messenger of Allah ﷺ taught us that, *'(Prophet) David would supplicate, saying: "O Allah, I ask you for your love and the love of those who love you and the deeds that will bring me your love. O Allah, make your love more beloved to me than myself and my family and even cold water."'* [Tirmidhī]

AL-GHANĪ – THE SELF-SUFFICIENT (69)

40

AL-GHANĪ – THE SELF-SUFFICIENT (69)

'Your Lord is self-sufficient and full of mercy.'

[6:133]

The champion boxer Muhammad Ali is reported to have said, 'I don't trust anyone who's nice to me but rude to the waiter. Because they would treat me the same way if I were in that position.'

Ali was pointing out something about the nature of some people: they treat others based on their social status, as well as on their need for them. If a person needs a cab driver to get home and he or she is short on cash, most people would likely be extra nice to the cab driver – they have a need that only this one person can fulfil. Indeed, though we all agree on ideal egalitarian values that everyone should espouse, regardless of social status or wealth, we are nonetheless impressed by the person who embodies these characteristics while not needing for others.

God is far above any analogy, but He is al-Ghanī, the Self-Sufficient, the Needless, the Rich. And despite having no need for anyone, He still bestows upon us His bounties, accepts us when we return to Him, and indeed calls us to come back to Him.

Al-Ghanī

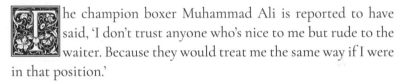

In human conceptions of a higher power, the unique attributes that are ascribed to deities usually concern immortality. Indeed, if we look at the Greek gods, though they had very human and very fallible temperaments, what made them 'gods' was essentially their immortality.

Part of the reason that Jesus is revered in Christianity is that he is believed to have died for the sins of others, essentially relinquishing what is perceived to be the most unique aspect of being divine – immortality – for the love of people.

But immortality is not in and of itself that exceptional. If human beings discover the proverbial fountain of youth – which scientists are working on – it would not make us in any way divine. It is true that Allah is immortal – He is al-Ḥayy, the Ever-Living, and al-Bāqī, the Everlasting – but if He so wills, He can give immortality to whomsoever He wishes. Would that mean that we were in any way equal to Him? We would still depend on Him for all our needs and for our very existence. Indeed, even our immortality would be dependent on Him!

Allah al-Ghanī, on the other hand, is the Self-Sufficient. He is completely free of need; He was not created nor does He need a cause to exist. He is al-Ḥayy al-Qayyūm – the Ever-Living, the Sustainer of all – and everything in this world is not only created by Him, but is sustained by Him in every nanosecond. He is not contained by time nor space – they are His creation and He is completely outside of them – and He has no limits. In our discussion of His names al-Samīʿ al-Baṣīr (the All-Hearing, the All-Seeing), we mentioned that our hearing and seeing are nothing like His hearing and seeing. We need a whole structure – light, soundwaves, frequencies, the mechanics of our hearing and sight – to come together in order to perceive using our eyes and ears. Allah's hearing and seeing are far beyond our comprehension because He needs nothing in order to hear and see.

When it comes to our worship, it is essential that we understand that Allah truly has no need for us, nor for our worship. We are the ones in need. Our prayers do not give Him anything, nor do our sins hurt Him. We do these things out of love and reverence;

because He has commanded them from us, we know that they are good for us. He is Needless and yet He understands our needs. So, He gives us the antidote to our illnesses. He teaches us the best way to fulfil the needs of our hearts, bodies and souls. God says in a hadith *qudsī*:

> "'*O My servants, you will not attain harming Me so as to harm Me, and you will not attain benefiting Me so as to benefit Me. O My servants, if the first of you and the last of you, and the humans of you and the jinn of you, were all as pious as the most pious heart of any individual amongst you, then this would not increase My Kingdom an iota. O My servants, if the first of you and the last of you, and the humans of you and the jinn of you, were all as wicked as the most wicked heart of any individual amongst you, then this would not decrease My Kingdom an iota. O My servants, if the first of you and the last of you, and the humans of you and the jinn of you, were all to stand together in one place and ask of Me, and I were to give everyone what he requested, then that would not decrease what I Possess, except what is decreased of the ocean when a needle is dipped into it. O My servants, it is but your deeds that I account for you, and then recompense you for. So he who finds good, let him praise Allah, and he who finds other than that, let him blame no one but himself.*'" [Muslim]

Most human beings cannot forgive completely, because our slights against others harm them, whereas God forgives over and over; our sins do not harm Him – they only harm us. He accepts even the smallest of deeds; their size does not affect Him either positively or negatively. Rather, these deeds help us. And Allah can give us anything and everything; He does not need any of it. Ultimately, we are the ones in need. And so we take our needs to the only One who has none.

And this makes all of His other names even more meaningful. Allah pairs His name al-Ghanī with other names to highlight certain truths to us. For example, He tells us in the Qur'an:

- *'God is self-sufficient, forbearing.'* [2:263]
- *'Our Lord is self-sufficient and full of mercy.'* [6:133]
- *'God is self-sufficient, worthy of all praise.'* (14:8]
- *'Then my Lord is self-sufficient and most generous.'* [27:40]

He is al-Ghanī and al-Raḥīm (the Most Merciful), al-Karīm (the Most Generous), al-Ḥalīm (the Forbearing), and al-Ḥamīd (the Praiseworthy); He gives mercy, gifts in abundance; He is not hasty in punishment. These are His names that He has chosen for Himself, and this is how He chooses to treat us, not out of any need. Thus, His love is the most pure, His mercy is the most pure, and His giving is the most pure, because they are not given out of any need.

Al-Ghanī and you

No matter how far science takes us, we can never be completely free of need. At the very least, we require the means of this world – all that Allah has provided – to do anything. What then of our emotional needs to connect to others, our physical needs for nourishment and sustenance, and – most importantly – our spiritual needs? We need God. Him, on the other hand? He is al-Ghanī – completely free of need.

Allah tells us in the Qur'an: *'People, it is you who stand in need of God – God needs nothing (al-Ghanī), and is worthy of all praise (al-Ḥamīd).'* [35:15]

In truth, we all need God. Some of us may realize it and some may not. If we do not, we may seek to assuage the calling of our soul with quick fixes. But just like we cannot quench our thirst by eating dry foods, we can never fulfil our needs by ignoring the very nourishment we do need. Quick fixes may provide a temporary distraction, but the need will always remain. As Ibn al-Qayyim said: 'In the heart there is a void that cannot be filled except by His love, turning to Him, always remembering Him, and being sincere to Him. Were a person to be given the entire world and everything in it, that would never fill the void.'

And this may be our ultimate problem. We do not realize that we need Him, or how much we need Him. And so, we attempt to fill that void with things that were never meant to fill it.

Prophet Moses, we are told in the Qur'an, helped two women to get water from a well. Someone else might feel proud that he or she had just helped someone who was in need. But Moses understood something. He sat down in the shade and said: *'My Lord, I am in dire need of whatever good thing You may send me.'* [28:24]

He knew that he was impoverished before Allah, even when he had just helped someone else in need. Recognizing that Allah is al-Ghanī should humble us, as we come to the realization that we are truly dependents of Allah, while He is completely and truly independent. The impact of this on our hearts should be that we turn to Allah for all our needs, big and small. This recognition means asking His help to keep us on the straight path that leads to Him. It means seeing that, no matter how much power or wealth any person is given, that person is completely and utterly impoverished before God.

You and others

Knowing that Allah is al-Ghanī can help our relationships with others. It may seem counterintuitive: how can the realization that people cannot fulfil all your needs improve your relationship with them?

We recognize that all people have needs, and because of this, we all necessarily have limits. Loved ones may want to be there for you, but sometimes they just cannot; they may be dealing with their own issues, juggling too many things for you to be their sole focus, or they may not know how to help. When we realize that they have their own needs, and are thus limited, we can cease to project our unrealistic expectations onto them. Our expectations of others become measured, and we stop putting more pressure on people than they can handle. God gave us people in our lives as gifts, but they are not meant to, nor can they, fulfil our every need. So, when we find that those we love cannot give us what we need, it is time to direct that request to al-Ghanī Himself, and be forgiving and understanding of the situation of our loved ones.

Something amazing happens here. Because He is also al-Mughnī (the Enricher), He can enrich you. He can enrich you to the point that you can wholeheartedly love people, but ultimately your dependency is on Him.

Living with this name

1. Realize that you need Him, and cannot do anything without His help

This realization teaches us to turn to Him every step of the way, and recognize that whatever means we have at our disposal are from Him. These means could disappear in an instant if He so willed, or our ability to utilize them could similarly be disabled. We learn to be humble in our souls and be grateful for what God has given us, as well as finding encouragement and energy when we are blessed with means to use.

This also helps to enhance our worship, because we understand that Allah has no need for us but it is truly us who need Him. When we understand that, for example, prayer is to fulfil a certain need of our soul, we can make more of a conscious effort to improve and beautify our prayer, and through it, connect to the Most High. Moreover, our *du'ā'* (supplication) also has more meaning when we realize that we are the ones truly in need.

2. *Understand that people have needs, because only He is free of needs*

This will ensure that our ultimate dependency is not on other people, and that we will not have unrealistic expectations of them. When we feel that others have let us down, we can direct ourselves to the One who has no needs.

3. *Busy yourself with His worship*

The Prophet ﷺ said, *'Allah Almighty said: "O son of Adam, busy yourself with my worship and I will fill your heart with riches and alleviate your poverty. If you do not do so, I will fill your hands with problems and never alleviate your poverty."'* [Tirmidhī]

The Prophet ﷺ taught us that when we busy ourselves with this world, we are essentially assuming that those things can fulfil our needs, and that we have no need for God. However, our hearts and minds should be filled with God and this should be evident in how we worship Him. This does not mean that we are not required to work, or that we isolate ourselves solely to pray. Rather, 'busying ourselves with worship' means prioritizing worship, because we recognize that our ultimate need is God, and also turning our day-to-day mundane activities into worship by checking our intentions.

AL-WĀSI' – THE VAST (70)

41

AL-WĀSI' – THE VAST (70)

'Such is God's favor. He grants it to whoever He will. God has endless bounty (wāsi') and knowledge.'

[6:133]

The word *wāsi'* means to be vast, spacious, without limit, and all-encompassing. God says in the Qur'an: *'And to Allah belongs the east and the west. So wherever you [might] turn, there is the Face of Allah. Indeed, Allah is all-Encompassing (wāsi') and Knowing.'* [2:115]

We are told that, wherever we turn, God is there. He is vast and cannot be contained in space. His vastness includes vastness in His essence, in His names, in His attributes, and in His actions. In whatever realm we can conceive, God is vast; whether that is to do with His expansive knowledge, dominion, forgiveness, blessings, or kindness – all of these are vast beyond comprehension.

There is room for you

This means something very beautiful for all of us who feel excluded or out of place: it means that there is room for us, with all of our struggles, our mistakes and our faults – God is vast. No matter how broken we are. No matter where we have been. No matter how many times we have messed up. There is room for everyone. Allah says in the Qur'an: *'My punishment – I afflict with it whom I will, but My mercy encompasses (wāsi'at) all things.'* [7:156]

The word used here for 'encompasses' is from the same Arabic root as Allah's name al-Wāsiʿ, *wāw-sīn-ʿayn*. His mercy encompasses everything. Every single thing. God also says: *'Indeed, your Lord is vast (wāsiʿ) in forgiveness.'* [53:32]

Do you feel as though your sins are too heavy? Do you find that you always give in to Satan's temptations? God's forgiveness is all-encompassing. The Prophet ﷺ said: *'Satan said: "By Your might, O Lord, I will continue to mislead the children of Adam, as long as their souls are in their bodies." The Lord said: "By My might and majesty, I will continue to forgive them, as long as they seek My forgiveness."'* [Aḥmad] The Prophet ﷺ also told us that Allah said, '*O son of Adam, were you to come to Me with sins nearly as great as the earth and were you then to face Me, ascribing no partner to Me, I would bring you forgiveness nearly as great as it.*' [Tirmidhī]

Allah tells us in Sūrat al-Tawbah: *'And [He also forgave] the three who were left behind [and regretted their error] to the point that the earth closed in on them in spite of its vastness and their souls confined them and they were certain that there is no refuge from Allah except in Him. Then He turned to them so they could repent. Indeed, Allah is the Accepting of repentance, the Merciful.'* [9:118]

The description in this verse is apt. It speaks about the three Companions we learned about in chapter 22, who abandoned the Muslims in their time of need, how they regretted it and how they felt like the earth was closing in on them, and that their souls were confined. But what happened? There is no refuge from God except to Him, so when they remained steadfast in their turning to God, He accepted them. That constriction that they felt was released. They could breathe.

God's vastness allows you to breathe.

Allah is all-encompassing when you ask from Him. Sheikh Akram Nadwi once said (paraphrased): 'If you were to ask me for a penny, how hard would it be for me to give it you? It would be almost like giving nothing. When you ask Allah, what you are asking of Him is even less to Him than that one penny is to me.' So, do not confine Allah in what you think He can give. Remember that He is limitless.

God also teaches us that He is expansive when we go through difficulty. He tells us that *'if husband and wife do separate, God will provide for each out of His plenty: He is infinite in plenty (wāsiʿ), and all wise.'* [4:130] We know that divorce is not forbidden in our religion, even if couples are generally recommended to initially try to reconcile. God tells us that if they do decide to separate, they should not be afraid of loss; rather, He will provide for each from His bounty. They may remarry or they may not, but they are not restricted, because God will provide.

And there is another meaning here. Allah's religion is vast. We all have things that are obligatory upon us – such as prayer, fasting and good character – but beyond that, we have all been given different talents and passions. We are told of so many different ways to come close to God with good deeds: smiling, helping others, being an honest business person, even having good intentions. This religion is for *you*. You can contribute in your own way, as long as it is within what is permissible.

Once, Imam Mālik was rebuked in a letter for wearing nice clothes. He was told that he should spend his time fasting during the day and praying during the night. Aside from the fact that wearing nice clothes does not preclude one from extra praying and fasting, Imam Mālik responded in the most beautiful way. He responded that God has apportioned acts of worship like He has apportioned sustenance. And Allah might have put a deep love of voluntary fasting and prayers in the heart of the author of the letter, but Allah had also put love in Imam Mālik's heart for learning and teaching. And there is good in all of these deeds.

Accordingly, connect to God with the obligatory, avoid what is impermissible, and then use whatever inspires you within the immense spectrum of permissible deeds to go deeper into that love. Just remember that He is vast, and so is His religion. In His mercy, there is enough space for you, with all of your mistakes. There is enough space for your talent. We all have deeds that are required of us, like prayer, and deeds we must decisively avoid, such as consumption and selling of alcohol. But God is all-encompassing and boundless, and He accepts our own journey to Him. You do not have to be an Islamic scholar, but you can if you want to be. You can be the honored cleaner of the mosque. You can be the member of your family who always brings people together. You can be a person known for his or her integrity. You can be like the Follower (*tābiʿī*) Uways al-Qaranī, who was said to be *'unknown to the people on earth, but well-known to those in the heavens'*[51] because of his sincerity. Those are all beautiful paths to God.

So, what is your way to God?

Living with this name

1. Learn your religion

It is important to learn our religion from qualified scholars who are familiar with the context we live in. We will find that our religion calls us to the most beautiful ethics and principles, and teaches us how to engage in the wide range of permissible acts, which increase our blessings in this life and the next. God's vastness does not mean that we act in accordance with our whims and desires, nor do deeds that He does not love. Rather, it means that if we try our best to obey Him and come close to Him in the ways that He has prescribed, even when we find it difficult, we will find acceptance.

2. Direct your intentions

We all have hobbies or interests that may seem 'secular', or unrelated to religion, which we love – for example, cooking, writing fictional stories, and so on. God's vastness teaches us that even these

[51] Mentioned in al-Dhahabī's *Siyar Aʿlām al-Nubalā*, 4/27

seemingly 'neutral' activities can be beloved to Him, when our intentions are in the right place.

If you love cooking, for instance, you can intend to feed others with food that you made with love – something the Prophet ﷺ specifically recommended for us to do – or bring people together around a nutritious and delicious meal, as that too is loved by God. If you love writing stories, you can infuse your writings with ethical principles and life lessons, or intend that people have a wholesome alternative to the vast array of material that exists.

3. Show people God's vastness through kindness

Part of Allah being Vast is that His kindness is also vast. There are some, even many, who may not know about God's endless mercy, kindness, knowledge and power. They may feel constricted by their understanding of this religion, and feel that they are excluded from it. Thus, it is important for us to show that Allah is vast, and that His religion encompasses all of us, through words and action. Our kindness should reflect the kindness Allah has bestowed upon us, thus enabling others to see the effect that belief in Him has on one's demeanor.

AL-ḤASĪB – THE ACCOUNTANT, THE SUFFICIENT (71)

42

AL-ḤASĪB – THE ACCOUNTANT, THE SUFFICIENT (71)

'God keeps account of everything.'

[4:86]

We are taught, as Muslims, to pay attention to our actions and our intentions, while understanding that Allah is the One who quantifies them. We know that the reward for one good deed is multiplied by Him at least ten times, up to seven hundred times or more, while a bad deed is counted as just one sin. Allah is al-Ḥasīb.

Ḥasīb is an aggrandizement of the verbal noun *ḥ*āsib, which means 'one who takes account'. *Ḥasīb* encompasses the meanings of counting, calculating, being sufficient, and honor. For example, in the Qur'an, Allah says of the gifts of Paradise: *'A recompense from your Lord, a sufficient (ḥāsiban) gift.'* [78:36]

The word used for 'account' is *ḥisāb.* Allah says in the Qur'an: *'But when you are offered a greeting, respond with a better one, or at least return it: God keeps account of everything (ḥasība).'* [4:86]

Thus, at one level, God tells us that He is *ḥasīb* over everything, meaning that He accounts for everything, even the tiniest of deeds. We sometimes make the mistake of belittling our deeds, whether good or bad. We belittle a sin because it is small, or think that doing a small good deed does not amount to anything, so we forego it or do it mindlessly. Knowing that God is al-Ḥasīb should make us aware that, no matter the size of our deeds, God takes them into account. Of course, we should try to do marvelous, grand good deeds, and avoid the greatest sins. But in a world where people's greatest achievements are celebrated on social media, we should not forget the small deeds that people might consider insignificant, which are nonetheless appreciated and loved by Allah. Similarly, we must try to avoid the so-called 'minor' sins because, as one scholar said, 'Mountains are made up of small stones.' Allah says in the Qur'an: *'Whoever has done an atom's-weight of good will see it, but whoever has done an atom's-weight of evil will see that.'* [99:7-8]

All of our deeds will be reckoned on the Day of Judgment, and thus 'Umar ibn al-Khaṭṭāb famously said, 'Take yourself to account before you are taken to account.' This means that we should be vigilant over ourselves and our actions, and try to improve. We should not be disheartened when we find that we make many mistakes, because while God is al-Ḥasīb, *He is also the Most-Forgiving* to those who return to Him and seek His forgiveness. The important thing is that we try.

At another level, since God is al-Ḥasīb, *He also takes others to account* – another translation of this name is the Reckoner – for their deeds. Whether they are the most powerful people in the world, who seem to act with impunity, or those who are weak and whose struggles seem unnoticed, al-Ḥasīb *is not ignorant of them.* Everyone will have to reckon with what they have done.

Sufficiency

Another meaning of al-Ḥasīb is that He alone is sufficient. The general meaning is that He is sufficient for all of His creation, as He has created them, given to them, and provided them with all of the means to achieve the purpose for which they were created.

He is also sufficient specifically for those who put their trust in Him. Allah says in the Qur'an: *'And whoever relies upon Allah - then He is sufficient for him (fa huwa ḥasbuh).'* [65:3]

This basically means that Allah will be enough for you in your worldly and spiritual matters, and if you have trust in God by relying on Him in your heart, and constantly think well of your Lord, you will truly taste the meaning of this sufficiency.[52]

Thinking well of Allah means having a good opinion of Him in all situations. It means that when we are given good, we thank Him for His favors, knowing that they have come from a giving, generous, affectionate Lord. When we are tested, we show patience knowing that the test is from the Most Wise, the Forbearing, the Merciful, the Generous, the Affectionate, and the Sufficient. He is what we need during the trial.

But what does it really mean for Allah to be sufficient, or enough for us? Think of the feeling that you get in your heart when you feel that what you have is enough for you. It could be knowing that all your financial needs are covered – you would feel tranquil and content. Or imagine the peace in your heart if you had someone in your life whom you felt was enough for you – he or she understood and loved you, and, despite your troubles, truly sufficed you; you felt that you could handle anything with this person by your side. Now, take a step back: Allah is telling you He is al-Ḥasīb – He is the Sufficient. Trust in Him, and He will be enough for you. It does not mean that you will not be tested, but it does mean that Allah will be enough for you to withstand whatever comes your way. And, if you have trust in Him, that same peace and tranquility we described will be multiplied, even in the face of tribulation – because you have Allah.

Think about this: a sixteen-year-old boy was put in front of a fire. The fire was so huge that he had to be placed into a catapult in order to be thrown from a safe distance. This boy was the Prophet Abraham, whose people wanted to burn him alive because he challenged their views on God and their way of life. Before he

[52] Abdelrazzaq bin Abdelmuhsin al-Badr, *Fiqh Al-Asmā Al-Ḥusnā*, 3rd ed. (Riyadh: Dār Ibn Al-Jawzī, 2019), 281.

was thrown in, he said the following words with a heart full of conviction: '*Sufficient is Allah for us, and He is the best Trustee (ḥasbunā Allāhu wa niʿm al-Wakīl).*' [Bukhārī]

And then the response came from none other than God Himself, the Sufficient: '*But We said, "Fire, be cool and safe for Abraham." They planned to harm him, but We made them suffer the greatest loss.*' [21:69-70]

We may have had small – or great – moments, when we faced something unbelievably difficult, and yet our hearts were calm. That calmness came from knowing that God is there for us, no matter what. It came from knowing that the ultimate source of everything is God, and only He gives and takes away. And it came from knowing that God is sufficient, because everything is from Him. It came from feeling that 'I have Allah, and I have all I need.'

Training ourselves to have this conviction in times of ease, or during minor difficulties, will strengthen our hearts so that we feel this same conviction during larger tribulations. Allah tells us: '*Those whose faith only increased when people said, "Fear your enemy: they have amassed a great army against you," and who replied, "God is enough for us: He is the best protector."*' [3:173]

In this verse, people were told to fear because others had gathered against them. But instead of fearing, they said that God was enough – sufficient – for them, and that He is the best protector. The next verse explains what happened next: '*[They] returned with grace and bounty from God; no harm befell them. They pursued God's good pleasure. God's favor is great indeed.*' [3:174]

We are advised to say those words, said by the Prophet Abraham and the believers described above, every morning and evening, in order affirm them in our hearts and live by them. The Prophet ﷺ said that whoever says the following '*seven times in the morning and evening, Allah will spare him what worries him: "Sufficient is Allah for me, there is no god but He, in Him I put my trust and He is the Lord of the*

Formidable Throne (ḥasbiya Allāh, lā ilāha illā huwa, 'alayhi tawakkaltu wa huwa rabb al-'arsh al-'aẓīm).'" [Abū Dāwūd]

When explaining this statement, we usually focus on Allah's Name al-Wakīl – the Trustee – and we learn about *tawakkul* (relying on God). But that only accounts for the second half of the statement. The first half tells us that God is enough for us.

This name reminds us where we should place our trust and our hope. It reminds us that there is no scarcity with Him. It reminds us that if we have God, we have everything. 'Umar ibn al-Khaṭṭāb is reported to have said that, when he was faced with a calamity, he would thank God that the calamity was not in his religion. He valued his relationship with God because he knew that with God by his side, he could face whatever hardship came his way. Being with Allah meant that he could see beyond the hardship and, indeed, even see the blessing within it.

Knowing that God is enough – that He is al-Ḥasīb – should empower us. But we should not misunderstand; it does not mean that we should not seek help from worldly means. If we are going through depression, for example, we should find a trained therapist to help us. Knowing that Allah is al-Ḥasīb means knowing that these remedies are ultimately from Him, and He has provided them for us. When we feel better, we thank God who provided a therapist for us, and we thank the therapist for helping us. We know that it is Allah who created the means by which the therapist was able to help us. The Prophet ﷺ taught us to: '*Make use of medical treatment, for Allah has not made a disease without appointing a remedy for it, with the exception of one disease, namely old age.*' [Abū Dāwūd]

When we truly internalize that Allah is al-Ḥasīb, we are able to shed whatever internal shackles are holding us back. We are able to act because we know that everything is in His Hands, and not in the hands of people. God suffices those who trust in Him, and in order for our trust to be true, we need to work with the means that we have been given. And if we are truly without any means, knowing that Allah is al-Ḥasīb means not despairing, seeing beyond the trial, and recognizing that those who are with Allah will be given ultimate bliss in the Hereafter.

Living with this name

1. Remember that Allah is the source of everything you need, and so trust in Him

Al-Ghazālī reminded us that we need to see beyond the immediate: when we think that we need food, drink or anything else, it does not mean that we do not need Him, because He is the one who supplies all that we need. He also emphasized that this realization and affirmation – that God suffices us – should lead us to desire nothing else but Him, and so we should direct our intention and our will towards Him.

2. Do not belittle what you consider to be small

The Prophet ﷺ said, '*Do not belittle any good deed, even meeting your brother with a cheerful face.*' [Muslim] Small deeds add up, and your intention can even magnify these seemingly small deeds. Allah is al-Ḥasīb, and He both takes into account and magnifies the ostensibly small actions.

3. Take yourself to account

Knowing that Allah counts all of our deeds should motivate us to be vigilant over ourselves, our hearts, and cause us to guard against the major and minor sins. We should take ourselves to account for our misdeeds and shortcomings through reflection, seeking forgiveness, and establishing the resolve to be better.

4. Remember that He is sufficient through daily remembrance (dhikr)

One of the remembrances (*adhkār*) of the morning and evening that we already learned is to recite seven times: '*Sufficient is Allah for me, there is no god but He, in Him I trust and He is the Lord of the*

Formidable Throne.' Moreover, when the Prophet ﷺ retired to his bed, he would say, *'All praise is due to Allah who has fed us, given us drink, sufficed us, and sheltered us. How many are those who do not have enough and have no shelter?'* [Muslim]

Finally, the Prophet ﷺ also said, *'Whoever says when he leaves his house, "In the name of Allah, I trust in Allah for there is no power or might but with Allah," then it will be said to him that you have been sufficed and protected, and the devils will be far from him.'* [Tirmidhī]

AL-QĀDIR, AL-QADĪR, AL-MUQTADIR – THE MOST POWERFUL, THE MOST ABLE, THE OVERPOWERING (72-74)

43

AL-QĀDIR, AL-QADĪR, AL-MUQTADIR – THE MOST POWERFUL, THE MOST ABLE, THE OVERPOWERING (72-74)

'Look, then, at the imprints of God's mercy, how He restores the earth to life after death: this same God is the one who will return people to life after death -- He has power over all things.'

[30:50]

Even before going into the linguistics of the names of God discussed in this chapter, many of us are at least theoretically aware of them. He is able to do all things, and we see this every day in our very own existence. We read the Qur'an and know that God created this world from nothing, and He has the power to make it disappear. He only says, *'"Be!" and it is.'* [2:117]

For others among us, this attribute is not just an abstract notion. The knowledge that God is able to do anything and everything is precisely why we call on Him with so much certainty in our supplications. We might not call on Him with these names specifically, but we ask Him because we know that He has the ability and power to respond to us and give us more.

Allah is al-Qādir (the Most Able), al-Qadīr (the Omnipotent) and al-Muqtadir (the Perfect in Ability), all from the same Arabic root, *qāf-dāl-rā*. This root can mean two things: power and ability on one hand, and measuring, or making manifest the measure of something, on the other.

As names of God, all three words are found in the Qur'an. Allah says:

> *'Do they not see that God, who created the heavens and earth, is [the one] Able (al-Q̱ādir) to create the likes of them [anew]?'* [17:99]

> *'It is He who creates human beings from fluid, then makes them kin by blood and marriage: your Lord is all powerful (Q̱adīr)!'* [25:54]

> *'The righteous will live securely among Gardens and rivers, secure in the presence of a Sovereign, Perfect in Ability (Muqtadir).'* [54:54-55]

Sheikh Māhir Muqaddim explains the nuances of these names. Al-Q̱ādir is the One who is able to do everything, from causing things to exist to ceasing their existence, and causing them to change or to return to what they were. Al-Ghazālī adds that its meaning encompasses Allah's ability to bring about the resurrection now, and He would bring it about if He willed it – God appraises, and then through His power, brings events about. Al-Muqtadir is an intensive form of the shared root, while al-Q̱adīr is the One with absolute power, which no one can stop or oppose.

These meanings encompass God's power to decree and carry out His decree. When we talk about *Laylat al-Q̱adr* (The Night of *Q̱adr*), scholars disagree over whether *qadr* here means the Night of Power or the Night of Decree, because the shared root can give rise to both meanings.

One may wonder why Allah would have three different names from the same root that are very similar in meaning. Would it not have sufficed that He revealed only one of them? Allah, in His wisdom, emphasizes to us through all three names His absolute, all-encompassing, unopposable power. Many times in life we may feel helpless and unable to make change; we may not know where to turn, and we see others who appear to have power in this world.

Perhaps this causes us to fear the seemingly powerful of this world more than al-Qadīr. Perhaps we lose hope because we feel powerless to change our condition or the world around us. But Allah teaches us: have certainty in Allah's all-encompassing power and, when you are not able, seek strength from the One who is able.

He has power over all things

Indeed, we all have moments when we look at a seemingly insurmountable obstacle and think to ourselves: 'How can it be overcome? It does not seem possible.'

A prophet once thought the same thing. He stood in front of a barren land to which he was sent, and asked the question, '"*How will God give this life when it has died?*"' [2:259]

Allah showed him how He could. He caused the Prophet 'Uzayr to die for a hundred years, then resurrected him. And when the prophet saw the town, which had once been razed to the ground, filled with people and homes and markets a mere hundred years later, he exclaimed, '"*Now I know that God has power (qadīr) over everything!*"' [2:259]

This example is mentioned to us to remind us that we should always plant seeds. Even if we have no idea how a seed will grow, it could become something which we could never have imagined, by the power and will of Allah – just like this town. Do not let your own limits cloud what you think is possible with God.

I know that God is capable of all things, but I am limited

There are two ways of looking at these attributes of God. We can view them in an abstract way, perhaps feeling great awe, yet not allowing the meaning of these names affect our behavior. 'Sure,' we may think, 'God is capable of all things, but we humans are limited. So, what is the point of trying?'

Then there is another way of looking at these names. God is able to do all things, and so whatever difficulty we face, we can overcome it if we seek strength from Him. At times, we are our own worst enemies. We stop ourselves from attempting to reach our goals because we believe that 'there is no way this could happen'. We close doors that may have been open to us, had we just tried.

When you believe that God is capable of all things, you are open to more possibilities. Believing in possibility is not simply an abstract notion, nor does it mean that you will something to happen, solely based on this belief. Rather, this belief means knowing that, because Allah is able, and He has revealed this attribute to you, you can derive strength from God, and you have possibilities. Ponder over the supplication of the prayer of *istikhārah* (guidance):

> *'If one of you feels inclined to do something then let that one pray two units of optional prayer, then say: "O Allah! I seek Your guidance by virtue of Your knowledge, and I seek ability by virtue of Your power, and I ask You of Your great bounty. You have power; I have none. And You know; I know not. You are the Knower of hidden things. O Allah! If in Your knowledge, (this matter**) is good for my religion, my livelihood and my affairs, immediate and in the future, then ordain it for me, make it easy for me, and bless it for me. And if in Your knowledge, (this matter*) is bad for my religion, my livelihood and my affairs, immediate and in the future, then turn it away from me, and turn me away from it. And ordain for me the good wherever it may be, and make me content with it."'* [Bukhārī]

We say to Allah, *'I seek ability by virtue of Your power.'* We recognize that we have no power, but that does not debilitate us. We put in the effort anyway, and seek strength from the Source of all strength.

Going back to the story of the Prophet 'Uzayr, God shows His power to both us and His prophet, by bringing a dead town back to life. He shows us possibility where we could only perceive impossibility. Allah teaches us that He is able, and this has consequences for the way that *we* perceive situations. We do not limit ourselves to one limited interpretation of the circumstances, but realize that there could be multiple paths. This affects our actions.

Take the example of the Prophet Muhammad ﷺ. If you had asked anyone in Makkah during the first few years of revelation whether they could imagine that the religion he taught could span the lands between China and Spain, he or she would have called you called crazy and delusional. You would probably have understood why – it seemed impossible at the time. But the Prophet ﷺ knew who God is. He was reminded in verse after verse about Allah's ability, and he derived strength from that knowledge.

When a situation became difficult, he never saw a dead end in front of him. He was able to see the whole picture and take alternative routes. When he was persecuted in Makkah, and knew that the persecution would get worse after his uncle passed away, he did not despair; rather, he made plans to leave. When he was rejected in Ṭā'if, he did not tell himself that there was no use; he used the Hajj season, when all the tribes would congregate in Makkah, to seek help. When they were in Madinah and an attack by the Makkans was imminent, he was not paralyzed into inaction because of the Muslims' perceived weakness; he was open to the idea of building a trench, which eventually led to victory. When the Makkans proposed a peace treaty at Ḥudaybiyyah, and negotiated terms that appeared to be disadvantageous to the Muslims at the time, he did not concentrate on those terms; he focused on what this peace treaty would enable the Muslims to do: secure long-peace with Makkah, and Hajj unopposed in future years.

This is the secret of all of the prophets and the righteous. When Moses was being hunted down by Pharaoh and his army, he said, "'*No, my Lord is with me: He will guide me.*'" [26:62]. The army of Saul (Ṭālūt in Arabic), when faced with the much larger army of Goliath, said: "'*How often a small force has defeated a large army with*

God's permission! God is with those who are steadfast.'" [2:249]. When Hājar was left in the desert with her infant son, she ran back and forth between the mountains of Ṣafā and Marwah. A person might have seen her and thought, 'what is the use?' But when you believe that God is capable of all things, you are able to be open to different possibilities and alternative paths. And Hājar was given the well of Zamzam.

Living with these names

1. Recognize that Allah is capable of all things

By simply recognizing this, we should increase our certainty in God's promise: of the Day of Judgment, of justice, and of hope. Allah is the Powerful and He is more powerful than anyone who appears to have power in this world, even those who misuse it. Allah is easily able to gather every single soul on the Day of Judgment. Knowing that He is All-Powerful means knowing that nothing we go through is too great for Him to overcome, and He is able to change what is seemingly impossible.

2. You are powerful if you derive your power from Him

Knowing that we have a Lord who is All-Powerful should strengthen our hearts. Āsiyah was objectively weaker than Pharaoh, but she was able to stand up to Him and declare her faith in God, because her strength was derived from the All-Powerful and not from herself.

3. When you supplicate, have certainty because you know that Allah is al-Qadīr

Ask Allah based on His ability, not on yours. Remember that God gives not only based on His power, but on His wisdom and mercy as well (See chapter 21).

4. Do not be reckless

This should go without saying, but knowing these names is not a call to recklessness. It is not about jumping from a window, because you believe that God has the power to ensure that your bones do not break. Rather, it means following the example of the Prophet Muhammad ﷺ, who planned and executed those plans using all of the means he possessed, no matter how small, because He knew that Allah could give success through any route.

5. Be open to possibilities

There are certain things that, due to the nature of the world, we cannot imagine being possible. Yet, if people always limited their imagination, we would not be flying on airplanes, nor finding cures for the most dangerous of diseases. Certainty that God is capable of all things should make us open to possibilities, and should encourage us to work towards innovative solutions.

6. Pray istikhārah about matters of importance

When you make the supplication of *istikhārah*, you are reminding yourself of your limited ability and God's limitless power. You recognize that, although you have no power over the matter about which you are asking, God does. And you have faith that He will help you, and will give you strength to choose the right way.

AL-JAWĀD AL-MANNĀN – THE MAGNANIMOUS, THE BESTOWER (75-76)

44

AL-JAWĀD AL-MANNĀN – THE MAGNANIMOUS, THE BESTOWER (75-76)

'God is magnanimous (jawād) and He loves those who are magnanimous in giving. He loves excellent moral character and detests meanness.'

[Bayhaqī]

There are different names of God that show us clearly how Allah gives to us: He is al-Karīm (the Most Generous), who gives above and beyond what is expected or even imagined; He is al-Wahhāb (the Bestower of Gifts), who gives without any compensation; and He is al-Razzāq (the Provider) who has apportioned for us everything that benefits us in this world. All of these names highlight to us the different ways and the extent to which Allah bestows upon us His gifts every day. They teach us to truly reflect upon the blessings that we have in our lives, and connect them to the Giver of these blessings.

God is also al-Jawād and al-Mannān, which highlight to us further the degree to which Allah constantly gives to us. It should truly warm our hearts that the Most High Himself has taken it upon Himself to give to each and every one of us personally.

Al-Jawād (the Magnanimous) comes from the Arabic root *jīm-wāw-dāl*, which means 'plentiful' or 'magnanimous'. *Jawād* is the name given to a strong and fast horse, while *jawd* is heavy, pouring rainfall. The Prophet ﷺ taught us that, *'God's Hands are full, and that fullness is not diminished by His giving day and night.'* [Muslim]

God's giving is like a heavy rain that falls and nourishes everything – and even more. Blessings rain on us every single day and we do not even notice. From the air that we breathe, to our ability to move, and every small or large blessing we have, al-Jawād is the One who is magnanimous in spirit and magnanimous in giving. If we simply reflect on everything we have, or even a portion of it, we can begin to appreciate this name.

While al-Jawād manifests His name in every moment of every day, we can see this name even more clearly when we are truly patient with difficulties, or during times when we feel that we are *not* being given what we want or need. When Hājar was steadfast in her hope in God, after being left alone in the desert with her infant son, He did not simply give her 'enough'. Rather, He gave her the well of Zamzam, which benefited her in her moment of need, and benefited all the believers after her too. When the Prophet Job lost everything – his children, his wealth, and his health – yet did not decrease in His love for Allah, al-Jawād *'answered him, removed his suffering, and restored his family to him, along with more like them, as an act of grace from Us and a reminder for all who serve Us.'* [21:83]

Allah tells us that the story of Job is a reminder: in times of constriction, He is still giving, and after we show patience, He gives even more. Indeed, we can see the extent of God's magnanimity during periods in which we know that we are not in the best spiritual state, and still He gives to us. We may feel ashamed to ask Him, but we do anyway, knowing that we are especially undeserving in that moment; He responds anyway. That is God al-Jawād, who rains down His blessings even on sinners. He is magnanimous in spirit and magnanimous in His giving. We all breathe in the air around us out of His magnanimity, whether we are doing good deeds or bad. Allah gives freely, as we are told in the Qur'an: *'Nay, both His Hands are widely outstretched. He spends (of His Bounty) as He wills.'* [5:64]

Favors: the greatest blessings

In another hadith, one of the Companions of the Prophet ﷺ once called to Allah, saying: 'O God, I ask you as all praise is Yours. There is no god except You, You are al-Mannān (the Bestower of Favors, the Benefactor), the Originator of the Heavens and Earth, Possessor of Majesty and Honor. O the Ever-Living, O Self-Subsisting.'

The Prophet ﷺ heard him and said: *'He has supplicated to Allah using His Greatest Name; when supplicated with this Name, He answers, and when asked with this Name, He gives.'* [Abū Dāwūd]

The Arabic root of the word *mannān* – *mīm-nūn-nūn* – means to cut something and leave with it. Allah says in the Qur'an: *'You will have a never-ending reward (ajrun ghayru mamnūn).'* [68:3]

The word *mamnūn* also comes from this root and has been translated as 'never-ending' or, in other translations, 'uninterrupted', meaning a reward that is not 'cut off'. Al-Mannān is an intensified form of the root, and means to give freely or liberally, as well as to do someone a favor. In general, favors are requested because we need them, from those who can oblige us in the best way. For example, Allah says in the Qur'an: *'Certainly, did Allah confer great favor [manna] upon the believers when He sent among them a Messenger from themselves, reciting to them His verses and purifying them and teaching them the Book and wisdom, although they had been before in manifest error.'* [3:164]

God reminds us of the status of the Prophet ﷺ by using the word *mann*, from the same root; indeed, we *need* the example of the Prophet ﷺ, and only God could have sent us the Prophet as a favor to help us on our path to Him. When we look at the world around us, we realize that in terms of material things, God has favors to different categories of people. Some of the most corrupt people are extremely wealthy, and so are some generous philanthropists. Material wealth, which we understand as coming ultimately from God, does not reflect one's spiritual standing with Him. When God refers to His favors as *mann*, an intense giving, He talks about those favors related to the Hereafter – indeed, the blessing they bring is uninterrupted because they relate to otherworldly life. He tells us that He has favored us by giving us a messenger who is from us, who purifies us and teaches us. In another verse, Allah says: *'They think they have done you [Prophet] a favor by submitting. Say, "Do not consider your submission a favor to me; it is God who has done you a favor (yamunnu 'alaykum), by guiding you to faith, if you are truly sincere."'* [49:17]

Our submission to God is a not a favor we are doing the Prophet ﷺ, because he does not need our Islam for his salvation; rather, our submission to God is a favor from *Him*, because ultimately it is what *we* need. And we should we grateful for this favor. It is easier to remember to be grateful for material and emotional blessings, because we reap the benefits in the present. But God reminds us of everything He gives us, and particularly the favors related to our connection with Him in this life, which lead us to be with Him in the Hereafter. It is a blessing we sometimes take for granted. The ability to turn to Him, to seek wisdom and comfort from the Qur'an, and to learn from the example of the Prophet ﷺ; these are all great gifts from al-Mannān.

God also tells us in the Qur'an about people on the Day of Judgment: *'They will say, "Indeed, we were previously among our people fearful [of displeasing Allah]. So Allah conferred favor (fa manna) upon us and protected us from the punishment of the Scorching Fire."'* [52:26-27]

The greatest *mann* (favor) from God is ultimately Paradise. For the very little that we do, we are given a reward that no language has the words to describe. It is indeed a favor, one which we need, and which only God can give us.

Living with these names

1. Be magnanimous

It was said about the Prophet ﷺ that, *'when it came to doing good, he was the most magnanimous (ajwad) of people, and he was at his utmost magnanimity during the month of Ramadan.'* [Bukhārī] Be magnanimous in spirit, and be magnanimous in giving. Nothing you give is ever lost – you will be rewarded for it.

2. Reflect on the material gifts and emotional gifts, but also reflect on and be grateful for the spiritual gifts

The greatest gifts we have been given are spiritual gifts. Wealth may or may not be accompanied by peace of mind in this world, and ultimately, we will be asked about that on which we spent our wealth. But the gift of closeness to God is truly the gift to be cherished. Reflecting on these blessings is one of the ways to increase our love for God.

3. Ponder over the gift of the Prophet ﷺ

God reminds us that one of His favors upon us is the Prophet ﷺ. Learn from the character of the Prophet ﷺ and study his *sīrah* (biography) to understand why Allah told us that he was given to us as a favor from the Most High.

4. Do not be a person that constantly reminds people of the favors that you have done for them

When God reminds us of His favors, it has a sweetness, because these reminders alert us to the value of these favors as blessings that we truly need, and they cause us to return to Him. This *mann* as a positive action is specific to God because of the perfection of His gifts and the good to which they lead. Then there is the *mann* of speech, when people remind you of their favors upon you. Allah tells us, *'Do not invalidate your charities with reminders (mann) or injury.'* [2:264]. When you give, remember that your intention is for God, and do not remind people of the things you have done for them in order to make them feel bad or that they owe you.

AL-NAṢĪR, AL-GHĀLIB – THE HELPER, THE CHAMPIONER (77-78)

45

AL-NAṢĪR, AL-GHĀLIB – THE HELPER, THE CHAMPIONER (77-78)

'So keep up the prayer, give the prescribed alms, and seek refuge in God: He is your protector – an excellent protector and an excellent helper (al-Naṣīr).'

[22:78]

We all go through periods in our lives when we feel embattled, physically or emotionally, and maybe even defeated. These are times of darkness, when we become acutely aware of our need for help and victory. Allah knows this and comforts us with His names al-Naṣīr and al-Ghālib.

The Arabic root of al-Naṣīr, *nūn-ṣād-rā*, means helping the oppressed, and the word for victory, from the same root, is *naṣr*. Allah says: *'And victory (naṣr) is not except from Allah, the Exalted in Might, the Wise.'* [3:126]

Naṣīr is an aggrandizement of the root word, and thus refers to help of both utmost quality and quantity – God helps us repeatedly, with both big and small problems. He reminds us that true help and victory are only from Him. Not only does Allah aid you and give you victory, but He is al-Ghālib, whom no one can defeat. These attributes are often mentioned together in the Qur'an. God tells us: *'If Allah should aid you (yanṣurkum), no one can overcome you (lā ghāliba lakum).'* [3:160]

These names are for everyone who has ever felt defeated or powerless. Indeed, the Prophet Noah, who was abused by his people for 950 years, felt this way, *'and so he called upon his Lord, "I am defeated (annī maghlūb): so help me (fantaṣir)!"'* [54:10]

What was the result?

> *'So We opened the gates of the sky with torrential water, burst the earth with gushing springs: the waters met for a preordained purpose. We carried him along on a vessel of planks and nails that floated under Our watchful eye, a reward for the one who had been rejected. We have left this as a sign: will anyone take heed?'* [54:11-15]

Upon hearing these names and this story, many of us might be comforted. Some of us might have questions: What help will come? When will it come? Will victory actually be given to the oppressed?

Types of victory: the external

There are different types of victory and aid. God gives us examples in the Qur'an that can very clearly be classed as victories and help from Allah. For example, God tells us:

> *'And already had Allah given you victory [naṣarakum] at [the battle of] Badr while you were few in number. Then fear Allah; perhaps you will be grateful. [Remember] when you said to the believers, "Is it not sufficient for you that your Lord should reinforce you with three thousand angels sent down?" Yes, if you remain patient and conscious of Allah and the enemy come upon you [attacking] in rage, your Lord will reinforce you with five thousand angels having marks [of distinction]. And Allah made it not except as [a sign of] good tidings for you and to reassure your hearts thereby. And victory (al-naṣr) is not except from Allah, the Exalted in Might, the Wise.'* [3:123-126]

During the Battle of Badr, the Muslims were few in number. They prepared as best as they could and put their faith in God, as a much larger army from Makkah was ready to attack them. God told them that He helped them by sending down angels – though

He also reminds the Muslims that, while the angels are there for reassurance, victory and help are only from God.

The beautiful thing about the Qur'an is that it talks about reality. It tells us about when a manifest victory occurred, and then shows us instances of what might appear to be losses. For example, Allah tells us in Sūrat al-Burūj of a people who were thrown into a fire for no reason except that they believed in one God [85:8]. So some might ask, where was the help? Where was the victory? Allah tells us: *'But for those who believe and do good deeds there will be Gardens graced with flowing streams: that is the great triumph.'* [85:11]

It may sometimes appear that injustice has won. But God gives victory in this life to whom He wills and gives victory in the Hereafter for those who live in accordance with their faith with dignity. Allah tells us: *'Indeed, We will support Our messengers and those who believe during the life of this world and on the Day when the witnesses will stand – The Day their excuse will not benefit the wrongdoers, and they will have the curse, and they will have the worst home.'* [40:51-52]

Injustice and oppression will never have the ultimate victory, and as Muslims, we are commanded to defend the oppressed against any and all forms of oppression. There are many lessons in the story in Sūrat al-Burūj – one is that we should never to allow oppression to flourish. The deeper the roots of oppression, the harder it is to uproot it. While the general rule is that Allah will help the oppressed – even in this world – we are reminded of our responsibility to stand against injustice, as well as our hope in ultimate justice. The Prophet ﷺ said, *'Help your brother whether he is an oppressor or is being oppressed.'* It was said, 'O Messenger of Allah, we help the one being oppressed but how do we help an oppressor?' The Prophet ﷺ said, *'By seizing his hand.'* [Bukhārī and Muslim]

Allah also teaches us through these names that there is purpose in everything that happens in this world, even if some events appear outwardly to be bad. Conviction in these names means knowing that what appears to prevail externally is actually Allah prevailing. How so? In the story of the Prophet Joseph, it appears that those with the worst intentions prevailed throughout his whole ordeal. It seems that his brothers got away with throwing him in the well, and the wife of the governor got away with her attempt to seduce him and then blaming him. Indeed, it seems that everyone moved forward but him; even the prisoner who shared his cell was released much earlier than him, and forgot about Joseph once he was released. But Allah reminds us that *'God always prevails (ghālibun) in His purpose, though most people do not realize it.'* [12:21]

We then realize that every single hardship was purposeful and, of course, Allah had not forgotten about Joseph. Every step led to his eventual release, being given authority over the food rations, and being reunited with his family. When people thought that they were accomplishing their own purpose – his brothers, for example, threw him in the well and succeeded in separating him from their father – in fact, Allah was prevailing in *His* purpose. Knowing that Allah is al-Ghālib is to know that, even when it appears that wrongdoers are 'winning', they can never prevail over God's plan. Their plotting can never override what Allah wills, and even if God allows them to execute their plans, this will only be held against them. Indeed, Allah is al-Ghālib on the Day of Judgment, the day when no one will prevail but Allah.

Internal victory

God helps us to overcome our external enemies, and He also helps us to overcome our internal foes, such as our lower selves, as well as Satan. In Sūrat al-Nās, we ask God for just this: '*Say, "I seek refuge with the Lord of people, the Controller of people, the God of people, against the harm of the slinking whisperer –– who whispers into the hearts of people –– whether they be jinn or people."*' [114:1-6]

The Prophet ﷺ would say the following supplication in the mornings and evenings: '*O Allah, Knower of the unseen and the evident, Maker of the heavens and the earth, Lord of everything and its Possessor,*

I bear witness that there is none worthy of worship but You. I seek refuge in you from the evil of my soul and from the evil of Satan and his helpers. (I seek refuge in You) from bringing evil upon my soul and from harming any Muslims.' [Abū Dāwūd]

Remember that when you feel troubled internally, God can help you. If you are battling sadness, Allah can help you overcome it. If you are having difficulty battling your own demons, Allah is there for you. When you are not able to overcome challenges, seek help from the One who is able to (see chapter 43). Another supplication that the Prophet ﷺ taught us to say in the morning and evening is: *'O Allah, I seek refuge in you from worry and sadness. I seek refuge in you from weakness and laziness. I seek refuge in you from cowardice and miserliness. And I seek refuge in you from being overwhelmed by debt and the tyranny of men.'* [Abū Dāwūd]

Part of seeking God's help is that we use the external means available to us, because ultimately, He provided them to help us.

When does God's help come?

Victory requires three things: faith, action, and *ṣabr* (patience and perseverance).

As people of faith, we can fall into *expecting* miracles to happen, without our hard work. We look at the story of Moses and see how, astoundingly, he was saved, so we wish that the sea would be parted for us too. We read the trials of Mary and see that she was given a child as a virgin, so we know that miracles are easy for God. We focus on His miracles, but forget that they came after much effort from His servants. The result is that when things do not go our way, and we feel that we have not been helped, we give up. But in the stories of the Qur'an, God shows us something amazing. It is when the righteous exhaust all their means – both internal and external – that the help of God finally comes. When Moses did everything he could to win Pharaoh over, and he was being literally chased by an army, *that* is when God split the sea [26:63]. When Mary was at the point of wishing that she was dead during her labor pains [19:23], she was given help. When Hājar ran seven times back and forth looking for help, God gave her the well of Zamzam. The Prophet ﷺ reminded us: *'Know that victory comes with patience, relief with affliction, and hardship with ease.'* [Tirmidhī] We must keep this in mind when seeking God's help.

Moreover, the life of the Prophet Muhammad ﷺ is full of examples of him working within his means. Miracles came to support him, but they never stopped him working, and in that is a lesson for us. The Prophet ﷺ planned his escape from Makkah. The Prophet ﷺ prepared for battles. He spent years in Makkah calling people to Islam and to justice in society. He did not expect that things would 'just happen'.

Finally, God giving us His help does not mean that there will not be hardships, as the examples above clearly show. Allah asks this question in the Qur'an:

> *"Or do you think that you will enter Paradise while such [trial] has not yet come to you as came to those who passed on before you? They were touched by poverty and hardship and were shaken until [even their] messenger and those who believed with him said, "When is the help [naṣr] of Allah?"'* He then answers at the end of that same verse: *'Unquestionably, the help of Allah is near.'* [2:214]

Remember that tests and hardships, as well as help, come to you from the Most Wise, the Equitable and the Most Merciful.

Living with these names

1. Have faith that God's victory will come, and none can prevail over Him or His will

Always have faith in al-Naṣīr al-Ghālib, and be mindful of Him wherever you are. The Prophet ﷺ taught us:

> *'Be mindful of God, and He will take care of you. Be mindful of Him, and you shall find Him at your side. If you ask, ask of God. If you need help, seek it from God. Know that if the whole world were to gather together in order to help you, they would not be able to help you except if God had written so. And if the whole world were to gather together in order to harm you, they would not harm you except if God had written so. The pens have been lifted, and the pages are dry.'* [Tirmidhī]

2. Work until the very end

Remember that help came to the righteous when they had exhausted each and every one of their means. They had faith in the help of God, and their perseverance was rewarded with His aid. We should avoid being lazy and complacent, and indeed, the Prophet ﷺ taught us to seek refuge from laziness every day. [Bukhārī]

3. Remember that your efforts will never go to waste

Whatever good you do, God records it for you. Your effort could be the seed that grows to help future generations. Even if you feel that you were not victorious in this life, remember that your effort counts in gaining you the ultimate victory in the Hereafter.

4. Allah aids the oppressed, whoever they may be, so do not be an oppressor

Never ever oppress people. The Prophet ﷺ tells us to *'Beware of the supplication of the oppressed, even if he is an unbeliever, for there is no screen between it and God.'* [Aḥmad] Allah does not discriminate between oppressed people, and your professed faith – if you are an oppressor – will not help you when you are unjust towards others.

5. Help others

The Prophet ﷺ said, *'God helps the servant as long as he helps his brother.'* [Muslim] If you want Allah's help to come, then help others. Be there on the front lines in the battle against injustice. Justice should be fought for everyone.

AL-FATTĀḤ – HE WHO OPENS ALL THINGS (79)

46

AL-FATTĀḤ – HE WHO OPENS ALL THINGS (79)

'No one can withhold the blessing God opens up for people, nor can anyone but Him release whatever He withholds.'

[35:2]

Inevitably, we all face 'doors' in our lives that seem to be closed – doors that we believe will lead us to somewhere better, or doors that will enable us to escape the difficult situations in which we find ourselves. It could be that we have exerted all of our efforts and, still, that one door that we want to open remains closed. We may simply see a closed a door, and so we do not even attempt to open it. These are situations which are seemingly impossible, or appear to be completely blocked.

For these circumstances, God invites us to know Him by His name al-Fattāḥ, which comes from the three-letter Arabic root *fā-tā-ḥā*. This root means 'to open or unlock', and can give rise to meanings such as 'to judge or to decide', because you are opening up a way forward, or giving relief to the oppressed party, when you make a decision or judgment. Indeed, the opposite of *fatḥ* (opening), from the same root, is for something to be closed. In the Qur'an, those who are accused unjustly make this supplication: *'Our Lord, decide (iftaḥ) between us and our people in truth, and You are the best of those who give decision.'* [7:89]

Iftaḥ has been translated in the above verse as 'decide', because God's just decision is an opening.

Al-Ghazālī explains that every closed thing can be opened by al-Fattāḥ. If one were to tell you to open a door, it would seem like a strange request if the door was already open; it must mean that the door is closed, since it needs someone to open it. Therefore, al-Fattāḥ tells us that He opens what is closed: whatever seems impossible, situations in which we need relief, and anything whose workings we cannot even understand. A door has to be closed in order for someone to open it.

The types of opening

This name is extremely vast in meaning, touching upon different parts of our lives and the experiences we have. Allah opens the doors of mercy and blessings, showering them upon us. He says, '*No one can withhold the blessing God opens up for people.*' [35:2]

Indeed, He is the Opener – when He wants to give, no one can stop Him. We experience the clear manifestations of this when a person who is ill is given two months to live, but ends up living for another ten years. In this scenario, Allah opens the doors of health and blessings, despite what people, even experts, thought was impossible. Allah also opens up opportunities for people, or provision for them through permissible and ethical means, when everyone else had told them that they would fail if they did not engage in forbidden methods of earning.

Allah also opens by facilitating opportunities and opening doors which we did not even know existed. He can open up a path that is filled with obstacles, or shrouded in darkness. When you are embarking on a new journey, ask God to open doors for you so that you do not encounter unanticipated difficulties, or, if you do face challenges, ask Him to open them for you so that are able to work through them. You can call on al-Fattāḥ in relation to marriage, a new job, or even the start of Ramadan.

He can also open hearts. We might feel upset and give up on people when we feel that they have closed their hearts to us, to guidance or to advice. But we repeatedly see people whose closed hearts open up, by the grace of God. This applies to us all. Whenever we feel that our hearts are closed, and that we do not taste the sweetness of faith or worship, we should ask Allah to open up our hearts.

This name also has a meaning that is related to al-Naṣīr and al-Ghālib. God gives victory – He opens and grants relief – to those who strive for Him and for justice, when they see a dead end in front of them. The Prophet Noah called upon his Lord, saying '"*I am defeated (annī maghlūb): so help me (fantaṣir)!*"' [54:10] Allah responded: '*So We opened the gates of the sky with torrential water, burst the earth with gushing springs: the waters met for a preordained purpose.*' [54:11]

This opening was physical, but we can extrapolate from it lessons for our lives. Prophet Noah was facing what appeared to be a dead end – all he could see was closed doors. His people had persisted in their rejection of God for 950 years. Only a few people had believed in Him. Nonetheless, he persevered for centuries, in spite of them. He never lost faith in God. And in the moment when he finally felt defeated and broken, He asked God for victory – for an opening, for respite. And Allah opened up the skies with torrential rain. Similarly, our opening might not come after days, or months. The opening might come after years, when we finally reach our lowest point, but still maintain faith in the Almighty. It is in those moments that we must hold on to al-Fattāḥ and call upon Him.

Sometimes, an opening is simply the feeling of relief that comes with a kind word from someone, a tear that we shed, or even a verse from the Qur'an. We may recite a verse we have read a hundred times before, yet one day, we hear or read that same verse from a completely different perspective – that understanding becomes an opening or a solution.

Moreover, on the day of Judgement, Allah will judge between His servants who said, '*Our Lord, decide (iftaḥ) between us and our people in truth, and You are the best of those who give decision.'* [7:89] Everything will be laid bare on the Day of Judgment – our books of deeds will be open, and nothing will be hidden. Allah will open up the way for those who were oppressed in this world.

Finally, when God sends us a solution in this world, He may give us a response that exceeds our expectations. When Moses was in a new city after fleeing the only home he knew, and did even know what he needed or what an opening would like in his situation, he prayed to God, saying 'My Lord, indeed I am, for whatever good You would send down to me, in need.' [28:24] Allah gave him, for the righteous act of helping the two women, refuge with the family of Shu'ayb, marriage to one of his daughters, dignified work, and stability. Indeed, he then received revelation years later, which is a unique opening for those whom God has chosen to be of His prophets.

The Opener, the All-Knowing

In the Qur'an, God's name al-Fattāḥ is paired with His name al-'Alīm: *'Say, "Our Lord will gather us together, then He will judge justly between us; He alone is the All-Knowing (al-'Alīm) Judge (al-Fattāḥ)."'* [34:26]

When Allah opens, He does so with full knowledge of *everything* – what is and what is not, what was and what was not, what will be, and all possibilities, past, future, and present. When we ask God to open doors for us, we do so with the certainty that He knows realities that we do not know. When it appears to us that the doors are not opening, we must also know that He has knowledge and insight that we lack. Moreover, God acts with wisdom and mercy; thus, He will give you the opening that is best for you, even if it does not feel like an opening to you in that moment. Indeed, when the Prophet Joseph was picked up by a lost caravan and subsequently sold to a wealthy governor in Egypt, no one would have imagined that it was actually an opening! An opening, we might have thought, would have been that the caravan rescued him from the well and then returned him to his family – not sold him into slavery. But al-'Alīm knows what we do not, and He opened for Joseph a path to eventually becoming a governor himself. An opening might look like a closed door in that moment, but only later do we realize that it was an opening all along. Allah tells us that *'He has the keys (mafātiḥ) to the unseen: no one knows them but Him.'* [6:59]

Similarly, when the Prophet Muhammad ﷺ and his Companions wanted to go on *'umrah* (the lesser pilgrimage), they were prevented from doing so by Quraysh. Instead, the Prophet ﷺ signed a treaty at Ḥudaybiyyah, which appeared to be disadvantageous to the Muslims. This verse was then revealed: *'Truly We have opened up a path to clear triumph for you.'* [48:1] The Companion 'Umar was astounded; how could the treaty's terms be an opening? The Muslims were given less than they requested, *and* they were not allowed to go on *'umrah* that year! However, this treaty opened up a period of calm, which enabled people to listen to the message of the Prophet ﷺ without fear, and when the treaty's terms were violated, the Muslims were able to return to Makkah. Remember that openings can come through events that look like problems to begin with, but they require our perseverance and trust.

Our responsibilities towards al-Fattāḥ

Knowing that Allah is al-Fattāḥ means working hard to achieve the result that we want. God alone decides when to open those doors, and He may delay solutions to test our sincerity and trust, to build our character, or to raise our station – so we should never lose hope. Imagine if the Prophet ﷺ had given up after being attacked with stones at Ṭā'if? He had gone there to seek refuge and protection, and was denied in the cruelest way. Yet he persevered, planned his next steps, and sought refuge with other tribes until he was given shelter in Madinah. Similarly, the Prophet Joseph remained steadfast and never lost hope in God. He did not use his hardship as an excuse to turn away from God or to give in to whims. In these stories, we see Allah's amazing openings for His people.

Living with this name

1. Have great hope in God's openings

Remember that God can open all doors, even those that are seemingly locked. The Arabic word for key is *miftāḥ*, from the same root as al-Fattāḥ, and He holds the keys. He is the All-Knowing, the Opener, so He only opens the doors for you that are best for your life in this world and the Hereafter. Trust in that.

2. Work towards the opening if you can

God is al-Fattāḥ, but He has also created a world of physical means. We should work and strive with whatever means we have towards an opening, as all the prophets and righteous did, while in our hearts knowing that it is God who ultimately opens.

3. Faith and God-consciousness can lead to openings

Allah tells us in the Qur'an: *'And if only the people of the cities had believed and been mindful of Allah, We would have opened upon them (lafataḥnā) blessings from the heaven and the earth.'* [7:96]

When we become so consumed with an issue or a goal, some of us forget Allah. We forget Him and forget to be mindful of Him, de-prioritizing our duties towards Him, neglecting to thank Him for His blessings or seek His help. This can even cause us to be heedless, and take means that are religiously and ethically dubious. The closed doors that we face might be due to our lack of faith and God-consciousness, but one only needs to return to God for those doors to be opened by al-Fattāḥ.

4. Remember that openings vary

Openings look different depending on the situation. Sometimes they can be obvious and apparent, like when Hājar was gifted with the well of Zamzam. Sometimes they can look like new obstacles, such as when Joseph was rescued from the well but sold into slavery in a new land. Sometimes they can simply be a kind word that opens your heart and gives you hope. These are all openings.

5. Be a key to good

It is reported that the Prophet ﷺ said, *'Among the people are those who are keys to goodness and locks to evil. And from among the people are those who are keys to evil and locks to goodness. So glad tidings to the one who Allah puts the key to goodness in his hands, and destruction to the one who Allah puts the key to evil in his hands.'* [53] [Ibn Mājah] We should always try to be keys to goodness, in every sense of the word. Moreover, an important principle to remember is to always treat people as we would like to be treated by God. If we want God to open up the way for us, then we should open up the way for other people. We should not make things unnecessarily difficult for others.

---

[53] Al-Albani graded this hadith as fair, though there is some dispute among the scholars of hadith about its authenticity.

AL-WALIYY, AL-MAWLĀ – THE GUARDIAN ALLY (80-81)

47

AL-WALIYY, AL-MAWLĀ – THE GUARDIAN ALLY (80-81)

'It is He who sends relief through rain after they have lost hope, and spreads His mercy far and wide. He is the Protector, Worthy of All Praise.'

[42:28]

We have different types of relationships with people whom we love, and who love us. Some are fun to hang out with, but we cannot exactly rely on them. Others may truly want to be there for us in the best way possible, and they support us as best as they can, but they may not always give us the best advice. But there are those – or maybe just that one person – who love us and truly have our backs. They would bail us out no matter how much trouble we were in. They are actually protective of us.

God is al-Waliyy and al-Mawlā. Al-Waliyy is generally translated as the Ally or the Guardian, while al-Mawlā is translated as the Protector and the Patron, although the translations are sometimes interchangeable, as they both come from the same Arabic root, *wāw-lām-yā*. This root means 'to be very close, without any barrier'. For example, the person sitting right next to you (*yalīk*) – not separated by anyone else – is your *waliyy*. This root also means 'to plan and have authority over something'. Hence, it has all of the following meanings: to be an ally and a helper; to defend and to guard.

The difference between them is that al-Waliyy is the One who takes care of your affairs. A minor's guardian in Arabic is referred to as *waliyy amr* (guardian of affairs), because they take care of the affairs of that child; a guardian is usually someone who is trusted and close. Ibn al-Qayyim states that the basis of this relationship of *wilāyah* (guardianship and allyship) is love, because the opposite of *wilāyah* – to be an enemy to someone, and far from him or her – has its basis in hatred. Therefore, allyship and closeness has love as its basis. This is why al-Ghazālī stated that al-Waliyy is also the lover and protector.

Al-Mawlā, on the other hand, is the One towards whom a person inclines, relies upon, and with whom he or she seeks protection. A *mawlā* is also someone with authority. So, there is a difference in how we relate to these names: al-Waliyy takes care of our affairs, and al-Mawlā is the One upon whom we rely. This is also why some scholars have said that al-Waliyy has a relationship of *wilāyah* with both believers and disbelievers, since He takes care of the affairs of all, albeit in different ways, whereas al-Mawlā is only for the believers, since they turn to Him. Allah says in the Qur'an, *'That is because Allah is patron (mawlā) of those who believe, and because the disbelievers have no patron.'* [47:11]

However, on the Day of Judgment, we are told that *'they will all be returned to God, their true Lord (mawlāhum al-ḥaqq).'* [6:62]

Because these names indicate authority, as well as closeness and care, Allah is al-Waliyy and al-Mawlā for the believers in His care for them, while He is al-Mawlā over those who reject Him in His authority over them. Indeed, during the Battle of Uhud, one of the disbelievers boasted that they had all the might, while the believers had none. The Prophet ﷺ instructed the believers to say *'Allah is our patron (mawlānā) and you have no patron (lā mawlā lakum).'* [Bukhārī]

What does it mean for Allah to be your *waliyy* and *mawlā*?

It means that He is your guardian, He has your back, and He will take care of your affairs with His love and care. Anyone can claim to care about you, but even those who care about you can sometimes be flaky or unreliable. The companion Abū ʿAbdullāh ʿAmr ibn al-ʿĀṣ said that he heard the Messenger of God ﷺ saying that *'the family of so-and-so (i.e., Abū Ṭālib) are not my supporters (awliyā'). My supporter (waliyy) is God and the righteous believing people. But they (that family) have kinship with whom I will maintain the ties of kinship.'* [Bukhārī and Muslim]

God is the true *waliyy*, demonstrating His closeness to you and His protectiveness of you. This beautiful verse encapsulates how Allah manifests this attribute in our lives: *'God is the ally of those who believe: He brings them out of the depths of darknesses and into the light.'* [2:257]

Allah says that He is the ally of those who believe. Because He did not use the word *mu'minūn*, meaning 'the believers', but rather mentioned 'those who believed (*alladhīna āmanū*)', the verse includes people who have entered into Islam, but faith has not fully settled in their hearts yet. God is the ally of those people – not the perfect people, but those who struggle; those who are not quite there yet. And how is He their ally? He has the constant attribute of pulling them – pulling us, those who go up and down in our faith – out of the different darknesses, and bringing us into the light. Not just once, but over and over again. Just like He forgives you over and over, He has your back always.

This is the general meaning of God being al-Waliyy. There is the general meaning of this name, and then the specific one – the *wilāyah* of those who are close to Him. Look at what Allah al-Waliyy said to the Prophet ﷺ: *'Wait patiently [Prophet] for your Lord's judgment: you are under Our watchful eye.'* [52:48]

While we all enjoy this closeness and protection from God, those who take their relationship with Him seriously, and do what they can to cultivate this relationship and be true slaves of the Most Merciful, receive special protection and friendship. God says in the Qur'an: *'Wrongdoers only have each other to protect them; the righteous have God Himself as their protector (waliyy).'* [45:19]

The way to this closeness and protection is alluded to in the hadith *qudsī*, in which God tells us that:

> *'Whosoever acts with enmity towards a closer servant of Mine (Waliyy), I will indeed declare war against him. Nothing endears My servant to Me than doing of what I have made obligatory upon him to do. And My servant continues to draw nearer to Me with the supererogatory (nawāfil) so that I shall love him. When I love him, I shall be his hearing with which he shall hear, his sight with which he shall see, his hands with which he shall hold, and his feet with which he shall walk. And if he asks (something) of Me, I shall surely give it to him, and if he takes refuge in Me, I shall certainly grant him it.'* [Bukhārī]

By focusing on *what* God loves – the obligatory acts – we begin on this journey of closeness to Him. And it is not just by doing the right actions, but understanding the true meaning behind them: seeking to connect to Him with our prayer; restraining the lower self when we fast; being humble when we give charity; and remembering that we are brothers and sisters when we perform Hajj (the greater pilgrimage). Then, by moving beyond these to add voluntary deeds, *we* become beloved *to* Him, and become recipients of His special friendship and protection. Al-Ghazālī states that the one who is a *waliyy* of Allah befriends His friends, and shows enmity towards His enemies. And who did he tell us are the enemies? 'One's own [lower] self and Satan.' The fruit of this *wilāyah* is that *'unquestionably, [for] the allies of Allah there will be no fear concerning them, nor will they grieve.'* [10:62]

We have countless examples from the life of the Prophet ﷺ. The people of Quraysh in Makkah were planning to assassinate the Prophet ﷺ. On that night, he escaped Madinah with his closest friend, Abū Bakr, but they were followed by the would-be assassins. So the Prophet ﷺ and Abū Bakr hid in the Cave of Thawr, but they were followed there too. They were inches away from being discovered by their persecutors, but with calmness, the Prophet ﷺ said to Abū Bakr: *"'Do not be sad, God is with us.'"* [9:40] And they were not discovered, so were able to make it to the security of the city of Madinah.

In understanding this concept of *wilāyah*, we need to go beyond the superficial. It is not just external protection that God gives us; He also gifts to us the internal strength and tranquility that enables us to withstand external hardships. There will always be external struggles in this world, especially when we are striving to do good.

The life of the Prophet ﷺ was not easy, nor was it easy for the Companions or those who strived, and continue to strive today, for justice and goodness for His sake. But the *awliyā'* (recipients of His special closeness and protection) are given tranquility to continue, and vision to see beyond the superficial nature of things.

So, do not worry. Allah is your Protective Ally. He has your back. Strive for Him and be ambitious in your goals, and do not let fear prevent you from doing good. As the Qur'an tells us: *"'My protector (waliyyiya) is God: He has revealed the Scripture, and it is He who protects the righteous.'"* [7:196]

Living with this name

1. He is your ally even as you struggle

God is the protecting ally of all of those who believe, and of all of those who struggle in faith. Remind yourself that He is there for you always, even as you struggle and try for His sake. He will bring you out of the darkness and into His light.

2. Work to become one of His special people

Those who are special to God – who love and strive for Him – are those whom He is with always, and whom He protects. We should prioritize Him and the deeds that He loves. We can start by investing in understanding the pillars of our faith, especially prayer, as they are the foundation by which we build a relationship with God. We should aim to increase in beneficial knowledge – i.e. sound knowledge of the religion – so that we can truly live in a God-conscious manner. We should take the time to recite and understand His book, as well as learn from the example of the beloved Prophet Muhammad ﷺ.

3. Keep company with the righteous

Allah has His special people on this earth – His *awliyā'* – and keeping their company is one way that we can ensure that we are in an environment that constantly drives us to righteousness, and reminds us of God. The Prophet ﷺ said, '*A man is upon the religion of his best friend, so let one of you look at whom he befriends.*' [Tirmidhī] However, it should be remembered that one should be wary of those who claim to be *awliyā'* of God, because no one knows their station with Allah. We judge based on action, and if someone who is claimed to be a *waliyy* engages in prohibited practices, we should know that these are not the actions of the true *awliyā'*. Unfortunately, some claiming to be *awliyā'* have used their position and the vulnerability of those they have standing with to spiritually abuse them, asserting that practices that are known to be prohibited are acceptable for them to engage in because they have achieved the station of those close to God. Remember that the sign of the true *waliyy* is his or her adherence to the rules set by God, and not transgression of them.

AL-'AFUWW – THE PARDONER (82)

48

AL-'AFUWW – THE PARDONER (82)

'God may well pardon these, for He is most pardoning and most forgiving.'

[4:99]

It is difficult to move forward from a past of which we are not proud. It may be that our past was public, and people still see us in the same way. It could be that no one knows how we used to live or what we did, but we find it hard to forgive ourselves and move on. We carry guilt, or resentment, or fear over our past deeds. Even when we wrong someone, and ask for their forgiveness, we feel bad that we wronged them to begin with. Even if they say they forgave us, it may permanently alter our relationship.

While this may be the case with people, and it is rare to find someone who can truly forget our negative past, it is not so with God. He has given us a way of starting anew. He is al-'Afuww – the Pardoner.

The meaning

'Afw comes from the same Arabic root as al-'Afuww, *'ayn-fā-wāw*. One of the meanings of *'afw* is the complete removal of something – removing even its traces. For example, land with no traces or is untouched is called *'arḍ 'afw*.

Sometimes it is not easy to distinguish between those of God's names that appear to have a similar meaning. If God is the Pardoner, is that not the same as His being the Forgiving?

There is a subtle and important difference between *maghfirah* and *'afw*. When we ask for forgiveness or *maghfirah*, we are asking God to cover up our sin for us, and to protect us from the effects of our sin. Even though we committed that sin, we ask God not to punish us for it. When we ask for *'afw*, we are asking Allah to completely erase the sin, such that its traces are also removed. This means that our slate is literally wiped clean – there will be no questioning for those sins on the Day of Judgment.

The Prophet ﷺ teaches us about this difference in two narrations. In the first hadith, the Prophet ﷺ tells us about a person who is questioned by God on the Day of Judgment. Allah tells His servant, "'*O my servant, do you remember when you did such and such a sin?*'" and the servant will lower his head in shame, nodding, thinking that surely, he will be punished. Then God tells him, "'*I concealed these sins from people in world (dunyā), and I will not shame you here. I have forgiven you (ghafartu lak).*'" [Aḥmad]

That is *maghfirah*.

In the second hadith, the Prophet ﷺ is told that 70,000 of his nation will enter Paradise without reckoning [Bukhārī]; this is the meaning of *'afw*. And then the Prophet ﷺ asks for more, so with every thousand people of those pardoned, God will pardon 70,000 more. And Allah is Al-'Afuww – He named Himself this to let us know that He is indeed the One who completely erases our sins. He knows everything that we do, yet He chooses to wipe our slate clean.

Indeed, when God tells us about *'afw* in the Qur'an, it is usually in reference to a major wrongdoing – as if to tell us that no sin is too great. It can all be wiped away. When the Children of Israel worshipped the calf, Allah tells us: '*We appointed forty nights for Moses [on Mount Sinai] and then, while he was away, you took to worshipping the calf – a terrible wrong. Even then We pardoned [ʿafawnā] you, so that you might be thankful.'* [2:51-52]

Allah pardoned and wiped away the greatest sin – the sin of *shirk* (associating partners with God). So if we come to God sincerely, if we come to the One who *loves* to pardon, then He will erase that sin we are so worried about, and those many sins for us.

Al-ʿAfuww in the last ten days of Ramadan

Ramadan is a special month for Muslims around the world, when the global community of Muslims fasts from the first light of dawn to sunset. The last ten nights are particularly important, and contain *Laylat al-Qadr* (the Night of Power, or Decree). ʿĀʾishah, the wife of the Prophet Muhammad ﷺ, realized the magnitude of these nights, and asked him: 'O Messenger of Allah ﷺ, if I know what night is the night of *qadr*, what should I say during it?' He said: 'Say: "O Allah, You are the One who pardons, and You love to pardon, so pardon me (*Allāhumma innaka ʿafuwwun, tuḥibbu al-ʿafwa faʿfu ʿannī*)."' [Bukhārī]

Out of all of the supplications which the Prophet could have advised, he taught us to ask for *ʿafw*. *ʿAfw* is sometimes translated as 'forgiveness,' but so is *maghfirah* (e.g. when we say *astaghfirullāh*, from the same root as *maghfirah*, meaning 'I seek forgiveness from God'). Unfortunately, there is something that is lost in translation, because *ʿafw* is more expansive than *maghfirah* – it is, as we explained, a complete erasure of the mistake.

Sufyān al-Thawrī said, 'During this night [*Laylat al-Qadr*] the most beloved thing to me to ask for is what the Prophet ﷺ told us to ask for.'

Indeed, it signals a reset: with Allah and with ourselves. We can start from the beginning. We do not need to be consumed by the mistakes of the past, creating a barrier of shame or guilt between ourselves and Allah. We do not need to define ourselves by what we used to do, even if others choose to define us in that way. We can be washed clean, with no traces of our wrongdoings, and start fresh, on a new page.

Living with this name

1. Do not let your past prevent you from moving forward

When God tells us that He is al-'Afuww, He is truly telling us that nothing or no-one is like Him. People may remember what you once did, or who you once were, and therefore continue to doubt you because of a less-than-perfect past. But God tells us that whatever our past may have been – even if it was truly horrible – He can erase its traces. So do not doubt yourself, and do not think that you are beyond help. Any small step forward that you take is appreciated by God, and He can completely transform you, if you are sincere in your efforts. Indeed, some of the most righteous, like Mālik ibn Dīnar, lived publicly depraved lives, and ended up being of the great scholars. Their transformation signals their conviction in Allah's name al-'Afuww – they knew that they could transcend their past.

2. Ask God during the last ten nights of Ramadan to pardon you

This name has a special relationship with the last ten nights of Ramadan, as God pardons more people during these nights than at any other time of the year. The last ten nights are a culmination of the effort that we put in during the first two-thirds of Ramadan, and God pardons those who continue to strive and be sincere.

AL-WAKĪL – THE TRUSTEE (83)

49

AL-WAKĪL – THE TRUSTEE (83)

'Sufficient for us is God, and [He is] the best Disposer of affairs.'

[3:173]

Trust is important for any relationship. It is defined as 'firm belief in the reliability, truth, or ability of someone or something.'[54] When used generically, we may say that we trust our parents, perhaps a best friend or a spouse, because we know that we can rely on them. That trust gives us confidence, conviction and peace.

Yet if we look at trust in its comprehensive meaning, we do not fully trust them. We might trust them to be there for us, or trust them not to judge us harshly when we make a mistake. But would we trust our best friend to be our lawyer in court if, for example, she is a banker and is not particularly eloquent? Thus, even with those closest to us, the trust we have in them is specific. For trust to be truly comprehensive, it must have three main elements:

1. The person is an expert in what he or she does: you might not trust your banker best friend to be your lawyer, but you would trust the Ivy League-educated lawyer who is known never to have lost a case.

2. The person is a moral person: even if the person is an amazing lawyer, if you were not sure about his or her moral character, you would still not be completely at ease. You might be afraid that they will cheat you out

[54] Oxford English Dictionary

of your money, for example, or take advantage of your vulnerability. But if this person is also an amazingly upright human being, you would be happier to give them power of attorney.

3. The person cares about you specifically: now imagine if the person with the above qualities also happened to be your close relative, who always treated you as their own child, or your best friend, who grew up with you and is practically your sister or brother. Would that not increase your trust, confidence and certainty in this person? You absolutely know that the person who possesses all of these qualities will get you through it all.

While God is far above any analogy, the example of selecting and trusting a lawyer breaks down the concept of trust for us. We may compare the trust we have in people to the trust we place in God al-Wakīl – the Trustee – but when we define trust in its comprehensive sense, trust in God is not like trust in people. When God tells us to trust Him, it is because He possesses all of the attributes required to truly place our full trust in Him, knowing that we will not be let down. Al-Ghazālī explains that al-Wakīl is the only One to whom all matters are entrusted, because our trust in people is necessarily deficient, since they cannot perfectly fulfil that trust. So our friends or family may have *some* of our trust, for particular matters, but they cannot be called 'trustees', because they do not have all the necessary qualities. Only God is capable of having all matters entrusted to Him.

Trusting someone in a complete sense, in all circumstances, can be hard, and this is why Allah puts us at ease. He says: *'Yes, indeed, everything in the heavens and the earth belongs to God, and He is enough for those who trust in Him.'* [4:132]

God tells us that everything in this world is His. He reminds us of that fact to comfort us. He also says: *'Put your trust in the Living*

[God] who never dies, and celebrate His praise. He knows the sins of His servants well enough.' [25:58]

Further, He tells us: *'[He is] the Lord of the East and the West; there is no deity except Him, so take Him as Disposer of [your] affairs.'* [73:9]

In these verses, God reminds us of His Power. To Him belongs everything, and moreover, He does not die. Even the human being you trust the most could pass away. Allah does not – so when you trust in Him, do not worry: *'Put your trust in God: God is enough to trust.'* [33:3]

The impact of this name

In practical terms, this name teaches us two things. First, that we should work as hard as we can with the means given to us. This might seem like a recurring theme in this book: this is because He teaches us, through His names and attributes, that we need to strive to the best of our ability. Being intimately acquainted with God means having conviction, confidence and internal tranquility as we strive, because we have already surrendered to Him.

The second lesson is that, as we work for a particular result through the avenues available to us, we should have absolutely no doubt that God will get us through to whatever outcome is best, because indeed He is the Trustee. The Prophet ﷺ said: *'If you were to rely on Allah as He should be relied on, He would provide for you as He provides for the birds. They go out in the morning hungry and return in the evening full.'* [Tirmidhī]

The bird does her part. She flies out in the morning in search for food, though she has no reason to believe that she will find any food. She wakes up without any food at all, but still she leaves her nest. God provides. Most of us stop ourselves doing the right thing because we are afraid that we will not be able to follow through, or that it will be too difficult. But Allah tells us to strive and have trust. The result is from Him.

Hājar, the wife of the Prophet Abraham, was truly an epitome of what it means to have trust, as we mentioned several times in this book. When Abraham left her and their infant son in the desert, she was baffled. But then she asked him, 'did God command you to do this?' and Abraham responded in the affirmative; so she accepted the decree [Bukhārī]. She knew that God would not leave her or her son – she was a person who knew Allah. This did not stop her from striving; on the contrary, it inspired her to strive. When baby Ishmael started crying, she ran back and forth between the mounts of Ṣafā and Marwah seven times, without being bitter or resentful. She continued to search, because she knew that God had a plan for them. And God rewarded that trust with the well of Zamzam, from which we still drink today. Allah does not want us to forget that lesson, which is why when Muslims go on Hajj (the greater pilgrimage) or *'umrah* (the lesser pilgrimage), we follow in the steps of Hājar, going seven times between the mounts of Ṣafā and Marwah. It is called *al-sa'ī* – 'the striving'.

A question that may be on our minds is: 'what if we work, but after having strived, we find ourselves worse off – does that mean that God has not fulfilled His trust?' To answer this question, we can go back to the example of the lawyer. If the lawyer who possesses expertise, morals, and love for you, tells you to enter into a plea bargain instead of fighting to be exonerated, would you not trust his or her advice? It might seem like a temporary failure, and it is not what you want, but in actual fact, it is actually the best way to ensure you remain free. Of course, a lawyer might just be unable to help you, and so the plea bargain is the best that he or she can do. But you still trust that this lawyer knows what he or she is doing.

For God, the concept of impossibility does not exist, and our trust in Him should be infinitely greater than in the example of the lawyer, because whatever happens is out of His wisdom, and has nothing to do with ability.

Look at the example of the Prophet Joseph. He was unjustly treated by his brothers, the people who found him in the well and sold him, and the family he lived with – eventually going to jail for years. 'Where was God?' some may ask. He was there all along: Allah brought two cellmates to Joseph. It was through the advocacy of the prisoner who was released that Joseph was then able to interpret the dream of the king, be declared innocent, and reunite with his family. While from the outside, his journey might have seemed like a punishment, the hardships he faced were simply stops along the road. Having *tawakkul* (trust in God) is the difference between despairing in those moments of hardship, and pushing through with a hopeful soul.

Moreover, sometimes we make mistakes in our striving, and we have to face the consequences of our mistakes and learn from them. Miscalculating in our striving does not mean that God will leave us. When some of the Muslims disobeyed the Prophet in the Battle of Uhud, and as a result suffered severe losses, it was not the end for them. It was a setback, but they learned. So, do not let your own mistakes make you lose hope – but do not ignore the fact that you made mistakes either. Learn from them, move on, and have trust.

Living with this name

1. Remember God al-Wakīl, even in difficult circumstances

Remembrance of God should be constant, whether we are in situations of ease or hardship. The Prophet Abraham was sixteen years old when his people planned to throw him in the fire. Abraham was calm, and simply said, '"*God is sufficient for me, and He is the Best Trustee.*"' [Bukhārī] He was always with Allah. So, Allah said '"*O fire, be coolness and safety upon Abraham.*"' [21:69]

2. When your means decrease, your hope should not

Sometimes our hope is dependent on our means. If we see that we have few means, then we do not strive; we lose hope. But *tawakkul* means that the conviction in our hearts does not falter, even when our means do. When God took Khadijah and his uncle Abū Ṭālib from the Prophet ﷺ, he did not give up on his journey. He went to Ṭā'if to seek shelter. Even after he was kicked out, he sought help from other tribes during the Hajj season. The means had to change, and there was a period of waiting before he got the result, but in his heart, the Prophet ﷺ still had complete trust in God. Ten years after having to leave Makkah, he returned to it victorious and merciful.

3. Do not use sin as your means

Your income *has* to be from permissible means. If you pursue your livelihood through religiously forbidden means, it negates part of your trust in God, because it means that you do not believe that He can provide for you through permissible means alone. The only exception is in circumstances of dire need (a technical term that has its own conditions in Islamic jurisprudence; this needs to be discussed with a trained scholar).

4. Lessen your worry about the future

All of us worry a little, and that is natural. But some of us are paralyzed by that fear, constantly in a state of worry about our futures, whether it is fear for our livelihoods or our children, and so on. This is not healthy for us, and may even cause us to do things that are unethical because of that worry. This state of agitation simply creates another problem – and why have two problems instead of one? God reminds that *'Unquestionably, by the remembrance of Allah hearts are assured.'* [13:28]

5. Strive with your limbs, submit with you heart

The Prophet ﷺ planned and worked hard. He put 'Alī in his bed as a decoy when he was going to migrate to Madinah. He waited until the evening so that they could leave discreetly. They covered their tracks. This is the external effort that is required of all of us when we undertake a task. At the same time, he knew that only God could save them. This is where the internal component of trust comes in. God tells us what happened when they were in the cave, hiding from the Quraysh, and Abū Bakr was worried that they would see him and the Prophet ﷺ:

> *'Even if you do not help the Prophet, God helped him when the disbelievers drove him out: when the two of them were in the cave, he [Muhammad] said to his companion, "Do not worry, God is with us," and God sent His calm down to him, aided him with forces invisible to you.'* [9:40]

6. Supplicate to al-Wakīl

The Prophet ﷺ trained us to have this trust in God, through various supplications that he used to make. He told us: *'Whoever says, when he leaves his house, "In the name of Allah, I have relied on Allah and there is no power nor strength except by Allah (bismillāh tawakkaltu 'alā Allāh wa lā ḥawla wa lā quwwata illā billāh)," will be told, "You have been guided, spared and protected," and Satan will be kept far from him.'* [Abū Dāwūd, at-Tirmidhī, an-Nasā'ī and others]

The Prophet ﷺ also said that whoever says the following seven times in the morning and evening, Allah will spare that person whatever worries him or her: *'Sufficient is Allah for me, there is no god but He, in Him I put my trust and He is the Lord of the formidable throne (ḥasbiya Allāh, lā ilāha illā huwa, 'alayhi tawakkaltu wa huwa rabb al-'arsh al-'aẓīm).'* [Abū Dāwūd]

AL-MUQADDIM AL-MU'AKHKHIR – HE WHO BRINGS FORWARD, HE WHO DELAYS (84-85)

50

AL-MUQADDIM AL-MU'AKHKHIR – HE WHO BRINGS FORWARD, HE WHO DELAYS (84-85)

'You are The One Who brings forward and who delays, there is no deity worthy of worship but You.'

[Muslim]

When we look at the world around us, or even at the people we know in our own lives, we see people who seem to be moving forward with their lives. It may have to do with their education, the opportunities that they have seized, their accumulation of wealth, their marriage, or having children. And we might look at our own situation and wonder why our own fortunes seem to be delayed.

Perhaps we are working hard but are not able to earn much, or fast enough. Maybe we want to get married but it just does not seem to be happening for us. Perhaps we want to have children, but we are facing issues. It seems that everyone else is moving forward, but we are being left behind.

At other times, some opportunities might come to us when we feel we are not ready for them, and we wish that they could be delayed.

It is in these moments that we need to get acquainted with Allah al-Muqaddim al-Mu'akhkhir; He who brings forward and He who delays. This name appears in the following supplication of the Prophet ﷺ: *'O Allah! Forgive my past and future sins and whatever I have done in secret, and whatever I have done in public, and what You are more knowledgeable of than I. You are The One Who brings forward and Who delays, there is no deity worthy of worship but You.'* [Muslim]

Another beautiful supplication attributed to the Prophet ﷺ conveys a similar meaning:

> *'O Allah, make me content with Your decree, so that I may not love to hasten what You have delayed, or delay what You have hastened.'* [Ṭabarānī]

Sheikh Muhammad al-Najdi made a beautiful point about the Prophet Joseph in relation to 'delays'. When Joseph was in jail, he was considered the best person there, even by those who shared his cell. They said to him, '"*Indeed, we see you to be of those who do good.*"' [12:36] Yet, even though he was better than them by their own admission, he remained in jail for longer than them; his release was 'delayed'. His first cellmate was released and went on to become a servant; the second was executed. When Joseph was finally released many years later, he became a minister and was reunited with his family.

So if you ever feel that your dreams are delayed, and everyone else seems to be moving forward, just remember the example of Joseph. Stay true to Allah and to yourself, and remember that *'Allah does not allow to be lost the reward of the doers of good.'* [9:120] Indeed, He is al-Muqaddim, al-Mu'akhkhir; the One who brings forward and the One who delays. And when things seem to be coming and you cannot keep up, remember that God brings events forward or expedites them for a reason: we can handle it.

The Promoter, the Delayer

There is another meaning to these names. Al-Ghazālī says about these names that God promotes – elevates – those servants of His whom He brings close to Him, and He banishes those whom he pushes away. This means that those who strive to come close to God, He brings them forward – He promotes them – before and above anyone else, while those who disobey and reject, He pushes them back.

Sheikh Rātib al-Nabulsī teaches us that Allah might give people gifts, such as wealth or intelligence, such that it appears that they are promoted or preferred. But this is not necessarily so; the true measure of a person is their hearts and deeds. Indeed, most of us have been given some gifts of this world, but these gifts should not delude us into thinking that we have been preferred because of them. Rather, we should look to our hearts and actions.

Living with these names

1. Trust in God's timing and do the best you can, wherever you are

We do not know what is in the unseen world, and thus we do not know what will be delayed and what will be hastened. The key is to trust in God's timing, and make the best of – indeed, appreciate and find the beauty in – wherever you have been placed right now. However, knowing these names of God should not cause us to be lazy; sometimes delays may simply occur because we are not working hard enough, so we have to strike a balance between action and trust in Allah.

2. Remember that God has given all of us good, and He brings forward those who do good

If someone seems to be promoted because of her wealth, or another because of his intelligence, remember that God has given each of us gifts. We should be grateful for and appreciate His gifts, and we should remember, as al-Ghazālī says, that truly the one promoted is the one who is close to God. As the Prophet ﷺ said: '*Whoever is slowed by his deeds will not be hastened forward by his lineage.*' [Muslim]

3. Bring forward or expedite the good

Sheikh Abdelrazzaq al-Badr said that one of the fruits of knowing these attributes of God – His bringing forward and delaying – is that we should strive to 'bring forward' or hasten our good deeds, and that we should delay and forego sins.

AL-ḤAFĪẒ, AL-MĀNIʿ, AL-QAWIYY, AL-MATĪN – THE PRESERVER, THE PREVENTER OF HARM, THE ALL-POWERFUL, THE FIRM (86-89)

51

AL-ḤAFĪẒ, AL-MĀNI', AL-QAWIYY, AL-MATĪN – THE PRESERVER, THE PREVENTER OF HARM, THE ALL-POWERFUL, THE FIRM (86-89)

'God is the Provider, the Lord of Power, the Firm.'

[51:58]

Watching the news, we are bombarded with images of violence and danger. Many of us may feel unsafe and weak in the face of the potential hazards of this world.

In moments of danger and crisis – whether in a conflict zone, or pandemonium in an otherwise 'safe' place – there is little we can do. In those moments, we turn to God because we recognize our own impotence. We turn to Him because innately we know that He possesses the attributes that can help us. We may not be able to protect and preserve, but He can. We may not be able to prevent harm, but He can. We may not have any power, but all power belongs to Him. We may find it hard to stand firm, but He strengthens us.

When you are in the depth of helplessness, when you feel overpowered, when you feel unsafe, call on the All-Preserver, the Preventer of Harm, the All-Powerful, the Firm.

Al-Ḥafīẓ, al-Mānī', al-Qawiyy, al-Matīn

Al-Ḥafīẓ is the Guard. The Arabic root of the word, *ḥā-fā-ẓā*, means 'to guard against loss', and it is also the opposite of forgetfulness. When the brothers of the Prophet Joseph asked their father to send their youngest brother with them, Prophet Jacob said: *'Am I to entrust him to you as I did his brother before? God is the best guardian and the Most Merciful of the merciful.'* [12:64]

He said that Allah is the best guardian (*khayrun ḥāfiẓa*), and both meanings mentioned above are present in this example. Despite knowing that his sons had something to do with the disappearance of his son Joseph, he knew who the ultimate protector was – al-ḤAFīẓ does not forget those who do good. And God guarded both Joseph and his younger brother and returned them to their father. Joseph had undergone extreme hardship, and some might have thought that he was 'forgotten' by God. But Allah was with him all along, guiding him by preserving his morals and character from corruption, and protecting him from any serious bodily harm, until finally he was made a minister and reunited with his family. Such is His preservation, even in the most difficult circumstances.

The Prophet ﷺ said, *'Be mindful (iḥfaẓ) of Allah and He will protect you (yaḥfaẓuk). Be mindful of Allah and you will find Him before you. If you ask, ask from Allah. If you seek help, seek help from Allah.'* [Tirmidhī].

The English translation perhaps does not do justice to the Arabic, as the Prophet ﷺ advises us to do *ḥifẓ* of God – this means that the more mindful we are of our duties towards God, and understanding His presence in our lives, the greater His divine protection over us will be. Allah describes the believers as those who *'observe (ḥāfiẓūn) God's limits. Give glad news to such believers.'* [9:112]

Al-Mānī' is the Preventer or the Defender. The Arabic root of al-Mānī', *mīm-nūn-'ayn*, means 'to prevent, restrain or deny'. The broad meaning is that God prevents or restrains out of His wisdom. He is also the One who prevents harmful actions from reaching you. When a lifeguard rescues a drowning child, it is God who prevented the drowning. Allah prevented Surāqah ibn Mālik, a man who wanted to capture or kill the Prophet ﷺ for the reward, from reaching him.

Al-Qawiyy indicates 'perfect power', according to Imam al-Ghazālī, and includes both physical and moral power. It is the opposite of weakness. This name is mentioned numerous times in the Qur'an, as we are told: *'Indeed, Allah is Powerful (Qawiyy) and Exalted in Might.'* [57:25]

Indeed, we frequently say, 'there is no power or might but with Allah (*lā ḥawla wa lā quwwata illā billāh*)', to remind ourselves that only God possesses true power. Anyone who appears to be strong or mighty can in fact have their strength and might obliterated by Allah the Powerful. It also reminds us to seek strength from Him in all our endeavors. Indeed, the Prophet ﷺ said to one of the Companions, *'Say: "there is no power or might but with Allah." Verily, it is a treasure among the treasures of Paradise.'* [Bukhārī and Muslim]

The first battle which confronted the Muslims was the battle of Badr. They were few in number (313, according to the narration) and faced the more powerful army of Quraysh of about 950 strong men. God tells us: *'God helped you at Badr when you were very weak. Be mindful of God, so that you may be grateful.'* [3:123]

This is the other meaning of al-Qawiyy: you may not be powerful yourself, but you are made powerful because your protector is the Most Powerful. Relying on the Most Powerful also means doing our due diligence. The Prophet ﷺ did not go to battle unprepared. He did as much as he could with what was given to him, was frequently innovative, and always asked the opinions of his Companions.

Finally, al-Matīn means 'being firm in strength, completely unshakeable and irresistible'. When al-Matīn decrees something, nothing can hold it back or prevent it – unless He so decides. We all have worries and fears, and we might even consider giving up on our values and principles for worldly gain. But whenever you feel your resolve wavering, hold on to Him. When you feel weak, seek strength from the One who is the Most Strong. When you feel that you cannot be steadfast, hold on to the One who is Firm.

Ponder over the protection in your life

Remember a time, if you can, when you escaped a major accident with minor bruises. When you broke your bones, but God al-Jabbār healed you. When you said goodbye to your child as they went away for college, worried, but he or she was safe. When you feared getting sick, but you were spared illness.

We do not often remember that most of our life is spent under the protection of God; accidents and harm are usually an anomaly. In the twenty-four hours that we have in a day, we are under protection for most or all of them. Because we take this for granted, we are often unaware that God's protection is an active act, and is constant. The Prophet ﷺ reminded us: '*Whoever wakes up safely in his home and is healthy in his body and has provisions for his day, would have acquired all the worldly possessions he is in need of.*' [Tirmidhī]

Tests and weakness

Sometimes we may be harmed and experience pain. That is the nature of this world – in order that we do not forget to strive for our Hereafter; in order that we turn to God and recognize our need for Him; in order to teach us; and in order for us to exhibit patience and other praiseworthy attributes that bring us closer to God. When we do go through difficulties, the Prophet ﷺ told us: '*No fatigue, nor disease, nor sorrow, nor sadness, nor hurt, nor distress befalls a Muslim, even if it were the prick he receives from a thorn, but that Allah expiates some of his sins for that.*' [Bukhārī]

Even when we are harmed, there is wisdom, as well as compensation for the harm – nothing that happens to us is overlooked by God.

In situations of war, it may seem that Allah's protection is absent. But this is why the rules of our religion command us to protect the weak and establish justice. In essence, the true application of Islam brings about the very visible manifestation of all of God's names and attributes. When we build a shelter for women who are escaping abuse, we embody this characteristic of protection, which is commanded from us. When we follow the example of Muhammad Ali, who was not only a world-famous boxer but also an outspoken critic of the Vietnam War, we actively try to protect the lives of innocent. When we work to stop violence in our communities, we are the shining light that our faith commands us to be. After all, why else were the Quraysh so angry when the Prophet ﷺ commanded that the weak be protected and justice be served? They benefitted from the unjust system they had set up, and the Prophet ﷺ came to obliterate it.

We may suffer hardship, as these roles are not easy, but there is no strength like the inner strength that comes with conviction of purpose and faith in God.

Some other meanings

Another meaning of al-Ḥafīẓ is that God has guarded and preserved the Qur'an. Allah says: '*We have sent down the Qur'an Ourself, and We Ourself will guard it.*' [15:9]

It is a great honor and gift to be able to memorize the Qur'an. The Prophet ﷺ tells us: '*It will be said to the companion of the Qur'an after he has entered Paradise, "Recite, and rise!" For every verse he recites he will rise one level (in Paradise), until he recites the last verse with him [i.e. in his memory].*' [Abū Dāwūd]

One becomes a *ḥāfiẓ* – in essence, a preserver or a guardian of the Qur'an – by memorizing and preserving it within his or her memory.

Meanwhile, Al-Māni' not only prevents physical harm from coming to you, but spiritual harm as well. So, ask Him to protect your soul and your faith.

As for al-Qawiyy, God pairs this name with al-'Azīz in the Qur'an. God says: *'so that God could mark out those who would help Him and His messengers though they cannot see Him. Truly God is powerful (qawiyy), almighty ('azīz).'* [57:25]

God tells us that He will mark out who helps Him and His Messengers, and the significance of these two names following afterwards is that they remind us that He is the One who is Powerful and Almighty. He is invincible and dignified; He does not *need* our help. Rather, we are tested to see whether we will help, and if we do, this ultimately benefits us. Moreover, we are encouraged to build strength. The Prophet Muhammad ﷺ said:

> *'The strong believer is more beloved to Allah than the weak believer, but there is goodness in both of them. Be eager for what benefits you, seek help from Allah, and do not be frustrated. If something befalls you, then do not say: "If only I had done something else." Rather say: "Allah has decreed what he wills." Verily, the phrase "if only" opens the way for the work of Satan.'* [Muslim]

While we are encouraged to build physical strength, this hadith shows us that internal strength and fortitude are important too. Indeed, in praising the strong believer, the Prophet ﷺ tells us to seek help from God and not be frustrated when things do not go our way. This requires internal strength.

Finally, Allah pairs al-Qawiyy (the Powerful) with al-Matīn (the Firm) in this verse: *'Indeed, it is Allah who is the [continual] Provider (al-Razzāq), the firm possessor of strength (dhūl quwwat al-matīn).'* [51:58]

Al-Ghazālī says that His *quwwah* (strength or power) indicates perfect power, while firmness (*matānah*) indicates firmness of strength. God does not waiver in His strength. Moreover, God says: *'And I will give them time. Indeed, My plan is firm (matīn).'* [7:183]

When the world gets too hard to bear, and all we see and hear are stories of injustice and pain, remember this verse: *'My plan is firm.'* [7:183] No one will escape His justice. While He gives everyone time, and He gives everyone an opportunity to turn back, if people persist with injustice, they will not escape the plan of God and will ultimately be brought to justice. No one, no matter how untouchable they might seem in this world, will escape the plan of Allah.

Pharaoh was a tyrant for many years. In all that time, there may have been people who wondered how Pharaoh could be allowed to do such acts, such as murdering infants. There may have been people who passed away before they saw Pharaoh and his armies destroyed. God gave them time, but finally justice caught up with them.

Even if it appears that someone has escaped justice in this life, remember that this is why there is an afterlife. So never forget that Allah's plan is firm, and no one can escape it.

Living with these names

1. Seek strength from the Strong

It is natural for us to be or to feel weak. In these circumstances, we should seek both internal and external strength from God Himself, and ask Him to help us.

2. Be a preventer of harm

God tells us to enjoin good and forbid evil; in this way, we also help to prevent harm. We can do so in different ways, like the everyday act of driving safely or removing harmful things from the street, or greater acts such as supporting processes or organizations that help to keep people safe and out of harm's way.

3. Observe the limits of God

Allah commands us to preserve or be mindful of His limits, and specifically mentions that we should protect our prayers, our words and promises, and our chastity.

4. Memorize and understand the Qur'an

The best type of guardianship you can embody is to make your heart a preserver of the Qur'an. Even memorizing a small amount benefits you.

5. Stand firm

It can be hard to stick to your principles. But remember that those principles are the foundation of faith, and we are commanded to stand for justice. Allah tells us that He is al-Matīn to remind us that, when we feel weak, we can hold on to Him to stay firm and steadfast. The Prophet ﷺ knew when to compromise (when there was a greater good at stake that did not violate fundamental principles), and when to stand firm (when justice would be violated). He refused to give in to wealth or power, at the expense of leaving God's message, yet he compromised with Quraysh at Ḥudaybiyyah when they wanted to forbid the Muslims from entering Makkah to perform *'umrah* (the lesser pilgrimage). He knew that to enter by force might cause bloodshed, and the proposed treaty was supposed to ensure at least ten years of peace. So he agreed to their conditions. It may have seemed disadvantageous at the time, but in fact it enabled the Muslims to enter Makkah the following year because the Quraysh violated the terms of the treaty, without any blood spilt. That is wisdom.

6. Strength should not result in or be based on injustice, and do not forget gentleness

The Messenger of God ﷺ said, *'Verily, this religion is matīn, so enter its depth with gentleness.'* [Aḥmad] While it is important to stand firm, remember to be gentle. Standing firm is not synonymous with being stubborn or harsh or unjust. The Prophet ﷺ said, *'No nation is blessed unless its weakest members can demand their rights without hesitation.'* [Ibn Mājah]

AL-AWWAL, AL-ĀKHIR, AL-ẒĀHIR, AL-BĀṬIN – THE FIRST, THE LAST, THE MANIFEST, THE HIDDEN (90-93)

52

AL-AWWAL, AL-ĀKHIR, AL-ẒĀHIR, AL-BĀṬIN – THE FIRST, THE LAST, THE MANIFEST, THE HIDDEN (90-93)

'He is the First and the Last; the Outer and the Inner; He has knowledge of all things.'

[57:3]

Imagine that you do not know who God is, or what His attributes are. Sūrat al-Ḥadīd starts by telling us that, *'Everything in the heavens and earth glorifies God –– He is the Almighty, the Wise. Control of the heavens and earth belongs to Him; He gives life and death; He has power over all things.'* [57:1-2]

Reciting this puts us in awe of the power of God, but it may also make us feel that Allah is far away. He is so Grand and Great, does He even understand us? Do we have a relationship with Him? Does He understand what goes on in our hearts and our world?

Then, in the following verse, God addresses these very thoughts: we are told that He is the First and the Last, the Ascendant and the Intimate. Seemingly divergent qualities come together in a beautiful way, as though God is telling you that there is nothing, big or small, that escapes His knowledge. He is the First and the Last, and thus He encompasses time, and He is the Ascendant and the Intimate, encompassing all forms of space.

These are the pillars of knowledge and knowing. These names cover everything. He is First before everything, and the Last after everything; the Manifest who is above everything, and the Intimate who is close. They combine His attributes of greatness and closeness, cutting across time and space. In a *du'a'* (supplication), the Prophet ﷺ said: *'He is the First, nothing is before Him, the Last, nothing is after Him, the Ascendant, nothing is above Him, and the Intimate, nothing is nearer than Him.'* [Muslim]

The First, the Last

The Prophet ﷺ said: *'Any matter of importance which is not begun with 'bismillāh' (in the name of Allah) remains defective.'* [Ibn Ḥibbān]

What is the first thing you think of when you wake up in the morning?

That you need coffee?

The tasks you have to do that day?

Social media? Your emails?

Allah?

It is said that if you want to know what your priorities are, reflect on the first thing you think of in the morning. Whatever is foremost in your mind not only sets the tone for your day, it also determines your destination. A person who wakes up thinking about money will then seek out and prioritize those things that lead him or her to money. A person who wakes up thinking of a loved one will probably talk to him or her first thing in the morning, and remain connected all day if they can.

God tells us that He is the First and the Last. Al-Ghazālī explains these two names beautifully, saying: 'When you ponder the order of existence and consider the ordered chain of beings, God the most high is first with respect to it... Whenever you ponder the order of wayfaring and observe the states attained by those journeying towards Him, He is the last, for He is the final point to which the levels of the 'knowers' ascend.... the first beginning was from Him; and to Him is the return and destination.'[55]

God is, quite literally, the First. He was before anything was, but we cannot conceptualize this, because He is not limited by time. He is also the Last because He is our destination and He remains when everything else goes away. There are deeper meanings here too. We prioritize things before God, and then we wonder why we feel a spiritual void. We may wonder why bad things happen, why we cannot seem to get something right, or why nothing satisfies us despite our pursuit of material means. To know that God is al-Awwal (the First) is to see Him before seeing anything else, because even the physical means start with Him.

This is why, for example, we do not simply drive to a destination; we start with the supplication for travel. Living the reality of this name is to seek God first even before we seek the means, because the means can only work with His blessing. This is one of the reasons for the prayer of *istikhārah* (seeking good): we ask Allah for the best choice when embarking upon a course of action. As Ibn al-Qayyim says, worshipping Allah by this name is to realize our complete need for Him, because we realize that He came before everything and He created the means to be able to do anything.

And this leads us to His being al-Ākhir (the Last), because as Ibn 'Aṭā'illāh said: 'He who is illumined at the beginning is illumined at the end.' God is the destination. We start with Him in everything that we do, so that we can end up with Him. We praise Him at the end of every matter and seek forgiveness from Him for any shortcomings. Ibn al-Qayyim says that worshipping Allah by His name al-Ākhir is to be unattached to results, and rather to be attached to God, who remains always, no matter the results. If our intention starts with Him, then no matter the outcome, our efforts

[55] Al-Ghazālī, *The Ninety-Nine Beautiful Names of God: Al-Maqṣad Al-Asnā Fi Sharḥ Asmā' Allāh Al-Ḥusnā*, 133–34.

are recorded by Him and are appreciated because they were for Him. In the Qur'an, Allah asks, *'So where are you going?'* [81:26]

So we need to ask ourselves – where are we going?

Everything leads to Him

As believers, it may be easy to conceptualize that Allah is the beginning of everything and the end. However, if we consider the example at the beginning of the article, about the first thing we think of when we wake up, living this name requires more than just *knowing*.

For us to begin thinking of God like this, every morning when we wake, there has to be something in our hearts – there has to be love. Many of us may know someone who has been in love: she talks to her beloved in the morning, and last thing at night. Simply connecting to his beloved sets the tone for his whole day. Do we have that kind of relationship with God, and if we do not, how can we start one?

The secret is living the knowledge that Allah is al-Awwal and al-Ākhir. It is making a conscious effort to remember Him at the beginning and at the end of everything. The fruits of this will be immediate. Allah tells us in the Qur'an: *'Unquestionably, by the remembrance of Allah hearts are assured.'* [13:28] He also tells us: *'So remember Me; I will remember you.'* [2:152]

The Prophet ﷺ tells us: *'Remember Allah during times of ease and He will remember you during times of difficulty.'* [Tirmidhī]

Just like a person who is in love finds comfort in the mention of his or her beloved, imagine the effect on your heart of remembering the absolute Source of love and peace before you do anything. Putting into practice the knowledge of God's attributes as the First and the Last brings us back to our ultimate purpose, until the meanings of these names are truly etched into our hearts, and we are confronted with reality. We then become the person in love, and for us, Allah is the First in our hearts and the Last in our journey. Allah reminds us that: *'Everyone on earth perishes; all that remains is the Face of your Lord, full of majesty, bestowing honor. Which, then, of your Lord's blessings do you both deny?'* [55:26-28]

The Manifest, the Intimate

Allah is manifest in His existence, yet hidden from our sights. He is al-Ẓāhir in His transcendence, obvious to anyone who reflects, and He is above all; He al-Bāṭin in His subtlety. Ibn 'Ajībah states that these names mean 'the One whose Lordship is clear with demonstrations and proofs, but who is inaccessible through modality, imaginings, and surmise."[56]

Part of the meaning of al-Ẓāhir is that He aids and supports His righteous servants. Allah says in the Qur'an, *'So We supported those who believed against their enemy, and they became dominant (ẓāhirīn).'* [61:14]

Al-Bāṭin is not only hidden from our sights, but He knows of every hidden thing in this world, what goes on in our hearts and what goes through our minds. Al-Ẓāhir al-Bāṭin knows what is manifest and what is hidden.

We fluctuate between two extremes: one that focuses solely on the external, in which we forget the spirit of the law, and the other, which is manifested in the trend of proclaiming that 'only Allah knows what is in my heart' and forfeiting external forms of obligations or worship. But God sees our external and our internal. They are both important, and both part of our submission to Him. When we worship God through His Names al-Ẓāhir al-Bāṭin, we become more conscious of both these elements. Allah tells us in the Qur'an, *'And do not approach immoralities - what is apparent (mā ẓahara) of them and what is concealed (mā baṭan).'* [6:151] He also says,

[56] Ahmad Ibn Ajiba, *Allah: An Explanation of the Divine Names and Attributes.* Translated by Abdulaziz Suraqah, (USA: Al-Madina Institute, 2014), 164.

'Avoid committing sin, whether openly or in secret (ẓāhir al-ithmi wa bāṭinah), for those who commit sin will be repaid for what they do.' [6:120]

We should focus both on inward and outward goodness. In one incident, the Prophet Muhammad ﷺ pointed to a man three nights in a row saying that he was of the people of Paradise. The Companion 'Abdullāh ibn 'Amr was adamant to find out what was so special about this man, so he stayed over at the other Companion's house for a few nights. When we think of a pious person, we usually think only of extra prayers, fasts and charity, which are commendable. This is what 'Abdullāh thought too, yet he did not see the man do any additional acts, so he decided finally to ask him. The man himself said that all the outward worship he did was what 'Abdullāh had seen, but added that he never allowed himself to carry any grudge in his heart against anyone, and would empty it of envy and resentment every night. 'Abdullāh ibn 'Amr said, *'This is what you have achieved and it is something we have not accomplished.'* [Aḥmad]

Of course, this does not mean that external actions are not important. The man may not have done any *additional* devotional acts of worship, but he most certainly was consistent in his obligatory actions. Indeed, God praises those who do, over those who do not do. The Prophet ﷺ would pray long devotional prayers in the night. Indeed, he reminded us that prayer is the foundation of every other deed. Moreover, we are told that actions are judged according to their intention, but an intention coupled with a wrongful action does not suffice. Sincerity is doing one's utmost to fulfil that intention.

Ibn al-Qayyim stated that when we worship Allah by His Name al-Ẓāhir (the Ascendant), we know where to direct our prayers, because there is no one above God. Worshipping Allah while knowing that He is al-Bāṭin (the Intimate) is something that you have to taste, because it is something that words cannot describe. That is why Ibn 'Abbās advised someone to recite the verse cited [57:3] when he faced doubts in the religion [Abū Dawūd], because it reminded him that Allah is the Intimate. He knows what is in your heart, so let go of the anxiety that you feel.

Living with these names

1. Start with Him, end with Him

Remember Allah at the beginning of everything, and praise Him and seek forgiveness at the end. This will ensure that you are always in remembrance of Him and that, for you, He is the First and the Last in all your endeavors. Moreover, ensure that you work towards deeds that will remain with you, because only Allah will remain after everything perishes.

2. Memorize the supplications for the start of a matter and its end, then incorporate them into your everyday routine

This is related to the first point, but it entails memorizing those remembrances and supplications from the Qur'an and the tradition of the Prophet ﷺ, which should be recited at specific points – for example: the start and end of your day; starting a journey; the beginning and end of a meal; and the conclusion of prayers. Many of these supplications can be found in the book *ḤIṣn al-Muslim* (Fortress of a Muslim).

3. Memorize this supplication that contain Allah's Names 'the First' and 'the Last'

'O Allah! Lord of the seven heavens and Lord of the Magnificent Throne. Our Lord and the Lord of everything; Splitter of the grain and the date-stone; Revealer of the Torah and the Gospel and the Furqān (the Qur'an), I seek refuge in You from the evil of everything that You shall seize by the forelock. O Allah, You are the First and nothing has come before You, and You are the Last, and nothing may come after You. You are the Most High, nothing is above You and You are the Most Near and nothing is

nearer than You. Remove our debts from us and enrich us against poverty.' [Muslim]

4. See how God manifests His attributes in everything

Sheikh Abdelrazzaq al-Badr said that, in order to connect to Allah's Name al-Ẓāhir, you have to *see* Allah's attributes as they reflect in this world. Al-Ẓāhir also means something that is manifest, so take the time to go out to nature to see how God is the Creator, while contemplating His beauty and the beauty of what He created. Remind yourself of the times when Allah responded to you, because He is al-Mujīb. Reflect on the times that something was denied to you, and then you actually saw the wisdom later on. Only once you realize that God is with you – He is the First and the Last, the Ascendant and the Intimate – can you actually gain closeness to Him, and see how He manifests His attributes in your life.

5. Direct everything to Him

Ibn al-Qayyim stated that knowing that God is above everything means knowing where to direct yourself – your prayers, your hopes, your goals and your fears. There is nothing above Him, so why turn to what is below Him?

6. Crave intimacy with Allah

Ibn al-Qayyim said that this attribute of Allah— al-Bāṭin —cannot be described, only felt. It is interesting that, when you start to see Allah's attributes as they manifest in the everyday and the mundane, as well as in the extraordinary, your heart naturally moves closer to Him. You realize how close He is, and the fruit of this realization is that you work to purify your heart, as well as praying more, because you know that those are your moments with Allah. That is why the Prophet ﷺ would pray in the night even though it was not obligatory: he loved doing so, because he loved being with God.

7. Let your inward match your outward

One of the scholars said, 'Verily, when the inward state of the servant matches his public behavior, Allah says: This is my true servant.' [al-Zuhd li Hannād Ibn al-Sarī]

AL-WĀRITH – THE INHERITOR (94)

53

AL-WĀRITH – THE INHERITOR (94)

'It is We who give life and death; it is We who inherit [everything].'

[15:23]

What are we leaving behind? This is a question that should cross our minds at some point in our lives. Most of us want to leave a good inheritance for our children in order to make sure that they are taken care of after we pass. A more comprehensive way of thinking about 'inheritance' is to ask: what is the good that we are leaving behind, and what will benefit us and others after we pass?

God tells us that He is the Inheritor, who remains after all is gone. Allah is the one to whom possessions return after the temporary owner passes, as He is the One who remains, so everything returns to Him. There will not be a single claim to ownership alongside Him.

Everything is God's – we are temporary possessors

God says in the Qur'an: *'The Day when they will come out and nothing about them will be concealed from God. "Who has control today?" "God, the One, the Prevailing."'* [40:16]

This verse reminds us that ultimately the true Possessor is Allah, and everything we have returns to Him. Sheikh Rātib al-Nabulsī states that knowing that God is the Inheritor changes our relationship with what we perceive to be 'ours'; it ceases to be a relationship based on ownership but rather one of responsibility and trusteeship. In this way, we are not entitled to our possessions, doing with them whatever we please, but rather we see them as items entrusted to us temporarily. One story tells of a Bedouin who was leading a camel, and was asked who owned the animal. He replied, 'It is God's, in my hands.' Anything that we have is Allah's, simply in our hands for the time being.

Imagine treating all your transactions as transactions with God. How would that impact the way you conduct yourself? What about seeing your own body as a gift from Him – would you take care of it better? Would you be as possessive with the cash in your pocket? Would it be so hard for you to give something away?

Indeed, God warns against our attachment to our possessions. He says,

> *'No indeed! You [people] do not honor orphans, you do not urge one another to feed the poor, you consume inheritance greedily, and you love wealth with a passion. No indeed! When the earth is pounded to dust, pounded and pounded, when your Lord comes with the angels, rank upon rank, when Hell is that Day brought near –– on that Day man will take heed, but what good will that be to him then?'* [89:17-23]

We will not take any of our possessions with us, and none of it will benefit us – only that which we gave for the benefit of others.

What do you want to leave?

Sheikh Abdelrazzaq al-Badr says that every believer should know that our good deeds are the best things we can leave behind, because they are the true inheritance that actually remains. The Prophet ﷺ gave us some examples of those things that remain:

> *'The good deeds that will reach a believer after his death are: knowledge which he learned and then spread; a righteous child whom he leaves behind; a copy of the Qur'an that he leaves as a legacy; a mosque that he built; a house that he built for*

> *wayfarers; a canal that he dug; or charity that he gave during his lifetime when he was in good health. These deeds will reach him after his death.'* [Ibn Mājah]

The Prophet ﷺ also said, *'Whoever gives charity and that is the last of his deeds will enter Paradise.'* [Aḥmad]

The righteous caliph 'Umar ibn 'Abd al-'Azīz said in his last sermon:

> 'O people, you were not created in vain, nor will you be left to yourselves. Rather, you will return to a place in which Allah will descend in order to judge among you and distinguish between you. Destitute and lost are those who forsake the all-encompassing mercy of Allah, and they will be excluded from Paradise, the borders of which are as wide as the heavens and the earth.
>
> Don't you know that protection tomorrow will be limited to those who feared Allah [today], and to those who sold something short-lived for something permanent, something small for something great, and fear for protection? Don't you realize that you are the descendants of those who have perished, that those who remain will take their place after you, and that this will continue until you are all returned to the Best of Inheritors?'

If you focus on planting the seeds of good wherever you are, you can be of the people Allah speaks about: *'That is Paradise, which We give as inheritance to those of Our servants who were fearing of Allah.'* [19:63]

When you are righteous

God says: *'And verily we have written in the Scripture, after the Reminder: My righteous slaves will inherit the earth.'* [21:105]

There are implications for this life in this name as well. God reminds us that, ultimately, those who inherit the earth are not the powerful. He shows us the opposite: while they may have temporary power, they eventually fall, as many seemingly great but unjust empires did in the past. He reminds us to stick to the lofty characteristics of this religion, because injustice never wins. In the Qur'an, Allah tells us about a conversation between Moses and his people: '*Moses said to his people, "Turn to God for help and be steadfast: the earth belongs to God – He gives it as their own to whichever of His servants He chooses – and the happy future belongs to those who are mindful of Him."*' [7:128]

The counsel of Moses is important. He is speaking to the Children of Israel at a difficult time, in which they are being oppressed. He reminds them to seek help through patience and prayer, and that this Earth ultimately belongs to God. The oppressors will not last, so never take your values from them.

That is why the Prophet ﷺ also reminds us, '*Do not be imma'ah (imitators)... One who says, "I am with the people. If they do good, I do good also; and if they do evil, I also do evil." Rather, train yourselves to do good when others do good, but if they do evil, to refrain from their evil.*' [Tirmidhī]

Living with this name

1. Think of what you are leaving behind

What impact have you left? Will the earth testify for you or against you? In Sūrat Yāsīn, God tells us, '*We record what they send ahead of them as well as what they leave behind.*' [36:12] All of us have the opportunity to leave good behind us, and we should take this into account before it is too late. Moreover, we should guard against leaving evil or destruction behind, because that will testify against us.

2. Remember that God will cause the righteous to inherit the good

Even if it seems like injustice has reigned over the earth, this is only temporary. In the end, God will cause those who are righteous to inherit all that is good, as well as the ultimate good: Paradise. Indeed, the Prophet Abraham made this supplication: '"*And place me among the inheritors of the Garden of Pleasure.*"' [26:85]

3. Be an inheritor of the Prophets through seeking knowledge

The Messenger of Allah ﷺ said, '*The scholars are the successors of the prophets. Verily, the prophets do not pass on gold and silver coins, but rather they only impart knowledge.*' [Bazzār]

4. Your children are inheritors of your values

Our heirs inherit our material wealth, but they also inherit our values. The Prophet Zachariah called upon Allah's name al-Wārith, when he said, '"*My Lord, do not leave me alone [with no heir], while you are the best of inheritors.*"' [21:89] He also said, ' "*And indeed, I fear the successors after me, and my wife has been barren, so give me from Yourself an heir Who will inherit me and inherit from the family of Jacob. And make him, my Lord, pleasing [to You].*"' [19:5-6]

The inheritance the Prophet Zachariah was alluding to here was the inheritance of prophethood and knowledge. Indeed, we are also told about two prophets who were father and son, '*And Solomon inherited David.*' [27:16]

If we want Allah to bless us with children, we should ask Allah by His name al-Wārith, and pray for them to inherit what is good from us.

AL-MUBĪN – THE EVIDENT (95)

54

AL-MUBĪN – THE EVIDENT (95)

'They will realize that God is the Truth, the Evident.'

[24:2]

There are some things that are crystal clear and evident to us. According to some scholars, one of Allah's Names is the Evident - al-Mubīn. Others have looked at the verse above and interpreted it as God being the evident Truth (i.e. the word for 'evident' is an adjective describing His being the Truth, not a separate name in itself).

God uses this word, from the Arabic root *bā-yā-nūn*, in its verb form many times in the Qur'an. He says: *'In this way God makes His revelations clear (yubayyin) to you, so that you may grow in understanding.'* [2:242]

Allah then tells us the purpose of making things clear in this verse and in many others: so that we might use reason, reflect, be guided, and be grateful.

The Evident

Sheikh Rātib al-Nabulsī says that Allah's Name al-Mubīn tells us two things: the first is that He is evident in His essence, similar to His Name al-Ẓāhir. God makes Himself evident by revealing His names to us so we may know Him. Whatever misconceptions one may have about God, they are dissipated as He shows us and makes clear to us who He is – this has been the purpose of this book. Whoever may have thought that God had anthropomorphic qualities only has to understand that Allah is al-Quddūs (the Pure, the Holy); whoever thinks that tyrants have escaped justice only needs to understand that Allah is al-'Adl (the Just) and al-Muqsiṭ (the Equitable); and whoever believes that God is far from us, He contradicts that notion by letting us know that He is Near.

Evident in His actions

The second meaning of this name is that He makes things evident. Sheikh Abdelrazzaq al-Badr explains that the root *bā-yā-nūn* means to make something separate. From it comes the word *mubīn*, which means to make clear. And thus al-Mubīn is the One who makes everything clear, and *bayyinah* is the clear and evident proof.

We are constantly told to reflect on God's signs. In the Qur'an, what we translate as a 'verse' is actually the word for 'sign' – *āyah*. Thus, Allah's signs are His words (i.e. the Qur'an), as well as what He has created: from the universe, to the sun and the stars, to trees and the mountains, to our very own selves – and all of these require our reflection. Once we ponder over these things, the natural conclusion is to see Allah's attributes in everything, and to internalize that God is indeed the Evident Truth.

He clarifies

God makes the way clear to us through His rules. He establishes the rules for justice, the imperative for compassion, how to pray, and our general conduct on this Earth. We have been given all this guidance, and more importantly, the way to Him. He makes the path to Paradise clear, as well as the way to avoid Hellfire. He warns us against the very real enmity of Satan, whom He describes as *'a clear enemy ('aduwwun mubīn).'* [numerous, e.g. 2:168, 2:208, 6:142, 7:22, 12:5]

He has clarified all of this through the Qur'an and the example of the Prophet ﷺ. We are told in the Qur'an, *'There has come to you from Allah a light and a clear Book.'* [5:15]

Whenever we feel confused, we should turn to the Qur'an and the example of the Prophet ﷺ.

He will show you

The verse cited in the beginning of this chapter tells us that God will make everything clear for those who doubt on the Day of Judgment. But there is also another lesson here. Many times, we may not see the wisdom in a certain event. We might wonder why we did not get what we specifically asked for, or that goal for which we worked hard. The wisdom is actually not evident – at least, not in our limited view.

Knowing that God is al-Mubīn actually enables us to *ask Him* to show us this wisdom. There are times when we feel like we do not understand, and in those moments, it is important to put our trust in Allah and ask Him to show us His wisdom. He can make it clear, and perhaps we will end up being more grateful that our lives took that unexpected route. Sometimes it takes time, but be certain: Allah will make the wisdom evident, either in this life or the next.

'Ā'ishah, the wife of the Prophet ﷺ, was slandered and gossiped about by her own community. She must have wondered why this was happening to her, what the wisdom in it was, and when people would see the truth. When she was declared innocent, the Qur'an made sure to teach people the lessons from this incident. After admonishing the believers [24:11-20], God says: *'God makes His messages clear (yubayyin) to you: God is all knowing, all wise.'* [24:28]

Sometimes the wisdom is that we need to take responsibility for our actions. Oftentimes, we behave as though our actions have absolutely no relevance, but God teaches us that they do. The Prophet Joseph had opportunities that were within his control, and circumstances which were not. When his brothers threw him in the well, and when he was sold as a slave, there was nothing he could do. These were outside of his control. But when he was in prison, he interpreted the dreams of his cellmates, and then told the prisoner he knew would be freed to advocate for him with the king. He could have waited in prison and prayed to see God's wisdom in it, but he did not rely solely on that course of action. He knew that he had to act too. And God made clear that both these elements – what happened to him and what he made happen – added up to the final outcome. And this is the reality for all of us.

Living with this name

1. Reflect

God exhorts us in the Qur'an to reflect on His signs. Ponder over His signs in the universe, and over His names and their manifestations in the world around us, so that you can see how He is Evident in His creation.

2. Ask God

Remember that you can – and should – ask al-Mubīn to show you what you cannot see or understand. Allah says *'Call upon Me; I will respond to you.'* So ask Him to make matters clear for you. And remember that when you wonder 'why did this happen to me?', He might show you that your actions have consequences, and that what happened was as a result of what you yourself did. The wisdom in those situations are the lessons we learn.

It will be made clear

Have certainty that the One who makes it all clear will clarify every single thing on the Day of Judgment, leaving no one in doubt. God says: *'On the Day of the Resurrection He will make clear to you those things you differed about.'* [16:92]

AL-SHĀFĪ – THE HEALER (96)

55

AL-SHĀFĪ – THE HEALER (96)

'He heals the hearts of a believing people.'

[9:14]

All of us become ill. We may be inflicted yearly with the flu, get a fever or an infection from time to time, or suffer from something more serious, or more frequently – may God protect us all and ease the suffering of those who are ill. At the time of writing, the world had come to a halt due to the COVID-19 pandemic, with the virus infecting millions, and hundreds of thousands of people passing away as a result. While restrictions eased up to protect the economy, most people still took precautions to avoid becoming ill. We were suddenly and collectively confronted by how weak we are as human beings, in the face of a virus that cannot even be witnessed by the naked eye. When people feel helpless – particularly when they are ill and there appears to be no cure, or they are facing a disease like COVID-19, about which very little is known – they plead to God for healing. Indeed, as the Prophet Abraham said: *'And when I am ill, it is He who cures me (yashfīn).'* [26:80]

'Āʾishah narrated that when someone would get ill, the Prophet ﷺ would put his right hand over the place of ailment and say: *'O God, the Lord of the people – Remove the trouble, for You are the Healer (al-Shāfī). No healing is of any avail but Yours; healing that will leave behind no ailment.'* [Bukhārī]

This supplication teaches that it is God who is the Healer: He is al-Shāfī.

Sheikh Abdelrazzaq al-Bader said that the meaning of Allah al-Shāfī is that He is the healer of the physical diseases of the body, and of the spiritual diseases of the heart and the soul – such as rancor, envy, doubt, and hatred. God says in the Qur'an: *'And [God will] heal the hearts of a believing people.'* [9:14]

The healing of the body

The Prophet ﷺ taught us that, *'Every disease has a cure. So, if the treatment is applied to the disease, the disease is cured by the Will of Allah.'* [Muslim]

Al-Shāfī is the Healer, as He has created the means by which disease is defeated or cured. When we take medicine that heals us, we have to remember that it is Allah who created the different elements of that medicine that acts as a remedy. Indeed, as Muslims, we are required to search for cures for our illnesses because we have certainty that there is a cure. The Prophet ﷺ told us: *'Allah did not send down any disease but that he also sent down the cure.'* [Bukhārī]

He also specifically instructed people to seek treatment. A Bedouin asked, 'O Messenger of Allah, shall we not seek treatment?' The Prophet said, *'Yes, O servants of Allah, seek treatment.'* [Tirmidhī]

The Prophet ﷺ led by example. He set up a makeshift hospital in the form of a tent in Madinah and appointed a woman, named Rufaydah al-Aslamiyyah, to run it. 'Ā'ishah stated that the companion Sa'd ibn Mu'ādh was injured during the Battle of the Trench, and it was Rufaydah who tended to him. [Muslim] Moreover, the scholar Ibn Ḥajar al-'Asqalānī praised Rufaydah's skill and wisdom, as she realized that the arrow that had hit Sa'd was too deep to pull out, and so she worked on stopping the bleeding instead.

Al-Shāfī is the source of all cure and healing. God created this world and its laws. He decreed that when a chemical reaction occurs between oxygen and a fuel at a certain temperature, the result is fire. He also decreed that water puts out most fires. Similarly, the laws dictate that when certain things occur – injury, infection, an unhealthy lifestyle, or inheritance of particular genes – we become ill. And those same laws provide us with the means to prevent or cure disease.

Seeking these cures, or making use of preventative measures, and prayer are complementary, when we understand that al-Shāfī is the source of healing. He heals us through the laws that He created in the universe – which is why we are commanded to seek cures for our illnesses – and through our asking for His healing. Indeed, the Prophet Job prayed to Allah: '"*Suffering has truly afflicted me, but you are the Most Merciful of the merciful.*"' [21:83]

And God healed him.

We must remember as well that we can cause our own illnesses. Think of a person who is a heavy smoker and is then afflicted with diseases in his or her lungs and throat. Of course, God is al-Shāfī, and He can cure whom He wills, but we must also take responsibility for our actions. We cannot be resigned and say, 'well, God willed it', as an excuse to avoid accountability. Allah says in the Qur'an: *'Do not contribute to your destruction with your own hands.'* [2:195]

This verse is in specific reference to withholding charity, but commentators on the Qur'an such as Ṭabarī stated that the general meaning is also applicable to doing anything that may bring about your own destruction, including self-harm.

Illnesses, whether self-inflicted or not, also provide us with opportunities. We realize our need for God. There is nothing like illness to remind us of our weakness and how much we need Allah. It is important to be a worshipper of God in all circumstances, whether times are good or bad. Illnesses also purify us. The Prophet ﷺ told us that, *'No fatigue, nor disease, nor sorrow, nor sadness, nor hurt, nor distress befalls a Muslim, even if it were the prick he receives from a thorn, but that Allah expiates some of his sins for that.'* [Bukhārī]

In another narration, a Companion visited the Prophet ﷺ when he was ill. The Prophet ﷺ told him: *'No Muslim is afflicted with any harm but that Allah will remove his sins as the leaves of a tree fall down.'* [Bukhārī] Furthermore, being patient when harm befalls us raises our station with God. Allah says in the Qur'an: *'Indeed, the patient will be given their reward without account.'* [39:10]

When we strive to be patient and steadfast through illness – meaning that we continue to trust in God, pray to Him and persevere with treatment if possible – we have to know that God understands. He knows what we are going through. And nothing that we go through is wasted. The verse cited above tells us that those who are patient will be given their reward without having to go through the *mīzān* (weighing of deeds on the scale) on the Day of Judgment. Rest assured that your patience and perseverance has not gone unnoticed.

Realizing that al-Shāfī is the true Healer means knowing that the cure is from Him. We supplant medical treatment with prayers, and understand that nothing will come to pass unless God wills it. Death is a rite of passage for all of us, so we should not lose faith when treatment or our prayers 'don't work'. Allah has decreed an end for all of us. Indeed, when the Prophet ﷺ was severely ill during his last days, faint and in pain, no medicine nor prayers would avail him, because it was his time to return to his Lord.

The healing of the hearts

When the Prophet ﷺ told us that Allah did not send down any disease without also sending down the cure, Ibn al Qayyim commented that: 'This is generally true for diseases of the heart, the spirit, the body, and their cures.'

Indeed, God says in the Qur'an: *'The Day when there will not benefit [anyone] wealth or children, But only one who comes to Allah with a sound heart.'* [26:88-89]

While a person may be rewarded during their physical illness and forgiven for sins, there is no such reward for the diseases of the heart. The reward for the disease of the heart is in the effort put into its removal.

God tells us about a beautiful invocation in the Qur'an: *'Those who came after them say, "Lord, forgive us our sins and the sins of our brothers who believed before us, and leave no malice in our hearts towards those who believe. Lord, You are truly compassionate and merciful."'* [59:10]

Allah tells us about those who came after the *muhājirūn* (people who emigrated from Makkah) and the *anṣār* (the helpers, who were native to Madinah), and the beautiful supplication that they made. They asked God to not allow any resentment in their hearts towards others. Knowing that Allah is al-Shāfī means turning to Him first in our quest to purify our hearts.

Many scholars have enumerated the diseases of the heart. They can manifest themselves in many ways, such as arrogance, envy, following base desires, miserliness, ostentation, heedlessness and others. The cure is in a) seeking knowledge – because knowledge empowers us to identify these diseases; b) remembering and returning to God frequently – as that connects us to Him, reminding us of our love for and fear of Him; and finally, c) obeying Him and performing good deeds – as they give us a spiritual light and teach us discipline. Moreover, one of the scholars stated, 'The cure of the heart is in five things: reading the Quran with contemplation, emptying the stomach, standing for prayer at night, humbly supplicating at dawn, and sitting with the righteous.'

What is beautiful is that there is a relationship between the healing of the heart and the healing of the body. In relation to following desires and discipline, for example, an article in the

Journal of Personality found that exerting self-control can make you happier both in the long-term and in the present moment, because disciplined people are able to avoid situations of temptation. Indeed, the Prophet ﷺ taught us: *'There lies within the body a piece of flesh. If it is sound, the whole body is sound; and if it is corrupted, the whole body is corrupted. Verily this piece is the heart.'* [Bukhārī]

Indeed, hope in God can also build our resilience, which helps in the face of physical illness. Numerous studies show that people who are hopeful, content and positive tend to recover better from illness, and are better protected from the inflammatory issues caused by stress. And how could one not be hopeful and content when they know that their Lord is al-Shāfī, the Most Affectionate, the Most Merciful, the Most Wise?

Living with this name

1. *Seek cures for your illnesses*

Pay attention to both the diseases of the heart and the body, and seek the appropriate cure with Allah and through the means that He has created. Allah created cures for all diseases, and our responsibility is to seek them out if we are able.

2. *Pray to God for healing*

Turn to al-Shāfī and remind yourself that healing is with Him. Enforce your seeking of physical cures with prayers to the One who is the Source and Creator of those cures.

2. *The Qur'an is a healing.*

Allah says about the Qur'an: *'And We send down of the Qur'an that which is healing and mercy for the believers.'* [17:82]

The Qur'an is a physical healing and is an ultimate spiritual healing for our hearts. The scholar Qatādah said, 'Verily, this Quran tells you about your diseases and your cures. As for your diseases, they are your sins. As for your cures, it is seeking the forgiveness of Allah.' [Bayhaqi]

AL-BARR, AL-ṬAYYIB, AL-MUḤSIN – THE DOER OF GOOD, THE GOOD, THE BENEFICENT (97-99)

56

AL-BARR, AL-ṬAYYIB, AL-MUḤSIN – THE DOER OF GOOD, THE GOOD, THE BENEFICENT (97-99)

"'We used to pray to Him: He is the Good (al-Barr), the Merciful One.'"

[52:28]

There are many names of God that relate to His goodness, His mercy, and His kindness. One might wonder why this is so, and would not one name suffice? But Allah reveals all His names for a reason, and part of it is so that we understand His all-encompassing goodness and affirm it. Moreover, human language is limited, and there are truly no words that can adequately express the magnificence of God's attributes. So, Allah reveals His beautiful names, some of which might on the surface appear to be synonymous, but when we look deeper, we can appreciate the beauty in their nuances.

This chapter explores three beautiful names that relate to His goodness. God is al-Barr, al-Ṭayyib and al-Muḥsin.

Al-Barr

Linguistically, *barr* is the expansion of good and of benevolence; wilderness or vast desert is called *barriyah*, from the same Arabic root *bā-rā-rā*, because of its expansiveness. Allah al-Barr, according to Al-Ghazālī, is the Doer of Good, the One from whom every good deed and beneficence comes, and this name brings together all kinds of goodness at the very highest level. Ibn 'Ajībah states that He delivers goodness with benevolence and excellence, and Ibn al-Qayyim says that one of the signs of Allah's *birr* is that He covers your mistakes from people.

Al-Barr refers to every form of goodness, charity, generosity and kindness, and indeed everything in existence benefits inwardly and outwardly from Allah al-Barr. Allah says in the Qur'an, *'[People], do you not see how God has made what is in the heavens and on the earth useful to you, and has lavished His blessings on you both outwardly and inwardly?'* [31:20]

From the goodness of al-Barr is that He multiplies the reward for one good deed, while a sin is only counted as only one wrong act, and indeed He frequently forgives and overlooks the mistakes of the wrongdoer. Al-Barr does not 'cut off' sinners, and loves when sinners return, rewarding them and blessing them when they do. Al-Barr's goodness is not simply in spiritual matters, but also in worldly matters, as He expands areas of goodness for us, such as our health, wealth, children, and support.

The culmination of His goodness is in Paradise, where the people who enter it say, '"*We used to pray to Him: He is the Good (al-Barr), the Merciful One,*"' [52:28] because they see before their eyes and experience this expansiveness in good and mercy. This verse pairs His names al-Barr and al-Raḥīm and reinforces the all-encompassing nature of His goodness and mercy, and that His goodness comes from His mercy.

Al-Ṭayyib

The Prophet ﷺ also told us about God: *'O people, Allah is ṭayyib (pure or good) and He accepts only what is pure. Verily, Allah has commanded the believers as He commanded his messengers. Allah said: "O messengers, eat from good things and act righteously, for I know what you do."* [23:51] *And Allah said: "O you who believe, eat from good things We have provided for you." [2:172]'* [Muslim]

Linguistically, the root *ṭā-yā-bā* means 'purity', and it is the opposite of malevolence or wickedness. It is also used to describe someone who is good-hearted or kind, and perfume, because of its beautiful scent, is also called *ṭīb.*

Allah is al-Ṭayyib, who is not tainted with evil or corruption, and He is *ṭayyib* in all aspects; His essence, His names, His attributes and His actions are all pure and good. This is similar to His names al-Quddūs and al-Salām, in the sense that His names and attributes are free from any deficiency, but it also informs us that, because He is good and pure, He expects us to be good and pure. Because He is al-Ṭayyib, we can only draw nearer to Him by what is good. Allah says, *'Good words (al-kalim al-ṭayyib) rise up to Him and He lifts up the righteous deed.'* [35:10]

Moreover, what emanates from Him is necessarily *ṭayyib,* and He makes permissible what is pure and good, and prohibits what is impure and bad. This is something to reflect upon. For example, conventional medical advice previously stated that drinking some red wine was good for the heart. And indeed, the Qur'an is nuanced with regards to alcohol, stating that, *'There is great sin in both [alcohol and gambling], and some benefit for people: the sin is greater than the benefit.'* [2:219]

The Qur'an acknowledges that there is some benefit, but that the harm greatly outweighs the benefit; so, it is not just the consumption of alcohol that is prohibited, but also dealing in it and being in its presence. Contemporary medical advice now states that whatever small benefit there is in alcohol is greatly outweighed by the harms – for example, drinking causes shrinkage of the brain in areas of cognition and learning,[57] and alcohol also adversely affects gut health.[58] Even the benefit of red wine for the heart is due to

[57] Merz, Beverly, *This is your brain on alcohol*, 14 July 2016, Available at: https://www.health.harvard.edu/blog/this-is-your-brain-on-alcohol-2017071412000
[58] Mutlu, E., et al, Colonic microbiome is altered in alcoholism, *American Journal of Physiology*, Vol. 302 No. 9, 1 May 2012, available at: https://www.ncbi.nlm.nih.gov/pmc/articles/PMC3362077/

resveratrol and antioxidants which can be found in the skin of red grapes, blueberries, cranberries and peanuts. One can benefit from those without coming close to alcohol; it is not *ṭayyib.* Furthermore, many psychologists and therapists recommend staying away from alcohol due to its effect on mental health and human behavior; even episodes of violence can be caused or exacerbated by consumption of alcohol. This brief example should cause us to contemplate over what Allah has made permissible, recommended, or mandatory, and the goodness or benefit they contain, as well as those things that He has made impermissible.

Finally, because He is al-Ṭayyib: *'God has promised the believers, both men and women, Gardens graced with flowing streams where they will remain; good (ṭayyiba), peaceful homes in Gardens of lasting bliss; and – greatest of all – God's good pleasure. That is the supreme triumph.'* [9:72]

Al-Muḥsin

Additionally, the Prophet ﷺ said, *'Allah is muḥsin and He loves those who exhibit excellence.'* [Ṭabarānī] This means that God is the Giver of Good, who goes above and beyond. Indeed, *iḥsān* (excellence) – from the same Arabic root as *muḥsin, ḥā-sīn-nūn* – is a level higher than justice. If, for example, some youth vandalize your home, and you take your right from them, this would be justice (*'adl*). *Iḥsān* would be if you not only forgave them, but tried to help them too. Indeed, this is how al-Muḥsin deals with us daily.

He is the Giver of Good and Excellence in our lives. The Prophet Joseph, despite facing significant hardships, was also honored by Allah throughout his trial, finding moments of respite. At the end of his journey, when his family was returned to him and he was made a governor, Joseph said, '"*My Lord has made it [the dream] come true and has been gracious to me (aḥsana bī) – He released me from prison and He brought you here from the desert – after Satan sowed discord between me and my brothers.*"' [12:100]

Moreover, He is al-Muḥsin in every sense of the word. He tells us that He is the One *'who perfected (aḥsana) everything which He created and began the creation of man from clay.'* [32:7]

We can see the signs of His excellence in His creation. One only needs to step out into nature to be completely in awe of its beauty; that is from Allah's *iḥsān*, because He is al-Muḥsin. Its beauty is way above and beyond what is needed to be to fulfil its purpose.

He is good, His actions are good and He accepts only good

God is good in all aspects – in His essence, in His actions and in what He accepts from us. Allah tells us what He wants for and from us in the Qur'an: *'God wants ease for you, not hardship.'* [2:185]

He also says, *'He wishes to make His laws clear to you and guide you to the righteous ways of those who went before you. He wishes to turn towards you in mercy – He is all-knowing, all-wise – He wishes to turn towards you, but those who follow their lusts want you to go far astray. God wishes to lighten your burden; man was created weak.'* [4:26-28]

Allah also tells us what He does not want. He says: *'These are God's revelations: We recite them to you [Prophet] with the Truth. God does not will injustice for His creatures.'* [3:108]

Throughout this book, we have been introduced to God's love, His generosity, His mercy, and His wisdom. Allah leaves no room for doubt; He encompasses all forms of goodness at their very highest levels. This is why thinking well of God is considered an act of worship; you are affirming these attributes of goodness in your heart and in how you interpret events. Thinking well of Him means having hope that He will accept you when you return to Him after you mess up, that He will overlook your faults, that He will help you overcome challenges, and that He is teaching you through hardship. This is what all the prophets and the righteous knew about God, and this is why they persevered. The Prophet Jonah turned to God in the belly of a whale, Hājar accepted that there was good in being left in the desert with her son, and Prophet Moses could say with utter certainty while being chased by Pharaoh and his army, '"*No, my Lord is with me: He will guide me.*"' [26:62]

Moreover, He *expects us* to be good. That is why Allah addresses both our inner and outer state. He tells us to purify our hearts and purify our actions. He tells us to have faith in our hearts and live that faith in everything we do.

Sometimes the best way to understand God's attributes is to see how beautiful they are when expressed by human beings, and then remember that whatever good we exhibit is nothing compared to God's goodness. So as Muslims, we are encouraged to have *birr* (piety), *ṭīb* (purity or goodness) and *iḥsān* (excellence). God says in the Qur'an that it is He '*who created death and life to test you [people] and reveal which of you does best – He is the Mighty, the Forgiving.*' [67:2]

Birr

Allah tells us: '*You who believe, when you converse in secret, do not do so in a way that is sinful, hostile, and disobedient to the Messenger, but in a way that is good (al-birr) and mindful [of God]. Be mindful of God, to whom you will all be gathered.*' [58:9]

Birr has many meanings. One of the meanings is truthfulness, as that is part of goodness. The expression *barra fī yamīnih* means that the person was truthful in their oath. The Prophet ﷺ said, '*You must be truthful. Verily, truthfulness leads to righteousness (birr) and righteousness leads to Paradise.*' [Muslim]

Another meaning is that *birr* is a type of goodness accompanied by gentleness. Allah shows us that *birr* is not easily attained unless we give what we love. He says: '*None of you [believers] will attain true piety (al-birr) unless you give out of what you cherish: whatever you give, God knows about it very well.*' [3:92]

We sometimes assume that giving is just about giving money, but it is about giving from whatever we love. We might love our time, or our possessions, but are we willing to part with them for others? Indeed, Allah warns against making *birr* all about rituals, without faith in the heart or goodness towards others. He says to the Christians and the Jews, when the direction of prayer was changed from Jerusalem to Makkah:

> *'Goodness (al-birr) does not consist in turning your face towards East or West. The truly good are those who believe in God and the Last Day, in the angels, the Scripture, and the prophets; who give away some of their wealth, however much they cherish it, to their relatives, to orphans, the needy, travelers and beggars, and to liberate those in bondage; those who keep up the prayer and pay the prescribed alms; who keep pledges whenever they make them; who are steadfast in misfortune, adversity, and times of danger. These are the ones who are true, and it is they who are aware of God.'* [2:177]

Everything described in the verse above is part of the *birr* that we as Muslims, as worshippers of al-Barr, should embody. The Prophet ﷺ also said, *'Piety (al-birr) is what the hearts feel comfortable with, while sin is what disquiets the heart and makes it hesitate, even if people say it is alright.'* [Aḥmad] One whose heart is with al-Barr, and who seeks knowledge to gain closeness to God and soundness in action, will naturally be predisposed to be comfortable with good and uneasy with bad. But we need to build this consciousness through knowledge of God and His religion, as opposed to following our base desires.

We are also told to exhibit *birr* specifically towards our parents. The Prophet ﷺ was asked, 'which deeds are best?' He responded, *'Prayer on time.'* He was then asked, 'then what?' The Prophet ﷺ replied, *'Good treatment (birr) of your parents.'* He was asked again, 'then what?' And he said, *'That people are safe from your tongue.'* [Ṭabarānī]

In the Qur'an, God tells us to treat our parents with *iḥsān*. He says: *'And your Lord has decreed that you not worship except Him, and to parents, good treatment (iḥsānan). Whether one or both of them reach old age [while] with you, say not to them [so much as], "uff," and do not repel them but speak to them a noble word.'* [17:23]

Having *birr* and *iḥsān* is not simply a case of obedience versus disobedience. Both are much more nuanced than that. Having *birr* and *iḥsān* with our parents means being good to them, treating them kindly, and having some sort of companionship with them, as God tells us to *'accompany them in [this] world with appropriate kindness.'* [31:15] A person may be obedient yet unkind; this is not *birr*. The converse may also be true, where a person is kind and honors their parents, but may not obey them strictly in what they want for their worldly life. The latter is closer to *birr*.[59]

Birr is additionally mentioned in another context in the Qur'an. Allah says, '*And cooperate in righteousness (birr) and piety (taqwā), but do not cooperate in sin and aggression*' [5:2] This verse concerns cooperation between people of others faiths. This verse is clear that we must work with each other in matters that are good and will bring benefit to all; this can include, for example, the aiding of refugees, banning pornography, better recourse to justice, and so on. Indeed, the Prophet ﷺ was witness to the Pact of Fuḍūl before Islam, a pledge to protect the oppressed, and he said that it was '*more beloved to me than a herd of expensive red camels. If I were called to it now in the time of Islam, I would respond.*' In another narration, he said, '*Make such pacts to restore rights to their owners and that no oppressor has strength over the oppressed.*' [Bayhaqī] The Prophet ﷺ wanted to cooperate with others, no matter their creed, on what was righteous and just, and encouraged us to do the same. We must also guard against working with others on causes that are based on sin or aggression.

[59] Parrott, Justin, Obedience to Parents its Limits, 16 January 2020, available at: https://abuaminaelias.com/obedience-to-parents-limits/

Ṭīb

Allah tells us: *'You who believe, give charitably from the good things (ṭayyibāt) you have acquired and that We have produced for you from the earth.'* [2:267]

Before the Prophet ﷺ received revelation, the Quraysh rebuilt the Ka'bah. They were adamant to only use money from good or pure sources – for example, not from usury or gambling – so the Ka'bah was built in the cube shape we know today, and not a rectangular one, because they did not have enough money from pure sources to complete it.[60] The Ka'bah was so sacred to them that they knew they could only give for God what was good and pure.

Indeed, the Prophet ﷺ reminded us that God *'accepts only what is pure (ṭayyib).'* [Muslim] In the same hadith, the Prophet ﷺ mentioned a man who traveled far, becoming disheveled and dusty and *'he raises his hands to the sky, saying, "O Lord! O Lord!" while his food is unlawful, his drink is unlawful, his clothing is unlawful, and he is nourished by the unlawful, so how can he be answered?'* This is a reminder for us that our earning must be from good and pure sources; if not, our prayers may not be answered by Allah. Earning money from impermissible means suggests that we trust more in the means than we do in God, that we care more about material wealth than spiritual wealth, and that we do not really believe that Allah is the Provider – al-Razzāq. What is impermissible, as we mentioned, is necessarily not good, as Allah is al-'Alīm al-Khabīr – He knows both the outward and inward realities.

In the Qur'anic context, the word *ṭayyib* is frequently used in relation to words, or to food that we consume. As we mentioned above, God is good in His essence and in His actions, and He commands the same from us. With regards to food, when we think of halal (permissible) meat, we often define it only by how the

[60] Originally, it also encompassed an area called "Ḥijr Ismail", which today is a small area outside the Ka'ba.

animal is slaughtered – which is important. But the way in which the animal is treated in its life is critical as well. We may be missing the point when we focus solely on the technicalities of the law, to the exclusion of its spirit.

Allah frequently describes words as either *ṭayyib* or *khabīth* (foul). He says in the Qur'an,

> *'Do you not see how God makes comparisons? A good word (kalima ṭayyiba) is like a good tree whose root is firm and whose branches are high in the sky, yielding constant fruit by its Lord's leave –– God makes such comparisons for people so that they may reflect ––but an evil word (kalima khabītha) is like a rotten tree, uprooted from the surface of the earth, with no power to endure. God will give firmness to those who believe in the firmly rooted word, both in this world and the Hereafter, but the evildoers He leaves to stray: God does whatever He will.'* [14:24-27]

The exegetes of the Qur'an clarified that the *'good word'* is in fact the testimony of faith – there is not deity but Allah (lā *ilāha* *illā Allāh*) – because once these words are firm in our hearts, they cause us to do good things. The *'branches high in the sky'* are our good works that reach God. Indeed, Allah tells us, *'good words (al-kalim al-ṭayyib) rise up to Him and He lifts up the righteous deed.'* [35:10]

God describes the believers who enter Paradise as being *'guided to good speech (al-ṭayyib min al-qawl) and to the path of the One Worthy of all Praise.'* [22:24] Good speech has a general meaning, as well as referring specifically to the Qur'an and words of praise for God, as they are truly the best and purest speech. In prayer, we say: *'Greetings, blessings, prayers, and all good are for Allah (al-taḥiyyāt lillāh wa al-ṣalawāt wa al-ṭayyibāt).'* [Muslim]

From His honoring of His righteous servants, He has derived from His name al-Ṭayyib a description of those who beautify their speech and actions with good: *al-ṭayyibīn* and *al-ṭayyibāt*. [24:26]

Another way to embody *ṭīb* is to ensure that all that we do for God is good, and purified from any insincerity. Allah loves for us to try to emulate His characteristics of mercy and beauty. Elsewhere in this book, we have mentioned that if we want God's infinite mercy, then we need to have mercy towards people. If we want Allah's vast forgiveness, then we must forgive others. If we want to be a recipient of His good, then we should do good to others. This is what will be said to those who were mindful of God and are granted Paradise: '"*Peace be upon you. You have been good (ṭibtum). Come in: you are here to stay.*"' [39:73]

Iḥsān

One of the beloved characteristics to God is *iḥsān*, and the Qur'an is full of praise for those who embody this trait. For example, we are told: '*Spend in God's cause: do not contribute to your destruction with your own hands, but do good (aḥsinū), for God loves those who do good (al-muḥsinīn).*' [2:195]

If we talk about *iḥsān* outside of its religious context, its basic meaning is 'to do something to its best'. If an event organizer consistently organizes functions to the highest standards, this would be described as *iḥsān*. In a famous narration, the Prophet ﷺ taught us the motivation behind doing things to their best: knowing that God sees you. When you know that Allah sees you, no deed is too small, and every act can be enhanced with excellence and perfection. Religiously, *iḥsān* is both an internal and external state – and God tells us that He *loves* those who show *iḥsān*. He speaks about those '*who give, both in prosperity and adversity, who restrain their anger and pardon people – God loves those who do good (al-muḥsinīn).*' [3:134]

Even if we feel that our efforts are in vain, God assures us that they are not. Prophet Joseph spent years in hardship, but never compromised his integrity. God says of him: '*In this way We settled Joseph in that land to live wherever he wished: We grant Our mercy to whoever We will and do not fail to reward those who do good (al-muḥsinīn).'* [12:56]

Allah repeated this in the Qur'an to remind us to be steadfast, and to banish any thought that are our deeds are wasted when we are good. Allah says, *'God never wastes the reward of those who do good.'* [9:120] Allah reminds us that *'those who strive for Us – We will surely guide them to Our ways. And indeed, Allah is with the doers of good.'* [29:69] Remaining steadfast in spite of hardships is one of the traits of a *muḥsin.* He also describes the *muḥsinīn* as those, *'Who spend [in the cause of Allah] during ease and hardship and who restrain anger and who pardon the people - and Allah loves the doers of good.'* [3:134]

Embodying this trait requires effort, but the blessings are immeasurable. Allah tells us that He *'is with those who are mindful of Him and who do good (muḥsinūn),'* [16:128] and that His mercy *'is near to the doers of good (al-muḥsinīn).'* [7:56]

At the end of our lives, we are told that, *'For them who have done good (alladhīna aḥsanū) is the best [reward] and extra. No darkness will cover their faces, nor humiliation. Those are companions of Paradise; they will abide therein eternally.'* [10:26]

Because, indeed, *'Shall the reward of good be anything but good?'* [55:60]

Living with these names

1. Reflect on God's goodness in His creation and His actions

We all become so busy with life and its stresses that we sometimes to forget how God has honored us and given to us. Knowing these names should encourage us to take a step back in order to reflect on and be grateful for all the good we have been shown by Him.

2. Pay it forward: Give from the good that you have been given.

Allah tells us in the Qur'an, *'And do good as Allah has done good to you.'* [28:77] Part of showing gratitude to our Creator is to give from the good that He has given us.

3. Do things with birr, ṭīb and iḥsān

When we see whatever we do as ultimately a transaction with God – doing good to be rewarded with good – it can help us display these characteristics in our dealings with people too. We can display *birr* and *iḥsān* towards our parents by being gentle with them and befriending them. Even if we have a tense relationship with them, there are common points that we can focus on to enhance our relationships. For example, if we know that one of our parents likes a certain sport, we can try to bond with them over that sport. This might seem like something minor, but it shows that we are trying our best and doing what we can. Part of this *birr* and *iḥsān* towards parents is also to supplicate for them after they are gone, as this is something that benefits them beyond this life [Ibn Mājah]. Moreover, the Prophet ﷺ said, *'The best act of righteousness [birr] is to maintain relations with a man loved by his father.'* [Muslim] These are some examples of *birr* towards parents.

We can exhibit *ṭīb* by being conscious of using good words when speaking, and being in the remembrance of Allah. We should try to purify our good deeds of anything that might taint them, such as a lack of sincerity.

We can try to emulate the *muḥsinīn* by looking for where they are mentioned in the Qur'an, and the characteristics cited in the verses about them, as well as infusing excellence in everything we do because we know that Allah sees us.

4. Cooperate in righteousness, not in sin

The verse cited above exhorts us, in no uncertain terms, to cooperate with others on matters of righteousness. It is equally clear from that verse that we must not work with each other in sin and aggression. In the time we live, many matters may contain both elements; elements of righteousness and elements of sin. Other matters might be dressed in the robes of righteousness but are far from it. In these cases, it is very important to be connected to a community of involved, learned people. It is inevitable that we might make mistakes and misjudge, but this is why having knowledgeable and righteous mentors, as well as a community around us, is so crucial. One of the foundations of engaging in social justice issues is having knowledge of what defines good and evil based on our creed. Indeed, we must learn *before* engaging in certain issues and causes. A wonderful resource in this regard is the book, 'Towards Sacred Activism' by Imam Dawud Walid, as well as his website by the same name (see bibliography).

5. Beautify your relationships with goodness

Be good to people, good to animals and good to the environment. The Sufis would say, 'The kind person [*barr*] is the one who is affable and gentle in nature, who has a smiling face and gentle words.'[61]

[61] Ahmad Ibn Ajiba, *Allah: An Explanation of the Divine Names and Attributes* (USA: Al-Madina Institute, 2014), 172.

ALLAH

(100)

57

ALLAH (100)

The Qur'an says in one of the first verses: *'Praise belongs to Allah.'*

[1:2]

Now that we have understood God's many names and attributes, it is fitting to come to His unique name: Allah. We praise God for being Allah, because it encompasses all His names and attributes. We are not just praising His wisdom or His giving, but rather His entire essence.

This is the name that is most commonly on the tongues of Muslims, and this name brings together all of His attributes such that, when we call on Him by this name, we bring together all of the names and attributes mentioned in this book, and more. When we say '*Allāhumma*', we are calling out to Allah. Ibn Al-Qayyim says that when someone calls to Allah saying, '*Allāhumma*, I ask you,' he or she is saying, 'I am asking Allah who possesses the best names and the highest attributes by those names and attributes.'

Allah says in the Qur'an, *'Allah – there is no deity except Him. To Him belong the best names.'* [20:8]

When you simply utter 'Allah', know that you are calling the One who possesses all the greatest attributes. This name is unique because it is Allah's alone. His other names may also be attributes by which people are sometimes described, but this name can only refer to Him. According to many scholars, this is the greatest of Allah's names. It is the name most mentioned in the Qur'an, and it is the name that is mentioned in every hadith that talks about God's greatest name.

The beauty of Allah

Just hearing this name of Allah should change something in us and soothe our hearts. Ibn al-Qayyim quotes Ibn Fūrak, who said that the name 'Allah' starts with the 'a' sound, which originates in the chest, and ends with the 'h' sound which goes back to the chest. The chest contains the heart, and thus the name 'Allah' begins in the heart and ends there. It is light on the tongue and easy for anyone to say.

Who is Allah?

Allah is the One whom we worship; the One to whom we go with hope, reverence, and love. He is the Lord, the Sustainer and the Originator of this whole universe. If you want to feel in awe of Allah, go out somewhere in nature and just be with yourself. Reflect on the vastness of this universe and its beauty, and our small place in it.

The world appears to be so grand, yet Allah created each soul personally. He knows you better than your parents, your spouse, or your best friend. He hears you before you speak, and He hears the unspoken words trapped in your heart. He knows everything you have been through and everything you are going through. His door is always open to you no matter your state. The Prophet ﷺ tells us:

> *'Allah is happier with His servant who turns back to Him than the happiness one of you would feel if he was wandering in a barren wasteland to find his steed had wandered off with all his food and provisions. Then, after the heat and his thirst become severe, he falls asleep in the same place and wakes to find his steed standing before him, so that he grabs its reigns and says: "O Allah! I am your Lord and You are my servant," mixing up his words on account of his extreme joy.'* [Muslim]

He is greater than any of our problems, our fears or worries. This is why we say, *Allāhu akbar!* (Allah is greater!) at the start of every prayer to remind ourselves: He is greater. He gifted the daily prayers to us so that we can be brought back to our center and purpose at least five times a day, remembering that He sets the standards for greatness and loftiness as we recite these attributes in our bowing and prostration.

Our hopes and dreams are not too big for Him. He says in a hadith *qudsī* (narration of the words of Allah via the Prophet ﷺ):

> *'O My servants, were the first of you and the last of you, the human of you and the jinn of you to rise up in one place and make a request of Me, and were I to give everyone what he requested, that would not decrease what I have, any more than a needle decreases the sea if put into it.'* [Muslim]

He is the Vast, and so He encompasses all of us, with all our mistakes and brokenness. Do not ever believe that you are too broken for Him. Never think that there is no room for you. When Allah tells you to turn back to Him and seek forgiveness, it is because you have the potential to be better. You are not defined by your mistakes. The Prophet ﷺ told us: *'Allah extends His hand at night to give forgiveness to those who sinned during that day, and He extends His hand during the day to give forgiveness to those who sinned during the night. This will continue to be the case until the Sun rises from the west.'* [Muslim]

Knowing that instructions may be theoretical, He sent us a Messenger from amongst us to teach us and show us the way. Allah says about the Prophet ﷺ: *'It was only as a mercy that We sent you [Prophet] to all people.'* [21:107]

He put in the Prophet ﷺ the perfect example: worshipping Allah with love, hope and fear; kindness and compassion to everyone; communal and individual responsibility; and justice in society. Knowing that we might sometimes feel as though it is all too much, the Prophet ﷺ advised his daughter, Fāṭimah, to say in the morning and in the evening: *'Yā Ḥayyu yā Qayyūm (O Ever-Living, O Sustainer), by Your Mercy I seek help, rectify for me all of my affairs and do not leave me to depend on myself, even for the blink of an eye.'* [Ḥākim]

By remembering that Allah is sustaining this world at every moment, we realize how fragile we are, and how much we need Him, and thus we ask Him not to leave us alone for even a second.

Allah sent us different trials to know Him and to experience His attributes through both the good times and those that we perceive to be bad. He knows of our efforts and assures us that they never go to waste, teaching us to be ambitious in our good intentions and actions. Tests and hardships may come our way, but they come to alert us, strengthen us, elevate us and teach us. With His wisdom, justice and mercy, the whole world moves. He commands us because He is our Creator, but in the end, everything commanded from us or prohibited to us actually benefits us in the long-term, in both the metaphysical and physical realms. He is the Acquainted One – who knows the inner and outer realities of everything – and the Most Wise.

He reveals to us that He is the Source of Peace, so that we can turn to Him to be at peace, and emulate His attributes by being agents of peace in this world. He is so Generous that He has prepared for us a paradise that not only satisfies our material wants, but also our emotional wants and needs. It is a place in which we will be with those whom we love, where our hearts will know no pain, and where we will finally be with Allah.

He is the First and the Last, the Ascendant and the Intimate. Once we realize that, we can start everything with His remembrance, and understand that it will all go back to Him; we can start to see His attributes in the minutiae of our everyday.

He is Allah.

Living with this name

1. Start with this name and end with it

The Prophet Muhammad ﷺ told us that, *'Any important work that does not begin with 'bismillāh' is imperfect.'* [Ibn Ḥibbān] *Bismillāh* simply means, 'in the name of Allah'. We should remember Him at the beginning of any important act or matter.

2. Be in awe of the magnitude of this name

This name is unique and can only refer to Him. It should cause awe and love in our hearts, which should lead us to respect the utterance of His name. We should be vigilant that the same tongue that says 'Allah' is not used inappropriately, in ways that He detests.

3. Reflect on the meaning of this name through understanding His other names

All the names discussed in this book are contained in His name 'Allah'. Thus, when we want to know who Allah is, we can return to this book, as well as other teachings on His name, in order to connect to Him.

WHAT NEXT? LIVING WITH THE NAMES OF ALLAH

With the conclusion of this book, it is fitting to end in the same way we ended each chapter: with advice on how to live with these names. I hope that this will be useful to you in your journey to know God.

1. Reflect on God's manifestations of His names in your life

Carve out time on a regular basis to think about and reflect on these names, and how Allah has manifested His names in your life. You can do this on a daily, weekly, or monthly basis, in which you reflect upon how Allah manifested Himself to you through the events of your life, and which of His names resonate with your experiences.

2. Reflect on His names as they appear in the Qur'an

The Qur'an is the word of Allah, and nothing can ever be more important in shaping how we understand Allah. Many verses end with His names, and part of our study of the Qur'an can be to reflect on how and why particular names are mentioned at the end of these verses.

3. Start a 'Names of Allah' journal

While journaling is recommended for a number of reasons, it is particularly useful to start a journal with your own personal reflections on the names of Allah. It will ensure that you capture your thoughts on paper, and that you are able to return to them when you forget. It is also a way to bring together everything you have learned from different sources, and whatever lessons you found most relevant from each of these, in one place.

4. Start a study circle

Allah loves for Muslims to be together, to encourage and remind one another to do good. The Prophet ﷺ said that, '*Allah Almighty said: "My love is assured for those who love each other for my sake, who sit together for my sake, who visit each other for my sake, and who spend on each other for my sake."*' [Aḥmad]

Being with one another to reflect on the names of Allah, encouraging one another to memorize these names, and helping one another to see their manifestations in our lives, brings us closer to God and closer together. Indeed, the Prophet ﷺ praised the believers, describing them in this way, '*Verily, the believers are like a structure, each part strengthening the other.*' [Bukhārī and Muslim] Through reflecting on the names of Allah together, we can strengthen one another's faith.

Moreover, there are immense spiritual blessings in gathering regularly to remember Him. The Prophet ﷺ tells us:

> '*Verily, Allah Almighty has caravans of angels who have no other work but to follow gatherings of remembrance. When they find such gatherings in which there is remembrance, they sit with them and some of them surround the others with their wings until the space between them and the heavens is covered.*'

Thereafter, the angels have a conversation with God about the desires of these people – that they desire Paradise, seek refuge from the Hellfire, and want Allah's forgiveness and blessings. The hadith continues:

> '*Allah says: "I will pardon them, give them what they request, and grant them protection." They say: "Our Lord, there is one among them, a simple servant who happened to pass by and sit there alongside them." Allah says: "I will also grant him pardon,*

for whoever sits with these fellows will not suffer misery."' [Bukhārī and Muslim]

The blessings in these gatherings are such that, even if someone just happens to sit in them, he or she is also included amongst those who are forgiven. Moreover, meeting regularly with others can help to keep us committed to learning and remembrance.

5. Memorize the names

'Allah has ninety-nine names and whoever preserves them will enter Paradise.' [Muslim] One of the meanings of this hadith is that we should memorize the names. You could memorize one name a day for three months, or three names a week for around eight months, until you are someone who knows the ninety-nine names of Allah by heart, fulfilling one meaning of the hadith.

6. Go beyond this book

While this book builds upon the knowledge and reflections of many others, it is only one humble effort. There are many resources on the names of Allah, including book translations, articles, audio and video lectures, and classes or courses. We should not stop at this book, but rather use it as a starting point to further explore the meanings and manifestations of the names of Allah. Some of these resources can be found in the bibliography section.

الحمد لله الذي بنعمته تتم الصالحات

All praise is due to God, by whose favor good deeds are completed

SUPPLICATIONS FROM THE QUR'AN AND SUNNAH

People often ask me how to call on Allah by His names in their supplications. Understanding these names means that we can, and should, speak to Allah from our hearts and in our own words, calling upon Him with those of His names which are relevant to our situation and our requests of Him. Allah says, *'And to Allah belong the best names, so invoke Him by them.'* [7:180] Knowing Him should enable us to know when and how to call upon Him.

If we feel anxiety, for example, we may want to connect to His name al-Salām, knowing that true peace can only come from Him, and ask Him to calm the agitation in our hearts. We can further supplement this by following the *'ways of peace'* mentioned in the Qur'an [5:16], like understanding and reciting the Qur'an, remembering Him, praying, and reflecting upon the life of the Prophet ﷺ, all because we have faith that He is al-Salām and from Him comes *salām*. When we go through difficulties, we can turn to al-Ḥakīm, with conviction that there is wisdom in what we are going through and that we should learn from our experiences. We can call on Him by His name al-Ḥakīm, asking Him to teach us the lessons that we need. If we lose a possession, we can call upon al-Jāmiʿ to reunite us with what we lost, because we know that He can bring together anything.

That said, there are many examples of supplications in the Qur'an and Sunnah, which encompass the most beautifully-worded prayers for so many of our needs. What follows is a selected compilation of these supplications:

Al-Asmā al-Ḥusnā

اللهمَّ إني عبدُك ابنُ عبدِك ابنُ أمَتِك ناصيَتي بيدِك ماضٍ فيَّ حُكمُك عَدْلٌ فيَّ قضاؤُك أسألُك بكلِّ اسمٍ هو لك سميت به نفسَك أوْ علَّمْتَه أحدًا مِنْ خلقِك أو أنزلته في كتابِك أو استأثرتَ به في علمِ الغيبِ عندَك أنْ تجعلَ القرآنَ ربيعَ قلبي ونورَ صدري وجلاءَ حُزني وذهابَ همّي

Allāhumma innī ʿabduka, ibnu ʿabdika, ibnu amatika. Nāṣiyatī biyadik, māḍin fiyya ḥukmuk, ʿadlun fiyya qaḍāʾuk. As'aluka bi kulli ismin huwa lak, sammayta bihi nafsak, aw anzaltahu fī kitabik, aw ʿallamtahu aḥadan min khalqik, aw ista'tharta bihi fī ʿilm al-ghaybi ʿindak, an taj ʿal al-qur'āna rabīʿa qalbī, wa nūra ṣadrī, wa jalā'a ḥuznī, wa dhahāba hammī.

The Messenger of Allah ﷺ said, *'If any Muslim is afflicted with distress and makes this supplication, then his supplication will be answered:*

> *"O Allah, I am your servant, the son of your servant, the son of your maidservant. My forelock is in your hand, your command concerning me prevails, and your decision concerning me is just. I call upon you by every one of the beautiful names with which you have described yourself, or which you have revealed in your Book, or you have taught to any of your creatures, or which you have chosen to keep in the knowledge of the unseen with you, to make the Qur'an the delight of my soul, the light of my heart, and to remove my sadness and dispel my anxiety."*

If he says this, Allah will remove his affliction and replace it with joy and happiness.'

The Companions said, 'O Messenger of Allah ﷺ, should we not learn it?' The Prophet ﷺ replied, *'Yes, whoever hears it should know it.'* [Aḥmad]

Allāh

بِاسْمِ اللهِ يُبْرِيكَ وَمِنْ كُلِّ دَاءٍ يَشْفِيكَ وَمِنْ شَرِّ حَاسِدٍ إِذَا حَسَدَ وَشَرِّ كُلِّ ذِي عَيْنٍ

Bismillāhi yubrīka wa min kulli dā'in yashfīk wa min sharri ḥāsidin idhā ḥasad wa sharri kulli dhī 'ayn

'In the name of Allah, may he cure you, may he heal you from every ailment, from the evil of the envier when he envies, and from the evil of every eye.' [Muslim]

Al-'Aẓīm al-Ḥalīm

لا إله إلا اللهُ العظيمُ الحليمُ، لا إله إلا الله رَبُّ العرش العظيم، لا إله إلا الله رَبُّ السماوات وربُّ الأرضِ، لا إله إلا الله رَبُّ الْعَرشِ الكريم

Lā ilāha illā Allāh al-'aẓīm al-ḥalīm. Lā ilāha illā Allāh rabb al-'arsh al-'aẓīm. Lā ilāha illā Allāh rabb al-samāwāti wa rabb al-arḍ. Lā ilāha illā Allāh rabb al-'arsh al-karīm.

'None has the right to be worshipped but Allah, the Majestic, the Most Forbearing, none has the right to be worshipped but Allah, the Lord of the Tremendous Throne. None has the right to be worshipped but Allah, the Lord of the Heavens and the Lord of the Honorable Throne.'

The Prophet ﷺ would make this supplication in times of difficulty. [Bukhārī]

Al-Wahhāb

رَبَّنَا لَا تُزِغْ قُلُوبَنَا بَعْدَ إِذْ هَدَيْتَنَا وَهَبْ لَنَا مِن لَّدُنكَ رَحْمَةً ۚ إِنَّكَ أَنتَ الْوَهَّابُ

Rabbanā la tuzigh qulūbanā ba'da idh hadaytanā wahab lanā min ladunka raḥmah innaka anta al-wahhāb

'Our Lord, let not our hearts deviate after You have guided us and grant us from Yourself mercy. Indeed, You are the Bestower.' [3:8]

Al-Razzāq

وارزُقنا وأنتَ خيْرُ الرّازقين

Warzuqnā wa-anta khayru al-rāziqīn

'And provide for us, and You are the best of providers.' [7:23]

Al-Samīʿ al-Alīm

بِسْمِ اللَّهِ الَّذِي لَا يَضُرُّ مَعَ اسْمِهِ شَيْءٌ فِي الْأَرْضِ وَلَا فِي السَّمَاءِ وَهُوَ السَّمِيعُ الْعَلِيمُ

Bismillahi alladhī lā yaḍurru maʿa ismihi shay'un fīl-arḍi wa lā fī al-samā'i wa huwa al-samīʿ al-ʿalīm

The Messenger of Allah ﷺ said, *'No servant says this three times in the morning every day and in the evening every night but that nothing will harm him: "In the name of Allah, in whose name nothing can be harmed on earth nor in the heaven, for He is the Hearing, the Knowing."'* [Tirmidhī]

رَبَّنَا تَقَبَّلْ مِنَّا ۖ إِنَّكَ أَنتَ السَّمِيعُ الْعَلِيمُ

Rabbanā taqabbal minnā innaka anta al-samīʿ al-ʿalīm

'Our Lord, accept [this] from us. Indeed You are the Hearing, the Knowing.' [2:127]

Al-Samīʿ

رَبِّ هَبْ لِي مِن لَّدُنكَ ذُرِّيَّةً طَيِّبَةً ۖ إِنَّكَ سَمِيعُ الدُّعَاءِ

Rabbī hab lī min ladunka dhurriyya ṭayyiba innaka samīʿ al-du'ā

'My Lord, grant me from Yourself a good offspring. Indeed, You are the Hearer of supplication.' [3:38]

Al-Wārith

رَبِّ لَا تَذَرْنِي فَرْدًا وَأَنتَ خَيْرُ الْوَارِثِينَ

Rabbī lā tadharnī fardan wa anta khayr al-wārithīn

'My Lord, do not leave me alone [with no heir], while You are the best of inheritors.' [21:89]

Al-Ra'ūf al-Raḥīm

رَبَّنَا اغْفِرْ لَنَا وَلِإِخْوَانِنَا الَّذِينَ سَبَقُونَا بِالْإِيمَانِ وَلَا تَجْعَلْ فِي قُلُوبِنَا غِلًّا لِّلَّذِينَ آمَنُوا رَبَّنَا إِنَّكَ رَءُوفٌ رَّحِيمٌ

Rabbanā ighfir lanā wa li ikhwāninā alladhīna sabaqūnā bi al-īmān wa lā taj'al fī qulūbinā ghillan lilladhīna āmanū rabbanā innaka ra'ūfun raḥīm

'Our Lord, forgive us and our brothers who preceded us in faith and put not in our hearts [any] resentment toward those who have believed. Our Lord, indeed You are Kind and Merciful.' [59:10]

Al-Tawwāb al-Ghafūr

رَبِّ اغْفِرْ لِي، وَتُبْ عَلَيَّ، إِنَّكَ أَنْتَ التَّوَّابُ الْغَفُورُ

Rabbī ighfir lī wa tub 'alayy, innaka anta al-tawwāb al-ghafūr

'My Lord forgive me and accept my repentance, You are the Accepting of Repentance, the Forgiving.' [Ibn Mājah]

Al-Tawwāb al-Raḥīm

رَبَّنَا وَاجْعَلْنَا مُسْلِمَيْنِ لَكَ وَمِن ذُرِّيَّتِنَا أُمَّةً مُّسْلِمَةً لَّكَ وَأَرِنَا مَنَاسِكَنَا وَتُبْ عَلَيْنَا ۖ إِنَّكَ أَنتَ التَّوَّابُ الرَّحِيمُ

Rabbanā wa ij'alnā muslimayni laka wa min dhurriyyatinā ummatan muslimatan laka wa arinā manāsikanā wa tub 'alayna innaka anta al-tawwāb al-raḥīm

'Our Lord, and make us Muslims [in submission] to You and from our descendants a Muslim nation [in submission] to You. And show us our rites and accept our repentance. Indeed, You are the Accepting of repentance, the Merciful.' [2:128]

اللَّهُمَّ أَلِّفْ بَيْنَ قُلُوبِنَا وَأَصْلِحْ ذَاتَ بَيْنِنَا وَاهْدِنَا سُبُلَ السَّلَامِ وَنَجِّنَا مِنْ الظُّلُمَاتِ إِلَى النُّورِ وَجَنِّبْنَا الْفَوَاحِشَ مَا ظَهَرَ مِنْهَا وَمَا بَطَنَ وَبَارِكْ لَنَا فِي أَسْمَاعِنَا وَأَبْصَارِنَا وَقُلُوبِنَا وَأَزْوَاجِنَا وَذُرِّيَّاتِنَا وَتُبْ عَلَيْنَا إِنَّكَ أَنْتَ التَّوَّابُ الرَّحِيمُ وَاجْعَلْنَا شَاكِرِينَ لِنِعْمَتِكَ مُثْنِينَ بِهَا قَابِلِيهَا وَأَتِمَّهَا عَلَيْنَا

Allāhumma allif bayna qulūbinā wa aṣliḥ dhāta bayninā, wa ihdinā subul as-salām, wa najinnā min al-ẓulumāti ilā al-nūr, wa jannibnā al-fawāḥish mā ẓahara minhā wa mā baṭan, wa bārik lanā fī asmā'inā wa abṣārinā wa qulūbinā wa azwājinā wa dhurriyātinā wa tub 'alaynā, innaka anta at-Tawwāb ar-Raḥīm, wa ij'alnā shākirīna li-ni'matika muthnīna bihā qābilīhā wa attimahā 'alaynā.

'O Allah, bring our hearts together, reconcile between us, guide us to ways of peace, and deliver us from darkness into light. Keep us away from immorality, outwardly and inwardly, and bless us in our hearing, our seeing, our hearts, our spouses, and our children. Accept our repentance, for you alone are the Relenting, the Merciful. Make us grateful for your blessings, praising and accepting them, and give them to us in full.' [Abū Dāwūd]

Al-Ghafūr Ar-Raḥīm

اللَّهُمَّ إِنِّي ظَلَمْتُ نَفْسِي ظُلْمًا كَثِيرًا، وَلا يَغْفِرِ الذُّنوبَ إِلاَّ أَنْتَ، فَاغْفِر لِي مغْفِرَةً مِن عِنْدِكَ، وَارحَمْني، إِنَّكَ أَنْتَ الْغفور الرَّحِيم

Allahumma innī ẓalamtu nafsī ẓulman kathīran wa lā yaghfir al-dhunūba illā ant. Fa ighfirlī maghfiratan min ʿindik warḥamnī, innaka anta al-Ghafūr al-Raḥīm

'O Allah, I have wronged myself with many great wrongs and none forgives sin but you, so forgive me and have mercy upon me. Verily, you alone are the Forgiving, the Merciful.' [Bukhārī and Muslim]

Al-Raḥīm

رَبَّنَا آمَنَّا فَاغْفِرْ لَنَا وَارْحَمْنَا وَأَنتَ خَيْرُ الرَّاحِمِينَ

Rabbanā amannā fa ighfir lanā wa irḥamnā wa anta khayr al-rāḥimīn

'Our Lord, we have believed, so forgive us and have mercy upon us, and You are the best of the merciful.' [23:109]

Al-Mawlā

رَبَّنَا لَا تُؤَاخِذْنَا إِن نَّسِينَا أَوْ أَخْطَأْنَا ۚ رَبَّنَا وَلَا تَحْمِلْ عَلَيْنَا إِصْرًا كَمَا حَمَلْتَهُ
عَلَى الَّذِينَ مِن قَبْلِنَا ۚ رَبَّنَا وَلَا تُحَمِّلْنَا مَا لَا طَاقَةَ لَنَا بِهِ ۖ وَاعْفُ عَنَّا وَاغْفِرْ
لَنَا وَارْحَمْنَا ۚ أَنتَ مَوْلَانَا فَانصُرْنَا عَلَى الْقَوْمِ الْكَافِرِينَ

Rabbanā lā tu'ākhidhnā in nasīnā aw akhṭa'nā rabbanā wa lā taḥmil ʿalaynā iṣran kamā ḥamaltahu ʿalā alladhīna min qablinā rabbanā wa lā tuḥammilnā mā lā ṭāqata lanā bihi waʿfu ʿannā wa ighfir lanā wa irḥamnā anta mawlānā fa unṣurnā ʿalā al-qawmi al-kāfirīn

'Our Lord, do not impose blame upon us if we have forgotten or erred. Our Lord, and lay not upon us a burden like that which You laid upon those before us. Our Lord, and burden us not with that which we have no ability to bear. And pardon us; and forgive us; and have mercy upon us. You are our protector, so give us victory over the disbelieving people.' [2:286]

Al-Waliyy

أَنتَ وَلِيِّي فِي الدُّنْيَا وَالْآخِرَةِ ۖ تَوَفَّنِي مُسْلِمًا وَأَلْحِقْنِي بِالصَّالِحِينَ

Anta waliyyī fī al-dunyā wa al-ākhirati tawaffanī musliman wa ilhiqnī bi al-ṣāliḥīn

'You are my protector in this world and in the Hereafter. Cause me to die a Muslim and join me with the righteous.' [12:101]

Al-Waliyy al-Ghāfir

أَنتَ وَلِيُّنَا فَاغْفِرْ لَنَا وَارْحَمْنَا ۖ وَأَنتَ خَيْرُ الْغَافِرِينَ

Anta waliyyunā fa ighfir lanā wa irḥamnā wa anta khayr al-ghāfirīn

'You are our Protector, so forgive us and have mercy upon us; and You are the best of forgivers.' [7:155]

Al-'Azīz al-Ḥakīm

رَبَّنَا لَا تَجْعَلْنَا فِتْنَةً لِّلَّذِينَ كَفَرُوا وَاغْفِرْ لَنَا رَبَّنَا ۖ إِنَّكَ أَنتَ الْعَزِيزُ الْحَكِيمُ

Rabbanā lā taj'alnā fi›natan lilladhina kafarū wa ighfir lanā rabbanā innaka anta al-'azīz al-ḥakīm

'Our Lord! Make us not a trial for the disbelievers, and forgive us, Our Lord! Verily, You, only You are the All-Mighty, the All-Wise.' [60:5]

Al-Raḥmān al-Raḥīm

أَنِّي مَسَّنِيَ الضُّرُّ وَأَنتَ أَرْحَمُ الرَّاحِمِينَ

Innī masanīya al-ḍurru wa anta arḥam al-rāḥimīn

'Indeed, adversity has touched me, and you are the Most Merciful of the merciful.' [21:83]

Al-'Afuww

اللَّهُمَّ إِنَّكَ عَفُوٌّ تُحِبُّ الْعَفْوَ فَاعْفُ عَنِّي

Allāhumma innaka 'afuwwun tuḥibbu al-'afwa fa'fu 'annī

'O Allah, you are pardoning and generous. You love to forgive, so forgive me.' [Tirmidhī]

Al-Fattāḥ

رَبَّنَا افْتَحْ بَيْنَنَا وَبَيْنَ قَوْمِنَا بِالْحَقِّ وَأَنتَ خَيْرُ الْفَاتِحِينَ

Rabbanā iftaḥ baynanā wa bayna qawminā bi al-ḥaqqi wa anta khayr al-fātiḥīn

'Our Lord, decide between us and our people in truth, and You are the best of those who give decision.' [7:89]

Al-Muqaddim al-Mu'akhkhir

رَبِّ اغْفِرْ لِي خَطِيئَتِي، وَجَهْلِي، وَإِسْرَافِي فِي أَمْرِي كُلِّهِ، وَمَا أَنْتَ أَعْلَمُ بِهِ مِنِّي، اللَّهُمَّ اغْفِرْ لِي خَطَايَايَ وَعَمْدِي، وَجَهْلِي وَهَزْلِي، وَكُلُّ ذَلِكَ عِنْدِي، اللَّهُمَّ اغْفِرْ لِي مَا قَدَّمْتُ وَمَا أَخَّرْتُ، وَمَا أَسْرَرْتُ وَمَا أَعْلَنْتُ، أَنْتَ الْمُقَدِّمُ وَأَنْتَ الْمُؤَخِّرُ، وَأَنْتَ عَلَى كُلِّ شَيْءٍ قَدِيرٌ

Allahumma ighfir-lī khaṭī'atī, wa jahlī, wa isrāfī fī amrī kullah, wa mā anta a'lamu bihi minnī. Allahumma ighfir-lī khaṭāyāya wa 'amdī, wa jahlī was hazlī, wa kullu dhālika 'indī. Allahumma ighfir-lī mā qaddamtu wa mā akhart, wa mā asrartu wa mā a'lant, anta al-Muqaddim wa anta al-Mu'akhir wa anta 'alā julli shay'in qadīr.

'O Allah, forgive my mistakes, ignorance, transgression in my matters, and what You are more knowledgeable of than me. O Allah, forgive me for my mistakes made unintentionally or intentionally; in earnestness and in jest; as I have committed all of these (types of sins). O Allah, forgive me for what I have already done, what I am yet to do, what I did privately,

what I did publicly. You are the One who brings forward and You are the One who defers. You are All-Powerful over everything.' [Bukhārī and Muslim]

اللَّهُمَّ اغْفِرْ لِي مَا قَدَّمْتُ وَمَا أَخَّرْتُ، وَمَا أَسْرَرْتُ وَمَا أَعْلَنْتُ، وَمَا أَنْتَ أَعْلَمُ بِهِ مِنِّي، أَنْتَ الْمُقَدِّمُ وَأَنْتَ الْمُؤَخِّرُ، لَا إِلَهَ إِلَّا أَنْتَ

Allahumma ighfir-lī mā qaddamtu wa mā akhart, wa mā asrartu wa mā aʿlant, wa mā anta aʿlamu bihi minnī. Anta al-Muqaddim wa anta al-Mu'akhir, lā ilāha ilā ant

'O Allah! Forgive my past and future sins and whatever I have done in secret, and whatever I have done in public, and what You are more knowledgeable of than I. You are The One Who brings forward and Who delays, there is no deity worthy of worship but You' [Tirmidhī]

Al-'Aẓīm al-Ḥalīm

لا إله إلا اللّه العظيمُ الحليمُ، لا إله إلا الله ربُّ السماواتِ والأرضِ ورب العَرشِ العظيم

Lā ilāha ilā Allāh al-'Aẓīm al-Ḥalīm, lā ilāha ilā Allāh rabb al-samāwāti wal-arḍi wa rabb al-'arsh al-'aẓīm

'None has the right to be worshipped but Allah, the Majestic, the Most Forbearing, none has the right to be worshipped but Allah, the Lord of the Tremendous Throne. None has the right to be worshipped but Allah, the Lord of the Heavens and the Lord of the Honorable Throne.'

The Prophet ﷺ would make this supplication during difficulty [Bukhāri]

Al-Aḥad al-Ṣamad; al-Ghafūr al-Raḥīm

اللَّهُمَّ إِنِّي أَسْأَلُكَ يَا أَللَّهُ بِأَنَّكَ الْوَاحِدُ الصَّمَدُ، الَّذِي لَمْ يَلِدْ وَلَمْ يُولَدْ وَلَمْ يَكُنْ لَهُ كُفُوًا أَحَدٌ، أَنْ تَغْفِرَ لِي ذُنُوبِي، إِنَّكَ أَنْتَ الْغَفُورُ الرَّحِيمُ

Allāhumma innī as'aluka yā Allāhu bi-annak al-wāḥid uṣ-ṣamad, alladhī lam yalid wa lam yūlad wa lam yakun lahu kufuwan aḥad, an taghfira lī dhunūbī, innaka antal ghafūr ar-raḥīm.

'O Allah, I ask You by virtue of You being al-Wāḥid al-Ṣamad, who does not beget nor is begotten, nor is anyone comparable to Him—that you forgive my sins for me—for certainly, it is You Who are the Most Forgiving, Most Merciful.'

The Prophet ﷺ said upon hearing this, '*He has certainly been forgiven; he has certainly been forgiven; he has certainly been forgiven.*' [Aḥmad]

اللَّهُمَّ إِنِّي أَسْأَلُكَ بِأَنِّي أَشْهَدُ أَنَّكَ أَنْتَ اللَّهُ لَا إِلَهَ إِلَّا أَنْتَ الْأَحَدُ الصَّمَدُ
الَّذِي لَمْ يَلِدْ وَلَمْ يُولَدْ وَلَمْ يَكُنْ لَهُ كُفُوًا أَحَدٌ

Allāhumma innī as'aluka bi-annī ash-hadu annaka anta Allāhu lā ilāha ilā ant, al-Wāḥid aṣ-Ṣamad, alladhī lam yalid wa lam yūlad wa lam yakun lahu kufuwan aḥad

'O Allah, I ask you by my testimony that you are Allah, there is no God but you, al-Wāḥid al-Ṣamad, who does not give birth and was not born, and to whom no one is equal.'

When the Prophet ﷺ heard a Companion making the above supplication, he said, '*By Him in whose Hand is my soul, he has asked Allah by His greatest name, for which He answers when called upon and He gives when asked.*' [Tirmidhī]

Al-Ḥayy al-Qayyūm

يَا حَيُّ يَا قَيُّومُ بِرَحْمَتِكَ أَسْتَغِيثُ أَصْلِحْ لِي شَأْنِي كُلَّهُ وَلاَ تَكِلْنِي إِلَى
نَفْسِي طَرْفَةَ عَيْنٍ

Ya Ḥayyu Ya Qayyūm, bi-raḥmatika astaghīth, aṣliḥ lī sha'nī kullah, wa lā takilnī elī nafsī ṭarfata 'ayn

'Oh Ever Living One, Oh Ever Sustaining One, in your Mercy I seek relief. Set all of my affairs right, and do not leave me to myself even for the blink of an eye.'

The Prophet ﷺ taught this supplication to his daughter Fāṭimah, saying that one should not let a day or night go by without saying it. [Ḥākim]

Al-Ḥayy al-Qayyūm; Al-ʿAẓīm

أَسْتَغْفِرُ اللهَ العَظِيمَ الَّذِي لاَ إِلَهَ إِلاَّ هُوَ، الحَيُّ القَيُّومُ، وَأَتُوبُ إِلَيْهِ

Astaghfiru Allah al-ʿAẓīm alladhī lā ilāha illā hua al-Ḥayy al-Qayyūm, wa atūbu ilayh

The Prophet ﷺ said that whoever says it, *'then Allah will forgive him even if he fled from battle.'* [Tirmidhī]

Al-Ḥayy al-Qayyūm; Al-Mannān

اللَّهُمَّ إِنِّي أَسْأَلُكَ بِأَنَّ لَكَ الحَمدُ لا إِلَهَ إِلَّا أَنتَ المَنَّانُ بديعُ السَّمواتِ
والأرضِ يا ذا الجلالِ والإكرامِ يا حيُّ يا قيُّومُ

Allahumma innī asʾaluka bi anna laka al-ḥamd, lā ilāha illā ant al-Mannān, badīʿ al-samāwāti wal-arḍ, yā dhal-jalāli wal-ikrām, yā Ḥayyu yā Qayyūm

'O Allah, I ask you as all praise is Yours. There is no god except You, the Bestower, the Originator of the Heavens and Earth, Possessor of Majesty and Honor. O Ever-Living (Ḥayy), O Self-Subsisting (Qayyūm)'

The Prophet ﷺ heard a Companion supplicate with the above and said: "He has supplicated to Allah using His Greatest Name; when supplicated with this Name, He answers, and when asked with this Name He gives." [Abu Dawūd]

Al-'Aẓīm

أَنْ يَشْفِيَكَ الْعَظِيمَ رَبَّ الْعَرْشِ الْعَظِيمِ اللَّهَ أَسْأَلُ

As'al Allah al-'Aẓīm rabb al-'arsh al-'aẓīm an yashfīk

Du'ā' to be made when visiting the sick: 'I ask Allah the Mighty, Lord of the Mighty Throne that He cures you.' [Aḥmad, Tirmidhī]

Al-Ḥamīd al-Majīd

اللَّهُمَّ صَلِّ على مُحَمَّدٍ، وعلى آلِ مُحَمَّدٍ، كما صَلَّيْتَ على آلِ إبراهيمَ، إنَّكَ حميدٌ مجيدٌ، اللَّهُمَّ بارِكْ على مُحَمَّدٍ، وعلى آلِ مُحَمَّدٍ، كما بارَكْتَ على آلِ إبراهيمَ، إنَّكَ حميدٌ مجيدٌ

Allahumma ṣallī 'alā Muḥammad wa 'alā āli Muḥammad, kamā ṣalayta 'alā Ibrahīm wa 'alā āli Ibrahīm, innaka Ḥamidun Majīd. Allahumma bārik 'alā Muḥammad wa 'alā āli Muḥammad, kamā bārakta 'alā Ibrahīm wa 'alā āli Ibrahīm, innaka Ḥamidun Majīd

'O Allah, send prayers on Muhammad ﷺ, and on the family of Muhammad ﷺ, as you sent prayers on [Ibrahim, and on] the family of Ibrahim; You are indeed Worthy of Praise, Full of Glory. O Allah, send blessings on Muhammad ﷺ, and on the family of Muhammad ﷺ, as you sent blessings on Ibrahim and the family of Ibrahim; You are indeed Worthy of Praise, Full of Glory.' [Bukhārī]

Al-Awwal al-Ākhir al-Ẓāhir al-Bāṭin

اللَّهُمَّ رَبَّ السَّمَوَاتِ السَّبْعِ وَرَبَّ الْأَرْضِ، وَرَبَّ الْعَرْشِ الْعَظِيمِ، رَبَّنَا وَرَبَّ كُلِّ شَيْءٍ، فَالِقَ الْحَبِّ وَالنَّوَى، وَمُنْزِلَ التَّوْرَاةِ وَالْإِنْجِيلِ وَالْفُرْقَانِ، أَعُوذُ بِكَ مِنْ شَرِّ كُلِّ شَيْءٍ أَنْتَ آخِذٌ بِنَاصِيَتِهِ، اللَّهُمَّ أَنْتَ الْأَوَّلُ فَلَيْسَ قَبْلَكَ شَيْءٌ، وَأَنْتَ الْآخِرُ فَلَيْسَ بَعْدَكَ شَيْءٌ، وَأَنْتَ الظَّاهِرُ فَلَيْسَ فَوْقَكَ شَيْءٌ، وَأَنْتَ الْبَاطِنُ فَلَيْسَ دُونَكَ شَيْءٌ، اقْضِ عَنَّا الدَّيْنَ وَأَغْنِنَا مِنَ الْفَقْرِ

Allahumma rabb al-samāwāti wal-arḍi wa rabb al-ʻarsh al-ʻaẓīm, rabbanā wa rabbu kulla shay', fāliq al-ḥabbi wal-nawā wa munzil al-tawrat wal-injīl wal-furqān, al-ʻAẓīm al-Ḥalīm, lā ilāha ilā Allāh rabb

'O Allah, Lord of the heavens, the Earth, and the Mighty Throne! Our Lord and the Lord of all things; Who splits the seed and the kernel, Who sent down the Torah, the Gospel, and the Criterion. I seek refuge with You from the evil in everything, all of which you grasp by the forelock. O Allah! You are the First, so nothing precedes You. You are the Last, so nothing comes after You. You are the Manifest, so nothing comes above You. You are the Hidden, so nothing comes below You. Fulfil our debts for us and enrich us so we will not be poor.' [Muslim]

ʻĀlim al-Ghayb

اللَّهُمَّ فَاطِرَ السَّمَوَاتِ والأَرضِ عَالِمَ الغَيْب وَالشَّهَادةِ، ربَّ كُلِّ شَيءٍ
وَمَلِيكَهُ. أَشْهَدُ أَن لاَ إله إلاَّ أَنتَ، أَعُوذُ بكَ منْ شَرِّ نَفسي وشَرِّ
الشَّيْطَانِ وَشِرْكهِ

Allāhumma fāṭir al-samāwāti wal-arḍ, ʻālim al-ghayb wal-shahādah, rabba kulli shayin wa malīkah, ash-hadu an lā ilāha illā ant, aʻūthu bika min sharri nafsī wa min sharri ash-shayṭān wa shirkih, wa an aqtarifa ʻalā nafsī sū'an aw ajurrahu ilā muslim

O Allah, Creator of the heavens and the Earth, Knower of the unseen and the seen, Lord and Sovereign of all things, I bear witness that none has the right to be worshipped except You, I take refuge in You from the evil of my soul and from the evil and shirk of the devil, and from committing wrong against my soul or bringing such upon another Muslim

Abu Bakr asked the Prophet ﷺ to teach him some words to say in the morning and the evening. So, the Prophet ﷺ taught him the supplication above to say in the morning and the evening, as well as when one retires to his or her bed. [Tirmidhī]

Al-Nūr; al-Qayyūm; al-Haqq

اللَّهُمَّ لَكَ الحَمْدُ، أَنْتَ نُورُ السَّمَوَاتِ وَالأَرْضِ وَمَنْ فِيهِنَّ، وَلَكَ الحَمْدُ، أَنْتَ قَيُّومُ السَّمَوَاتِ وَالأَرْضِ وَمَنْ فِيهِنَّ، وَلَكَ الحَمْدُ، أَنْتَ الحَقُّ، وَوَعْدُكَ حَقٌّ، وَقَوْلُكَ حَقٌّ، وَلِقَاؤُكَ حَقٌّ، وَالجَنَّةُ حَقٌّ، وَالنَّارُ حَقٌّ، وَالسَّاعَةُ حَقٌّ، وَالنَّبِيُّونَ حَقٌّ، وَمُحَمَّدٌ حَقٌّ، اللَّهُمَّ لَكَ أَسْلَمْتُ، وَبِكَ آمَنْتُ، وَعَلَيْكَ تَوَكَّلْتُ، وَإِلَيْكَ أَنَبْتُ، وَبِكَ خَاصَمْتُ، وَإِلَيْكَ حَاكَمْتُ، فَاغْفِرْ لِي مَا قَدَّمْتُ وَمَا أَخَّرْتُ، وَمَا أَسْرَرْتُ وَمَا أَعْلَنْتُ، أَنْتَ إِلَهِي لاَ إِلَهَ إِلَّا أَنْتَ

Allāhumma laka al-ḥamd anta nūr as-samāwāti wa al-arḍi wa man fīhinna wa laka al-ḥamd, anta qayyūm as-samāwāti wal-arḍi wa man fīhinna wa laka al-ḥamd. Anta al-ḥaqq, wa wa'duka ḥaqq, wa liqā'uka ḥaqq, wa al-jannatu ḥaqq, wa al-nāru ḥaqq, wa al-nabbiyyūna ḥaqq, wa al-sā'atu ḥaqq, wa muḥammadun ḥaqq. Allāhumma laka aslamt, wa bika āmant, wa 'alayka tawakkalt, wa ilayka anabt, wa bika khāṣamt, wa ilayka ḥākamt, fa ighfirlī mā qaddamtu wa mā akhart, wa mā asrartu wa mā a'lant, anta ilāhī lā ilāha ilā ant.

'O Allah, our Lord, praise be to you, You are the Sustainer of the heavens and earth. Praise be to You, You are the Lord of the heavens and earth and all in them. Praise be to You, the Light of the heavens and the earth and all in them. You are the truth and Your word is the truth. Your promise is the truth and Your meeting is the truth. Paradise is the truth, Hellfire is the truth, and the Hour is the truth. O Allah, I surrender to You, I have faith in You, and I rely upon You. I have argued for Your sake and judged for Your sake. Forgive me for what I have done and will do, what I keep secret and what I do in public. None know me better than You, there is no God but You.' [Bukhārī and Muslim]

Al-Shāfī

اللَّهُمَّ رَبَّ النَّاسِ أَذْهِبْ الْبَاسَ اشْفِهِ وَأَنْتَ الشَّافِي لَا شِفَاءَ إِلَّا شِفَاؤُكَ شِفَاءً لَا يُغَادِرُ سَقَمًا

*Allāhumma rabb al-nās, adhhib al-bās, wa ishfih anta al-shāfī,
la shifā'a illā shifā'uk, shifā'u lā yughādir saqamā*

'O Allah, the Lord of the people! Remove the trouble, for You are the Healer (al-Shāfī). No healing is of any avail but Yours; healing that will leave behind no ailment.' [Bukhārī]

BIBLIOGRAPHY & FURTHER RESOURCES

Al-Azdi, Safwan bin Aḥmad. *Al-Imām an-Nawawī Wa Manhajihi Fi Asmā Allāh Al-Ḥusnā Min Khilāl Sharḥihi Li Ṣaḥīh Muslim.* Alexandria: Dar al-Eman, 2005.

Al-Ashqar, Umar Sulayman. *Sharḥ Ibn Al-Qayyim Li Asmā' Allāh Al-Ḥusnā.* Amman: Dar al-Nafā'is, 2008.

Al-Badr, Abdelrazzaq bin Abdelmuhsin. *Fiqh Al-Asmā Al-Ḥusnā.* 3rd ed. Riyadh: Dār Ibn Al-Jawzī, 2019.

Al-Fifi, Ali bin Jaber. *Li'annaka Allāh: Riḥla ilā as-Samā' as-Sābi'a*, Riyadh: Dar al-Hadharah, 2018.

Al-Fifi, Ali bin Jaber. *Yūsufiyyāt*, Riyadh: Dar al-Hadharah, 2019.

Al-Fifi, Ali bin Jaber. *Elā al-Ẓil: Qawānīn al-Ḥayāh*, Riyadh: Dar al-Hadharah, 2020

Al-Ghazali, Abu Hamid. *The Ninety-Nine Beautiful Names of God: Al-Maqṣad Al-Asnā Fi Sharḥ Asmā' Allāh Al-Ḥusnā.* Translated by David Burrell and Nazih Daher. The Ghazālī Series. Cambridge: The Islamic Texts Society, 1992.

Al-Nabulsi, Muhammad Ratib, *Asmā' Allāh al-Ḥusnā,* www.nabulsi.net (audio lectures and articles)

Al-Oadah, Salman. *In the Company of God: Closeness to Allah through the Beauty of His Names and Attributes.* 2nd ed. Islam Today, 2011.

Bradford, Joe. *Prayer as the Path to Knowing Allah: Finding Greater Meaning* (Houston, 2020), available at: https://www.subscribepage.com/prayerpath

Chapman, Gary D. *The five love languages: The secret to love that lasts*. Northfield Publishing, 2015.

Furber, Musa. *Beauty and the Sacred Law*. Tabah Essays 4. Abu Dhabi: Tabah Foundation, 2017.

Haley, Alex. *The Autobiography of Malcolm X*. Ballantine Books, 1992.

Hanuf, Safwan Mahmoud. *Al-Ism Al-Rabbānī Wa Atharuhu Fī as-Sulūk Al-Insānī*. 1st ed. Beirut: Dār al-Ma'rifa, 2004.

Ibn Ajība, Aḥmad. *Allah: An Explanation of the Divine Names and Attributes*. Translated by Abdelaziz Suraqah. USA: Al-Madina Institute, 2014.

Isaacson, Walter. *Einstein: His Life and Universe*. New York: Simon and Schuster, n.d.

Khaled, Amr. *Bismika Naḥyā*, Ramadan TV series on the Names of Allah, 2009

Khan, Nazir., Alkiek, Tesneem., and Chowdhury, Safiah,. Women in Islamic Law: Five Prevailing Myths, *Yaqeen Institute*, 24 July 2019. Available at: https://yaqeeninstitute.org/nazir-khan/women-in-islamic-law-examining-five-prevalent-myths/

Muqaddim, Maher. *Asmā' Allāh Al-Ḥusnā: Jalālahā Wa Laṭāif Iqtirānihā Wa Thamarātihā Fī Ḍaw' Al-Kitāb Wal-Sunnah*. 3rd Ed. Kuwait: Al-Imam al-Thahabi, 2014.

Murad, Abdal-Hakim. "Contentions 2." Masud.co.uk. Accessed January 7, 2017. http://www.masud.co.uk/ISLAM/ahm/contentions2.htm.

Parrott, Justin. Obedience to Parents its Limits, 16 January 2020, available at: https://abuaminaelias.com/obedience-to-parents-limits/

Parrott, Justin. *Heavenly Affection: Living the Love of Al-Wadūd*, Yaqeen Institute, 9 July 2020. Available online at https://yaqeeninstitute.org/justin-parrott/heavenly-affection-living-the-love-of-al-wadud/

Ratey, John J. and Hagerman, Eric. *Spark!* (United Kingdom: Hachette Publishing, 2010)

Walid, Dawud. *Towards Sacred Activism.* (USA: Al-Madina Institute, 2018); website: https://www.towardssacredactivism.org/resources

Yaqeen Institute, In Awe of Allah series, available online at https://yaqeeninstitute.org/mohammad-elshinawy/the-awe-of-allah-behind-the-scenes/ (various authors)

Yusuf, Hamza. *Purification of the Heart: Signs, Symptoms and Cures of the Spiritual Diseases of the Heart.* 5th Edition. Chicago: Starlatch Press, 2004.

Finally, thanks must also go to Justin Parrott for his hadith website – (https://abuaminaelias.com/dailyhadithonline/) – which made citing accurate English translations of sound hadith so much easier. May Allah reward you for this accessible website and your diligence.